MANAGING THE GLOBAL ECON

MANAGING THE GLOBAL ECONOMY

Edited by

JONATHAN MICHIE
and
JOHN GRIEVE SMITH

OXFORD UNIVERSITY PRESS

Oxford University Press, Walton Street, Oxford OX2 6DP

Oxford New York

Athens Auckland Bangkok Bombay
Calcutta Cape Town Dar es Salaam Delhi
Florence Hong Kong Istanbul Karachi
Kuala Lumpur Madras Madrid Melbourne
Mexico City Nairobi Paris Singapore
Taipei Tokyo Toronto

and associated companies in
Berlin Ibadan

Oxford is a trade mark of Oxford University Press

Published in the United States
by Oxford University Press Inc., New York

First published in hardback and paperback 1995
Reprinted in paperback 1995

British Library Cataloguing in Publication Data
Data available

Library of Congress Cataloging in Publication Data
Managing the global economy / edited by Jonathan Michie and John
Grieve Smith
Includes bibliographical references.
1. Economic policy. 2. Keynesian economics. 3. International
finance. 4. Economic history—1945— I. Michie, Jonathan.
II. Grieve Smith, John.
HD87..M273 1995 94–36912 338.9—dc20
ISBN 0–19–828969–3
ISBN 0–19–828968–5 (Pbk)

Printed in Great Britain
on acid-free paper by
Biddles Ltd., Guildford & King's Lynn

PREFACE AND ACKNOWLEDGEMENTS

Fifty years ago there was a widespread determination to prevent a return to the mass unemployment and currency instability of the 1920s and 1930s. This determination was the backdrop to the Bretton Woods agreement in 1944 for a new international financial system which aimed at providing the stability necessary for achieving and maintaining full employment. The working of this agreement, its breakdown, and what might emerge to replace it in the future are the topics of the following chapters. Suffice it here to say that the stark contrast with today is not so much that the policies thought necessary in the 1990s have moved on from those to which there was a commitment in 1944; the key difference today is the abandonment of the commitment to full employment and international economic cooperation on the scale envisaged at Bretton Woods.

All the chapters were commissioned specifically for this book and draft versions were discussed at a working conference in May 1994 at Robinson College, Cambridge. We are very grateful to Robinson College for hosting and helping to fund this event. We are also grateful to the contributors to our earlier book *Unemployment in Europe* (Academic Press, 1994) who kindly agreed that their royalty payments would go to the Robinson College Economics Research Fund which met the remainder of the expenses, and to the contributors to this book for similarly donating their royalties to help fund future such events. We are grateful for their participation to Daniele Archibugi, Tony Atkinson, Michael Best, Mike Bosman, Ha-Joon Chang, Ken Coutts, Serge Halimi, Alfred Maizels, Robert Neild, Gabriel Palma, Jonathan Perraton, Bob Rowthorn, Giles Slinger, Solomos Solomou, and Adrian Wood.

Our thanks as editors go to all the authors for the speedy incorporation of points made in May 1994 on their draft chapters; Jane Humphries, Francis Stewart, and Geoff Harcourt for chairing the sessions at the May conference; David Musson and Deborah Protheroe of Oxford University Press for the speedy turnround of the manuscript; Lesley Haird for typing and other help; and Brian Reddaway for contributing the Foreword. Our personal thanks for putting up with weekend editing go respectively to Carolyn and four-year-old Alex, and to Jean.

JONATHAN MICHIE
JOHN GRIEVE SMITH

CONTENTS

FIGURES

TABLES

CONTRIBUTORS

YILMAZ AKYÜZ is at the United Nations Conference on Trade and Development, Geneva.

MIKE ARTIS is Professor of Economics at the University of Manchester.

ANDREW CORNFORD is at the United Nations Conference on Trade and Development, Geneva.

JOHN EATWELL is Fellow of Trinity College, Cambridge.

JOHN GRIEVE SMITH is Fellow and Senior Bursar, Robinson College, Cambridge.

LAURENCE HARRIS is Professor of Economics, School of Oriental and African Studies, University of London.

GERALD HOLTHAM is Director, Institute for Public Policy Research, and Affiliated Professor, London Business School.

WILL HUTTON is Economics Editor of the *Guardian* newspaper.

RUTH KELLY is Economics Writer at the *Guardian* newspaper.

MICHAEL KITSON is Fellow, St Catharine's College and Lecturer in Economics, Newnham College, Cambridge.

RICHARD KOZUL-WRIGHT is at the United Nations Conference on Trade and Development, Geneva.

JONATHAN MICHIE is at the Judge Institute of Management Studies and Fellow of Robinson College, Cambridge.

MIĆA PANIĆ is Fellow and Bursar, Selwyn College, University of Cambridge.

BRIAN REDDAWAY is Professor of Economics Emeritus, University of Cambridge.

WERNER SENGENBERGER is at the International Institute for Labour Studies, Geneva.

AJIT SINGH is Fellow and Director of Studies in Economics, Queens College, Cambridge.

FRANK WILKINSON is Senior Research Officer, Department of Applied Economics, and Fellow of Girton College, Cambridge.

ANN ZAMMIT is at the South Centre, Geneva.

FOREWORD

Brian Reddaway

The title *Managing the Global Economy* is obviously one which must not be taken too literally. Apart from anything else, in the real world there is no supernational power which can force individual countries to behave in ways which will lead to some sort of ideal world; even within individual countries, governments are far from being able to force companies, individuals, trades unions, trade associations and the like to do all the things which a 'managing' government might consider desirable, and to refrain from doing things which it considered undesirable. Moreover, different people and different political parties have different views about numerous subjects for which it might seem desirable to have agreed objectives: in particular, there are some topics (such as the working of the welfare state) on which some people would like to see action increased, but on which others would like it to be minimized.

Nevertheless I am glad that the authors of the various chapters in this book have faced up to the difficult problems of future action, as well as setting out much of what has happened in the past. The main object in this foreword is to stress the numerous interconnections between the various topics, and hence the need to consider the picture *as a whole*. Not only do the objectives overlap, and indeed on occasions are contradictory, but the same is also true of the measures which may be taken in an attempt to achieve the preferred set of objectives. As an example, the need to improve a country's balance of payments might call for a lower exchange rate, but the desire to reduce inflation might indicate raising the exchange rate.

It is perhaps useful to start by casting one's mind back fifty years to the Bretton Woods decisions. These were based on a 'vision' of the world economy, which covered all its main problems—not just exchange rates, for example, but also growth, inflation, aid to the Third World countries, and so on. The proposals adopted were not necessarily the best for achieving each major objective considered separately, but they constituted a rounded package which made at least some contribution to each important problem; above all, they were put together in such a way that they could be accepted by each country as at least 'better than nothing'—not only for the world as a whole, but also for the country in question.

In part the functioning of the Bretton Woods decisions relied on consultation between individual countries and the relevant part of 'the Bretton Woods Organization' which emerged as permanent institutions to help with 'the continued managing of the global economy'. The general principles to be applied by these institutions were however fairly well specified, and in some cases are set out in later chapters of this volume.

Circumstances have changed in the world economy since the days when 'Bretton Woods' was launched, and also since it died in 1973. What seems desirable is that a new 'comprehensive vision of the world economy' should be developed, which would again cover all the major interrelated problems in a single picture. It would be unreasonable to expect anything like complete agreement between all nations or between all individuals, but hopefully a working agreement could be negotiated which would add up to a useful agenda for action—and this could be further elaborated in later years.[1] Some of the basic ideas to be embodied in such a 'vision' would be as follows.

LEVEL AND GROWTH OF OUTPUT

First, it would be crucial to get agreement on the basic idea that governments and international institutions can, by combined or separate actions, have a meaningful influence on the level of aggregate output in the world (including its average growth rate over long periods)—as indeed is suggested by past history, as set out (for example) in this book. Since there are so many interconnections between major economic variables it would also have to be recognized that actions aimed at influencing the level of economic activity and output would *also* have effects on other things about which governments and individuals have objectives—notably inflation and deficits or surpluses on budgets or the balance of payments.

Inevitably, people have different 'value judgements' about the relative importance of these economic variables, and also—unfortunately—about how economies work and government (or inter-government) policies influence them. But to my mind it is highly important, especially in a period like the 1990s, to secure full recognition that 'world-wide recessions' and 'long periods of stagnation' are not things like tornadoes which are inflicted on us inevitably by nature: in my view they are largely 'man-made', or at least 'man-tolerated'. And it is important that those who attach greater relative importance than I do to the evil effects of modest inflation should seek to adopt offsetting measures in such fields as wage-management, rather than falling back on policies to deflate demand and lower employment.[2]

---

[1] Personally, I am attracted by the idea of setting up an 'Economic Security Council' of the United Nations which would discuss and negotiate according to the same sort of procedures and voting rights as the existing Security Council adopts on primarily political matters.

[2] They should also study an article by W. Stanners entitled 'Is Low Inflation an Important Condition for High Growth?', *Cambridge Journal of Economics*, 17/1, Mar. 1993.

AGGREGATE EXCHANGE RESERVES

Secondly, the 'vision' of how to produce an effective global economy should include a conscious and more systematic set of actions to adjust the total of the world's exchange reserves, or at least to prevent it from becoming inadequate and pushing some countries into undesirable measures of deflation to keep their own reserves above a tolerable minimum.

This is too long a subject to discuss here in detail, but a few key points can be made. In the first place, most countries have held the greater part of their reserves in US dollars—i.e. in the currency of one particular country. This is, on the face of it, a somewhat peculiar arrangement, because it would seem more logical to use some international instrument, specially created for the purpose and managed in a way designed to suit the needs of the world economy. The use of the dollar has been, for countries other than the USA, a simple extension of the idea that it is the currency most commonly used in international payments, and there was a general tacit acceptance of the idea that it could be 'trusted' as a reserve asset: no single country had any incentive to devise something different. Moreover the supply of dollars available for central banks to buy (in order to meet the growing 'need', which sprang from the general growth in national products in real and money terms) was kept up by the deficits on the US balance of payments (taking capital and current accounts together).

All this has become much more precarious in recent years. Both in the USA and elsewhere the continued deficit on the US current account has been widely regarded as 'undesirable' for a number of very varied reasons— some concerned primarily with its effect on the USA, others with its effect on the rest of the world. If effective action were taken to eliminate the US deficit on current account, the available supply of 'international' money might become inadequate to meet the world's ever-growing need for exchange reserves, unless the USA had a series of large deficits on capital account. That *could* easily happen for a few years, if US institutions bought international assets on a large scale and paid in effect with dollars, which would go into the exchange reserves of the rest of the world. But there is no reason to suppose that this would happen 'automatically' on the appropriate scale—certainly not over a long period: there is indeed a natural tendency for financial institutions in the rest of the world to use part of their asset growth to buy (say) shares on Wall Street, in their search for a diversity of good assets. Thus there are strong forces tending to produce an *inflow* into the USA on capital account, which reduces the extent to which the rest of the world can add dollars to its exchange reserves.

It seems far more desirable that the USA should be treated more nearly like any other country (albeit a very important one) in these matters, and that there should be a conscious development of a mechanism for increasing each year the available amount of a truly international currency. There are many ways in which these adjustments of the total stock of international currencies might be made, which could best be decided as part of a general review of international institutions and how they fit together.[3]

One cheerful feature of any system designed to provide additional exchange reserves in the form of specially created international 'money' (possibly designated in World Currency Units) is that it can also help with another of the world's economic problems, by increasing the supply of funds available for soft loans to Third World countries. If Germany, for example, wants to add to its holding of exchange reserves it might buy (new) World Currency Units from the IMF (or possibly a new International Institution, set up under the general review of institutions) and pay in Deutschmarks or dollars or other convertible currencies: these could then be lent to the International Development Association at a nominal rate of interest, and so enable the IDA to increase the annual flow of 'soft' credits which it grants to Third World countries (provided they satisfy the IDA's criteria on economic policy etc.).

EXCHANGE RATES

In the main, I wish to leave the chapters in the book which deal with this subject to speak for themselves. It is, however, worth emphasizing that if one is considering a single country, exchange rates have to be examined in the light of *all* policies which have an important macroeconomic effect, whether or not they are regarded as primarily aimed at producing certain sets of exchange rates with other currencies, or whether they are regarded as 'primarily' concerned with (say) the level of employment, output, or inflation. And above all I wish to stress that the series of outcomes on exchange rates and all other macroeconomic variables may be greatly affected by changing events in the *other* countries of the world, as well as what happens in the country under consideration.

Finally, one negative point needs to be stressed, because it was widely believed, after the 'fixity' of exchange rates under Bretton Woods was abandoned, that floating rates would 'automatically' allow for differences in the economic policies of individual countries, and preserve 'balance of payments equilibrium': in particular, floating rates were regarded as enabling a country to maintain its desired level of employment, in the face of policies elsewhere which it considered 'too deflationary'.

[3] There is no space here for such a review, but it is highly desirable. Institutions have been changing their functions—often by including activities previously concentrated in other institutions—and a comprehensive review might lead to smoother and more effective operation on many problems.

The fallacy in this view is that the balance of payments 'position' of a
country depends largely on the *capital* transactions between its inhabitants
and those of other countries (giving a wide interpretation to 'inhabitants',
to cover for example both solid financial institutions and managers of speculative funds). These capital transactions are frequently both much *bigger*
than the sum total of current transactions and *much more variable*: the speculative transactions in particular are based largely on the speculators'
guesses about very short-term movements in exchange rates. There is no
presumption that the uncontrolled outcome of 'market forces' will be a
series of exchange rates which will achieve the sort of 'equilibrium' in the
real economy which the country desires.

THE GAINS FROM INTERNATIONAL TRADE AND OTHER TRANSACTIONS

The international division of labour brings substantial benefits to the
world's inhabitants, which will normally—at least in the long run—be
shared by all countries, so long as reasonable rules of behaviour are followed by all traders. It is clearly possible, however, for the government of
a single country to try to divert a bigger share of the benefits to people in
its own country, by imposing its own rules on those over whom it has
control—even though the aggregate benefit to the world will normally be
reduced by such interference.

Under the Bretton Woods 'system' the member countries recognized the
all-round benefit from general agreements to observe certain rules of behaviour, and established various organizations to help them to negotiate further improvements. In particular, the 'General Agreement on Tariffs and
Trade' limited the levels of tariffs and the scope of quantitative restrictions
on trade, and the institution (GATT) set up to run this has called confer-
ences, at which member countries have negotiated further reductions.

Initially, the arrangements made in this way had as a central feature a
rule against discrimination by any country in the tariffs charged on any
commodity according to the country from which it was imported. There
were special exceptions (for example for countries in a Customs Union) but
this 'most favoured nation clause' ruled out a lot of 'ganging up' by pairs
of countries to hamper imports from third countries; goods would be
bought from the country best able to supply them, and the total gain from
trade would be broadly maximized. But on the other hand nothing would
be done to give special help to Third World countries to enlarge their markets—except that in the process of bargaining about reductions of barriers
there was a general convention that Less Developed Countries would not
be expected to make reductions in *their* tariffs in order to enjoy the general

reductions which the developed countries regarded as 'about equally valuable' to each of them.

Later, however, the developed countries agreed to a system whereby each designated certain goods which it would admit duty free (or at reduced duties) from Third World countries. Although the lists were drawn up in most countries so as to have the minimal effect on competing domestic producers, this principle of giving the poorer countries of the world special assistance is to be welcomed.

Broadly speaking, our 'vision' for the future of the global economy should include further international agreements to lower trade barriers and improve the 'rules of behaviour', so as to increase the benefits from the international division of labour, and these should in the main respect the non-discriminatory principle: but further progress in helping the Third World to increase its share of the market is highly desirable. 'Trade as well as Aid' is a useful slogan to cover both better funds for international development assistance (as discussed above) and better openings for the LDCs to earn foreign exchange through exports (visible and invisible).

THE PROBLEM OF SPECULATIVE MOVEMENTS OF FUNDS

Our 'vision' for the future includes plenty of scope for positive action. Realism, however, suggests a conclusion on a warning note: the large speculative movements of funds across the exchanges have serious unsettling effects of various kinds, and it is far from easy to devise measures to deal with this problem which can be implemented without serious side-effects. On this, the chapters of this book may be left to speak for themselves, but the message is not a pleasant one.

INTRODUCTION

Jonathan Michie

The postwar era of full employment has been dubbed the 'Golden Age of Capitalism'; it is a description which appears increasingly appropriate with the continued failure of the advanced capitalist economies to return to the levels of economic growth and employment witnessed from 1948 to 1973. The demise of that era around 1973 has now been followed by more than twenty years of global instability and varying degrees of mass unemployment. Yet far from provoking a concerted effort to construct a new global economic framework for stability and growth, as was the case in 1944 with Bretton Woods, the past two decades of stagflation, recovery, and stagnation are instead ushering in what threatens to be a period of still greater economic and political danger. The end of the Cold War has been marked by regional conflicts and open wars. The 'freeing of the market' in the former Soviet Union and Eastern Europe has destroyed many existing institutions without developing effective alternatives, resulting in economic regression and falling national income.

Increased global competition from the Newly Industrialising Countries has been blamed for aggravating unemployment in Western Europe and North America. It has led to calls for an abandonment of the welfare state and the associated social security and other provisions which are alleged to make Western Europe, in particular, uncompetitive, and to policy proposals for 'managed trade' or similar measures. What was seen by some as an alternative economic system of 'social corporatism', explaining a relative escape from mass unemployment by the Scandinavian economies, has also crumbled in the face of domestic political developments and global economic pressures.[1] The Third World debt crisis may have slipped out of the news but is hardly resolved. And the world economy seems set to enter the twenty-first century with the industrial world divided between three main trading blocs: the European Union, the North American Free Trade Area and the Pacific Rim countries.[2] This tripolar division could either form the

[1] For a discussion of which see J. Pekkarinen, M. Pohjola, and R. Rowthorn, *Social Corporatism: A Superior Economic System?* (Oxford University Press, 1992) and J. Michie, 'Global Shocks and Social Corporatism' in R. Delorme and K. Dopfer (eds.), *The Political Economy of Complexity: Evolutionary Approaches to Economic Order and Disorder* (Aldershot: Edward Elgar, 1994).

[2] James Abbeglen argues that East Asia under Japanese financial and industrial leadership is just establishing itself as a self-sustaining independent economic trading bloc no longer reliant on the West: it now accounts for a quarter of world trade, with eight of its ten economies among the twenty-five top traders in the world (J. Abbeglen, *Sea Change* (New

basis for negotiation and cooperation, or else for the sort of unstable economic and political developments only before witnessed in the preludes to
the two world wars.[3]

The situation demands action from national governments to tackle economic recession and unemployment: this requires cooperation between
governments towards these ends, and calls for new international institutions to facilitate such cooperation. The following chapters set out some of
the policy options available. They aim to make sense of current economic
developments and to give an account of the key trends in the world economy, both to indicate what sort of new institutional arrangements might
be appropriate and to allow judgements to be made as to their feasibility.

The global economy can be imagined to be a self-equilibrating mechanism of the textbook variety, or it can be recognized as subject to processes
of cumulative causation whereby if one or more countries fall behind the
pack, there may be dangers of them falling further behind rather than
enjoying an automatic ticket back to the equilibrium solution path. These
two-alternative, conflicting views of real world economic processes have
very different implications regarding institutional needs and arrangements.[4]

LESSONS FROM HISTORY

In considering how to achieve a situation of global economic and social
development, one thing is clear: we would not choose to start from here.
How we did come to get here, though, is examined in Part I of this book,
'Lessons from History'. Is there a previous 'Golden Age' to which we
should be attempting to return? Could the conditions of the immediate
postwar era be recreated? Could the success of the pre World War One gold
standard provide a model for global financial stability today? Does the
interwar period offer any clues as to how cooperation and conflict impact
negatively or positively on domestic economies, either from the damage
inflicted on economies by the operation of the interwar gold standard, or

York: Free Press, 1994)). Japanese aid flows are now second in scale only to the USA, with
the six biggest recipients of Japan's aid being in East Asia. As ever, 'aid' is not unconnected
with trade: a third of Japan's aid to its East Asian neighbours is used to finance infrastructure spending that supports trade, including ports and transport systems, all the better for
receiving Japanese goods.

[3] For a discussion of the three-way struggle for global supremacy which picks a different
winner than does Abbeglen, see Lester Thurow, *Head to Head* (London: Nicholas Brealey
Publishing, 1994); reissuing his 1992 book in 1994, Thurow still sees Europe as the likely
winner. For a discussion of the present struggle for hegemony in its historical context see
G. Arrighi, 'The Three Hegemonies of Historical Capitalism', chapter 5 of J. Iivonen (ed.),
The Future of the Nation State in Europe (Aldershot: Edward Elgar, 1993), as well as Chapter
1 of this volume.

[4] I am grateful to Geoff Harcourt for having made this point.

from the partial economic success enjoyed by countries which broke free from that regime? These questions are investigated by Michael Kitson and Jonathan Michie in Chapter 1, 'Trade and Growth: A Historical Perspective'.

Within this historical analysis, Mića Panić in Chapter 2, 'The Bretton Woods System: Concept and Practice' analyses the specific case of Bretton Woods; he points out that international financial crises since the early 1970s have frequently produced calls for the Bretton Woods system to be revived, but that it is rarely clear whether this is supposed to mean the 'system' as conceived at Bretton Woods or the 'system' as it actually operated. Yet this distinction is of critical importance, as the blueprint produced by Keynes, White, and others was never applied in practice in the form originally envisaged. Panić's chapter considers the extent to which the original plans for a new global financial system were influenced by the problems experienced in the interwar period and analyses the most important aspects of the articles of agreement signed at Bretton Woods, looking critically at their limitations. After examining the principles, the chapter turns to the practice—the factors that made the system successful early on, but then progressively deteriorated, creating many of the difficulties that the architects of the Bretton Woods system had tried to ensure would never again arise. Panić concludes with some suggestions as to why any new Bretton Woods system would have to be different from the old one and the obstacles which he believes will make it difficult to achieve another such agreement on a global scale in the foreseeable future.

Chapter 3, 'Taming International Finance' also analyses many of the new features of the world economy; in it Yilmaz Akyüz identifies three basic deficiencies underlying the increased instability in the world economy: first, the explosion of speculative international capital movements, secondly the policy approach prevailing in the major countries, and thirdly the absence of effective international institutions. The currency speculation unleashed by deliberately deregulatory policies has not only exacerbated economic instability, but has itself also been fostered and encouraged by the very instability which free market policies have promoted and which has provided profitable betting opportunities for the speculators. Economic instability and currency speculation have proved self-reinforcing.

LABOUR AND CAPITAL

Having considered how we got to where we are, any consideration of how we might try to get to a more rational economic system needs to start from an evaluation of the current balance of forces in the global economy; this is considered from a number of angles by the various chapters in Part II,

'Labour and Capital'. The global context is set by Ajit Singh and Ann Zammit in Chapter 4, 'Employment and Unemployment, North and South'. In 1943 Kalecki argued that if the sort of policies which both he and Keynes had developed for the maintenance of full employment were actually implemented:

a strong opposition of 'business leaders' is likely to be encountered. Lasting full employment is not at all to their liking. The workers would 'get out of hand' and the 'captains of industry' would be anxious to 'teach them a lesson'. In this situation a powerful block is likely to be formed between big business and the *rentier* interests, and they would probably find more than one economist to declare that the situation was manifestly unsound. The pressure of all these forces, and in particular of big business would most probably induce the Government to return to the orthodox policy of cutting down the budget deficit. A slump would follow.[5]

Whether the timescale Kalecki had in mind for this reaction was the generation or so which it actually took is open to question, but the process has no doubt occurred, and the 'more than one' economist willing to play the role cast by Kalecki have in fact proved too many to enumerate.[6] This process depicted by Kalecki is most often thought of in domestic economic terms—giving managers 'the right to manage'. But similar forces are at work on a global scale, with Third World countries being weakened by recession. This political economy of slow growth on a world scale, with powerful interests opposing any return to economic development and full employment, has been highlighted before by Ajit Singh.[7] His chapter here with Ann Zammit stresses this close interconnection between employment in the North and South. The practical implication is that both problems—of mass unemployment in the North and the South—need to be tackled jointly. In dealing with this interrelation, Singh and Zammit challenge the idea that unemployment in the North is caused by the industrialization of the South, and in particular of the Newly Industrializing Countries. These countries not only export, they also import, and there is no reason why industrialization should reduce employment; of course, there may be trade surpluses and deficits, but not all the countries of the North have deficits, and in the case of those that do, such as Britain, this has more to do with failures of industrial management and government policy than with economic success in South East Asia.

Nevertheless, the growing competition in international trade has produced an added impetus to employers and governments to cut wages and

[5] M. Kalecki (1943), 'Political Aspects of Full Employment' in *Selected Essays on the Dynamics of the Capitalist Economy* (Cambridge University Press, 1971), 144.

[6] A key additional factor since Kalecki wrote this piece has been the vastly increased power and significance of financial institutions resulting from the growing mobility of capital as postwar restrictions on capital movements were abandoned.

[7] See A. Singh, 'The Political Economy of Growth', in J. Michie (ed.), *The Economic Legacy: 1979-1992*, London: Academic Press, 1992.

increase the intensity of work in an attempt to undercut others. This process is analysed by Werner Sengenberger and Frank Wilkinson in Chapter 5, 'Globalization and Labour Standards'. They contrast the present state of affairs with the decades following the Second World War when the achievement of decent social welfare, training, health and safety at work, and environmental standards played a part in the rapid and sustained levels of economic growth and consumption; egalitarianism was no obstacle to effective competition. Their warnings of the danger of global competition leading to attempts to win short-term competitive advantage by deteriorations in pay and working conditions, and by violating established trade union rights is timely.[8] Their warnings of the price to be paid by growing inequality are also borne out by a range of recent studies not only documenting the growing inequality witnessed nationally and internationally over the past decade and more, but also demonstrating the deleterious economic as well as social consequences of these developments.[9]

The scope for pursuing such policies has been increased not only by the effect of free market policies in creating mass unemployment domestically and globally, but also by the further development by firms of their global production networks, thereby increasing the ease with which they can play off one group of workers against another. This development of transnational corporations is documented by Richard Kozul-Wright in Chapter 6, 'Transnational Corporations and the Nation State'. National governments are not only faced with the global power of transnational corporations, though, they are also faced with global capital markets which are analysed by Yilmaz Akyüz and Andrew Cornford (Chapter 7, 'International Capital Movements: Some Proposals for Reform') who also discuss different techniques and instruments which are available for regulating international capital movements, and discuss proposals for curbing speculation.

INTERNATIONAL FINANCE AND EXCHANGE RATE POLICY

In addition to the disruptive potential discussed by Akyüz and Cornford, global financial markets impinge on national monetary and exchange rate policies. These constraints are analysed in the various chapters in Part III, 'International Finance and Exchange Rate Policy'. Laurence Harris in Chapter 8, 'International Financial Markets and National Transmission

---

[8] For a catalogue of anti-trade-union repression fuelled by a wave of free market capitalism, see the International Confederation of Free Trade Unions (1994), *Annual Survey of Violations of Trade Union Rights 1994*, ICFTU: Brussels.

[9] See e.g. the various chapters in A. Glyn and D. Miliband (eds.), *Paying for Inequality: The Economic Cost of Social Injustice*, London: Rivers Oram Press/Institute for Public Policy Research, 1994.

Mechanisms', traces through the constraints which are imposed by global financial markets on interest rates and hence on domestic investment levels, setting out at each stage of the supposed transmission mechanism the extent to which this constraint actually impinges, and what scope there is in practice for national government action to overcome these constraints.

In addition to the existing room for manoeuvre identified by Harris, there may be scope for taming the Frankenstein monster created by governments in the 1980s, of speculation-dominated international financial markets, thereby directly reducing many of the constraints. This is considered by Ruth Kelly in Chapter 9, 'Derivatives: A Growing Threat to the International Financial System', who argues that policy should aim to reduce volatility in financial markets by curbing speculation both through attempts to reach international agreement and by pursuing a national strategy to limit the damage currently being wreaked.

A more free-market view is taken in Chapter 10, 'Managing the Exchange Rate System' by Gerald Holtham who opposes putting any sand in the wheels of the international capital markets. Nevertheless, he identifies various ways in which the exchange rate system could and should be managed. This is developed by Mike Artis in Chapter 11, 'Lessons of Exchange Rate Targeting', who discusses the numerous forms which exchange rate targeting may take and the variety of objectives and motivations lying behind these alternatives.

THE ROLE OF GOVERNMENT: NATIONAL AND INTERNATIONAL

There has been a false and damaging dichotomy drawn in policy discussion between action by individual national governments, on the one hand, and international cooperation on the other. The argument has tended to run something like this: national, 'go it alone' policies were all very well in the past, but, in the modern era of global financial markets and transnational corporations, individual governments are powerless; instead, international cooperation is the only way forward. The striking thing about this characterization is that we had far more international cooperation in the immediate postwar era when apparently it was not needed than we have had since, when supposedly it is the only option. A more honest distinction would be between, firstly, the present era when governments have in practice attempted very little intervention in the operation of the free market, whether national or global, and secondly, previous eras when they were less inhibited.

The view that governments could and should act both nationally and internationally is set out in the chapters in Part IV, 'The Role of

Government: National and International'. John Eatwell argues against the view that unemployment has been caused by technology, or by the Newly Industrializing Countries, and sets out in Chapter 12 ('The International Origins of Unemployment') not only the role played by macroeconomic policy in allowing the growth of global unemployment, but also the sort of policy changes which would be required to begin to tackle the problem. These are dealt with in detail by John Grieve Smith in Chapter 13, 'A Programme for Reform' which sets out a series of policy actions which could and should be pursued at the international level but which at present are hardly even seriously discussed. Finally, in 'A Postscript', Will Hutton depicts possible future scenarios for the development of the global economy and the implications these would have for policy.

CONCLUSION

The new orthodoxy rules out any successful intervention, nationally or internationally, on two counts. It asserts first that countries are now so interdependent, and capital so mobile, that no single country can operate an effective macroeconomic policy. It then rejects the idea of effective inter-national macroeconomic policy coordination on the grounds that monetary policy is the only valid instrument for influencing demand, and financial markets can be relied upon to ensure that interest rates will move in rela-tive harmony. The first argument, that we now live in a brave new global-ized world, might be characterized along the following lines:

All old-established national industries have been destroyed or are daily being destroyed. They are dislodged by new industries, whose introduction becomes a life and death question for all nations, by industries that no longer work up indigenous raw material, but raw material drawn from the remotest zones; industries whose products are consumed, not only at home, but in every quarter of the globe. In place of the old wants, satisfied by the productions of the country, we find new wants, requiring for their satisfaction the products of distant lands. We have universal inter-dependence of nations. And as in material, so also in intellectual production.

True, of course. But new? This characterization of globalization was actu-ally written almost 150 years ago.[10] And, of course, policies for macroeco-nomic expansion to tackle unemployment would best be pursued internationally. But again this is nothing new; Kalecki's call in 1932 for expansionary policies to tackle unemployment made precisely this 'new realist' point: discussing the possibility of increasing employment by 'major public investment schemes, such as construction of canals or roads', financed by borrowing or increasing the money supply, he stressed the

---

[10] Written in 1847 (published 1848) by K. Marx and F. Engels, *The Communist Manifesto*.

effects on the trade balance of increasing output—'if it were to be carried out on a large scale, it would have to be co-ordinated by an international agreement of the individual capitalist governments, which, given today's quarrelling imperialisms, is almost out of the question.'[11]

The real question, then, is not whether it is best to act at the national or international level; it is how best to secure international action. For all to remain frozen until such time as everyone else moves is inadequate, however eloquent the calls for movement being made might be. Action at the local, regional, national, or bloc level, far from being a utopian alternative to the real international stage, might in reality prove a prerequisite to cooperation.

But why, finally, should the world be stuck in such an impasse when there was by contrast such a more active policy agenda pursued in the mid to late 1940s, from Bretton Woods to the Marshall Plan? One clue is to look at what was pushing the ruling powers in that previous era, as compared to the lack of any such push today. When in 1948 the West European countries were struggling to recover from the devastation of war, Marshall Aid was introduced against a background of significant Communist support in many of the countries of Europe and beyond, including Communist Party participation in the governments of France and Italy. As suggested in Mića Panić's chapter, whether the Bretton Woods system would have been constructed without the Cold War is open to question; the lack of any such external pressure helps to explain today's general failure to act.

The necessary policy action will not be taken, nationally or internationally, until the prevailing fatalistic economic ideology has been discarded and the dissatisfaction of voters puts sufficient pressure on the political establishment. The following chapters demonstrate that the global financial markets are not God-given: they were created by financial institutions as governments freed financial markets from control over the past decade or so, and they can be remade in a more socially responsible image. Mass unemployment has been created and can be overcome. There has been no shortage of international cooperation when it has been a matter of freeing markets and limiting the power of democratically elected governments; that priority can be reversed. As Keynes argued back in 1926:

'Many of the greatest economic evils of our time are the fruits of risk, uncertainty, and ignorance. It is because particular individuals, fortunate in situation or in abilities, are able to take advantage of uncertainty and ignorance, and also because for the same reason big business is often a lottery, that great inequalities of wealth come

---

[11] M. Kalecki (1932), 'Is a Capitalist Overcoming of the Crisis Possible', and 'On the Paper Plan', in J. Osiatynski (ed.), *Collected Works of Michael Kalecki* (Oxford University Press, 1990): see particularly pp. 53 and 61; cited by A. Glyn and B. Rowthorn, 'European Employment Policies', ch. 12 of J. Michie and J. Grieve Smith (eds.), *Unemployment in Europe* (London: Academic Press, 1994), 198, n. 13.

about; and these same factors are also the cause of the unemployment of labour, or the disappointment of reasonable business expectations, and of the impairment of efficiency and production. Yet the cure lies outside the operations of individuals; it may even be to the interest of individuals to aggravate the disease. I believe that the cure for these things is partly to be sought in the deliberate control of the currency and of credit by a central institution . . .

'I believe that some coordinated act of intelligent judgement is required as to the scale on which it is desirable that the community as a whole should save, the scale on which these savings should go abroad in the form of foreign investments, and whether the present organisation of the investment market distributes savings along the most nationally productive channels. I do not think that these matters should be left entirely to the chances of private judgement and private profits, as they are at present.'[12]

[12] J. M. Keynes, 'The End of *Laissez Faire*' in *The Collected Writings of John Maynard Keynes, Vol. IX, Essays in Persuasion* (Cambridge: Macmillan and Cambridge University Press for the Royal Economic Society, 1984), 291–2.

Part I

Lessons from History

1. Trade and Growth: A Historical Perspective

Michael Kitson and Jonathan Michie[1]

'There has developed a growing realization that stability of income and employment calls for policies operating not merely on prices and the credit base but on the volume of effective demand; and this affords a new hope for stability on a wider front. While the synchronisation of national policies required under the gold standard conflicted at times with the demands of internal stability and was for this very reason gradually abandoned, a synchronisation of policies aimed at sustaining and steadying effective demand in the various countries would promote both internal stability and stability of exchange rates at the same time.' Ragnar Nurkse (League of Nations, 1944).

The 'hope for stability' expressed fifty years ago by Ragnar Nurkse was central to the international monetary system conceived at Bretton Woods in 1944.[2] The collapse of Bretton Woods in 1973 marked the end of the postwar boom—the 'Golden Age of Capitalism'—and ushered in two decades of instability. The resulting series of economic recessions and large-scale unemployment demands action from national governments, cooperation between governments, and new international institutions to facilitate such cooperation. This chapter raises in its concluding section some of the options for such policy action, but these are dealt with in more detail in other chapters. We should make clear from the outset that of course we recognize that there are many new and unique features to the present world economic and political scene, without historic precedent. There are, however, lessons that can be drawn on the key issues of economic rivalry, dominance, leadership, and blocs; of regionalism; of free trade and protectionism; and of currency stability. The history of world capitalism has been one of dominant powers in relative economic decline being challenged by the growing economic—and, in the past, military—strength of newly emerging powers with growing world market shares and ambitions. This has led to leadership or dominance passing from one country (the UK) to another (the USA) but not without an inevitable interregnum with no dominant power able to underpin a world monetary and trade system. The interwar period was one such interregnum and in many ways the 1990s is

---

[1] We are grateful for comments from John Grieve Smith, Jonathan Perraton, and Solomos Solomou; and to John Wells for unpublished data.
  [2] Although, as discussed by Miċa Panić in Ch. 2, there were significant differences between the system that was conceived and the system that was actually implemented.

another. It is from this historical context that the chapter attempts to give an account of how we have arrived at the controlled chaos that character-izes the world economy today.

The principal aims of this chapter are threefold. Firstly, to document the relationship between the growth of world trade and world output since 1870. Secondly, to evaluate the effectiveness of alternative international monetary regimes. And thirdly, to consider the trends in world trade and power that will shape the future path of the world economy and any attempts to foster global economic cooperation. These issues are considered sequentially in the following sections. Section 1 presents some of the mech-anisms that link trade and growth. Section 2 presents some comparative statistics on the pre World War One, the interwar, and the post World War Two periods. Section 3 considers the role played by the differing trade pol-icy regimes across these periods. Two of the issues which will shape the future of the world economy—'regionalism' and world economic leader-ship—are considered in sections 4 and 5. Section 6 considers the current state of the world economy and section 7 evaluates what lessons might be drawn regarding future policy and institutional arrangements.

1. TRADE AND GROWTH: THE MECHANISMS

The postwar 'Golden Age of Capitalism' was founded on a stable interna-tional monetary system which helped ensure a rapid growth of trade and output. The benefits of international trade are well known and frequently cited. Firstly, trade leads to specialization, improving the allocation of resources. Secondly, trade, as an important and increasing component of demand, can raise output through export-led growth.

The potential impacts of increased trade are, however, not universally positive. Increased dependence on trade can make countries more vulnera-ble in general to external shocks—shocks which may be initiated by national or international factors but whose impact is transmitted through trade. More specifically, the distributional impact of exchange rate move-ments increases as economies become more open on capital and current account, with any given exchange rate movement causing a greater redis-tribution of income within the domestic economy.[3] Additionally, increased international integration may constrain the growth and weaken the eco-nomic structure of some trading nations. Whereas exports are an injection into the foreign trade multiplier, imports are a leakage. Thus, a high depen-

---

[3] See J. A. Frieden, 'Exchange Rate Policies: Contemporary Lessons from American History', *Review of International Political Economy*, 1/1 (1994) 82 who also argues that it is the internationally oriented economic groups within any country which will in general prefer fixed exchange rates, while domestically based groups will prefer floating rates.

dence on imports—a high import propensity—may constrain the growth of a domestic economy. Moreover, variations in trade performance in an increasingly integrated world economy may lead to persistent divergences in growth, with success in international trade becoming cumulative as increasing demand for net exports allows countries (or more specifically, the firms and industries within them) to exploit economies of scale, improving their competitiveness and leading to further improvements in their trade performance. Conversely, weaker trading nations may fail to maintain balance of payments equilibrium at a high level of economic activity, with deflationary policies then pursued in an attempt to maintain external balance. The combined impact of poor trade performance and domestic deflation is likely to lead to a cumulative deterioration in relative economic growth as countries fail to exploit the increasing returns associated with a high level of economic activity.[4] These twin processes of virtuous cycles of growth and vicious cycles of decline have been clearly identified by many economists, principally Myrdal (1957) and Kaldor (1972), who illustrate that the benefits of trade may not be evenly spread and that the trading system must take account of the initial conditions of its members. (Sawyer, 1994, discusses these processes of vicious cycles and uneven spreading of benefits as among the factors which have made full employment a relatively exceptional state of affairs under capitalism.) What is required is a system with mechanisms that maintain the balanced development of the world economy and allow countries in difficulty some means of adjustment.

2. TRADE AND GROWTH: SOME EVIDENCE

In this section we consider the growth of world trade and output in three periods. Firstly, the pre World War One period, from 1870–1913, the era of the classical gold standard. Secondly, the interwar period which saw the rise of a reconstructed gold standard in the 1920s and its subsequent collapse in the 1930s leading to a series of discretionary and uncoordinated trade policies. And thirdly the post World War Two period which was dominated by the Bretton Woods system until its collapse in 1973 and which has been replaced by a number of attempts at establishing stability in trade and foreign exchange.

---

[4] This argument has similarities to that advanced by A. P. Thirlwall, 'The Balance of Payments Constraint as an Explanation of International Growth Rate Differentials', *Banca Nationale del Lavore Quarterly Review*, Mar. 1979. Thirlwall, however, assumes that income elasticities (for exports and imports) are constant over time so although countries' growth rates differ, due to the balance of payments constraint, they do not diverge. Our suggestion is that due to cumulative causation processes, including the Verdoorn effect, the income elasticities may shift and this may lead to diverging growth rates. This process will, of course, be affected by any countervailing processes of convergence such as appropriating technology and production systems from the leading country or countries.

(i) Pre-1913

During the 1870 to 1913 period there was an almost continual increase in world trade and world output (see Figure 1.1). As shown in Table 1.1 world trade increased by an average of 3.5 per cent per annum whereas world output increased by an average of 2.7 per cent per annum. There were cyclical variations in trade[5] and output, and significant differences in national growth rates (see Solomou, 1988 and Eichengreen, 1994a) but only in four years did world trade decline (1885, 1892, 1900, and 1908) and only in three years did world output decline (1876, 1893, and 1908).

The interdependence between world trade and growth is indicated by the high positive correlation between the two variables. Additionally, Figure 1.2—which provides an indicator of the trade orientation, or 'openness', of the world economy—suggests that despite some significant downturns dur-

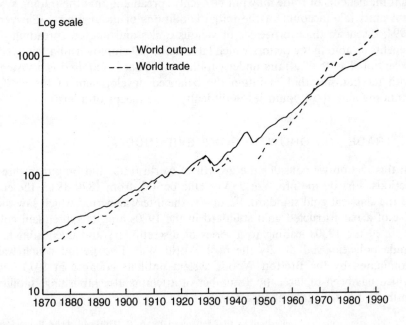

Fig. 1.1 World output and world trade, 1870–1990
Key: World output
          World trade
Sources: See Table 1.1.

---

[5] For instance the growth of trade accelerated from the early 1900s to 1913.

Table 1.1. Growth of world output and world trade, 1870–1990 (Annual % growth rates, calculated peak to peak)

	Output	Trade
Pre-WW1: 1870–1913	2.7	3.5
Interwar: 1913–1937	1.8	1.3
1913–1929	2.3	2.2
1929–1937	0.8	–0.4
Postwar: 1950–1990	3.9	5.8
1950–1973	4.7	7.2
1973–1990	2.8	3.9

Sources: Authors' calculations from the following:
  World Trade—Based on volume of world exports from:
    1870–1913—Lewis (1981), Appendix III, Table 4
    1913–1950—Maddison (1962), Table 25
    1950–1991—Wells (1993), Appendix
  World Output—based on constant price GDP series from:
    1870–1950—Maddison (1991), Table 4.7
      (Computed from annual growth rates of sixteen countries.)
    1950–1990—Wells (1993), Appendix

ing the early 1890s and at the turn of the century, the world economy was becoming progressively more open. Evidence of the volatility of the growth rates of output and trade is presented in Table 1.2 which gives figures on absolute dispersion (the standard deviation) and relative dispersion (the coefficient of variation). The long-term perspective suggests that trade growth during this period was less volatile than during the disrupted period of the 1930s and the post Bretton Woods period but was relatively more volatile than during the Bretton Woods period itself. Similarly, output growth was less volatile than during the turbulent 1930s but was more volatile than during the entire post World War Two period, including post-1973.[6]

[6] Eichengreen (1994a) examines the volatility of GDP across countries during the operation of different exchange rate regimes. He concludes that 'There is no evidence that output volatility increased with the shift from pegged to floating rate regimes after 1972: if anything the opposite may have been true', B. Eichengreen, 'History of the International Monetary System: Implications for Research in International Macroeconomics and Finance', in F. Van Den Ploeg (ed.), *The Handbook of International Macroeconomics*, Oxford: Blackwell, 1994, 172. This conclusion may be dependent on Eichengreen's use of standard deviations (of de-trended series) as the measure of volatility, since the transition to floating exchange rates led to lower growth of world output (see Table 1.1) and a lower mean growth rate for most industrialized countries.

Table 1.2. The growth and volatility of world output and world trade, 1870–1990

	Output			Trade		
	mean average growth rate (%)	standard deviation (%)	coefficient of variation	mean average growth (%)	standard deviation (%)	coefficient of variation
Prewar: 1870–1913	2.8	2.1	0.75	3.6	2.5	0.71
Interwar: 1924–1937	2.1	4.8	2.26	2.2	7.5	3.48
1924–1929	3.7	0.8	0.22	5.7	2.2	0.39
1929–1937	1.3	5.9	4.53	0.5	8.5	16.65
Postwar: 1950–1990	3.9	1.8	0.45	5.9	4.6	0.78
1950–1973	4.7	1.6	0.34	7.5	4.2	0.56
1973–1990	3.1	1.6	0.53	4.5	4.9	1.09

Sources: As Table 1.1.

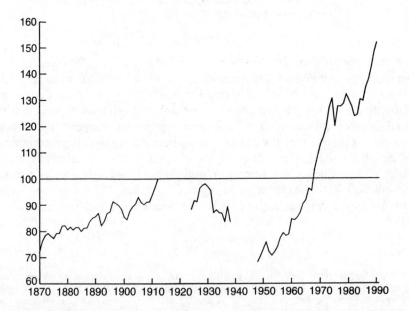

Fig. 1.2 Index of the trade orientation ('openness') of the world economy, 1870–1990
Sources: See Table 1.1.
Note: A rise in the index indicates that the world economy is becoming more open, a fall in the index indicates that the world economy is becoming more closed

(ii) The Interwar Period

Discontinuities in growth and trade characterize the interwar period, with the relative stability of the 1920s followed by the turbulence of the 1930s. As shown in Table 1.1, during the 1913–29 period world trade grew at an average annual rate of 1.3 per cent, whereas output grew at an average annual rate of 1.8 per cent. Much of this slow growth can be explained by the disruptions and dislocations of World War One. The international trading system was in considerable disarray and only recovered slowly; by 1924 the volume of world trade was only 7 per cent above the 1913 level. From 1924 onwards output and trade grew at a faster rate and experienced less volatility than in the pre-1913 period.

During the 1930s, or more precisely from 1929, the world economy suffered severe disruptions. The Great Depression of 1929–32 was the most severe depression in the world economy since the Industrial Revolution. During these three years world trade collapsed at an average annual rate of 9.9 per cent and world output declined at an average annual rate of 6.2 per cent. As shown in Figure 1.2, the disintegration of the world trading system was reflected in a movement towards a more closed world economy, a reversal of the 1920s trend towards increased openness. From 1932 there was a world recovery, albeit one with large inter-country variations (see Kitson and Michie, 1994). During the period 1932–7, world output grew at an average annual rate of 5.2 per cent and world trade at 5.8 per cent, although this failed to return trade to its 1929 level. For the 1929–37 period as a whole, as shown in Tables 1.1 and 1.2, growth of output and trade was very slow and, as expected given the experience of the Great Depression, highly volatile.

(iii) Post World War Two

During the 1950–90 period world output and trade grew at a faster rate than in any of the previous periods. As shown in Table 1.1, world output grew at an average annual rate of 3.9 per cent and world trade grew at an average annual rate of 5.8 per cent. Only in one year (1982) did world output fall;[7] and only in four years did world trade fall (1952, 1958, 1975, 1982).

The postwar period can be broadly divided into two sub-periods. The Bretton Woods period, from 1950 to 1973, and the post-1973 period. The former witnessed a rapid growth of trade (average annual growth of 7.2 per

---

[7] As pointed out by J. Wells, 'Factors Making for Increasing International Economic Integration' (unpublished manuscript, Cambridge University, 1993), on the more demanding criteria of per capita output there are six years of absolute decline.

cent) and output (average annual growth of 4.7 per cent), with a significant rise in the openness of the world economy. The openness indicator increased at an average annual rate of 2.4 per cent during this period, three times the increase during the pre-1913 period. In part this can be explained by a catching-up process as the world economy adjusted from the dislocations of World War Two: it was not until 1968 that openness reached the level achieved in 1913. It also reflects, however, the increasing integration of the world economy based on an effective and stable international trading system. This integration promoted openness despite the growing contribution of non-tradable activity to domestic output in advanced economies.[8] As shown in Table 1.2, trade and output were less volatile during this period than during any other period apart from the late 1920s. Moreover, comparison with the 1920s is not strictly appropriate as the Bretton Woods period was significantly longer—the stability of the system over twenty-three years being added testimony to its success.

The collapse of the Bretton Woods system ushered in a period of slower growth of world trade and output. From 1973 to 1990, world trade grew at an average annual rate of 3.9 per cent, around half that achieved in the Bretton Woods period, and output increased at an average annual rate of 2.8 per cent. Within this period there were major setbacks in the mid-1970s and the early 1980s; the former caused by the first OPEC shock and the latter by 'OPEC 2' and the 'monetarist' shock of deflationary policies being adopted in a number of the leading industrialized countries.[9] The impact of these disruptions was to impede severely the openness of the world economy. As shown in Figure 1.2, the post-World War Two trend towards a more open world economy was halted from the mid-1970s and only resumed from the mid-1980s. It has since, again, been halted.

3. TRADE AND GROWTH: THE ROLE OF TRADE POLICY REGIMES

(i) Pre-1913

The classical gold standard formed the foundation of the international trading system in the pre-1913 period. From 1880, the four major industrial countries—Britain, France, Germany, and the US—belonged to what

---

[8] During the post World War Two period there was an increase in service sector activity in both the private and public sectors, much of which was not internationally tradable.

[9] Japanese economic policy also shifted towards austerity in 1981. It is true that the Japanese budget deficit continued to increase, but this was due to depressed tax revenue (see M. Itoh, 'Is the Japanese Economy in Crisis?' *Review of International Political Economy* /1 (1994) 1: 37).

was effectively a fractional-reserve, gold coin standard.[10] Under this system notes and coins issued by government and commercial banks circulated alongside, and were convertible upon demand into, gold coins. For many economists the growth of trade and output in the world economy can be attributed to the successful operation of the pre-1913 gold standard. It is argued that it was a system that provided stability and an automatic adjustment mechanism, via gold flows, to correct payments imbalances. For some, the main issue concerning the effectiveness of the classical gold standard is simply which monetarist adjustment mechanism it supposedly embodied, the Humean price-specie-flow mechanism or its close cousin, the monetary approach to the balance of payments.[11]

Others, however, have questioned the success of the system. Firstly, the system did not actually operate according to the 'rules of the game' commonly supposed. Central banks, rather than allowing gold flows to adjust their domestic money supplies, intervened either by varying their discount rates or by expanding domestic credit (Bordo, 1992).[12] Secondly, the operation of the system depended not on gold flows but on a series of other adjustment mechanisms, such as deflation, migration, long-term capital flows, and protectionism (Panić, 1992). The system did not provide an adjustment mechanism that ensured the attainment of internal and external balance. Any shock, domestic or international, which caused a deterioration in the balance of payments, required a tightening of monetary policy to maintain the gold parity. The impact of such a deflationary path is likely to have both price and quantity effects, the composition of which will depend on the structure of, and underlying conditions in, the domestic economy.[13]

The deflationary mechanism inherent in the classical gold standard depressed employment but widespread unemployment was prevented by

[10] There have been a number of alternative forms of gold standard in history, for a discussion of which see A. J. Schwartz, 'Alternative Monetary Regimes: The Gold Standard', in C. D. Campbell and W. R. Dougan (eds.), *Alternative Monetary Regimes* (Baltimore: Johns Hopkins University Press, 1986).

[11] See the arguments in favour of the price-specie-flow mechanism by W. E. Huffman and J. R. Lothian, 'The Gold Standard and the Transmission of Business Cycles 1833–1932', and arguments in favour of the monetary approach by P. M. McCloskey and J. R. Zecher, 'The Success of Purchasing Power Parity: Historical Evidence and its Implications for Macroeconomics', both contained in M. D. Bordo and A. J. Schwartz, *A Retrospective on the Classical Gold Standard, 1821–1931*, NBER Conference Volume (University of Chicago Press, 1984). The essence of the dispute is whether gold flows cause, in the first instance, price adjustments (the price-specie-flow mechanism) or expenditure adjustments (the monetary approach). There is thus disagreement over whether there can be transitory changes in relative prices—the invariance of the law of one price—but both retain the remaining monetarist assumptions.

[12] According to the monetary approach, the rules were inconsequential due to perfect arbitrage in goods and capital markets.

[13] In response to a shock, the unravelling of the price–quantity adjustment process will not necessarily lead to a return to the initial position; shocks can have persistent effects as well as altering and undermining the dynamics of growth.

migration. During the 1880s, 5 per cent of the British population emigrated and, after Austria-Hungary joined the system in the early 1890s, 6.5 per cent of its population fled before 1910. Furthermore, the system was sustained by large international capital flows which financed the development of the weaker countries. Within the orthodox theoretical framework, the movement of capital is explained by interest rate differentials, which themselves reflect gold flows. A more realistic approach would have also to embrace the impact of underconsumption, capital market biases, government policies,[14] the co-movement of capital and population flows and the role of empire(s), and the desire to obtain cheap food and raw materials. The prevailing economic, structural, and institutional conditions therefore encouraged a transfer of resources from richer to weaker countries—a transfer that helped accommodate, at least in the medium term, the flaws of the gold standard system.

An additional adjustment mechanism was protectionism. During the nineteenth century there had been a movement, albeit erratic, towards free trade. Britain led the way with the repeal of the Corn Laws in 1846 and the Anglo-French commercial treaty in 1860. During the late 1870s, contemporaneous with the emergence of the gold standard, this trend was reversed and there was a shift to increased protectionism and in particular the widespread use of tariffs. In the main, this shift was a response to specific industrial factors. In the case of the protection of European agriculture it was a defensive response to cheap grain imports from North America and Russia. For manufacturing it was often a case of protecting young, infant industries. In Germany, for example, throughout the 1880s large parts of heavy industry, especially iron and steel, pushed for tariff barriers in order to compete with established British industries (Kitson, 1992). During the late nineteenth century the cumulative impact of tariff protection as an industrial policy was to provided domestic economies—that did not have recourse to nominal exchange rate realignment—with an alternative tool of external adjustment.

The picture often presented of the classical gold standard era is of a free-trade, low-inflation world. A sort of monetarist nirvana. In reality, the stability of the international system was founded on deflation in weaker countries and enforced migration. Limiting the adverse impacts of the system required resort to protectionism and the transfer of savings from the richer countries. Moreover, this transfer of resources was not the result of some automatic mechanism causing gold flows but resulted rather from the specific historical circumstances of the time.

[14] Protectionism, through tariff-jumping, was one such policy which encouraged foreign direct investment during this period (P. Bairoch, *Commerce Exterieur et Dévélopment Economique de L'Europe au XIX Siècle* (Paris: Ecole des Hautes Etudes et Sciences Sociales, 1976); A. Bloomfield, *Patterns of Fluctuation in International Investment Before 1914* (Princeton University Press, 1968)).

(ii) The Interwar Period

Following the end of the First World War the world economy was in considerable disarray. Initially the international trading and payments system was dominated by flexible exchange rates but from the mid-1920s the cornerstone of international economic management was a reconstructed form of the gold standard, the operation of which encouraged beggar-my-neighbour deflation and which, after 1929, became a vehicle for transmitting recession. It was replaced by the use of independent and uncoordinated trade policies including managed exchange rates and various forms of protectionism.

The failures of the interwar gold standard were more apparent than had been those of its pre-1913 predecessor. The earlier variant survived, despite its failings, because it accommodated a number of adjustment mechanisms, such as migration and capital flows, to alleviate persistent trade imbalances, and, despite its deflationary bias and adverse effects on employment and wages, was not seriously challenged by organized labour. During the interwar period, however, there was not only an increasing political influence of organized labour but also a growing awareness of the impact of exchange rates—or more accurately of the monetary policies that accompanied them—on employment (Eichengreen, 1992).

As with the classical version, the success of the interwar gold standard depended on nominal convergence. However, its actual effect was to depress real variables such as output and employment and to undermine the capacity of individual governments to deal with domestic economic problems. As the main trading nations entered the exchange rate system with different domestic economic conditions, it was apparent that the efficacy of the adjustment process would be central to the regime's impact. The option of adjusting the nominal exchange rate was effectively precluded. As the adjustment of real exchange rates was slow and erratic, only two adjustment mechanisms remained: firstly, changes in the level of demand, with deflation in deficit countries and reflation in surplus countries; and secondly, as in the classical gold standard, the financing of trade deficits by capital flows from countries with a current balance of payments surplus.

Despite large capital exports from the United States during the 1920s, the ultimate burden of adjustment was borne by domestic deflation. The surplus countries were reluctant to reflate. The classical adjustment mechanism assumed that gold flows would provide the means of changing the level of demand, with the impact falling on prices. As noted above, price adjustment was slow; in addition, the reflationary impact of gold flows into France and the United States was negated by domestic monetary policy. Both countries, which by the late 1920s had accumulated 60 per cent of total world gold reserves, deliberately prevented these reserves from boosting their domestic money supplies. American policy makers were increasingly concerned with curbing stock market speculation whereas the French were wary of inflation. The prioritization of domestic economic issues transmitted deflation abroad. Low import demand, particularly in America, led to widening balance of payments deficits in many of the key European economies.

The growth of world trade was therefore limited by the domestic policies of the surplus countries. Whereas these nations could choose whether to reflate or to pursue other domestic policy concerns, deficit countries had no such options. The entire burden of adjustment fell on them—they could either deflate to eradicate balance of payments deficits or they could borrow to fund them. The effective approach of the UK economy was the former and Germany the latter.

Deflation could be achieved either through allowing reserves to flow out, depressing the money supply and domestic expenditure—the classical mechanism—or by policies that directly affected the components of demand. In Britain it was interest rates that acted as the key deflationary tool. From 1923 there was a trend rise in the Bank of England's discount rate as the authorities adopted policies consistent with the return and maintenance of the exchange rate to the pre-war parity. At the same time the general trend of other central banks' discount rates was downward (Eichengreen, 1991). The deflationary impact of the Bank of England's policy helped to keep the UK balance of payments in surplus and prevented the loss of gold.[15] The Bank of England also deployed gold market and foreign exchange operations to maintain its stock of international reserves (Moggridge, 1972). The impact on the real economy was to slow the growth rate, with the economy therefore failing to reap its growth potential (Kitson and Solomou 1990); despite the level of GDP in 1924 being significantly below what it had been in 1913, the rate of growth of the British economy from 1924 was significantly below the world average.[16] Similarly, unemployment remained persistently high, averaging just under 8 per cent for the period 1924–9 (Feinstein, 1972).

Unlike Britain, Germany maintained a persistent balance of payments deficit throughout the 1920s. Along with reparations, this deficit had to be

[15] The UK balance of payments on current account was in surplus from 1924 to 1929 apart from 1926 when the impact of the General Strike resulted in a small deficit (see C. H. Feinstein, *Statistical Tables of National Income and Expenditure and Output of the UK, 1855–1965* (Dept. of Applied Economics, Cambridge and Royal Economic Society, 1972)). The adverse impact of the overvaluation on competitiveness, however, led to smaller surpluses than had been achieved in the immediate pre-war period.

[16] During the period 1913–29, Britain's growth rate of 0.7 per cent per annum was approximately one third of the world average (M. Kitson and S. Solomou, *Protectionism and Economic Revival: The British Interwar Economy* (Cambridge University Press, 1990)).

financed and Germany became heavily reliant on foreign loans, particularly from the United States. Although initially able to attract sizeable capital inflows, the rising debt burden undermined creditworthiness. Germany became increasingly reliant on short-term funds and by 1931 had accumulated net debts equivalent to 25 per cent of national income (Kitson, 1992). The subsequent concern about the German economy, and the collapse of American lending abroad from 1928, led to capital flight, the loss of reserves, a credit squeeze, and the raising of interest rates. Germany had been able to cope with its balance of payments constraint in the short term by borrowing; ultimately, however, this only postponed the requirement to deflate.

Thus the deflationary bias of the gold standard not only failed to deal with the structural problems of constrained countries, it accentuated them. Countries, which had entered the system with major structural problems, left the system weakened as a result of having had to accommodate the burden of adjustment by deflating their domestic economies. This not only lowered growth and raised unemployment, it also hampered long-run competitiveness. The dampening of domestic demand reduced the benefits of mass production and the exploitation of scale economies. Deflation to maintain external equilibrium thus raised unit costs, generating a further loss of competitiveness and world market share. Such a process of cumulative causation lead the constrained countries to suffer a vicious cycle of stagnation. Locked into a fixed exchange rate system there were few policy options to reverse the process.

The operation of the gold standard thus hampered world growth in the 1920s; its shortcomings were also evident with the onset of the Great Depression, the severity of which can certainly be attributed to the operation of the gold standard; (see Eichengreen, 1992; and Temin, 1989). The impact of adverse shocks, such as the recession in the USA and the collapse in capital exports, were transmitted to the rest of the world through the exchange rate regime. As foreign loans were called in due to developments in the domestic economy, gold flows to the United States increased. The draining of reserves from the debtor countries caused monetary policy to be tightened in an attempt to ensure gold convertibility. Thus the deflationary bias of the gold standard system resulted in a perverse reaction to adverse demand shocks. Rather than facilitating an expansion of demand to ameliorate the depression, the system magnified the problem, leading to a collapse in world trade. The interwar gold standard placed a deflationary burden on deficit countries, and thus on the world economy as a whole, a burden which had persistent effects on productive capacity. The system failed to provide adjustment mechanisms to rectify payments imbalances which did not involve the loss of output and rising unemployment. Furthermore, the system restricted the policy options open to its members, limiting their ability to deal with changing domestic economic conditions or problems.

An analysis of inter-country variations in economic growth indicates that the pace of recovery during the 1930s was significantly dependent on countries untying themselves from the strictures of the gold standard and adopting independent expansionist policies (Kitson and Michie, 1994). Exchange rate regime was not the only factor; some countries also reaped the advantages of increased protectionism and fiscal expansion. What is apparent, however, is that the cooperative regime failed and uncoordinated policies were a vast improvement. This is not the same as saying that coordination *per se* is ineffective. What was ineffective, however, was a coordinated regime which depended for its success on nominal convergence, but which led to adverse impacts on the real economies of some of the participants.

(iii) Post World War Two

The design of the international trading regime established after World War Two was formulated in the context of the perceived failings of the interwar system: the disintegration of world trade in the early 1930s and the subsequent development of uncoordinated trade policies. The system took its name from the conference held in 1944 at Bretton Woods, New Hampshire, which put into place the rules that would regulate the international monetary and trading system in the postwar world. The characteristics of the system were subject to dispute between the British delegation led by Keynes and the American delegation led by White, with Keynes arguing unsuccessfully that the system should put the onus on surplus countries to reflate rather than deficit countries to deflate. Nevertheless, the Bretton Woods era was, for a number of reasons, one of rapid economic growth, as has been extensively analysed elsewhere (see in particular Glyn *et al.*, 1990, and Armstrong, Glyn, and Harrison, 1991).

Within the Bretton Woods system every country had to peg its currency to gold or the US dollar (which, in turn, was pegged to gold). Before it could change its exchange rate a country would have to show that it faced 'fundamental disequilibrium'. This term lacked adequate definition although in effect it was interpreted as that condition where the exchange rate parity was inconsistent with acceptable levels of unemployment or inflation. There was a resistance to making general exchange rate realignments (one notable exception was the realignments made in 1949 following the sterling devaluation). Furthermore, the exchange rate adjustments that were made tended to be devaluations by deficit countries rather than revaluations by surplus countries. As with its gold standard predecessors, the Bretton Woods system did not function symmetrically; the burden of adjustment was borne by the weaker deficit countries, with the stronger countries accumulating increased reserves.

Despite its asymmetry, the Bretton Woods system was relatively successful because it accommodated a number of adjustment mechanisms and was anchored by US monetary hegemony.[17] Two of the principal adjustment mechanisms, which complemented each other, were firstly, the discretionary use of domestic monetary and fiscal policy and, secondly, the use of capital controls. For some economists these policies and controls led to international instability (see the various contributions in Bordo and Eichengreen, 1993). A more realistic interpretation is that they provided some flexibility in a system that was approximating to a fixed exchange rate regime. The case for capital controls had been made by Keynes, prior to the agreement at Bretton Woods:

'It is not merely a question of curbing exchange speculations and movements of hot money, or even of avoiding flights of capital due to political motives; though all this is necessary to control. The need, in my judgement, is more fundamental. Unless the aggregate of the new investments which individuals are free to make overseas is kept within the amount which our favourable trade balance is capable of looking after, we lose control over the domestic rate of interest.' (Keynes, 1943a, 275; quoted in Pivetti, 1993.)

The stability of Bretton Woods was undermined, though, by the relative decline of the USA (evaluated in section 5 below) and the increasing inconsistency between US domestic policies and the needs of the world economy. For most of the life of the Bretton Woods system US monetary and fiscal policies were directed at domestic targets (Kenen, 1992); there are parallels here with the problems faced within the European Exchange Rate Mechanism, with German monetary policy dictated by domestic rather than European needs. Furthermore, the need for the USA to run balance of payments deficits to supply reserves to the rest of the world, such that its dollar liabilities exceeded its gold stock, undermined the viability of the system (Triffin, 1960). A series of exchange rate crises in the early 1970s signalled the demise of the system, the end coming in early 1973 with the floating of the Yen and the currencies of the six members of the European Community.

The collapse of Bretton Woods was followed by floating exchange rates, albeit with various attempts—some perhaps more 'half baked' than others—at reintroducing a degree of exchange rate stability. The impact of floating exchange rates in practice has been to increase uncertainty and misalignments ('overshooting') in foreign exchange markets. The challenge for

[17] The system was also supported, particularly during its early life, by resource flows from the USA to Western Europe and Japan (in the form of Marshall aid and other official transfers). While these flows helped to stabilize the international economy, their primary motive was to act as a bulwark against the spread of communism.

the latter half of the 1990s will be to design a new framework for international economic stability which does not impose deflationary adjustment mechanisms on participating countries.

4. REGIONALISM AND WORLD TRADE

The issue of regionalism requires clarification and elaboration. The key issues are firstly, to what extent has the degree of regionalism in the world economy increased over the 1980s and early 1990s; secondly, would such regionalism destroy or create trade; and thirdly, would it distort or promote multilateralism? Regionalism can perhaps best be defined in terms of preferential regional trade agreements (RTAs) amongst groups of countries, or trade within broadly defined geographic regions such as Europe and North America. It does seem to have emerged in the world economy in a significant way in two periods: firstly in the 1930s, and then again in the 1980s.

During the early 1930s the chaos in world markets led to an increased use of discriminatory trade policies and the *de facto* formation of trading blocs. These blocs, as indicated in Table 1.3, were usually centred on a dominant country. For countries such as the UK, France, the Netherlands, and Italy, a growing proportion of trade during the 1930s was conducted with their respective empires. Furthermore, currency blocs also grew in importance as countries sought exchange rate stability and made extensive use of exchange rate agreements and discriminatory exchange controls. However, despite the formation of trading blocs—or perhaps because of it, due to the dispersed location of Empires and Colonies—trade did not actually become regionalized on a geographical basis; the world did not see the development of 'natural' trading blocs. Table 1.4 shows the direction of merchandise trade in eight regions in 1928 and 1938. For most of the regions there was no increase in intra-bloc trade as a share of total trade, the one exception being Latin America.[18]

The first post World War Two wave of regionalism was from the mid-1950s with the establishment of the original European Economic Community (EEC) and European Free Trade Area (EFTA). The 1980s saw pressure for the formation of RTAs led by the United States which

---

[18] The shares of intra-bloc trade are a crude indicator of regional trade bias as they can be affected by the number of countries in the bloc, the openness of each country, the commodity composition of trade and variations in transactions costs. K. Anderson and H. Norheim, 'History, Geography, and Regional Economic Integration' in K. Anderson and R. Blackhurst, *Regional Integration and the Global Trading System* (Hemel Hempstead: Harvester Wheatsheaf, 1993), construct an index which adjusts for these factors. This index shows only a small increase in geographical intra-regional trade for the world economy from 1928 to 1938 (Anderson and Norheim, 'History, Geography and Regional Economic Integration', Table 2.2).

Table 1.3. The emergence of blocs in the 1930s

Country	Economic Bloc	Imports from 'Economic Bloc' as a % of total imports		Exports to 'Economic Bloc' as a % of country's total exports	
		1929	1938	1929	1938
United Kingdom	British Commonwealth, colonies, protectorates	30	42	44	50
	Other countries of the 'sterling bloc'[1]	12	13	7	12
France	French colonies, protectorates, and mandated territories	12	27	19	27.5
Belgium	Belgian Congo	4	8	3	2
Netherlands	Netherlands overseas territories	5.5	9	9	11
Italy	Italian colonies and Ethiopia	0.5	2	2	23
Portugal	Portuguese overseas territories	8	10	13	12
Japan	Korea, Formosa, Kwantung, Manchuria	20	41	24	55
Germany	Eastern Europe[2]	4.5	12	5	13
	Latin America	12	16	8	11.5

Source: League of Nations (1939), 186.
Notes: 1. Sweden, Norway, Finland, Denmark, Egypt, Estonia, Latvia, Portugal, Thailand, and Iraq.
  2. Bulgaria, Greece, Hungary, Rumania, Turkey, and Yugoslavia.

Table 1.4. Direction of merchandise trade in 1928 and 1938 (% shares, eight Geographical Regions)

	Africa 1928	Africa 1938	North America 1928	North America 1938	Latin America 1928	Latin America 1938	Asia 1928	Asia 1938	USSR 1928	USSR 1938	Continental Europe 1928	Continental Europe 1938	Non-Continental 1928	Non-Continental 1938	Oceania 1928	Oceania 1938
Imports from:																
Africa	7	6	2	2	—	—	1	2	4	—	6	8	6	6	1	—
North America	10	12	26	27	38	34	16	19	21	33	14	11	22	22	27	22
Latin America	2	2	21	20	13	18	—	1	8	—	9	9	12	11	—	—
Asia	9	11	24	22	3	4	46	45	22	22	8	8	9	12	13	17
USSR	—	—	—	1	—	—	2	1	—	4	2	1	2	2	—	—
Continental Europe	43	44	17	19	30	31	15	17	39	30	51	52	35	30	11	10
Non-Cont. Europe	28	25	8	8	16	13	18	13	2	11	8	9	7	5	43	43
Oceania	1	—	2	1	—	—	2	2	4	—	2	2	7	12	5	8
Total	100	100	100	100	100	100	100	100	100	100	100	100	100	100	100	100
Exports to:																
Africa	8	8	2	3	1	1	3	5	—	—	6	7	10	15	2	—
North America	8	5	23	20	35	27	23	17	5	8	7	6	11	9	9	4
Latin America	—	—	14	15	9	18	1	1	—	—	6	6	10	9	—	—
Asia	3	5	11	13	—	1	41	42	19	15	6	7	21	16	12	9
USSR	2	—	1	2	—	—	2	1	—	—	1	1	1	1	1	—
Continental Europe	54	59	27	21	35	33	19	18	56	46	58	57	27	29	33	17
Non-Cont. Europe	25	23	19	23	20	20	9	13	20	31	15	15	10	9	38	62
Oceania	—	—	3	3	—	—	2	3	—	—	1	1	10	12	5	8
Total	100	100	100	100	100	100	100	100	100	100	100	100	100	100	100	100

Source: League of Nations (1942)

Note: Figures in italic are the share of intra-regional trade in total trade.

negotiated a series of agreements culminating in the formation of the North American Free Trade Area (NAFTA).[19] It is too early to discern the impact of the NAFTA agreement on intra-bloc trade. The evidence for the European Community (EC, now European Union), however, does show a rise in intra-bloc trade since 1960 although most of the increase occurred in the period up to 1973 with a later spurt from the mid-1980s (Lloyd, 1992).[20] The intra-bloc share of the EFTA countries (the original six members) showed a moderate increase up to the mid-1970s, followed by a decline of a similar magnitude.

An alternative measure of regionalization is the regional share of world trade. Figure 1.3 shows the shares of world imports of the three principal RTA blocs (with membership as at the time) since 1960. The combined shares of the European Community and EFTA have not increased

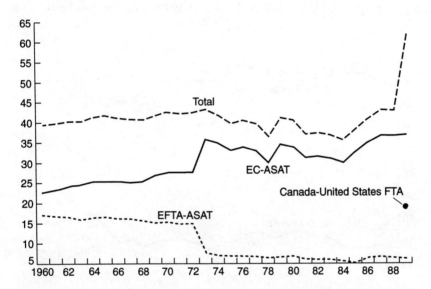

Fig. 1.3 Shares of world imports of the three leading regional trade agreement blocs, 1960–1990
Source: Lloyd (1992).

---

[19] See J. Bhagwati, 'Regionalism and Multilateralism: An Overview', ch. 2 of J. de Melo and A. Panagariya (eds.), *New Dimensions in Regional Integration* (Cambridge: Cambridge University Press, 1993), who argues that the USA, frustrated at the slow progress of the GATT talks, turned to regionalism instead.

[20] The intra-bloc share of the original six members of the EC also increased up to the early 1960s but subsequently it declined until the mid-1980s. This possibly reflected the trade diversion impact of new members to the bloc.

significantly over the period (the total for all three regions jumps upwards in 1989 with the formation of the Canada–United States free trade agreement). The share of the EC has increased but this reflects expansions of membership (Lloyd, 1992).

In addition to the explicit role of RTAs, regionalism can occur through the increased *geographic* concentration of trade. Attention has been focused on the development of a tripolar world economy dominated by North America, Europe, and Japan and the 'Asian Tigers'. There have been contrasting trends in intra-bloc trade since 1960 in these three areas: increasing in Europe and Asia but falling in North America since 1969 (Lloyd, 1992).[21] Figure 1.4 shows the share of world imports of the three poles. It illustrates their dominance—they account for nearly four-fifths of world imports in 1989—although it is noticeable that this dominance dates at least from the start of the period. The share of Europe has averaged over 40 per cent, although there was a fall from the mid-1970s until the mid-1980s. The

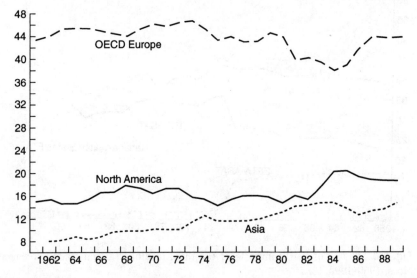

Fig. 1.4 Shares of world imports of the three leading geographical trading blocs, 1960–1990
Source: Lloyd (1992).

---

[21] The intensity of intra-regional trade index constructed by Anderson and Norheim ('History, Geography and Regional Economic Integration', Table 2.2), for various benchmark years, shows a continuous rise for Western Europe during the post World War Two period, a rise for North America until 1979 followed by a subsequent decline, and a decline for Asia since 1958. The apparent contradiction of the latter with the intra-bloc share evidence is probably due to the intensity index adjusting for the fast growth of the Asian economies.

share of North America has been relatively stable at around 16 per cent, although there was an increase in the early 1980s. The most significant change has been the rapid growth of the Asian share of world imports, almost doubling over the period.

The evidence provides some indication that both RTAs and the development of geographical blocs have led to an increase in regionalism. The evidence, however, is not conclusive and suggests that the pace of change has varied across the postwar period and within blocs. In part this may reflect the conflicting impact of the increasing globalization of the world economy on regionalization. On the one hand, regional arrangements develop as both a defensive and aggressive response to intensified international competition. On the other hand, globalization can counteract, or at least constrain, underlying trends towards regionalization as it encourages extra-bloc trade. Despite the uneven and erratic process of regionalization it is undoubtedly true that the world economy of today is dominated by three blocs, the policies of which will define the future path of the world trading system.

An analysis of the trade and currency blocs of the 1930s indicates that different discriminatory regional arrangements had different impacts on the trading system—some blocs created trade while others diverted trade (Eichengreen and Irwin, 1993). In addition, there is no empirical support for the contention that discriminatory trade agreements led to a collapse in the level of multilateral trade (Kitson and Solomou, 1991). Likewise, an analysis of the impact of contemporary regional blocs provides conflicting results: some studies have identified trade creation effects (Robson, 1984) while others have identified trade diversion effects (Pomfret, 1988). This conflicting evidence concerning the impact of regional blocs suggests that their overall impact will depend on the macroeconomic policies which they deploy. They can be a force for growth if they adopt expansionary policies, and in this context they can be particularly effective if they isolate the region from deflationary pressures which may emanate from the international trading system. If they merely replace a global form of monetarism with a regional form they will provide little benefit.[22]

---

[22] This is quite aside from the additional issue of what the effects would be of adopting a single currency in these areas; T. Bayoumi and B. Eichengreen, 'Monetary and Exchange Rate Arrangements for NAFTA', *Journal of Development Economics* 43/1 (1994) find that the North American Free Trade Area (NAFTA) is even less of an optimum currency area than is the European Union (EU), because, while most of the anticipated benefits apply with equal force, the underlying disturbances are more diverse across members of NAFTA and hence the costs of abandoning the exchange rate instrument are likely to be higher.

5. WORLD ECONOMIC LEADERSHIP

The leadership of the world economy has shifted during different epochs of international economic development. The pre World War One era saw Britain, the first industrialized economy, as the dominant economic power. Increasingly, however, its relative position declined—the 'diminished giant' syndrome (Bhagwati and Irwin, 1987)—with the rising economic might of the USA and Germany and others as 1914 approached. Table 1.5 indicates that Britain's share of the output of the world's capitalist countries (measured as the aggregate output of Maddison's sixteen capitalist countries) declined from 21.5 per cent in 1870 to 15.3 per cent in 1913 whereas the US share rose from 24.5 per cent to 40.8 per cent over the same period.[23] In addition, Britain's share of exports from these countries declined from 37.2 per cent in 1870 to 27.0 per cent in 1913 (Table 1.6).[24] During the same period the output of the USA increased rapidly so that by 1913 its share of the output of the capitalist countries was more than two and a half times that of the UK. Furthermore, although Britain remained the largest exporter in 1913, its share of total exports was only eight percentage points

Table 1.5. GDP shares of 'world' capitalist countries (%, benchmark years)

	UK	US	Germany	Japan
1870	21.5	24.5	8.6	5.0
1913	15.3	40.8	8.9	5.0
1929	11.8	46.1	7.5	6.2
1950	11.1	51.3	6.5	5.1
1973	7.9	41.5	8.7	13.9
1989	6.9	41.0	7.8	16.7

Source: Authors' calculations from Maddison (1991).
Notes: 1. 'World' is Maddison's 16 capitalist countries.
      2. GDP data are measured in 1985 US relative prices and adjusted to exclude the impact of boundary changes.

[23] These data do not cover the whole world economy. They are useful, however, in providing internally consistent comparisons over time of the changing shares of output between the group of countries covered.
[24] As with the GDP data, the export data series will underestimate the total of world exports. Using more comprehensive series (A. Lewis, 'The Rates of Growth of World Trade, 1830–1973' in S. Grassman and E. Lundberg (eds.), *The World Economic Order: Past and Prospects* (London and Basingstoke: Macmillan, 1981)), the share of UK merchandise exports is seen to have declined from 18.9% in 1870 to 13.7% in 1913. Although these shares are lower, the rate of decline is very similar.

Table 1.6. Export shares of 'world' capitalist countries (%, benchmark years)

	UK	US	Germany	Japan
1870	37.2	11.0	16.6	0.2
1913	27.0	19.1	21.1	1.2
1950	20.5	32.7	5.6	1.9
1973	8.8	23.5	14.5	9.1
1987	8.4	20.1	14.4	13.4

Source: Authors' calculations from Maddison (1991).
Notes: 1. 'World' is Maddison's 16 capitalist countries.
2. Export data are measured in 1985 prices and exchange rates.

greater than that of the US and only six percentage points greater than that of Germany.

During the interwar period Britain attempted to reimpose its hegemony, but its long-run relative decline continued. By 1929 the US share of the capitalist world's GDP was four times that of Britain and it had overtaken Britain as the world's leading exporter.[25] Britain could not maintain its leading role in the international monetary system; indeed, it has been argued that this, combined with the reluctance of the US to assume leadership, resulted in global instability which exacerbated the depth and duration of the great depression (Kindleberger, 1973).[26] What is certainly true is that the post World War Two 'Golden Age of Capitalism' was underpinned by the strength of the US economy, with the dollar thereby being able to act as the anchor to the international monetary system. As indicated in Tables 1.5 and 1.6, by 1950 the USA accounted for over half of GDP, and a third of exports, of the capitalist countries. However, the growth of the world economy and the emergence of other economies, in particular Germany and Japan, was to undermine the USA's relative position. In 1973, when the Bretton Woods system collapsed, the US share of output had fallen by ten percentage points since 1950 and its share of exports had fallen to less than the combined total of Germany and Japan.

Table 1.6 indicates that the US share of exports has declined since 1973

[25] Maddison's (1962) figures for the whole world economy indicate that in 1929 the US had 14.7% of world export markets whereas the UK had 8.6%.

[26] This argument has been challenged by B. Eichengreen, *Golden Fetters: The Gold Standard and the Great Depression, 1919–1939* (Oxford University Press, 1992) who argues that the problems of the interwar monetary system were primarily due to lack of cooperation amongst central banks rather than the absence of an effective hegemonic power.

whereas the Japanese share has increased significantly. In terms of shares of world manufactured exports, as shown in Table 1.7, Japan has certainly caught up with, if not overtaken, the USA, and while the European Union (EU) had, as recently as 1980, a share almost double that of Japan, it has since fallen significantly (see Table 1.7). On this measure, the balance of forces appears now to be very much a tripolar one. Figure 1.5 indicates the distribution of world income in 1990, with Europe, the USA, and Japan as the three clear concentrations. Although Japan accounts for a far lower share of world income than does either the EU or the USA, Japan's GDP per head was 119 per cent of the EU average in 1990 (Figure 1.6), with a faster growth rate than in either the US or the EU (Figure 1.7).

Table 1.7. Exports: shares of world exports of manufactures (%)

	1980	1986	1992
Japan	11.2	14.1	12.3
US	13.3	10.8	12.8
EU	21.9	19.4	17.6
Intra-EU	24.1	22.9	26.1
Rest of World	29.4	32.8	31.2

Breaking down manufacturing trade into high, medium and low tech, Japan can be seen from the figures reported in Table 1.8, not only to have captured a growing proportion of OECD trade, but to have done so particularly in high tech trade, with a concomitant decline in the USA's share of total manufacturing trade in the OECD, other than in low tech trade. These changes in relative shares have been accompanied over the past twenty years by a fall in OECD manufacturing employment of 8 per cent. Yet manufacturing employment actually rose in Japan over the same period by 2 per cent and was barely unchanged in the US. It is the EU which has had the big manufacturing job losses, amounting to 20 per cent over the past twenty years, with the worst case being the UK, suffering a 35 per cent fall. This in turn is reflected in the poor EU employment rates (Figure 1.8) and correspondingly high unemployment (Figure 1.9).

The key questions are firstly, what implications the present balance of international economic power will have for future developments politically and institutionally; and secondly, what if anything might replace the underpinning which was given to the world economic system by US dominance post World War Two, and which had been given pre World War One by British dominance, but which was lacking in the interwar period—without this underpinning, the Gold Standard eventually collapsed under the

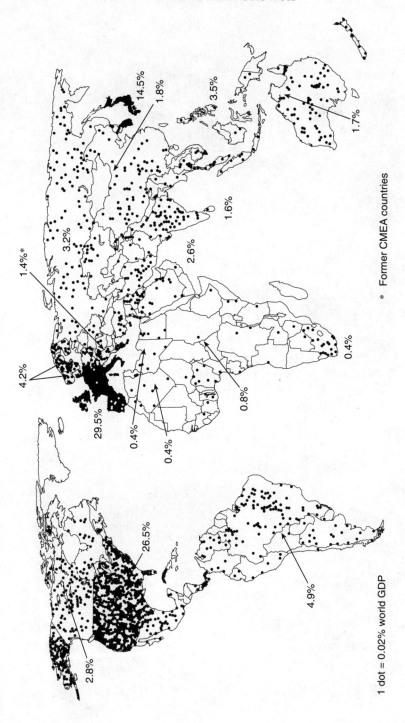

1 dot = 0.02% world GDP

Fig. 1.5 Distribution of world income, 1990
Source: CEC (1993*a*), 65.

* Former CMEA countries

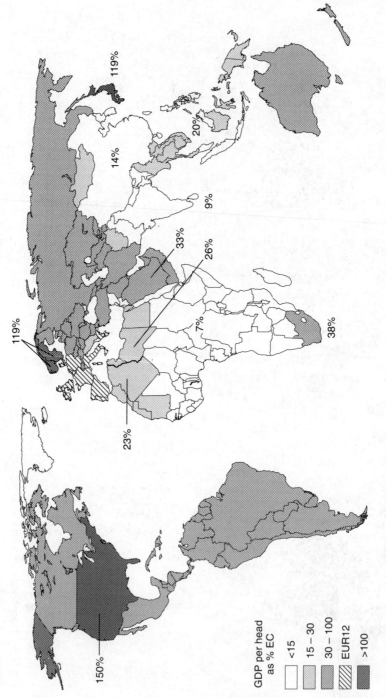

Fig. 1.6 Income per head compared to the Community, 1990
Source: CEC (1993*a*), 65.

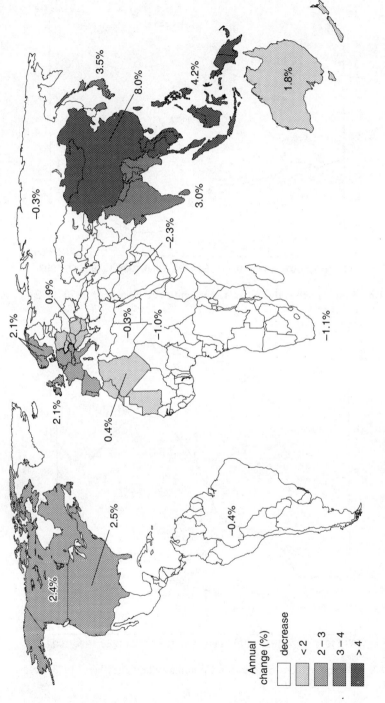

Fig. 1.7 Growth of income per head, 1980–1990
Source: CEC (1993*a*), 66.

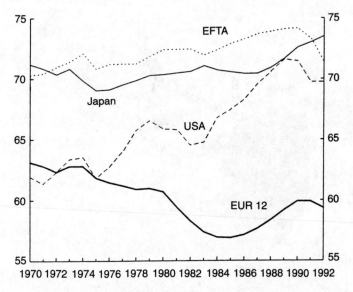

Fig. 1.8   Employment rates in the Community and elsewhere, 1970–1992
Source: CEC (1993*b*), 17.

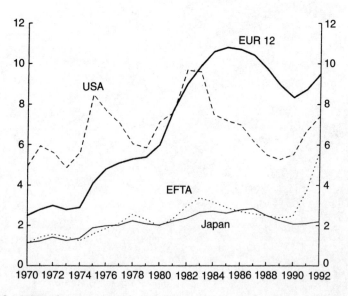

Fig. 1.9   Unemployment rates in the Community and elsewhere, 1970–1992
Source: CEC (1993*b*), 20.

Table 1.8. Shares of OECD trade in manufactures (%)

	1970				1980			
	Total	High Tech	Medium Tech	Low Tech	Total	High Tech	Medium Tech	Low Tech
US	20.3	31.1	21.7	13.4	17.4	26.3	15.4	13.3
Japan	11.0	13.2	8.5	13.2	15.0	21.1	16.9	7.1
Germany	18.9	17.7	23.1	15.0	20.6	16.2	24.7	17.9
France	9.3	7.7	8.5	10.7	10.3	8.7	10.0	12.1
Italy	7.3	5.5	7.1	8.5	8.6	5.1	7.7	12.8
UK	10.4	10.5	11.9	8.9	8.9	10.2	8.5	8.5

strains, even if these strains had been caused or at least exacerbated by bad institutional design.[27]

6. RECENT DEVELOPMENTS AND IMMEDIATE PROSPECTS

The 1994 Gatt agreement—the signing of the Uruguay Round—ended seven years of negotiations and created the new World Trade Organisation to police international trade, to be established on 1 January 1995. It is claimed that the freer trade in manufactures, services, textiles, and agriculture, which will follow what will be the biggest tariff cuts in history, will add $250 billion a year to world output in ten years time. Even on the assumption that such a figure might be plausible, there is some doubt as to what the differential impact would be, with suggestions that the benefits will be skewed towards the already industrialized countries. We have discussed above the dynamic links between trade and growth, but looking to the likely impact of the 1994 Gatt agreement, a key determinant of its effects on output will be the extent to which it impacts differentially on countries' trade balances, since if one or more countries or blocs are affected adversely, the resulting trade deficits may prove unsustainable, leading to deflationary policies being pursued to slow down the growth of import demand. The resulting slowdown in economic growth will also reduce the growth of trade—indeed, this

[27] Not that bad institutional design is simply the result of technical inadequacies; more likely it is caused by the underlying economic disparities themselves, with the stronger powers in a position to dictate that the brunt of adjustment mechanisms be borne by the weaker powers rather than by themselves, which would actually be more rational for the global system (and therefore, indeed, for the long-term interests of the dominant powers themselves, if only they could be forced to act in their own long-term interests instead of, at every turn, having to be forced to by pressure from, or fear of, outside forces).

latter result would be the purpose of the deflationary policies. From a static viewpoint it might be thought that reductions in output and trade brought about to correct imbalances caused by increased trade levels could not, logically, reduce world output levels below their initial levels; that is, could not reduce world output below what it was prior to the initial boost to trade. But this is, precisely, to ignore the dynamics of cumulative causation and the risks of countries—and even the global economy—slipping into a vicious circle of deflation. There is no necessary or logical floor to such a process, quite aside from the additional dangers which such imbalances carry of provoking trade wars and protectionism. Free trade is quite capable of creating the conditions for its own demise.[28]

The immediate prospects for the world's trading imbalances, though, are dominated by the US deficit and Japanese surplus. The US trade deficit in 1993 reached $115.8 billion, the worst for five years. Of this, just over one-half of the total was due to the deficit with Japan, which increased by 37 per cent on the 1992 trade imbalance between the two countries, reaching $59.3 billion. This is the background to the trade sanctions dispute between the USA and Japan which continued throughout the early months of 1994. The resulting pressure from the USA on Japan to open up its domestic market to American imports has led to fears from the EU that they will lose out in the three-way competition, with Japan opening up to US goods but not to European ones. And while the US deficit has led to pressure on Japan to open its markets to increased American imports, the trade balances between Japan, the US, and the EU will also inevitably be influenced by the relative growth rates of the three. Countries (or blocs) with relatively high growth will often see their trade balances deteriorate as rising demand sucks in imports while export markets stagnate. Yet the opposite correlation may also be found, with successful economies enjoying both higher than average growth rates and trade surpluses. In the immediate future, though, the USA is likely to see its trade deficit grow if it continues its current recovery from recession.[29] Europe's trade balance, on the other hand, is likely to do well, with a stagnant economy and correspondingly depressed demand for imports. That these deflated demand conditions apply equally to domestically produced goods means that the longer term performance of Europe in export and domestic markets may be hampered by correspondingly weak investment and poor product and process development.

[28] There have of course been a range of other concerns expressed regarding the debilitating effects of unrestricted free trade, most recently around the environmental implications of devoting resources to transporting goods around the world rather than producing them locally; see J. Lang and C. Hines, *The New Protectionism: Protecting the Future Against Free Trade* (London: Earthscan Publications, 1993).

[29] The US National Association of Business Economists estimate that the US trade deficit will deteriorate from the 1993 level of $116 billion, to $135 billion in 1994 and $137 billion in 1995.

As for relative output levels, it is hard to envisage any of the world's countries or blocs emerging as an economically dominant power within the next generation or so, certainly not to the degree that Britain was pre World War One and the USA was post World War Two. It might be supposed that Japan and the Newly Industrialising Economies will continue their relative rise, at the expense of the USA's continued relative decline. Whether the EU countries will continue with their chosen role as the world's stagnationists, glorying in price stability, is a matter for speculation. But even if Japan does become increasingly dominant, it would be a long time before Japan's economy alone could match NAFTA's or the EU's, and the possibility of Japan achieving the military dominance which went along with America's economic leadership—and Britain's before that—appears even more remote. Within the tripolar impasse with which the global economy will be entering the twenty-first century, relative shifts in economic and political power will no doubt continue. In a four-nation poll (conducted in the UK, Germany, Japan, and the USA) reported in April 1994, the strongest candidate for world leadership apart from the USA was thought by people in the UK and Germany to be the EU and by people in the USA to be Japan, while in Japan it was thought to be China.[30] Asked, 'Which country poses the biggest threat to world peace?', the most common reaction from those in the UK, Germany, and the USA was 'Russia', with Russia being outdone in people's minds as a military danger only in Japan, where the USA was considered the greater threat.[31]

7. SOME LESSONS

Conventionally, an evaluation of the history of the international monetary system has compared the efficacy of fixed versus flexible exchange rate regimes. This is a rather limited approach; the performance of alternative regimes depends not only on the exchange rate regime but on a range of other factors, including the power and impact of other adjustment mechanisms embedded in the system.

[30] Answering the question, 'Which will be the strongest candidate for world leadership apart from the US?', the percentage responses were as follows (reported in the *Guardian*, 2 April 1994):
In the UK: West Europe, 32; China, 23; Japan, 19; Russia, 10.
In Germany: West Europe, 53; Japan, 19; China, 13; Russia, 3.
In America: Japan, 28; West Europe, 26; China, 25; Russia, 11.
In Japan: China, 38; Japan, 24; West Europe, 12; Russia, 5.

[31] Answering the question, 'Which country poses the biggest threat to world peace?', the percentage responses were as follows (reported in the *Guardian*, 2 April 1994):
In the UK: Russia, 20; Middle East, 15; US, 11; China, 9.
In Germany: Russia, 27; Middle East, 10; Ex-Yugoslavia, 9; Israel, 6.
In America: Russia, 17; Middle East, 11; China, 9; Ex-Yugoslavia, 6; Iraq, 6.
In Japan: US, 22; Russia, 21; Korea, 13; China, 4.

The classical gold standard survived due to the existence of 'negative' adjustment mechanisms, such as domestic deflation and migration, and the benefits of specific historical conditions, such as the level of international capital flows and the lack of labour resistance to unemployment and under-employment. The interwar gold standard was short-lived due to its structural faults. It created a system of asymmetric adjustment which imposed a deflationary burden on the weaker countries and amplified the impact of recessionary forces during the great depression. The Bretton Woods system accommodated a number of positive adjustment mechanisms such as capital controls and the widespread use of fiscal policy to regulate domestic demand. Its effectiveness, however, was ultimately undermined by the reluctance to use exchange rate realignments, and by the changing world conditions which undermined the central position of the USA in the system. As with the gold standard systems, asymmetries developed which led to imbalances in world economic development. Of course, any international monetary system will face changes in global economic conditions; the point is that systems must therefore evolve and incorporate appropriate adjustment mechanisms.

The requirements of a balanced international monetary system are therefore twofold. Firstly, it must accommodate a series of positive adjustment mechanisms that do not impose domestic deflation, and that allow participating countries to adjust to national-specific conditions. Secondly, these adjustment mechanisms must reflect the characteristics and dominant forces of the global economy; as such they need to evolve over time. For instance, an exchange rate realignment may be an appropriate mechanism, but its effectiveness will be contingent on the behaviour of exchange rate markets. These markets are now dominated by transactions for speculative rather than trade purposes and, as shown by the ERM débâcle, the volume of these speculative flows alone can force through exchange rate adjustments, thus depriving the monetary authorities of much of their discretion over the choice of exchange rate parity. One response to this has been the advocacy of a 'a quick jump to monetary union' (Eichengreen, 1994b); a more appropriate response, we would argue, would be the introduction of capital and exchange controls to counter the threat of speculative attacks; (a variety of such proposals exist—see Harcourt, 1994, and Kelly, 1994). At the very least, it is necessary to throw 'some sand' in the wheels of international finance (Tobin, 1978) in order to reconcile international economic stability with some domestic policy autonomy.

A new 'Bretton Woods' would thus need to provide the capacity for exchange rate adjustment, exchange controls, the coordination of capital flows, and flexibility over the use of fiscal policy. International economic cooperation at present is, however, dominated by concerns with monetary and financial targets, the pursuit of which can impact adversely on the real economies of the participants; this was the experience of the gold standard regimes and, more recently, the ERM.

Cooperative systems which deploy the coordinated use of fiscal policy and the effective redistribution of resources to regions or countries of the world with difficulties is preferable but fraught with difficulties. The level of cooperation required would be significant, the 'rules of the game' would be complex, and the commitment to a large transfer of resources between countries (as opposed to within countries) would face political resistance. Furthermore, there is no longer one nation with the economic and political power to take centre stage. The lead must come from the three dominant trading blocs. This itself presents additional difficulties as there is not only potential conflict between the three main players but those countries outside the main blocs may also be disadvantaged. Institutional reform would also be required (for a discussion of which see Chapter 13), the most important of which would be to stop the International Monetary Fund from pedalling the myths of monetarism and free market economics as being the only effective means of economic management (for an example of which see IMF, 1994).

In the absence of a global growth strategy the alternatives are to adopt expansionary policies at the regional or national level. The experience of the 1930s indicates that these may be appropriate responses to a lack of coordination at the world level. As the experience of Maastricht and the ERM testify, though, regional blocs do not necessarily provide higher growth; outcomes depend on the objectives, implementation, and coordination of macroeconomic policy. In the absence of expansionary regional initiatives countries may have little option but to pursue independent growth strategies. Even at this level however, prospects will be tempered by the dominant forces in the world economy. Policies aimed at regulating product and labour markets to safeguard the interests of both consumers and workers could lead to attempts to relocate production by multinationals. Demand management policies aimed at increasing output and employment could also lead to capital flight and a free-falling exchange rate, although it needs to be remembered that this dual process may to some extent sort itself out: as the exchange rate falls, it makes capital flight increasingly costly to those who continue to sell the currency. In addition, it is not clear how long competitor countries would allow one economy to enjoy the massive gain in competitiveness which a hugely devalued currency would provide.

CONCLUSIONS

There are clear signs of the sort of policy responses which might be seen if present imbalances in trade and growth rates between countries continue.

On trade, Clinton was elected on a platform which included 'managed trade', and, while he has shown little sign of pursuing his election platform in office, disputes with Japan over the openness of the Japanese market to American goods have been a constant source of tension during the early months of 1994. On exchange rates, there has been little cooperation since the 'Group of Seven' Plaza Accord in 1985 to encourage a gradual depreciation of the dollar; indeed, far from cooperating, there were strong suspicions in February 1994 that the US had been deliberately pushing up the Yen on foreign exchange markets in order to reduce Japan's competitiveness. Certainly, with the EMS buckling under the strains of being transformed from an adjustable peg mechanism to a precursor for a single currency, there are no signs of any imminent move to international exchange rate coordination.

On regional economic integration, the political experience regarding the Maastricht Treaty's ratification has been mirrored in North America: during his election campaign, Clinton was critical of NAFTA, yet his first major policy action was to force it through in the face of widespread criticism, from trade unions among others. In Canada, the government, supporting NAFTA in its election campaign in face of criticism from the opposition, suffered perhaps the biggest election defeat in world history, being left with only two MPs, yet the incoming government, again, changed its tune and supported NAFTA wholeheartedly. This rise of regionalism is certainly, in part at least, a response to the new global competition. In some ways it can be seen as mirroring the response of countries and blocs to the previous demise of a global economic power capable of underpinning the world's economic, trading, and currency arrangements: when Britain failed to reimpose her leadership role, via sterling's 1925 return to the gold standard, new economic blocs began to emerge capable of pursuing their own policy agendas. One key difference today is that there has not, as yet, been the recourse to the protectionism witnessed in the 1930s. Fears of a 'fortress Europe' and American 'managed trade' have so far remained in the background, with the new Gatt agreement promising ever freer trade. Whether this can form the basis of a stable economic environment on which new global institutional structures can be built will depend crucially on whether the 'Third World' countries will be able to develop without recourse to the sort of interventionist measures which delivered economic development to the now industrialized countries, but which will be forbidden under Gatt. If not, imbalances will be exacerbated and the go-it-alone responses seen in the 1930s may once again be seen as the best route for economic growth and development.

2. The Bretton Woods System: Concept and Practice

Mića Panić

The first (discouraging) thought that occurs to anyone asked to write about the Bretton Woods system is that there is nothing, no aspect of the subject, that has failed to attract careful and lengthy scrutiny over the last fifty years. The existing literature must be at least as voluminous as that on the classical gold standard; and the number of devotees of the System is probably greater than the one that admired for so long its much debated nineteenth century precursor.

International financial crises since the early 1970s have frequently produced calls for 'a new' Bretton Woods System. The problem with this is that the system, like the gold standard, was a product of particular circumstances that cannot be reproduced easily. Moreover, it is never clear whether those who advocate a return to more orderly international economic relationships, such as those that existed in the 1950s and for most of the 1960s, mean the system as conceived at Bretton Woods or the system as it operated in practice.

Nevertheless, the conditions that inspired the search for a consensus in the conduct and control of economic relationships between nations in order to enhance their economic welfare, the solutions that were proposed in response to the specific problems that had destroyed in the 1930s the multilateral system of trade and finance created over the preceding half a century, and the obstacles that made it impossible to implement the whole of the Bretton Woods blueprint in practice—all have important lessons to offer to a world struggling with similar difficulties half a century later. Many of the problems that Keynes, White, and others tried to solve in the 1940s are still with us and will continue to lead to serious crises for as long as international economic integration and the growing interdependence to which it gives rise continue to increase in a world divided into a large number of independent states—all jealously guarding their national sovereignty.

This chapter analyses, first, the extent to which the original plans for a new global monetary system were influenced by developments between the two world wars. After the principles, the chapter turns to the practice: the factors that made the system successful early on, but then progressively deteriorated, creating many of the difficulties which the architects of the Bretton Woods system tried to ensure would never happen again. It concludes with some suggestions why a Bretton Woods Mark II would have to be different from the old one and of the obstacles which make it unlikely on a global scale in the foreseeable future.

THE SUPRANATIONAL BLUEPRINT AND ITS ORIGINS

As Machlup (1977) has shown, the idea of creating an international economic and monetary union has a long history. In spite of this, it remained for centuries only a dream for the simple reason that until the 1940s no government took a serious interest in any of the schemes proposed. For instance, in the 1920s a French economist, Nogaro, floated the idea of establishing an international bank to issue a new international currency (Gomes 1993, 215). A few years later, in 1929, Schacht, the President of the Reichsbank, proposed the creation of an international clearing union (Luke, 1985); and in 1930 Keynes (1971 (1930), 358–61) suggested a modified gold standard to be managed by a 'supernational bank' acting as the international lender of last resort. Nothing happened.

However, only a little over a decade later, both the allies and the Germans were incorporating these suggestions into their plans for a new international economic order to be established once the war was over (Van Dormael 1978, Gardner 1980). Two important, interrelated developments, which took place in the intervening period, played a major role in contributing to this change in official attitudes. The collapse of the international economic system at the beginning of the 1930s, followed by the Great Depression, the rise of Fascism and the Second World War destroyed the old order created by trial and error before 1914 in response to growing international economic integration. Most contemporaries were convinced that each step in this sequence of events was a direct result of the one preceding it. The events also demonstrated the fact that industrial countries, in particular, were too advanced, specialized, and interdependent to contemplate genuine, lasting improvements in economic welfare after the war without re-establishing some sort of a new economic order. Morever, the task was too important and urgent for the postwar recovery to be left to the slow, haphazard processes of the markets whose limitations had been exposed in the interwar period (Milward 1987a and 1987b). It had to be taken on, therefore, by governments; and the powerful vested interests that might have resisted this successfully were too shell-shocked and marginalized by the disastrous turn of events in the 1930s and early 1940s to put up an effective resistance to fundamental, far-reaching changes. Hence, such changes became not only essential but also feasible.

British, American, and other plans and, ultimately, the Bretton Woods blueprint for the postwar order reflect, therefore, these preoccupations rooted in the interwar experience. They were the outcome of a pragmatic approach to the major challenges of the time adopted by a remarkable generation of public-spirited politicians, administrators, and experts, often of widely differing ideological persuasions. However, they had one thing in common: most of them had lived through two world wars and the Great Depression; and it was this experience that made them determined to create economic and social conditions which would ensure that the world would never again have to live through similar man-made disasters.

The starting-point, which made all the subsequent development possible, was the widespread acceptance of the fact that economic interdependence requires consensus and cooperation if countries participating in the international division of labour are to achieve their national objectives; and that many of the problems experienced between the two world wars could be traced directly to a failure in this respect. Even the rather informal financial arrangements that had existed under the classical gold standard (see Eichengreen, 1992) broke down as, confronted with unprecedented economic and social crises, each country tried to solve its problems in isolation. In spite of this, very few of them managed to stage a genuine economic recovery before the outbreak of the Second World War; and those that did (for example Nazi Germany and the Soviet Union) achieved economic success at exceptionally heavy social cost.

The lessons that this experience had taught those who attended the Bretton Woods Conference were summarized in the opening speech by the US Secretary of the Treasury, Morgenthau (US Department of State 1948a, 81):

All of us have seen the great economic tragedy of our time. We saw the worldwide depression of the 1930s. We saw currency disorders develop and spread from land to land, destroying the basis for international trade and international investment and even international faith. In their wake, we saw unemployment and wretchedness—idle tools, wasted wealth. We saw their victims fall prey, in places, to demagogues and dictators. We saw bewilderment and bitterness become the breeders of fascism, and finally, of war.

The important conclusion, as he pointed out to a much wider audience in a radio broadcast, was that: 'We have come to recognise that the wisest and most effective way to protect our national interests is through international co-operation' (quoted in Eckes 1975, x). Keynes went even further in his closing speech at Bretton Woods (US Department of State 1948a, 1110): 'We have been learning to work together. If we can so continue, this nightmare, in which most of us here present have spent too much of our lives, will be over. The brotherhood of man will have become more than a phrase.'

What they had done 'working together' at Bretton Woods was to produce the first and, in many ways, the most ambitious blueprint for a global economic order ever attempted. It was designed to eliminate permanently a number of serious problems experienced in the interwar period (and, indeed, before 1914) within a basically supranational, centralized institutional framework.

The first problem that they had to solve in setting up a new international monetary system was that of agreeing on (a) what should constitute liquid assets which would be universally acceptable in settling international debts and (b) how they were to be created. The practice from about the 1870s until the Second World War was to rely for this purpose on gold and one or two national currencies, with a few other currencies in a minor, supporting role. The snag, as those attending the Bretton Woods Conference knew from experience, was that the production of gold might fail to expand sufficiently to finance the growth of world trade and investment. This had happened before 1914 and to an even greater extent in the interwar period—with the result that national currencies of the most important trading nations were used to fill the gap, effectively turning the international financial set-up into an extension of their national systems, mainly that of the dominant economy.

However, in a dynamic economic environment this only produces a temporary solution. In the medium to long term the relative position of countries in the international economy changes and with this the relative demand for their currencies. The once dominant country is overtaken by more dynamic economies whose firms become responsible for a larger share of international trade and investment. As a result, a high proportion of international exchange is conducted in its currency, in preference to that of the once dominant country. But, for the transition to be smooth, supporting a continuous expansion of world trade and investment, the authorities of the new leading economy have to be both willing and able to provide its currency in the quantity required. Otherwise, international trade, investment, and production will decline. The rate of decline may be slowed down for a time if the once dominant economy is determined to continue playing a major financial role and reduces the supply of its currency relative to the shrinking global demand for it, thus maintaining its exchange rate unaltered. The problem is that such a policy cannot be pursued for long because of its adverse effects on domestic output and employment.

All this is, of course, precisely what happened in the interwar period, though there were already some signs of the changing roles of major economies and their currencies towards the end of the classical gold standard. As Kindelberger (1973) has pointed out, after the First World War an economically weakened Britain was in no position to play the key role, and the United States, because of the virtually closed nature of its economy, was both unable and unwilling to take over.

Both the British and US plans prepared for Bretton Woods tried to deal with these weaknesses: the British by creating an international currency ('bancor') to be made available on demand; and the American by revising contributions to a new international organization at intervals according to changes in the relative size and importance of the countries in the international economy (US Department of State 1948*b*, 1536–7). The latter also proposed an international monetary unit ('unitas') for the new global organisation (ibid. 1543). In the end, it was the US 'contributory' plan (minus 'the unitas') that was adopted at Bretton Woods and enshrined in the IMF Articles of Agreement. But arguments about the relative merits of the two plans continued for years. Yet, as will be shown later, each had serious deficiencies and, therefore, little chance of success. (Both plans are reproduced in US Department of State 1948*b*.)

The next problem that architects of the Bretton Woods System set out to solve—that of establishing an international lender of last resort—was also prompted by their past experience. Even under the classical gold standard, a country with temporary liquidity difficulties depended on the self-interest of other countries to come to its rescue in order to prevent an international financial crisis (Eichengreen 1992, Bloomfield 1963). In other words, although, at least in the case of major countries, it was likely that other countries would help, there was no guarantee that they would do so. No central bank was under an obligation to act as a surrogate international lender of last resort, nor were there generally agreed rules according to which this should be done.

The British and US plans for, respectively, a 'Clearing Union' and an 'International Stabilization Fund' were intended to overcome these problems by creating a supranational institution that would act, effectively, as a central banks' Central Bank—by stepping in to help countries with temporary liquidity problems. The end result of these labours, the International Monetary Fund, was therefore instructed (Article I) to act in such a way as to enable countries 'to correct maladjustments in their balance of payments without resorting to measures destructive of national and international prosperity'. It was to do this (Article V.1) by dealing only with national monetary authorities (that is, central banks, ministries of finance, and stabilization funds).

Moreover, like national central banks, the IMF was to provide clearing facilities, as all central banks were to hold reserves with it. In addition, again like a national central bank, it was given the authority to ask a country applying for help to take certain corrective actions in order to qualify for assistance. (IMF Articles of Agreement are reprinted in US Department of State 1948*a*, 942–84).

All these powers were, in principle, both necessary and desirable. But to be effective in practice, the institution had to have sufficient resources, independence of the influence of any one country, and undisputed authority to discharge its responsibilities. The founding fathers of the Bretton Woods system were in no position to provide this. Hence, their blueprint contained another serious deficiency that was to make it unworkable in the form intended.

Another important issue which the forty-four countries participating at the Bretton Woods Conference were determined to resolve was that of preventing destabilizing capital flows and competitive exchange rate devaluations. Both were regarded—on the basis of prewar experience—as a major obstacle to creating the viable system of multilateral trade and payments which they believed to be essential if they were to achieve high levels of output and employment after the war. For instance, Nurkse (1944) expressed a widely held view when he argued, in his analysis of international finance in the interwar period, that floating exchange rates discouraged trade, led to misallocation of international resources, and encouraged destabilizing speculation. Hubert Henderson (1955, 291), another influential observer of economic disintegration in the 1930s, concluded that competitive devaluations were the least helpful policy instrument to the countries that employed them and most harmful to the rest.

Not surprisingly, both the British and US plans wanted member countries to hold a large proportion of their reserves with the new international organization. That would make it possible for the organization to clear external imbalances and thus avoid destabilizing flights of short-term capital from one financial centre to another, as happened in the 1930s. To ensure this, it was also essential—in the British but not the American view—to impose controls on international capital flows, especially those of a short-term, speculative nature. Keynes certainly believed, as Churchill explained in a letter written in 1941, that 'the exchange regulations and controls imposed during the war' would have to be maintained 'for some considerable time' (quoted in Van Dormael, 1978, 10). Experience had taught him that only in this way would it be possible to sustain over a long period a system of fixed exchange rates in which all currencies would be pegged to the new international currency advocated in the British plan; (see Moggridge, 1986.) At the same time, both British and American plans had provision for countries with persistent balance of payments difficulties to devalue their currency.

In the end, most of these proposals were incorporated into the IMF Charter. The Fund was given responsibility 'to promote exchange rate stability' and 'to avoid competitive devaluations' (Article IV.4a). Its members were allowed to devalue only 'to correct a fundamental disequilibrium' (Article IV.5a)—although no attempt was made either then or subsequently to define this concept (see Solomon, 1982). If a member changed the par value of its currency despite the Fund's objections it would become 'ineligible to use the resources of the Fund unless the Fund otherwise' determined (Article IV.6). What is more, a persistent offender in this respect might be required to withdraw from the IMF (Article XV).

There is obviously consistency and logic in these arguments and provisions. The problem is that their effectiveness depended critically on the Fund's ability to appropriate a significant part of member countries' national economic sovereignty. This was a much more important aspect of the Bretton Woods agreement than the often discussed fact that the system was a variant of the gold standard, as all the currencies were fixed to the US dollar which, in turn, was fixed to gold. The IMF, after all, was empowered to increase international liquidity, if its larger members approved, by altering the par values of members' currencies relative to gold (Article IV.7).

A system of fixed exchange rates, strictly and scrupulously observed, should in itself be sufficient to ensure that all countries participating in it have no alternative but to follow rigid stabilization and adjustment rules. That was certainly true of countries belonging to the classical gold standard—even though, for various reasons, the system was much more flexible than is generally believed (Panić, 1992). However, the risk with a quasi-monetary system (that is, a system of fixed exchange rates) is that there is no guarantee that when confronted with a serious internal imbalance a country will stick to the rules rather than change its exchange rate; or, alternatively, that a country earning current account surpluses will not simply increase its reserves rather than expand domestic activity and imports, invest abroad, or allow the rate of exchange to appreciate to the point at which it eliminates the surpluses.

All these practices had become so common in the interwar period that the British plan included a provision empowering the new international organisation ('the Clearing Union') to impose penalties on both deficit and surplus countries (US Department of State 1948b, 1554–5). The idea was that the organization should charge extra interest: in the first case if a country's reserves fell over a period of a year or so below a certain minimum; and in the second case if the reserves held by a country at the Clearing Union over a similar period were persistently over a specified maximum.

The Americans made no similar proposal—hardly surprising, as everyone expected them to be by far the most important surplus country for a long time after the war. Nevertheless, they agreed at Bretton Woods that a 'scarce currency clause' should be included in the IMF Charter. If there was a general scarcity of a currency, the Fund would try first to borrow it from the country concerned. However, if excess demand for the currency persisted, the Fund would declare it 'scarce' and start to ration it (Article VII.3a). The moment this happened, any member would have the right, after consulting the Fund, to impose restrictions on transactions with the country whose currency had been declared 'scarce' (Article, VII.3b)—for as long as the scarcity lasted. The restrictive measures were to be discontinued only when the Fund declared the currency no longer scarce (Article VII.3c)—in other words, after the country had taken appropriate steps to balance its external account.

In this way, the IMF was given extraordinary powers to force even its largest and most influential members to observe the stabilization/adjustment rules. It could do so in the case of a deficit country when asked to act as the lender of last resort; and in the case of a surplus country by declaring its currency scarce.

All the problems, proposals, and policy decision described so far were designed to deal with the short-term aspects of economic activity: international financial measures needed to facilitate high levels of activity and trade without which the most important policy objective that industrial countries were determined to pursue after the war—that of high levels of employment and income—could not be achieved. However, there was another important factor that had contributed to the disintegration of the international economy in the 1930s: the unprecedented collapse of international long-term capital flows (see Bairoch, 1976 and Panić, 1988, chapter 9).

The three nations which provided most international investment before 1914—the United Kingdom, France, and Germany—were in no position to play this role after the First World War. The Americans, on the other hand, had the resources but no inclination to take over the role on the scale required. Their financial institutions had little experience of investing abroad, as all but a small proportion of the country's savings were used to finance domestic investment. Moreover, those who borrowed from the United States found it difficult to service and repay their debts because of the country's highly protectionist policies.

It was this experience that led US Treasury officials, under Harry White, to propose the creation of a new institution whose task would consist of providing the long-term capital that would be required for the postwar reconstruction. The problem was obvious enough: after the war, economic and political uncertainties could be expected to be so great that private investors would be most unlikely to provide such finance, at least in the initial stages of postwar reconstruction. In the circumstances, as White put it: 'Only an international, non-profit institution with enormous resources can afford to undertake the task of supplying adequate amounts of capital on the gigantic scale that will be necessary after the war' (quoted in Eckes 1975, 52).

The International Bank for Reconstruction and Development was created, therefore, to perform the function of an international allocator of last resort. Its Charter, agreed at Bretton Woods, makes it clear that the Bank's task was to assist and supplement private international investment, not to supplant it. This is emphasized in Article III.4 which, among other things, specifies that the Bank would lend mainly if the funds could not be obtained from other sources on reasonable terms. The Bank's Charter was also specific about the ways in which it would either make loans from its own resources or underwrite loans ('in whole or in part'), including those made 'by private investors through the usual investment channels' (Article IV.1a). The role intended for the Bank is, in fact, reminiscent of that played by the Japan Development Bank in the extraordinary growth and modernization of the Japanese economy after the Second World War. (The IBRD Articles of Agreement are reprinted in US Department of State 1948a, 984–1014.)

Equally important for a *World* Bank, serving countries at different levels of development and with different political systems, it was not allowed (a) to specify in which country the proceeds of its loans should be spent (Article III.5a) and (b) to interfere in the political affairs of a country, or to be influenced in making its decisions by the political system of the member or members concerned (Article IV.10).

By agreeing on the Charters of the two institutions, delegates at the Bretton Woods Conference managed to achieve something that the world had never even attempted before: to create the basic framework of supranational institutions required to manage the economic and financial behaviour of a large number of nation states whose economies were closely integrated. As Keynes, White, and others involved in producing the Bretton Woods blueprint realised—and were to be proved right by subsequent events—the only viable, lasting framework for an integrated world economy is one that is managed by supranational organizations. For reasons that had become obvious during the interwar period, dependence on a single, dominant country could not be expected to guarantee long-term improvements in global economic welfare of the kind planned by national governments after the war.

The problem that they could not solve at Bretton Woods was the one central—then as now—to the effective running of an internationally integrated economy: how to ensure in the absence of a world parliament and government that supranational institutions perform the role that such a system demands. It was this, in fact, that made the system which operated from the late 1940s until the early 1970s depart significantly in a number of respects from the blueprint produced at Bretton Woods.

THE REVIVAL AND FATAL FLAWS OF A SYSTEM MANAGED BY A DOMINANT ECONOMY

Contrary to popular belief, the 'Bretton Woods System' never operated as intended by those who created it. Instead of being managed by the two supranational institutions, it was run by the dominant economic power after the Second World War: the United States. In that sense, its fortunes, like those of the classical gold standard, were directly linked to those of the relative economic performance and policies of the country responsible for the largest share of world industrial production, trade, and finance at the time—precisely the outcome that those attending the Bretton Woods Conference had been anxious to avoid.

As there are already numerous accounts of how the postwar system actually operated (see, for instance, Argy, 1981; Spero, 1981; Solomon, 1982; Scammell, 1987; and Tew, 1988), important lessons for the future can now only be gained by discovering the reasons why it departed from the original blueprint.

Warning signals that the system was unlikely to function as agreed at Bretton Woods were there from the start. For instance, a common complaint in the literature is that the founding fathers seriously underestimated the scale of the postwar reconstruction effort and the time that it would take; and that, as a result of this, the two international institutions were provided with totally inadequate resources to play the role for which they had been created. There is some justification in this, in the sense that it was commonly believed at the time that the postwar recovery would be accomplished within five years. In fact, in most cases it took ten to fifteen years (cf. Panić, 1991a). As for the financial resources given to the IMF and the IBRD, it was agreed at Bretton Woods that they should receive $8.8 billion and $10 billion respectively (US Department of State 1948a, 976 and 985). The two figures, although quite large at the time, would have been sufficient to cover the amounts provided in different forms to Western Europe and Japan by the United States (see Milward, 1987a) during the first six or so years after the war. But there would have been very little left for other countries or purposes—even if the IMF and the IBRD had been in a position to spend every dollar, or its equivalent in other currencies and gold, allocated to them.

In fact, political considerations and economic realities ensured that the sums that the two institutions could actually use were considerably smaller. When the World Bank started its operations after the war it had effectively only $570 million (that is, the US contribution) available for lending—less than 6 per cent of the resources that it was supposed to have (Spero, 1981, 36). Moreover, it could advance loans only in those cases where it was assured of repayment. IMF currency dealings between 1947 and 1952 amounted to no more than $850 million (Kenwood and Lougheed, 1983, 255). As its responsibility was limited to short-term stabilization, it refused to come to the aid of countries with serious adjustment (that is, reconstruction and development) problems even though it was in a position to help them. Not surprisingly, in 1947, soon after they had started their operations, the two organizations expected to be the pillars of the Bretton Woods System admitted that they had inadequate resources to deal with the mounting international economic problems (Mason and Asher, 1973, 105–7 and 124–35).

There were basically two reasons for this. First, in agreeing on contributions to be made by individual countries to the IMF and the IBRD the founding fathers had to consider carefully what would be acceptable to national parliaments, especially the US Congress, and the powerful interests that they represented. (See, for example, Mickesell, 1994). The agreed quotas reflected this as much as what was thought to be either necessary or within the ability of individual countries to contribute. Second, it was important for political reasons to assume at Bretton Woods that all national currencies were of similar importance and would, therefore, be equally in demand. To distinguish 'key' currencies from others would have made it virtually impossible to achieve the consensus needed to create the postwar system. At the same time, it was clear that only a few countries— in particular, the United States—would be able to provide the goods and services needed for postwar reconstruction, for the simple reason that the economies of the remaining nations were either destroyed and dislocated by the war, or not sufficiently industrialized. To make things worse, the grossly uneven productive capacities and competitive strength of individual countries made it essential for almost all members of the two institutions to continue with the inconvertibility of their currencies after the war in order to avoid major financial crises of the kind experienced by the United Kingdom in the summer of 1947 (see Milward, 1987a). The outcome was that the IMF and the IBRD had at their disposal a large stock of currencies which were for all practical purposes unusable.

The two supranational institutions were, therefore, in no position to manage the international financial system—the task for which they had been created in 1944. Not surprisingly, the supranational edifice which represented the Bretton Woods system as originally conceived collapsed almost as soon as it was created in 1946/47. The 'Bretton Woods system' that soon afterwards rose from the ashes was something quite different: managed by the United States because of its dominant economic position in the world, its fortunes were bound to be tied closely to that country's ability to maintain this supremacy. The problem is that no country can realistically be expected to sustain such a position for long in a dynamic world economy. Consequently, no international monetary system dependent on a dominant economy is likely to have more than a relatively short life span.

At the end of the Second World War, the United States accounted for half of world manufacturing output, half of world shipping, one-third of world exports and 61 per cent of total world reserves of gold (Kennedy, 1989, 461). In 1950 its reserves were 2.73 times greater than its liquid liabilities (Milner and Greenaway, 1979, 271). The dollar was not only fixed to gold but also, as an official reserve asset, convertible into it. In these circumstances, it is inconceivable that the bancor or any other international currency could have displaced the dollar as the international medium of exchange, unit of account, and store of value—unless its creation had coincided with the abolition of all national currencies. Even in the 1960s the dollar accounted for more than two-thirds of the official reserves of all countries, with its share rising to over 77 per cent in the early 1970s when the 'Bretton Woods System' finally collapsed (cf. Walter, 1993, 187).

With the US economy and currency in such a commanding position, it was also inevitable that it would be the US authorities and financial institutions that managed the international system rather than the two supranational institutions created at Bretton Woods for the purpose. In other words, as before 1914, the international monetary system became effectively an extension of the dominant country's system. It could hardly have been otherwise, as it was that country's authorities and financial insitutions that determined the supply of the world's key currency—influencing the ability of other countries to reconcile their internal and external balances at desired levels of output and employment. Consequently, it was the US authorities and financial institutions that had a major influence on the stability and growth of the world economy; and, under the global economic conditions that existed for a quarter of a century after the Second World War, no supranational institution would have been able to challenge this influence. Hence, the position occupied by the United States under the 'Bretton Woods system' was very similar to that played by the United Kingdom under the classical gold standard—in contrast to the original Bretton Woods concept and blueprint which were designed to provide a more permanent solution.

Initially, the system worked extremely well after the advent of the Cold War left the United States with little alternative but to take over its management in 1947 in order to prevent a major international economic and political crisis. US policies ensured a steady injection of dollars into the world economy, making it possible for imbalances in international payments to be adjusted in an orderly fashion, without imposing serious welfare costs either on the countries concerned or on their trading partners. In this way, the United States also helped preserve the system of fixed exchange rates, at least among industrial economies, for more than two decades.

Massive US economic assistance to other countries started with the European Recovery Programme (Marshall Aid) and other official transfers in the late 1940s. However, as the remarkable success of the programmes in Western Europe and Japan became apparent, official grants and loans for this purpose were reduced after the early 1950s without affecting adversely the supply of international liquidity provided by the United States. The reason for this was that the reduction in official transfers coincided with increases in the country's military expenditure and long-term investment abroad which, together, offset its large, persistent surpluses on trade in goods and services (cf. OECD, 1964). In that sense, the United States, like the United Kingdom before 1914, provided other countries with its currency on a scale that facilitated the growth of world output, trade, and investment without compromising the confidence that the dollar enjoyed internationally. It performed, therefore, the role of a surplus, creditor country in a way that benefited the rest of the world and would have made it unnecessary for the IMF to apply the scarce currency clause against the dollar even if it had been able to do so.

However, unlike the British in the interwar period and to a lesser extent before 1914, the Americans were unwilling to sacrifice any of their major economic and political objectives when their economic supremacy and, thus, their position at the centre of the 'Bretton Woods System' began to wane. As the rate of growth of the economy accelerated in the 1960s and unemployment levels fell, US current account surpluses decreased progressively. At the same time, the country's military expenditure and investment abroad continued at high levels, producing large deficits on the basic and overall balance of payments. The result was a sharp deterioration in the ratio of US reserves to liquid liabilities: from 2.73 in 1950 to 0.92 in 1960 and 0.31 in 1970 (Milner and Greenaway, 1979, 271). Not surprisingly, the dollar became vulnerable to speculative attacks, as doubts increased around the world about the country's ability to maintain the value of its currency fixed to gold at the existing parity ($35 to one ounce of pure gold).

The first run on the dollar occurred in 1960 when international speculators began to exchange it for gold on the London market. The general unease about US ability to manage the System and maintain the exchange rate of the dollar continued throughout the decade, intensifying after sterling's devaluation in November 1967. There was also increasing resentment in Europe that the Americans were deriving 'seigniorage' benefits from the role played by their currency and institutions under the 'Bretton Woods system'.

Clearly, to deal with these problems and complaints, the United States needed either to tighten macroeconomic policies to boost its surpluses on trade in goods and services, or to reduce its military expenditure and investment abroad. But, for domestic reasons, the successive administrations found it difficult to do either. Instead, they made some attempts in the mid-1960s to control capital outflows, tie foreign aid to orders from the United States, and introduce various schemes to encourage exports. Yet, despite the country's apparent determination to keep the dollar at the centre of the international system, no attempt was made to take the required stabilization/adjustment measures because of their potentially adverse effects on domestic output and employment.

In the end, as in the British case forty years earlier, the conflicting objectives and policies could not be sustained. In August 1971, the Nixon administration first abandoned convertibility of the dollar into gold and imposed a 10 per cent surcharge on imports; and a few months later, as part of the Smithsonian Agreement, devalued the dollar by 10 per cent—signalling, in effect, the end of the 'Bretton Woods system'. For the second time within a century, after initial success, a dominant country had failed to secure a viable, lasting international monetary system. The reason was the same in both cases: the inability of the country at the centre of the system to maintain its economic supremacy and, with it, the capacity to fulfill its international role without sacrificing domestic welfare. No international system can survive if the country responsible for managing it is unwilling to observe its basic rules.

One of the consequences of this is that international consensus will start to break down precisely at the moment when it is needed most, that is, when it becomes apparent that no country is capable of managing the system on its own.

The Americans played a major role in rebuilding international cooperation after the war, especially among the countries of Western Europe (see Milward, 1987a, and Panić 1991a and 1993). Marshall Aid was given on condition that the countries receiving it cooperated in designing and implementing it through the Organisation for European Economic Cooperation (set up in 1948). The United States actively promoted intra-European trade and the clearing of external imbalances by helping create the European Payments Union in 1950. The success of these and other initiatives made an important contribution towards the greater European integration which is still in progress. Later on, in the early 1960s, there was an increase in collaboration among the central banks of industrial countries in supporting each other's currencies in times of speculative attack. The 1960s also saw a significant liberalization of international trade (OECD, 1985).

However, as the decade progressed there were serious disagreements among industrial countries about the policies required to deal with the growing disparities in their external balances and who should bear the main responsibility for taking steps to correct them: deficit countries, such as the United States and the United Kingdom, or surplus countries of the European Community, notably West Germany. In other words, neither side was prepared to observe the rules of the international stabilization/adjustment game when they began to come in conflict with their national objectives and policies.

This could have only one outcome: greater uncertainty and, consequently, international financial instability—especially as the weakening of consensus and cooperation among the major industrial countries coincided with rapid growth of international investment flows.

The scope for such movements was limited until the second half of the 1950s by two factors: tight controls of capital exports, practised by almost all industrial countries; and, where this was not the case (the United States), the risks and uncertainties associated with investing in economies struggling to recover from the economic and other damage and dislocation caused by the war. But with the success of the recovery, the narrowing down of international income differentials, and improvements in transport and communications, there came a rapid growth of transnational corporations followed by transnational banks and other financial institutions.

By 1971 the value of liquid assets held by the top one hundred US transnational corporations (TNCs) exceeded the combined reserves of the largest industrial countries (Robbins and Stobaugh, 1974, 182–3). The growth of transnational banks (TNBs) was even more rapid. Between 1965 and 1974 the value of assets held abroad by branches of US banks had risen from $9 billion to $125 billion. Foreign banks operating in the United States held in 1974 assets worth $56 billion (United Nations, 1981). The gross size of eurocurrency deposits (that is, including interbank deposits) went up from $19 billion in 1964 to $210 billion in 1972 (Pilbeam, 1992, 312).

Given the resources at their disposal, it was sufficient for these transnationals to switch a relatively small proportion of their assets from one currency to another to cause a major exchange rate crisis. The growing discord among industrial countries provided them with the incentive to do precisely that in order to protect the value of their assets; and, although their actions interfered increasingly with the ability of different countries to achieve their economic objectives, the fact that transnationals operated globally made it more and more difficult for any one government to control their actions (see Panić, 1991b).

A system of fixed exchange rates cannot survive for long under these conditions, as Keynes and his contemporaries learned from experience, particularly when there are noticeable differences in the ability of different countries—including those whose currencies are used widely in international transactions—to reconcile their internal and external balances. Of the two reserve currencies, sterling was the first to be subjected to persistent pressure until it was devalued in 1967. The dollar followed four years later. The 'Bretton Woods system', resuscitated and managed with great success for a number of years by the United States, was no more.

An international monetary system, using a single global currency and run by supranational institutions, could have avoided the financial (though not the economic!) problems described in this section. As a result, it would probably be functioning even more effectively now than in the 1940s.

Keynes and many of his contemporaries realized this. Unfortunately, like all visionaries, they were far ahead of their time.

CONCLUSION: IS THE WORLD READY FOR A 'NEW BRETTON WOODS'?

The 'collapse' of the 'Bretton Woods system' in the early 1970s has been mourned ever since. However, as suggested in the previous section, the change has not been as dramatic or as complete as seems to be widely believed. The return of floating exchange rates—unavoidable in a world of massive capital flows—destroyed the quasi-monetary union (that is, the regime of fixed parities) that had existed from the late 1940s until the early 1970s. To that extent, the demise of the postwar system has increased economic uncertainty considerably by relaxing (though not removing!) the obligation to observe the well-known stabilization/adjustment requirements and, thus, weakening the need for international cooperation which such a system demands.

That has obviously imposed welfare costs on all countries. But the costs have been kept down by the fact that the industrial countries in particular have been careful to avoid competitive devaluations and other protective devices of the kind that caused so much damage in the 1930s. Thus, the Bretton Woods spirit of international cooperation has survived, though mainly in a negative form: national governments have, in general, taken considerable care not to repeat the worst mistakes of the interwar period, but have not made a genuine effort to create a new world economic and financial order. In the same spirit, the two international institutions created at Bretton Woods have not been abolished mainly because, as recognized in the 1940s, an integrated world economy needs supranational organisations. True, neither has been at the centre of international economic developments over the last twenty years. But this is neither surprising nor new. They had not been allowed to manage the international financial system during the preceding twenty-five years either.

All this may be unsatisfactory, but what is the likelihood of doing better by restoring a much needed order and predictability in international economic and financial relationships under a 'Bretton Woods Mark II'?

As I have argued elsewhere (Panić, 1988), the basic economic requirements of such a system are straightforward enough and, from a technical point of view, relatively easy to implement. The reason for this is that, in principle, they are not different from those that have been applied for many years in the most successful industrial countries, especially those with federal constitutions. Hence, if the world had a single political authority the same blueprint could be implemented globally—by fiat if necessary.

The problem is, of course, that the day when nation states are ready to hand over sovereignty to a world authority, because it is much more likely to satisfy the economic and social aspirations of their citizens, belongs to a very distant future. Consequently, the critical issue in creating an effective supranational institutional framework is still the same as in 1944: how to make it worthwhile for a large number of countries at different levels of development, often with widely different problems and priorities, to collaborate in a way that makes all of them noticeably better off than they would have been otherwise.

Given that there are even more sovereign states now than at the time of the Bretton Woods Conference, with huge differences in their efficiency and income levels, global consensus and active cooperation of a lasting nature are extremely unlikely. The best that one can hope for are mini 'Bretton Woods' at regional levels. Arrangements of this kind should be easiest to achieve among industrial countries with similar problems and objectives—though the European Union, the most promising candidate for a successful regional grouping, has been demonstrating in recent years the difficulties involved.

The familiar alternative, a global system managed by a dominant economy whose actions have a marked effect on the welfare of other countries, appears to be a thing of the past. No single country currently in existence is in a position to exert such an influence either at present or in the foreseeable future.

As a result, it is inconceivable that the global economy can be managed now either supranationally (as intended at Bretton Woods) or by a dominant economy (as practised effectively for a time after 1945 by the United States). A truly international currency ('son of bancor') is, therefore, as unlikely as it was fifty years ago; and it is even less realistic to expect a single national currency to fill the gap as successfully as sterling did before 1914 and the dollar after 1945. Nevertheless, given the size of the US economy, the dollar is bound to remain a major asset in settling international debts for quite some time—with its relative importance determined by the size and survival of regional blocs.

The existence of a number of major currencies—in a world in which transnational corporations and financial institutions can switch vast funds from currency to currency at short notice—makes it difficult to believe that any return to a system of fixed exchange rates would survive for long. As Keynes argued, controls of capital flows are essential for the viability of a global monetary union in a world of independent national currencies. Effective control of transnational enterprises is virtually impossible at a time when so many countries are desperate to attract their capital, and technical and managerial expertise; this, in turn, means that a global system of fixed exchange rates (that is, a global quasi-monetary union) would be unsustainable in the near future.

For all these reasons, the most likely prospect for quite some time is that of restrained anarchy, such as the world economy has been experiencing since the end of the 1960s. A new Bretton Woods—whichever aspect of the original model or its application in practice this represented—is not a practical proposition. But regional groupings, such as the European Union, though very much a second best, are more likely, if organized properly, to enhance global economic welfare than almost two hundred squabbling countries of varying degrees of impotence.

Whether or not regional groupings materialize and survive long enough to provide a stepping-stone to a truly global system of the kind contemplated at Bretton Woods will depend on the extent to which those forming them respect the guiding principle which prompted that remarkable conference in 1944: that international integration and, ultimately, world peace are unsustainable without close collaboration between independent, sovereign states directed towards improvements in economic welfare, widely diffused within and between countries.

3. Taming International Finance

Yılmaz Akyüz[1]

The past decade has witnessed many sharp and unpredictable shifts in the major monetary and financial variables, including the prices of financial assets, interest rates, and exchange rates, and flows of capital, both across borders and across markets for financial assets denominated in different currencies. There have also been periods in which these variables have persistently stayed at levels not compatible with their fundamental determinants; instability has thus been latent even when it has not actually occurred. As a result, serious strains have been put on international debtor–creditor relations, the banking system, capital markets, and the international payments and exchange arrangements. Many observers, analysing these developments from the standpoint of both the world economy and individual countries, have concluded that actions to make the monetary and financial system more stable and less susceptible to disruptions and crises should have high priority.

Monetary and financial disorder is not a new phenomenon. The international monetary and financial system has exhibited disorderly and sometimes even chaotic behaviour since the early 1970s—although the latter has fortunately been relatively short-lived. Until the early 1980s this behaviour could plausibly be explained by shocks and abrupt changes in the environment in which the international monetary and financial system operated. First, the early 1970s saw progressive disintegration and the eventual breakdown of the Bretton Woods system; currency market turbulence and exchange rate instability could thus be expected to persist until floating was generalized and the markets learned and established new rules of the game. Second, the inflationary experience following the oil price rises of the 1970s had destabilizing influences for the international monetary and financial system. On the one hand, not only did foreign exchange markets have to operate under conditions of price instability, but also relative price levels of major countries underwent drastic changes because of significant inter-country differences in rates of inflation. On the other hand, the trade imbalances that emerged as a result of oil price increases and terms-of-trade changes, together with policies designed to avoid contraction in economic activity, resulted in substantial increases in international liquidity and debt-financing of current account deficits which proved a major problem

[1] The views expressed in this chapter are personal and do not necessarily reflect those of the UNCTAD secretariat. I am grateful to Cape Kasahara for his assistance in section 1.

subsequently. Finally, the disinflationary process of the late 1970s and early 1980s entailed substantial instability in financial and currency markets because the mix and stance of policies in the major countries gave rise to large swings in key financial prices. The pace of disinflation also differed among the major countries, implying substantial changes in relative price levels.

However, such conjunctural and transitory factors are much less capable of explaining the continued instability in international money and finance over the last decade. This period has seen neither especially high inflation nor serious supply shocks, and the major market economies have increasingly converged in their growth performance and displayed increased willingness to undertake joint interventions to manage exchange rates. Even so, the international monetary and financial system has remained unstable, as witnessed by the sharp swings in stock prices, exchange and interest rates, continued failures of banks and other financial institutions, and persistence of strains in international debtor/creditor relations. As pointed out by the former President of the Federal Reserve Bank of New York: 'The past fifteen years have witnessed a greater number of financial disruptions with potential systemic implications than was the case over the postwar period prior to 1974. And if we divide the 1974–89 period roughly in half, the latter half of that interval has seen more disruption than the former.' (Corrigan, 1989, 9.)

These considerations suggest that deficiencies in the structure of the international financial and monetary system, and in the philosophy underlying policies, are more important factors in the observed behaviour of financial and currency markets. Disruptions and disorder in such markets have so far been contained in that they have not led to crises characterized by falling asset prices, widespread insolvency among debtors and financial intermediaries which seriously undermine the capacity of the markets to allocate capital and exert a visible and significant damage to the real economy. However, crisis management has been costly. For instance, an international banking crisis has been staved off at the expense of living standards, and stability and development in debtor developing countries, while exchange rate management has tended to raise world interest rates. The debt deflation process that emerged in the major industrial countries at the turn of the decade has undermined the willingness and ability of banks to lend, thereby forcing debtors to curtail operations or resort to distress sales of assets, and hence lowering incomes and asset prices further and prolonging the recession. More important, so long as the international monetary and financial system remains structurally vulnerable, the potential for an extremely costly crisis will remain: 'if a crisis were to develop ... its capacity to generate major damage to the real economy may be greater today than it was in the past. The fundamental reason for this is the nature, speed and complexity of the operational, liquidity and credit interdependences that bind together all major financial institutions and markets in the world.' (Corrigan, 1989, 9.)

Three basic deficiencies appear to underlie the increased instability. First, the main activity of financial markets has become not so much to intermediate between ultimate savers and investors, allocate resources on the basis of asset valuations reflecting long-term risk and profits, and facilitate transactions and payments needed for investment, trade, and production, but rather to create short-term opportunities for speculation in volatile and misaligned asset valuations. Speculation is not, of course, a new phenomenon; but the increased internationalization of finance has enhanced the scope for propagation of disturbances from one market to another within, as well as across, borders.

Second, the policy approach prevailing in the major countries has also tended to contribute to instability. Since the beginning of the decade many countries have effectively ceased to use the government budget, and prices and incomes policies for macroeconomic management, thereby overloading monetary policy and making different policy objectives more difficult to reconcile. Moreover, the conduct of monetary policy has changed significantly: not only have interest rates been deregulated, but, except at times of crisis, monetary policy has been directed at certain monetary aggregates rather than the management of financial asset prices and interest rates. Consequently, monetary and real shocks to financial markets have tended to generate sharp swings in financial asset prices and interest rates. Moreover, interest rate deregulation has not always been accompanied by increased prudential regulations; excessive risk-taking in the financial system has played a major role in financial failures in some major countries. Meanwhile the dismantling of quantitative and tax restrictions on movements of capital across countries, markets and currencies has accorded markets greater scope to generate and/or propagate speculative disturbances.

Finally, effective multilateral constraints and obligations on policy making in the major countries have been absent. Although existing institutional arrangements have been outmoded by the increased financial integration and internationalization of finance that has taken place, there has been no reform designed to ensure effective multilateral surveillance over the policies of countries which have a large impact on the world economy.

This chapter examines the extent, causes, and consequences of the internationalization of finance, and discusses possible ways of improving policies and the functioning of markets. It argues that governments need to commit themselves to defend a publicly announced pattern of exchange rates which should be internationally agreed and compatible with high levels of activity and employment. Multilateral surveillance of policies of major industrial countries should be much strengthened, and targets need to be set for demand growth and current account balances. The burden of adjusting policy when outcomes deviate from those targets should be clearly specified and shared between deficit and surplus countries[2] in such a way as to avoid bias towards deflation and high interest rates. More important, given the degree of development of the organization of financial markets, and the increased predominance of speculative activities, an appropriate design and coordination of policies would not be sufficient to avert financial disruptions and destabilizing capital flows. Consequently, there is a need to give serious consideration to possible ways and means of reducing the scope of markets to generate disruption and instability. These include prudential regulations to restrict banks' participation in currency speculation and an internationally agreed tax on foreign exchange transactions.

1. INTERNATIONAL FINANCIAL INTEGRATION

Strictly speaking, the term *domestic finance* covers only financial transactions among residents denominated in the country's own currency (the 'home currency'). By contrast, *international finance* involves either a non-resident or assets denominated in a foreign currency, or both—that is, financial transactions across borders or across currencies. *International banking* thus involves claims and liabilities *vis-à-vis* residents denominated in foreign currencies, as well as claims and liabilities *vis-à-vis* non-residents denominated in either home or foreign currencies. This definition of international finance is wider than Eurocurrency or offshore banking, which excludes international bank loans to and deposits of non-residents denominated in the home currency. It also includes bond and equity issues in Eurobond and Euroequity markets—that is, in a currency not that of the country in which the bond or the equity is issued; issues in the so-called foreign bond markets—that is, bonds issued by non-residents in a country in the currency of that country; and non-resident holdings of securities issued by residents in the home currency (that is, issued in the so-called national stock market).

However, domestic and international transactions are not segmented into separate markets. When the financial market of a country is opened to non-resident investors and/or borrowers, or when residents are allowed to deal in foreign currency assets and liabilities, these markets become interna-

---

[2] These concepts belong to the Bretton Woods era since they imply that exchange rate movements are governed by current account balances rather than autonomous capital movements. It would now be more appropriate to use weak- and strong-currency countries since deficit countries can experience appreciations and surplus countries experience depreciations. However, for simplicity, we shall continue to use the old terminology.

tionalized. As national and international financial transactions develop relations of substitutability and complementarity, financial transactions with purely domestic characteristics become subject to strong external influences.

The share of transactions with international characteristics can, in principle, provide a good indicator of the exposure to such influences.[3] Following Bryant (1987) Table 3.1 puts together some data on international banking, covering major financial markets and offshore centres. Almost one-third of total bank assets in this group of countries taken together qualifies as international. The share is very large in some countries—60 per cent in London and more than three-quarters in offshore centres—but relatively low in Germany. About two-thirds of international assets are interbank transactions. In general, claims on non-residents in foreign currencies account for a substantial portion of international assets, but banks in Germany and particularly the United States appear to have a stronger preference for the home currency in international lending.

Data for different years are not directly comparable, particularly in Germany and Japan. Between 1982 and 1988 the deutschmark appreciated against the dollar by nearly 40 per cent and the yen by more than 90 per cent, raising considerably the dollar value of total bank assets in these countries; between 1988 and 1992 both currencies remained relatively stable against the dollar. Nevertheless, they reveal a number of tendencies regarding changes in the importance of international banking. First, there has been a significant increase in the share of international banking in Japan despite the yen appreciation. Second, there has been a decline in the share of offshore centres in international banking, and in the share of international banking in some traditional financial centres such as London.[4] This probably reflects competition—financial deregulation and liberalization by other centres.

The combined size of world financial markets can be estimated at over $43,000 billion (Table 3.2), half of which is accounted for by commercial banks. Assets which are strictly international (that is, international bank assets, Euroequities, Eurobonds, and foreign bonds) account for 18 per cent of total world markets; but including those 'national' capital markets which have become more open to non-resident investors raises substantially the share of world financial markets having an international character.

The 1980s have seen a major shift in international financial intermediation

[3] There are serious practical difficulties in estimating financial transactions with international characteristics, and integrating national and international aspects of finance, since such data are not readily available in most countries. Thus, the estimates here need to be used with caution.

[4] It has to be pointed out that sterling depreciated between 1982 and 1988, and again between 1988 and 1992, i.e. figures in Table 3.1 underestimate the relative decline in international banking in the United Kingdom.

Table 3.1. Total and international assets of banking offices in selected industrial countries and offshore banking centres

Country/centre	Total assets[a] (\$ billion)			International assets as a percentage of total assets			Assets with international characteristics (as a percentage of total assets)								
							Claims on non-residents in foreign currencies			Claims on non-residents in home currency			Claims on residents in foreign currencies		
	1982	1988	1992	1982	1988	1992	1982	1988	1992	1982	1988	1992	1982	1988	1992
8 European countries[b]	3811	7136	10227	31.9	31.6	31.9	19.9	20.0	21.1	4.5	5.1	4.9	7.4	6.5	5.8
of which:															
United Kingdom	893	1841	2113	72.3	62.4	60.8	48.9	43.8	44.2	2.9	4.2	4.1	20.5	14.4	12.6
Federal Republic of Germany	1140	2238	3687	7.5	9.4	10.3	1.7	2.7	4.4	5.6	6.5	5.6	0.2	0.2	0.3
France	654	1271	1868	28.8	27.3	25.6	18.0	18.4	18.1	3.7	3.3	3.9	6.1	5.6	3.6
United States	2109	3048	3138	17.2	18.4	17.8	0.4	2.3	2.0	16.8	16.1	15.8	—	—	—
Japan	1157	4625	5825	15.4	25.0	26.2	5.7	8.4	7.5	2.2	7.4	7.6	7.5	9.1	5.9
11 industrial reporting countries[c]	7313	15213	19519	24.9	26.6	26.2	12.4	12.7	13.8	7.6	7.9	7.4	5.4	6.0	4.9
Eight offshore centres[d]	660	—	—	87.4	—	—	75.6	—	—	1.3	—	—	10.5	—	—

Source: 1982 data (except for Japan) from Bryant (1987); 1988 and 1992 data from BIS, *International Banking and Financial Market Developments*, and national sources. All data are end-year.

    [a] Gross size of banks' balance sheets.
    [b] Belgium, Federal Republic of Germany, France, Ireland, Italy, Netherlands, Switzerland and the United Kingdom.
    [c] The eight European countries plus Canada, Japan, and the United States.
    [d] Bahamas, Bahrain, Cayman Islands, Hong Kong, Lebanon, Netherlands Antilles, Panama and Singapore.

Table 3.2.   Size and structure of world financial markets

	1982		1988		1992	
	Value of assets ($ billion)	Per cent of total assets	Value of assets ($ billion)	Per cent of total assets	Value of assets ($ billion)	Per cent of total assets
Bank assets[a]	8,887	59.2	16,714	45.9	19,632	44.9
Domestic	6,218	41.4	11,209	30.8	13,503	30.9
International	2,669	17.8	5,505	15.1	6,129	14.0
Capital markets	6,127	40.8	19,717	54.1	24,133	55.1
Euroequity	—	—	40	0.1	71	0.2
International bond markets[b]	259	1.7	1,085	3.0	1,687	3.9
Stock markets	2,737	18.2	9,773	26.8	11,098	25.4
Bond markets	3,127	20.9	8,819	24.2	11,277	25.8
Total	15,010	100.0	36,431	100.0	43,765	100.0

Source: Bank assets as for Table 3.1. Euroequity from OECD *Financial Market Trends* (various issues). International bonds from BIS, *Annual Report* (various issues). Stock markets from IFC, *Emerging Stock Market Factbook* (various issues). Bond market information for 1982 and 1988 has been supplied by Salomon Brothers International; for 1992 from FIBV statistics.
[a] Gross size of banks' balance sheets.
[b] Eurobonds and foreign bonds.

from banking to security markets ('securitization'). International bank lending slowed down, reflecting the cutback of lending to developing countries and the increased recourse of international borrowers to direct security issues while Eurobond markets became important; Euroequity markets also emerged. While securitization has reduced the share of international banking in world financial markets, it has increased the involvement of banks in security transactions, greatly widening the grey area between banking and security market transactions, often in the form of off-balance-sheet business. Securitization has gone hand-in-hand with the introduction of a variety of new financial instruments (for example rate-issuance facilities, swaps, options, and forward rate agreements) designed to reduce investors' exposure to credit, liquidity and exchange rate risk.

The internationalization of finance has also meant financial deepening at a global level. Growth in world output, trade, and investment naturally tends to cause the volume of financial transactions to grow. However, over the last two to three decades the pace of growth of international financial transactions has been far in excess of that of real variables. This is demonstrated in Table 3.3, which compares two measures of international banking (the only time series available on a continuous basis) with indicators of 'real' world economic activity—production, trade, and investment. These

Table 3.3. International financial deepening: international banking in relation to world output, trade, and investment

	1964	1972	1980	1985	1991
	As a percentage of world output[a]				
Net international bank loans[b]	0.7	3.7	8.0	13.2	16.3[c]
Gross size of international banking market[d]	1.2	6.3	16.2	27.8	37.0[c]
	As a percentage of world trade[a]				
Net international bank loans[b]	7.5	31.5	42.6	80.4	104.6
Gross size of international banking market[d]	12.4	53.7	86.3	169.7	215.6
	As a percentage of world gross fixed investment[a]				
Net international bank loans[b]	6.2	25.6	51.1	103.7	131.4
Gross size of international banking market[d]	10.3	43.7	103.6	219.2	270.9

Source: 1964 and 1972 data on bank loans and gross size of international banking market are from Bryant (1987), and other years from BIS. *Annual Report* (various issues). Output and trade data are from UNCTAD *Handbook of International Trade and Development Statistics* (various issues), and investment data from UNCTAD data base.

Note: The table relates the stock of bank loans outstanding at the end of the year to world output, trade (imports cif) and gross fixed investment in current dollars during the year.

  [a] Excluding Eastern European countries.

  [b] Claims of banks in the BIS reporting area, excluding inter-bank redepositing.

  [c] 1990.

  [d] Claims of banks in nearly all European countries, the Bahamas, Bahrain, Canada, Cayman Islands, Hong Kong, Japan, Netherlands Antilles, Panama, Singapore and the United States, including inter-bank redepositing.

figures tend to underestimate the deepening since, as noted above, securities transactions have grown even faster than international banking.

Since the early 1970s, international banking has grown at about 20 per cent per annum, that is, almost twice as fast as international trade (12 per cent) and world output (10 per cent). Between 1972 and 1992 world trade increased by about $3,000 billion whereas the gross size of international banking expanded by $7,000 billion. In 1992 the stock of international bank assets was more than double the volume of world trade. A comparison of finance with capital accumulation provides an even better measure of financial deepening in view of the role of finance in converting savings into investment. Between 1982 and 1988 the annual increment in the stock of world financial assets was, on average, about $3,800 billion, whereas the annual average level of world fixed capital formation was around $2,300 billion. The ratio of the size of the international banking market to total global fixed investment doubled in less than a decade.

Deregulation and Internationalization of Finance

The strong tendency for the pace of the internationalization of finance to outstrip the growth of real activity has been facilitated by (and itself accelerated) developments in communication and transportation technology, particularly in electronics. These have allowed information to be acquired, processed, and disseminated much more rapidly and at very low costs, and to improve greatly the payments transmission mechanisms across countries. As a result, opportunities for cross-border arbitrage have increased, the costs of international financial transactions have been reduced and national markets have been brought closer together.

The progressive dismantling of policy barriers to capital movements has also played a cardinal role. Financial deregulation and liberalization quickened after the collapse of the Bretton Woods system, and has further accelerated in the 1980s. As a result, the financial system prevailing in the major countries now has the following broad characteristics: cross-border and foreign exchange credits (forex) are virtually unrestricted in all the countries concerned; cross-border and forex deposits are allowed in all major financial centres and the member countries of EU; and security transactions now enjoy a high degree of freedom. Since the early 1970s, freedom of capital movements has been increasingly viewed as an important policy objective. This trend is in stark contrast to government attitudes in the postwar years: the Bretton Woods era was based on a consensus that capital flows unrelated to foreign direct investment or trade should be discouraged (or even prevented).

By contrast, in the field of trade, restrictions of various kinds have proliferated. The tendency for financial policies to become less restrictive cannot be explained by considerations of efficiency; the efficiency argument has greater validity in respect of trade liberalization. A more plausible reason is that costs of financial openness (loss of policy autonomy, increased financial instability, and so on) being collective are anonymous in their incidence, whereas the benefits accrue to particular economic agents (especially international financial and non-financial enterprises, and *rentiers*). Political pressures by the latter for financial opening therefore do not meet significant resistance. By contrast, in the field of trade, it is the costs of restrictiveness that are borne collectively, and the benefits accrue to particular groups.

The failure of controls imposed under the Bretton Woods system to check capital movements also played an important role in changing official attitudes towards financial deregulation. Most controls and regulations were adopted *ad hoc* for macroeconomic reasons, and did not slow down the growth of unregulated offshore markets and the relocation of financial activities. This in turn entailed a more liberal treatment of financial operations in order to avoid a loss of competitiveness for domestic financial institutions.

Similarly, competition among national financial markets has also been an important factor in the proliferation of deregulation and the reduction or abolition of taxes. Examples include competitive abolition of withholding tax on securities held by non-residents; widespread decisions concerning non-resident issues in national capital markets; authorization given to foreign banks to lead-manage bond issues; and removal of restrictions on trading in certain financial instruments. When many major financial centres deregulate, the rest have little choice but to follow suit. The process tends to be circular and cumulative also because markets themselves generate pressures for further freedom; for deregulation generates fluctuations and turnover for many financial operators on which their profits depend.

Moreover, there has been a tendency for national financial regulations to become subject to international negotiations and agreements. These include the establishment of a single market in Europe; the Canada–United States Free Trade Agreement of 1989, which provides for the removal of restrictions on United States financial institutions operating in Canada and equal treatment of Canadian banks in the United States; and the 1984 United States–Japan agreement (which contributed to a massive increase in the Japanese portfolio and foreign direct investment in the United States instead of increasing the penetration of Japanese financial markets by United States institutions).

Such agreements have now gone beyond the regional or bilateral level; for the first time with the Uruguay Round, financial services have figured on the agenda of multilateral trade negotiations (Cornford, 1993*a*). Some major industrialized countries, notably the United States and the United Kingdom, have been advocating further liberalization of trade in banking services in the context of a multilateral agreement. This is largely a reflection of their belief that banks in these countries have a competitive edge compared to their counterparts in developing and other developed countries. The control that banks and other financial institutions can exert over the pattern and scale of production may be thought to help them to regain, at least partly, competitiveness in industry *vis-à-vis* Japan and Germany; it also explains why the United States and the United Kingdom have been putting pressure on these countries for greater financial openness.

Financial Openness in Developing Countries

In developing countries, the real degree of financial openness (that is, the ease with which residents can acquire assets and liabilities denominated in foreign currencies and non-residents can operate in national financial markets, including the enjoyment of market access by foreign banks) does not always correspond to the restrictiveness of regulations ostensibly in force. For one thing, these are not always fully implemented. For another, because financial institutions are underdeveloped, many financial transactions take place in informal, curb markets, which makes it relatively easy to circumvent regulations. Furthermore, a number of specific factors (such as high earnings from tourism and workers' remittances, the presence of transnational corporations, and physical proximity to hard-currency areas) can facilitate the access to foreign currency and financial transfers abroad through informal channels. Liberal treatment of financial inflows abroad, particularly in neighbouring countries, can also impede a country from limiting its degree of financial openness. For instance, in the late 1980s in Uruguay, where banks were free to accept forex deposits and banking secrecy prevailed, about one-half of such deposits were estimated to have belonged to Argentine nationals. Similarly, during the same years, tax exemption of foreign depositors in the United States (together with the tax deductibility of interest payments in Mexico) gave Mexican enterprises an incentive to shift their funds to the United States and recycle them back as loans to themselves, thereby avoiding taxes on interest income received while deducting interest payments from their taxable income.

Nevertheless, official policies and a resolve and capacity to implement rules and regulations play the most important role in determining the degree of financial openness. Since the early 1970s there has been a general easing of restrictions on three fronts. First, *inward* transactions: allowing residents to borrow freely in international financial markets, and non-residents to invest freely in domestic financial markets. Second, *outward* transactions: allowing residents to transfer capital and to hold financial assets abroad, and non-residents to issue liabilities and to borrow in domestic financial markets. Third, *domestic transactions in foreign currencies*: allowing debtor–creditor relations among residents in foreign currencies such as bank deposits and lending in foreign currencies.

The first wave of external liberalization in developing countries generally took the form of allowing the private sector to borrow abroad. The Southern Cone experience is the best known, and was set in a broad programme of liberalization. However, external borrowing by residents was liberalized also in a number of countries where domestic financial markets continued to be highly regulated (for example Turkey in the 1970s,

Yugoslavia, and the Philippines). Resident banks were often involved as intermediaries between international capital markets and domestic borrowers. In countries with a sizeable flow of workers' remittances, a particular form of such borrowing took place on a large scale, namely foreign currency deposits offering attractive terms and carrying government guarantees. In almost all these episodes there was a massive build-up of foreign exchange liabilities by private corporations which contributed significantly to the subsequent debt crisis and payments difficulties (Diaz-Alejandro, 1985; Rodrik, 1986; UNCTAD, 1991). Although controls over foreign borrowing by the private sector were subsequently reinstated during the financial crisis, these have been effectively lifted in the course of the 1980s. Inward transactions are now virtually free in a large number of countries in Latin America where external borrowing by the private sector is not subject to approval, except for capital market issues—a factor that underlies massive inflows of short-term capital during the last few years.

Regarding the entry of non-residents to domestic markets in developing countries, recent years have witnessed two major developments. First, recent deregulation of domestic financial markets in developing countries has often been accompanied by a relaxing of restrictions on the entry of foreign banks. Of equal and even greater importance is the substantially increased access of non-residents to national equity markets. This has been greatly facilitated by the debt crisis. In many highly-indebted countries, especially in Latin America, the 'market-based menu' has generated new prospects for international arbitrage, speculation, and windfall profits for a handful of operators in creditor and debtor countries. Various debt conversion facilities have significantly raised the amount of equities and domestic-currency debt assets held by non-residents in such countries (UNCTAD, 1989, 105–7).

More recently, access of non-residents to national equity markets has been encouraged in the context of privatization programmes. While one of the stated objectives of privatization has been precisely to develop capital markets, increased access to such markets has been granted to non-residents in order to boost demand. Some of the newly-emerging capital markets have come to depend on foreign portfolio investment which often accounts for a major part of capital inflows. In Mexico, for instance, equity holding by non-residents is estimated to have amounted to about a quarter of the market's capitalization in the second quarter of 1992 (*Latin American Economy and Business*, May 1992, 4), compared to about 5 per cent in the major capital markets (Morgan Guaranty, 1989, Table 1).

As for outward transactions, an increasing number of developing countries have adopted capital account convertibility in recent years—some to an extent not found in many industrialized countries. Liberalization of transactions among resident in foreign currency, however, has gone much further. Indeed, there has been a tendency to permit and encourage residents to hold foreign exchange deposits with banks at home, both in countries where such deposits were originally permitted for migrant workers and in others with an acute foreign exchange shortage. The interest rates offered on such deposits are usually above world levels; deposits are highly liquid; even sight deposits earn considerable interest; and they are much more easily accessible than their counterparts in most industrial countries, where minimum limits and/or charges and commissions are applied.

The effect of introducing foreign currency deposits is generally to increase the importance of foreign currency in the domestic monetary system, that is, encourage currency substitution and dollarization of the economy. In many developing countries where such deposits were introduced, there was not just a once-and-for-all shift from holding foreign banknotes; rather, foreign exchange deposits kept growing, often rapidly, even coming to exceed domestic currency deposits. The share of foreign exchange accounts in total deposits in recent years exceeded domestic currency deposits in a number of developing countries in Latin America and elsewhere. This figure is well above the levels found in some international financial centres such as London where the share of total bank claims (including inter-bank claims) on residents in foreign currencies barely exceeds 20 per cent (Table 3.1). Moreover, some developing countries have started issuing dollar-denominated or dollar-indexed paper in domestic markets. In short, the degree of financial openness of many developing countries is much greater than indicated by the degree of capital account convertibility.

2. SOME CONSEQUENCES OF THE INTERNATIONALIZATION OF FINANCE

The main argument put forward in favour of financial openness and internationalization of finance is that it would improve the allocation of resources internationally. The reasoning is that, if allowed to move freely, capital would flow to countries in response to opportunities for real investment, thereby equalizing rates of return on investment everywhere, and allow individual countries either to save more than they invest, or to invest more than they save, according to market disciplines. Whether openness and internationalization in practice have had these results can, in principle, be assessed in three ways: by comparing rates of returns on physical capital; by comparing returns on similar financial assets; and by examining the links between national savings and investment rates. A comparison of rates of return on capital investment among the Group of Seven countries shows that, on average, inter-country differences in rates of return (as measured by the coefficient of variation) during the 1980s have been as large as they were during the 1960s and early 1970s.[5]

The lowering of national barriers to financial flows has undoubtedly reduced substantially the degree of segmentation of financial markets and, hence, international dispersion of prices for financial assets denominated in the same currency but issued in different countries. Rapid dissemination of information, increased ease of market access, and greatly reduced transaction costs have indeed helped equalize yields on assets denominated in the same currency, and with identical default risk and term to maturity, in various parts of integrated financial markets (for example dollar CDs issued by London and New York banks).

But a similar tendency is not discernible for financial assets with identical risk and maturity characteristics but different currency denominations (for example United States Treasury bills in dollars and United Kingdom Treasury bills in sterling), even though certain financial intermediaries, institutional investors, and large corporations accounting for an important part of the market find them close substitutes. Convergence of rates of return implies a tendency for interest rate differentials to equal the expected change in the exchange rate of the currencies in which they are denominated. When assets are close substitutes, the forward rate reflects the expected future rate, and the forward premium (that is, the proportionate differential between the forward and spot exchange rates) the expected rate of currency depreciation. The evidence shows that the premium tends to be equalized with the interest rate differential over the same time interval, that is, 'covered interest parity' holds, but that forward exchange rates have failed to predict the future spot rates (that is, 'uncovered interest parity' does not hold). The deviations are too large to be explained by the risk premium, which implies that rates of return on assets denominated in different currencies are not equalized.

This strongly suggests that markets systematically leave unexploited opportunities for abnormal profits. Indeed, during the first half of the 1980s the dollar offered higher interest rates and sold at a discount in the forward markets against most other currencies, and yet dollar depreciation failed to materialize within the time frame of the contracts entered into; again, some European currencies have persistently offered higher interest rates *and* appreciated against the others during the same interval of time. Markets are inefficient in the sense that they fail to incorporate relevant information in the determination of exchange rates. Indeed, divergence between forward

[5] The figures are given by the OECD for the business sector (e.g. OECD, *Economic Outlook* 53, June, 1993). It should be noted that there are serious conceptual and practical difficulties in the measurement of rates of return, and they cannot always be compared across countries because of country-specific factors (e.g. taxation of earnings on capital assets). Thus, available estimates need to be interpreted with caution.

rates and future spot rates has taken place in a manner that is far from random; it can be related in a systematic way to the information available at the time the forward rates are established. This evidence, in combination with bandwagon-type exchange rate movements, strongly suggests that speculation has been predominant in the determination of exchange rates, and that it has been destabilizing.[6]

When nominal interest rate differentials do not cover exchange rate changes, there is no reason to expect real rates of interest to be equalized across countries. Such a process requires not only that exchange rates move in line with the relative purchasing power parity of the two currencies, but also that exchange rate changes are fully covered by interest differentials; that is, that differences between nominal interest rates are equal to changes in the exchange rate between the two currencies and that these are equal to changes in the relative price levels. The evidence shows clearly that neither the uncovered interest parity nor *ex ante* purchasing power parity has been attained. This tallies with the observation that there is no tendency for real interest rates to be equalized across countries (Pigott, 1993). Disparities in real interest rates among major countries are also reflected in continued differences in the cost of capital. Firms in the United States and the United Kingdom suffer from a decided disadvantage in this respect compared to those in Germany and Japan, and need a higher rate of return on their investment in order to cover financing costs (Kasman and Pigott, 1988; McCauley and Zimmer, 1989; Poterba, 1991).

This last observation suggests a relatively strong link between national savings and investment. Indeed, direct evidence on this link is in line with the evidence on relative rates of return and interest rates. They suggest that even among the OECD countries where capital has become increasingly mobile, the strength of the correlation between national savings and investment rates has not diminished, and a very large share of new domestic savings remains at home.

The recent pattern of cross-border capital flows does not tally with the original expectations that in a financially free world, capital would flow from developed countries with excess savings and low-return investment to low savings developing countries with ample investment opportunities. Over the past decade capital flows among developed countries have grown much faster than capital flows from developed to developing countries. More important, capital has flown primarily from countries with high investment rates (for example Japan) to countries with low investment rates (for example the United States); such flows have thus served to finance consumption rather than investment. On the other hand, rather than

---

[6] For a more detailed account of the speculative nature of foreign exchange markets see UNCTAD, *International Monetary and Financial Issues for the Developing Countries* (New York: United Nations, 1987), particularly 101–3 and 107–12.

penalizing inappropriate policies, capital flows have often helped to sustain them, as has been the case in recent years in the United States and Italy where inflows have helped to run chronic fiscal deficits.

The evidence does not mean that financial markets are not integrated, or that capital is not very mobile: to gauge the degree of financial integration and capital mobility in terms of the extent to which rates of return are equalized reflects a priori assumptions about the role of international finance and efficiency of markets which may not necessarily tally with reality. Massive flows of capital are not always motivated by opportunities for real investment. Indeed, a very large proportion of international financial transactions today is unrelated to trade and investment. The daily volume of foreign exchange trading in major currency markets has reached the average monthly volume of world trade (Kregel, 1994). International capital flows reflect portfolio decisions rather than business decisions, for example to establish a production base in a foreign country. International bank lending alone considerably exceeds total FDI made across all borders as well as the annual net capital flows across countries (Table 3.4). Moreover, there is no close correlation between their movements: until 1986–7, bank lending grew much faster than FDI and net capital flows, but slowed down considerably afterwards.

These transactions have increasingly come to be governed by perceptions of prospects of short-term capital gains and losses rather than long-term

Table 3.4. The growth of international banking relative to foreign direct investment and net capital flows across countries

	1973–1979	1980–1984	1985–1987	1988–1992
	As a percentage of foreign direct investment			
Net international bank loans	290	240	358	167
Gross size of international banking market	612	513	958	254
	As a percentage of net capital flows across countries[a]			
Net international bank loans	143	106	183	184[b]
Gross size of international banking market	301	225	490	295[b]

Source: Foreign direct investment from *Transnational Corporations in World Development*, third survey and the UNCTAD data base. Others as for Table 3.3. See also that table for definitions.

Note: The figures relate the annual average increase of international bank loans in each period to the average annual FDI or net capital flows across countries during the period.
    [a] Net capital flows are measured as the absolute sum of current-account balances divided by 2.
    [b] 1988–1991.

yields, and are capable of generating gyrations in exchange rates and secu-rity prices. These, in turn, increase profit opportunities and, hence, the spec-ulative component of the market. It is thus far from clear that the process of international financial deepening is contributing to efficiency in the allo-cation of resources internationally. The predominance of speculation over enterprise in the sphere of international finance is not very different from the operation of modern capital markets that Keynes described in chapter 12 of the *General Theory* with metaphors such as 'the game of Snap, of Old Maid, of Musical Chairs', and 'newspaper competitions', 'beauty contests', and 'casino games'.

Links between Currency and Financial Markets

The internationalization of finance and integration of financial markets have considerably increased the importance of securing an exchange rate system conducive to financial stability. For one thing, the increased denom-ination of assets and liabilities of financial intermediaries, debtors, and investors in foreign currencies means that the value of assets and liabilities is directly influenced by exchange rate changes. For another, events in exchange markets can exert a strong influence on asset (for example bond and equity) prices because exchange rate expectations can induce funds to be shifted among securities denominated in different currencies, and/or because policy measures taken to manage exchange rates or to deal with the inflationary or deflationary influences of exchange rate changes alter interest rates and security prices. Exchange rate instability can therefore increase the level of risk in the financial system. For instance, banks can incur substantial losses when there is a serious mismatch between currency denomination of their assets and liabilities, and many governments in major countries have introduced regulations restricting open positions. However, regulations do not generally require perfect matching: they often set aggregate limits to open positions, but allow net open positions for dif-ferent currencies or for different maturities in a given currency (see Chapter 7).

The impact of unexpected changes, and hence uncertainty, cannot be fully removed unless there are forward markets for all goods and assets for which there are current markets, and they reach far into the future. Since there are not, the financial system is subject to a systemic risk. Existing for-ward and futures markets and financial instruments (derivatives) simply transfer risk to those who are willing to take it at a price, rather than elim-inate risk by providing guidance as to the future course of prices. These instruments are used as much for gambling as for hedging; thus, they increase the risk associated with financial flows by increasing the volatility of short-term capital. Risk transfer may be possible for each operator taken individually, but not collectively, because the quality of assets held by financial intermediaries, or savers investing in direct securities, will remain vulnerable to unexpected changes in exchange rates since their debtors cannot be fully covered. Exchange rate uncertainty thus tends to raise the credit risks assumed by the financial system. As put by the former General Manager of BIS, 'you may argue that when risk-averse market participants shift risks associated with unexpected interest and exchange rate developments onto willing risk takers, everybody is going to be better off. This may well be the case, but increased collective happiness does not necessarily mean greater systemic stability.' (Lamfalussy, 1985, 411.)

The effects of monetary policy and interest rates on exchange rates are familiar: changes in interest rate differentials (current and/or expected) can lead to massive shifts of portfolios among financial assets denominated in different currencies, exerting a significant influence on exchange rates. What is less appreciated is the interrelation between exchange rates and security prices. Since the demand for securities denominated in different currencies depends, *inter alia*, on expected changes in exchange rates, changes in expectations can shift portfolios among securities denominated in different currencies, even causing sharp changes in their prices as well as in current exchange rates. Thus, expectations of exchange rate depreciations can trigger both a sharp decline in equity prices and an outflow of capital. Similarly, the mood in equity markets can exert a strong influence on the exchange rate—for example bullish expectations can trigger capital inflow, leading to appreciation. By contrast, a bearish mood in the capital market can not only prick the speculative bubble in the stock market, but also lead to a currency crisis.

Thus, the strengthening of the link between the two inherently unstable markets, namely, currency and stock markets, increases the potential for the emergence of foreign exchange and/or stock-market crises. Indeed, recent evidence suggests that chaotic feedbacks between financial and currency markets can easily develop. For instance the combination of low interest rates in Japan with rising rates in the United States and Europe in late 1989 and early 1990 exerted substantial downward pressure on the yen, and triggered massive shifts from yen-denominated assets, which accentuated the downward pressures on the value of the yen and also brought down bond and equity prices. Moreover, the continued decline of the yen triggered expectations of substantial increases in domestic interest rates, which fed into further declines in bond and equity prices. Eventually interest rates had to be raised, and in this process the Nikkei index dropped by about 25 per cent, government bonds by more than 20 per cent, and the yen by over 10 per cent.

Such feedbacks may prove to be much more serious in developing countries because of the greater presence of non-residents in their capital markets and a high level of dollarization. For instance, when the international credit rating of Turkey was downgraded by the major rating agencies in early 1994, not only the domestic currency but also stock prices collapsed as assets were moved into foreign currency: the stock market fell by one-half and the currency by one-third within a few days, forcing the government to devalue and raise interest rates considerably, and creating difficulties for banks having sizeable open foreign exchange positions. Similarly, a very close correlation has been observed in recent years between equity prices, exchange rates, and capital inflows in a number of the so-called newly-emerging markets (for example Mexico) where foreign presence is considerable.

Similarly, management of exchange rates under conditions of extreme volatility tends to generate considerable swings in interest rates and financial asset prices, particularly when domestic monetary policy is targeting certain reserve aggregates and exchange market intervention needs to be sterilized through domestic open market operations; such sterilization could have a significant effect on bond prices, particularly when the market pressure on the exchange rate is strong. Alternatively, when sterilization is too difficult, action may be needed on interest rates to check liquidity expansion. When pressures on the currency markets are due to serious inconsistencies in the mix and stance of policies in major countries, attempts to manage exchange rates through monetary policy and currency market intervention can prove highly destabilizing for the financial system, as exemplified by the events leading to the October 1987 crash.

Under asymmetry in international adjustment, exchange rate management can introduce a bias towards higher interest rates. If the burden of responsibility for policy action is put entirely on deficit countries and monetary policy is the only tool, defending the exchange rate and/or reducing demand will require interest rates to be raised, possibly to extremely high levels. This has recently been observed once more in Europe. In view of the reluctance of Germany to reduce its interest rates, members of the Exchange Rate Mechanism facing speculative attacks were obliged to defend their currencies by sharp increases in interest rates. This was true both for the United Kingdom which eventually suspended its membership, and the other countries which appeared to consider it necessary to preserve exchange rate stability in the run-up to the second phase of monetary union: thus, initially the Netherlands, France, Belgium, and Denmark all managed to defend their parities at the cost of extremely high real rates of interest, and of domestic output and employment foregone. Even after the ERM crisis of the summer of 1993 and the introduction of wider bands, countries such as France continued to maintain high interest rates and kept their exchange rates close to the old intervention bands.

Currency instability tends to generate a systemic bias towards higher interest rates also by intensifying the instability of interest rates arising from the way monetary policy is conducted. Such a tendency has become particularly visible since the late 1970s when many central banks switched to quantitative targets for certain monetary aggregates in order to influence the rate of inflation. Thus, the promise of greater price stability was exchanged for increased instability in interest rates and exchange rates. Indeed, during the past decade, interest rates in the major reserve currency countries have been extremely unstable by historical standards. The exchange rates of the major currencies, on the other hand, have been much more unstable than their interest rates, in large part due to autonomous speculative bubbles.

Financial instability tends to increase uncertainty and reduce the degree of confidence in the expectations held with respect to the future course of interest and exchange rates and security prices. Since uncertainty is the essence of liquidity preference, as uncertainty grows, liquidity preference increases. Not only are maturities shortened as the demand for capital-uncertain assets is reduced, but also interest rates, especially long-term rates, are pushed up to cover increased riskiness of interest-bearing financial assets.

In the 1970s, as instability and uncertainty increased significantly alongside inflation, markets started to innovate to meet the increased demand for interest-bearing short-term assets (such as the NOW and ATS accounts in the United States to by-pass regulations regarding interest rates on savings and demand deposits). Banks attempted to shorten the maturities of their assets by introducing variable-interest loans, in effect transforming the interest rate risk into credit risk (UNCTAD, 1985, 1988). Innovations have continued to burgeon and holdings of liquid short-term assets proliferated in more recent years even though inflation has been kept relatively low and stable. On the other hand, interest rates stayed persistently high in the 1980s, particularly in the United States (and on dollar assets), where financial instability was more pronounced than in the other major countries. The increase in long-term interest rates in most countries has been greater, and these rates have been less sensitive to fluctuations in short-term rates compared to past decades. This steepening of the yield curve cannot be explained by expectations of an acceleration of inflation; inflation has not only been falling sharply since the early 1980s, but it has been lower, on average, than in the 1960s. These factors could have been expected to push future short-term interest rates below the current rates. The steepening of the yield curve, together with the proliferation of holdings of liquid short-term assets, suggests that the increased instability of interest rates and the exchange rate of the dollar have been important factors in the increase in interest rates, which can also help explain the evidence that the ability of the term structure of interest rates to forecast future inflation is very much limited.

Financial Openness and Policy Autonomy

Increased financial openness and dismantling of barriers to capital flows have considerably strengthened the links among the financial markets of national economies. This has had significant implications for national policy autonomy and domestic and global effects of national economic policy. The degree of policy autonomy has declined everywhere, but most of all in smaller and/or less developed countries having a high degree of financial openness. On the other hand, the global effects of the policies pursued by the major countries have increased considerably, even though their policy autonomy too has diminished.

Policy autonomy refers to the ability of national policy makers to control national policy goals by using the policy instruments at their disposal. The degree of policy autonomy or the effectiveness of national policy instruments in controlling the ultimate goals of policy depends on the *strength* of the influence of these instruments on goals. It also depends on the *stability* of the link between instruments and goals and, hence, the predictability of the influence of the former on the latter. Financial openness reduces the degree of autonomy because it weakens the national policy influence on national goals while it raises the external influence. It also renders the link between national instruments and targets less stable and reliable, making the relationship dependent on the behaviour of policy makers and markets elsewhere.[7]

The more open an economy, the smaller is the impact of national policy instruments on national policy goals, because the effects of policy action tend to spill abroad. Thus, increased openness raises the impact of national policy instruments on variables in other countries relative to their influence on national variables. More important, foreign policy action and economic shocks originating abroad exert significant constraints on the conduct of national policy, and on its ability to attain policy goals.

Such cross-country influences, including those of policy instruments, are not usually known with a reasonable degree of accuracy. Knowledge about structural and behavioural relations that link the national economy to the rest of the world is extremely inadequate; available empirical models linking major countries differ not only as regards the magnitude but even the direction of cross-country policy influences (Frankel, 1988). Moreover,

---

[7] These passages draw on R. Bryant, *International Financial Intermediation* (Washington DC: The Brookings Institution, 1987) who gives a penetrating analysis of the effects of openness on policy autonomy.

access to information abroad is more difficult and costly, and developments in other countries are difficult to assess. An equally and perhaps more important source of uncertainty is the game-theoretic nature of decision making by policy authorities in an interdependent world. What constitutes an appropriate policy action of a home government depends on what is assumed of the behaviour of foreign policy makers; but the latter, in turn, depends on assumptions about the policy course in the home economy. This not only creates problems in policy making, but can also lead to serious conflicts when countries have incompatible objectives for the same and common variables such as exchange rates and trade balances. These difficulties arise from a variety of sources, among the more important of which is the fact that internationalization of finance and financial openness raise the degree of substitutability of assets denominated in home and foreign currencies, and issued by residents and non-residents. They also create increased possibilities for the private sector to circumvent various restrictions imposed by monetary authorities.

Indeed, in a financially open economy domestic monetary and credit aggregates become extremely difficult to define in a meaningful and useful way, that is, so as to provide reliable guidance to the conduct of monetary policy. For instance, there is no satisfactory and generally agreed way of dealing with the assets and liabilities of Eurobanks. Should a dollar deposit held in a London bank by a Colombian resident in Switzerland be included in the money supply of Colombia, the United States, the United Kingdom, or Switzerland? The same question arises also with respect to credits from Eurobanks. Here the difficulty is not a practical but a conceptual one—that of identifying the influence of such deposits and credits on spending decisions in the various countries involved, and thus interpreting movements in such aggregates in taking monetary policy action. These difficulties become particularly serious when monetary policy is targeting certain monetary and credit aggregates.

That increased financial interdependence leads to a loss of policy effectiveness and autonomy for national governments does not imply that influences due to financial openness always undermine the achievement of policy objectives. That depends on the objectives pursued, and actions taken at home and abroad. For instance, in a financially open economy, fiscal stimulus tends to leak abroad because the consequent rise in interest rates encourages capital inflow, thereby appreciating the domestic currency and reducing net exports. By contrast, monetary tightening can lead to currency appreciation, which can reinforce the disinflationary impact of the monetary policy. Again, the ability to attract capital through financial policies can help avoid taking deflationary action at times of serious external payments difficulties. However, in both cases there is a great deal of uncertainty as to the final outcome, not only because of the unpredictability of the response of international financial markets to such policy actions, but also because of their international repercussions and the policy response of foreign governments. This uncertainty and the associated costs of loss of control over national economies can only be reduced by collective action, involving management of international money and finance and of interdependence—a topic taken up in the final section.

Vulnerability of Developing Countries

For developing countries financial openness brings an even greater loss of policy autonomy. The exposure to short-term, speculative capital flows is much greater for developing than for developed countries because their instability provides greater opportunities for quick, windfall profits on short-term capital movements while their ability to influence capital flows through monetary policy is much more limited. This is clearly illustrated by serious problems of macroeconomic management that many Latin American countries have been facing in recent years as a consequence of massive speculative capital inflows. Sterilizing them by issuing domestic debt has imposed a serious burden on the public sector, particularly where the arbitrage margin is large (for example in Brazil). Furthermore, by increasing the stock of government debt, sterilization has tended to raise domestic interest rates and, hence, the arbitrage margin. Where the currency was allowed to appreciate considerably, it undermined the competitiveness of domestic industry and created large trade deficits, creating a potential for a sharp reversal in short-term capital flows. So far only very few countries have been able to overcome these dilemmas (UNCTAD, 1992, 1993).

More important, exposure to sharp swings in the direction of capital flows and greater instability of exchange rates can undermine the outward-oriented strategies that many developing countries have recently been urged to adopt. For investors in traded goods sectors, the real exchange rate is the single most important relative price affecting profits. One important consequence of sharp swings in the direction of capital flows and greater instability of exchange rates is to increase investor's risk. By raising the average rate of return required by investors to undertake investment, this will depress the level of investment corresponding to any given rate of interest. Since the influence of the exchange rate on investment decisions increases with the share of the foreign trade in the economy, it is ironic that the exchange rate is becoming increasingly determined by purely financial forces de-linked from trade and investment at a time when greater emphasis is placed on export-led growth.

Quite apart from loss of control over macroeconomic and development objectives due to greater financial openness, developing countries also suffer from many adverse consequences of international financial instability to which they are often unable to respond effectively. The stock of developing countries' external debt is the most important transmission channel for disruption and instability from world financial and currency markets into their domestic economies. Thus, the absence of a tendency for equalization of rates of return on assets denominated in different currencies means that the cost of servicing debt depends crucially on its currency composition, and is influenced not only by changes in the overall level of interest rates, but also by changes in exchange rates. This causes serious problems in the management of debt, and can give rise to significant losses when there is a mismatch between the currency composition of debt and foreign exchange receipts and reserves. On the other hand, since most developing countries do not have unlimited access to each of the major international capital markets, they cannot easily adjust the currency composition of their external debt or take forward cover to alleviate the effects of financial and currency market disturbances.

There can be little doubt that the systemic tendency of interest rates to remain high has been an important factor in the debt crisis of the 1980s. Its effects on developing countries have been aggravated because a large stock of debt had already been built up before this tendency emerged in force; interest rate increases were passed on to the debtors via the variable-interest loan practice, and rates of return on real domestic assets in debtor countries were depressed by deflationary adjustments, mainly because of investment cuts. The appreciation of the dollar also contributed to the crisis since the foreign exchange risk had also been assumed by the debtors as banks hedged exchange risk by lending in US dollars.

Equally important, developing countries suffer considerably from protectionism triggered by exchange rate misalignments and trade imbalances among the major industrial countries. Overvaluation of currencies gives rise to protectionist pressures, and ultimately to protectionist measures which are not removed when misalignment is corrected; often permanent protection is sought in order to compensate for long-term exposure to exchange rate risk. Similarly, currency undervaluation can lead to investment in industries which are otherwise uncompetitive; again, such industries could exert substantial pressure for protection when the exchange rate misalignment is corrected. Evidence strongly suggests that these effects have played a major role in the proliferation of non-tariff barriers in the 1980s.

3. STRENGTHENING THE INTERNATIONAL MONETARY SYSTEM

The adverse consequences of the increased instability of the international monetary and financial system are not always fully appreciated, in large part because visible and significant damage to the real economy of developed countries has so far been averted. However, the experience of the past decade shows that financial instability and disruption are costly and the financial system is susceptible to crisis. Thus, there is a need for action designed to attain a more stable system of international money and finance. The previous sections show that while the factors that generate disturbances and disruption are several and complex, and it is not always easy to assess accurately their relative importance, action will be needed to improve the exchange rate arrangements, the design and mutual compatibility of policies in the major OECD countries, and the functioning of the markets.

Exchange Rate Arrangements

There is now a widespread recognition that the floating exchange rate system has failed to promote stable and sustainable current account balances, and that there is a need to move to a more stable system of exchange rates. Such a system should be sufficiently flexible to allow exchange rates to adjust to underlying economic conditions, in particular to changes in prices and productivity and, hence, to avoid the mistakes of the Bretton Woods regime. It should also avoid the mistakes of the last two decades.

One of the arguments in favour of floating exchange rates was that they would give countries autonomy and independence in domestic policy making. The autonomy in question was partly with respect to monetary policy; since there would be no obligation to defend a particular exchange rate, monetary policy would have greater scope to deal with domestic objectives. However, this has proved rather illusory, because of increased financial integration of the countries and increased instability of exchange rates. It is no longer possible to ignore the consequences of exchange rates for domestic policy objectives, and pursue an autonomous monetary policy.

A broader issue of policy autonomy is related to trade adjustment. It was implicitly, and sometimes explicitly, assumed that external equilibrium could be attained primarily through movements in exchange rates, rather than in domestic demand and income, thereby allowing countries to pursue macroeconomic policies geared to full employment and growth. This expectation was based on two premises. First, there would be no major shortcomings in the conduct of policies both within and across the countries. Secondly, trade balances would respond swiftly to changes in exchange rates. However, as recent experience has shown, both of these assumptions have proved wrong.

There can be little doubt that no exchange rate system can work efficiently when there are serious macroeconomic policy shortcomings. As the experience of the United States has demonstrated, inconsistency in the mix of monetary and fiscal policies can cause exchange rate movements that aggravate trade imbalances. On the other hand, when trade imbalances are due primarily to major divergences between the overall stances of the macroeconomic policies of the major trading partners, and/or because trade policy is significantly restrictive in some of these countries, attempts to reduce trade imbalances through exchange rate movements would entail sharp swings in exchange rates; or, should exchange rates come under pressure, attempts to stabilize them could cause serious strains.

Regarding the second assumption of the floating system, recent experience has also shown that the response of exports and imports to exchange rates can be very sluggish. Markets for traded goods do not necessarily operate on the basis of the type of competitive pricing envisaged by the proponents of floating exchange rates. In particular, greater instability of exchange rates raises the average profit margin. The latter also becomes much more variable in order to allow prices to be adjusted to changes in exchange rates, thereby rendering exchange rate movements much less effective in correcting trade imbalances. The sharp depreciation of the dollar since early 1985 brought about much less improvement in trade imbalances among the major OECD countries than had been expected because exporters preferred to take cuts in their profit margins rather than reduce export volumes and lose their share of the United States market, whereas United States producers tended to respond to the dollar depreciation not always by raising their export volumes but also their profit margins.

These considerations show that the scope for attaining a stable pattern of exchange rates will depend, *inter alia*, on the degree of consistency of policies within and across the major countries. However, experience has shown that the discipline needed to eliminate policy inconsistencies is hard to obtain without effective multilateral surveillance, an issue that will be taken up in the following subsection.

The second important issue in the management of exchange rates is the need for an international commitment by the major OECD countries to an explicitly announced pattern of exchange rates that is compatible with underlying fundamentals, and to defend it by intervention in currency markets and regulation and control of financial flows. Such commitments would play an important role in achieving stability by providing an anchor for expectations, thereby influencing market behaviour, and by disciplining policy making.

In the post Bretton Woods period, the Plaza meeting in September 1985 marked for most governments a major reassessment of the roles to be assigned to markets and public policy in the determination of exchange rates. It marked the beginning of exchange rate management which played a major role in correcting the misalignment of the dollar, primarily through monetary policy and intervention in exchange markets. At the Louvre meeting in February 1987, consensus was reached among Group of Seven governments that the dollar should be stabilized, and the adjustment in trade balances be achieved through enhanced coordination of macroeconomic policies among the participating countries directed at changing the international pattern of domestic demand; the actions taken in pursuit of this objective were to include fiscal policies.

The period from February 1987 to September 1987 witnessed a degree of exchange rate stability unprecedented during the decade. The orderly decline in the dollar attained between the Plaza and Louvre meetings, and the subsequent success in keeping the dollar stable, gave impetus to new initiatives to manage exchange rates in the OECD area. The reasons for this move towards managed floating were clearly expressed by the Chancellor of the Exchequer of the United Kingdom at the annual meetings of the IMF and the World Bank in September 1987: 'The belief that markets would provide a stabilizing influence, through the operations of medium-term speculators, has not been borne out. . . . In particular, we have seen wild gyrations in the dollar that have clearly not been a reflection of economic fundamentals. . . . Moreover, these gyrations have damaged growth in world trade. . . . And the major uncertainties about exchange rate movements inhibited risk taking and required a switching of resources at a pace that was totally unrealistic.'[8] The regime of managed floating adopted at the Louvre meeting has worked because countries have 'been prepared in practice to give significant weight to exchange rates in the conduct of monetary policy . . . and to back up [the] agreement with co-ordinated intervention'. Moreover, the experience gained should be used 'to build up a more permanent regime of managed floating'.[9]

However, the exchange rate stability between February and September 1987 was attained at the cost of increased pressures on monetary policy. The Louvre agreement was translated only partly into actual measures, the United States trade deficit failed to improve, and, consequently, pressures on the dollar intensified. Thus, monetary policy had to bear the brunt of adjustment and soon became overburdened: it had to shift from one objective to another as actions to ensure stability in one market destabilized others. These shifts of direction in the conduct of monetary policy simply reflected the major dilemmas that the policy makers were facing; namely, too few policy instruments to attain many objectives simultaneously, in an

[8] See Press Release 44 of *The Annual Meetings* (*30 September 1987*), p. 3.
[9] Ibid, 5.

environment characterized by increased volatility of markets, and continued failure to coordinate policies in order to manage exchange rates and reduce trade imbalances. This created a situation of fragility in financial markets, culminating in the collapse of stock prices in October 1987.

The enthusiasm regarding exchange rate management faded away with the 1987 stock market crash. Immediately after the crisis, exchange rate instability rose again as monetary policy was focused first on the stability of the financial system and then on internal objectives. Foreign exchange market intervention was reduced and monetary policy largely lost view of exchange rates.

The experience with exchange rate management after the Louvre meeting (that is, the so-called reference ranges) constituted a direct targeting of exchange rates without, however, containing some of the above elements needed for durable stability. The ranges were not announced explicitly; they were agreed provisionally with a view to short-term adjustment needs, and not because they reflected fundamentals; there were no formal obligations and rules in the event of the divergence of the rates from the agreed reference ranges; and, more important, the agreement did not secure policy adjustments needed to reduce pressures on exchange rates.

Lack of a firm commitment to defend the agreed pattern of exchange rates is also a feature of a version of the target zones proposal which favours 'soft margins' in order to allow considerable flexibility and facilitate exchange rate management (Williamson, 1983). Wide margins (for example plus and minus 10 per cent) are advocated, *inter alia*, in order to absorb certain temporary shocks within the zones, and because of substantial uncertainty in calculating the appropriate pattern of exchange rates. However, wide margins make sense only if there is a commitment to defending the targets. Moreover, it is not clear if such a system can ensure the discipline needed, and thereby be regarded as credible by the markets.

A firm commitment among participating governments is essential for achieving greater exchange rate stability. The burden of adjustment should not be placed on exchange rates when external imbalances arise from inappropriate trade and macroeconomic policies. The question arises as to whether an adjustable peg system, with narrow ranges and predefined obligations regarding exchange rate and policy adjustment, would be feasible. Such a system can include automatic adjustment of nominal rates to allow for inflation differentials. Real exchange rates may be adjusted on a discretionary basis when current account balances persistently deviate from the agreed pattern of deficits and surpluses. Such a system, in combination with regulation and control of short-term capital flows, would leave much less room for speculative pressures and policy inconsistencies to build up, and could thus be more successful in preventing the emergence of misalignments. Moreover, if speculative capital flows are curtailed in the first place, markets themselves can help determine exchange rate configurations consistent with the underlying fundamentals. However, like other proposals for reference ranges and target zones, it would require not only agreed intervention rules but also a framework within which national monetary and fiscal policies would have to be conducted and coordinated.

Interdependence, Policy Coordination, and Surveillance

Since exchange rate instability is undesirable because of adverse effects of unpredictable and misaligned exchange rates on growth and development, it is essential that a system designed to attain exchange rate stability does not contain a deflationary bias. This clearly raises the question of assigning responsibilities and obligations to defend exchange rates and to undertake policy adjustment in order to correct destabilizing and unsustainable trade imbalances. Indeed, it evokes the whole question of the management of interdependence, which has become the central concept in recent discussions of policy coordination among the major OECD countries. However, actions have not always reflected its true meaning and policy implications. Interdependence among countries implies that the economy of each is both sufficiently *open* for it to come under considerable influence from abroad, and sufficiently *large* for its own policies to make a significant impact on others.

An appropriate management of interdependence implies that no country with a sufficiently open economy (even if it is too small to itself have an impact on other economies) should be expected to be able to put its house in order regardless of what the other countries are doing. Otherwise, the burden of adjustment would be put on deficit countries, thereby introducing a global deflationary bias. Nor should any country set its policies without paying attention to their possible international consequences, an approach that would lead to 'beggar my neighbour' policies designed to export unemployment or inflation, thereby creating considerable frictions in the international monetary and trading systems. The experience of the 1980s, leading to the emergence of serious exchange rate misalignments and large trade imbalances, and the subsequent failure to reduce them and to manage exchange rates, show that the major OECD countries have been unable to take proper account of interdependence, and to coordinate their macroeconomic policies accordingly.

Effective policy coordination necessitates agreement on certain goals, and on policy actions needed when outcomes differ from the agreed goals. First, certain objectives need to be set for each country concerned, including admissible rates of growth of domestic demand as well as exchange rates and current account balances. Consistency of objectives needs to be attained both within and across the countries concerned. It is particularly important to secure a pattern of demand generation consistent with trade and exchange rate objectives; and the latter need to be mutually consistent among the countries, since the number of exchange rates or current account balances that can serve as independent targets is less than the number of countries. There should be a clear understanding about the allocation of the burden of adjustment when the outcomes persistently deviate from the agreed targets.

Second, a set of global targets and indicators may be used to prevent a deflationary or inflationary bias in the overall policy stance, and to provide a basis for global action by all the countries concerned. A recent proposal in this respect is that of introducing a commodity price index as an indicator to help in 'monitoring the performance of the group (of industrial countries) as a whole',[10] and to serve 'as an early-warning signal of potential price trends'.[11] This proposal is based on the assumption that global demand pressures are reflected in movements in commodity prices; indeed deflationary policies have played a major role in the collapse of commodity prices in the 1980s. Since they still remain depressed, an important issue is the level to be taken as the basis for assessment of their future movements. An upward adjustment would certainly be necessary before embarking on the use of this index as an indicator of global demand pressures.

Coordination of policies within such a framework does not necessarily imply automatic policy reactions to developments in certain indicators. A considerable amount of flexibility and discretion may be introduced, based on extensive consultations among the parties concerned. However, it should also be recognized that it necessarily implies a certain degree of constraint on national policy making.

There can be little doubt that there are serious difficulties in attaining the required degree of coordination. Experience shows that coordination has been more successful when collective goals were pursued (such as the adjustment to the oil price rises in the 1970s), but it is not always possible to reach agreement on such goals. Often, policy coordination is required where the precise nature and causes of problems affecting several countries do not command consensus. For instance, in the present situation, the problem of trade imbalances is perceived differently by different countries. Moreover, there may be considerable differences in priorities attached to different ultimate goals by different countries. For instance, views as to what is sustainable in terms of output growth can differ according to per-

[10] The statement of Chancellor of the Exchequer Nigel Lawson at the Annual Meetings of IMF and the World Bank, Washington, DC, September 1987 (as reproduced in Press Release 44 of 30 September, p. 6).

[11] The statement of Secretary James Baker III at the Annual Meetings of IMF and the World Bank, Washington, DC, September 1987 (as reproduced in Press Release 50 of 30 September, p. 3).

ceptions regarding trade-offs with environmental objectives. Another major difficulty is that the contribution of a national government to international economic cooperation carries little weight in the formation of voters' opinion,[12] and the policy record of a government usually takes little account of external influences on the home economy. A basic requirement to overcome such difficulties is that policy makers and electorates in the major OECD countries understand that the international orientation of macroeconomic policy is a necessity stemming from the interdependence that the very same countries have been promoting by advocating more liberal policies and open economies; nor is it against their own country's interest, since the alternative would be serious disruptions to national and global economies.

Policy coordination among the major countries would also need to take into account its implications for *small* but *open* economies, and, particularly, for developing countries. As experience has demonstrated, these countries are affected not only by the the overall stance of macroeconomic policies in the major OECD countries, which exerts a major influence on their volume and terms of trade, but even by the mix of monetary and fiscal policies which, through its effects on interest rates, has a major influence on their external debt burden. This is perhaps one of the most important reasons why conduct of policies in the major countries should be subject to multilateral surveillance.

The record in this respect is extremely poor. Increased interdependence among the major OECD countries, increased dependence of economic performance in developing countries on the mix and stance of policies in the major OECD countries, and the greatly enhanced capacity of financial markets and capital flows to generate global disturbances, mean that the world economy today is considerably different from the one envisaged by the architects of the postwar monetary arrangements. This would have required the strengthening of the surveillance function of the IMF in order to help attain the objectives of growth and stability as laid down in article I of its Articles of Agreement. Instead, the last two decades have seen a considerable strengthening of the Fund's position *vis-à-vis* the developing countries while issues of great importance to the global economy have continued to be decided within the Group of Five or the Group of Seven countries.

The inadequacy of IMF surveillance is now widely recognized. The Group of Ten countries, for instance, agreed that 'surveillance has not been as effective as desirable in influencing national policies and in promoting underlying economic conditions conducive to exchange rate stability,' while also noting that some 'countries appear to have been able on occasion to

---

[12] This has been exemplified by the continued failure of many industrial countries (with some honourable exceptions) to comply with their commitments for ODA.

sustain policy courses not fully compatible with the goals of international adjustment and financial stability.'[13]

The Group of Twenty-Four has argued that surveillance should not be limited to members' exchange rate policies, but should also include the international adjustment process.[14] There is broad agreement that effective surveillance requires an assessment of all policies affecting trade, capital flows, external adjustment, and the effective functioning of the international monetary system, particularly of the major OECD countries.

The IMF has so far developed a number of medium-term economic indicators, and used them primarily for periodic bilateral consultations with governments. However, the surveillance function of the Fund has particular importance for the process of policy coordination itself; it should be conducted on a multilateral basis before issues regarding policies and indicators are taken up in bilateral consultations. In this way, it may help allocate the burden of adjustment between deficit and surplus countries, and ensure that coordination of macroeconomic policy in the major industrial countries leads to results for the world economy that are conducive to growth as well as stability.

Regulation and Supervision of Finance and Capital Flows

Given the degree of development of the organization of financial markets, and the increased predominance of speculative activities, it is not altogether clear that an appropriate design of policies both within and among the major OECD countries would be sufficient to avert financial disruptions and destabilizing capital flows. Consequently, there is a need to give serious consideration to possible ways and means of reducing the scope of markets to generate disruption and instability without undermining their ability to facilitate the proper allocation of investment.

This stands in sharp contrast to orthodox thinking which views convergence of macroeconomic policies and performance among the major industrial countries as both necessary and sufficient for currency stability. According to this view, interdependence does not even call for coordination of policies among major countries. So long as each and every country independently puts its house in order by pursuing appropriate policies, turmoil in currency markets would be avoided. Appropriate policies are defined in terms of 'non-inflationary growth', emphasizing price stability and fiscal equilibrium. This thinking also underlies the convergence indicators set by the Maastricht Treaty for the transition to monetary union.

While greater macroeconomic convergence may help attain stability, it is

---

[13] *IMF Survey*, Supplement on the Group of 10 Deputies' Report, July 1985, para. 36.
[14] *IMF Survey*, Supplement on the Group of 24 Deputies' Report, September 1985.

not altogether clear if the degree of convergence required is realistic. Nor is convergence always desirable since it can introduce a deflationary bias to the world economy. For instance the convergence rules of the Maastricht Treaty are inherently deflationary because they require countries with 'excessive fiscal deficits' to cut back without obliging other countries to expand, and without making it mandatory to adopt a more expansive monetary policy (Akyüz, 1993).

That macroeconomic convergence is not always sufficient for stability in currency markets is shown by the events leading to the crisis in the European Monetary System. While both the IMF (1993a, 19–26) and OECD (1993, 31–6) emphasize inadequate convergence in explaining the exchange market turbulence in Europe, they are unable to explain why so much pressure was put onto countries which satisfied the convergence criteria better than the others. Thus the IMF writes: 'But the intensity of the speculative pressure that developed against the French franc, in particular, is difficult to explain in view of the high degree of convergence of the French economy since the mid-1980s, and its relatively strong external competitive position in recent years.' (IMF, 1993a, 26.) The attack on the franc reflected the belief that France's ability to tolerate recession and unemployment was less than Germany's, and that France would eventually be forced to favour the pursuit of internal over external policy objectives; thus, markets did not consider convergence in deflation and unemployment as equally viable options for France and Germany.

By contrast there were numerous occasions during the Bretton Woods period when there were major differences among the industrial countries in their policy mixes and stances as well as in the strength of economic activity, without any serious exchange rate instability. What distinguished the period of relative stability of the Bretton Woods system from the situation today was, therefore, not so much the degree of divergence between the macroeconomic policies followed by particular countries, as the volume and volatility of private short-term capital flows.

Two main questions arise regarding regulation and supervision of international finance and capital flows: is regulation necessary to ensure stability? And does regulation undermine efficiency? Answers to these questions will clearly be shaped, *inter alia*, by the type of regulation being considered. In this respect a distinction can be made between three categories: (a) prudential regulations designed to limit the risk taken by financial institutions (such as capital adequacy and liquidity requirements, and diversification rules); (b) protective regulations designed to shelter investors, in particular depositors at commercial banks (for example, deposit insurance and the lender of last resort facilities); and (c) what may be called 'systemic (or macroprudential) regulations' designed primarily to reduce systemic disturbances and instability. Clearly, both prudential and protective regulations also serve this purpose, but their focus is more on specific institutions and investors. Among the types of measures included in systemic regulations are various controls and restrictions on capital movements, and taxation designed to discourage speculation.

Under conditions in which interest rates are fully deregulated, and restrictions are significantly eased on access to financial markets and types of transactions permitted, the importance of having an effective system of prudential regulations is considerably enhanced. However, in the 1980s, the tendency was to broaden protective regulations (through deposit insurance or *ex post* financial rescue operations) without matching this with pruden- tial regulation. This created a moral hazard problem and played a major role in financial disruptions in certain countries (for example the Savings and Loan Associations in the United States). There is now an increased consensus concerning the need for vigorous prudential regulations to avoid such disruptions, at least for financial intermediaries.

Prudential regulations often trigger innovations by markets to avoid them, and with increased financial openness such reactions tend to gravi- tate more to the international than to the national level. Recent efforts to harmonize the regulatory regimes for the financial systems of different countries reflect an awareness of this tendency. An important reason for improving international cooperation in the area of banking supervision is that differences in national regulatory regimes can generate international financial transactions with little or no underlying economic justification. Various evidence indicates that large capital movements frequently take place solely with the aim of circumventing monetary regulations such as minimum reserve requirements, prudential controls regarding capital ade- quacy and liquidity, and restrictions and rules concerning foreign exchange transactions. Moreover, during periods when confidence is adversely affected by financial turbulence, large movements of funds may be triggered from financial centres perceived as 'soft' to safer havens, principally the major financial markets in the OECD area. Thus, the Basle Agreement of July 1988 among the central bank governors of the Group of Ten countries and Luxembourg, concerning a common, risk-based standard of capital adequacy for international banks, constitutes a useful step in the process of reducing the incentive to international capital movements associated with divergences in national regulatory regimes (Cornford, 1993b).

The risk-based standard of capital adequacy needs to be applied also to the foreign exchange operations of international banks in order to restrict their participation in currency speculation. This would take the form of imposing capital charges on banks' open positions in foreign exchange, cov- ering both open positions in different maturities in a given currency as well as open positions for different currencies in a given maturity. Such a step would be consistent with the objective of covering banks' market risks with adequate capital. Non-interest-bearing reserve requirements may also be used to discourage banks from holding open positions in foreign exchange. Finally, specific absolute limits on open positions would need to be introduced when such measures prove to be ineffective (see Chapter 7).

Such agreements concerning prudential regulations need to cover all countries with significant banking centres as well as offshore markets. Otherwise, they may encourage further relocation of banking activities. This had indeed happened in the 1960s and 1970s and subsequently triggered competitive deregulation in the major money and capital market countries. Now the need for effective prudential regulation is increasingly recognized, but unless the regulatory regime becomes truly international, differential regulatory and tax treatment may continue to shift activity to offshore centres.

In the past decade, lack of adequate and effective safeguards against the assumption of excessive risks in securities markets gave rise to proliferation of high-risk instruments used primarily for speculative activities (such as corporate takeovers through junk bonds in the United States). Absence of prudential regulations in such areas also encouraged regulated institutions to enter into such transactions via off-balance-sheet business. A similar tendency has now become visible in the so-called derivatives market for futures, options, swaps, and other instruments associated with the management of foreign exchange and interest rate risks (Kregel, 1994). This market does not have the necessary transparency and the financial risks involved are far from being clear—factors that give rise to concerns that the next financial crack may well come from the derivatives markets. Such concerns may also underlie the views recently expressed by the President of the Federal Reserve Bank of New York as well as the members of the US House Banking Committee that rules and regulations concerning derivatives need substantial tightening (*International Herald Tribune*, 18 March 1994).

While prudential regulations designed to limit the risk taken by financial institutions in foreign-currency related operations help to deter speculation, they are not sufficient. There is also a need for regulation designed primarily to reduce systemic disturbances and instability, including particularly taxation designed to discourage speculation, that is, to deter short-term, as opposed to long-term, capital movements. Such a tax was advocated by Keynes in the context of domestic capital markets:

It is usually agreed that casinos should, in the public interest, be inaccessible and expensive. And perhaps the same is true of Stock Exchanges. That the sins of the London Stock Exchange are less than those of Wall Street may be due, not so much to differences in national character, as to the fact that to the average Englishman, Throgmorton Street is, compared with Wall Street to the average American, inaccessible and very expensive. The jobber's 'turn', the high brokerage charges and the heavy transfer tax payable to the Exchequer, which attend dealings on the London Stock Exchange, sufficiently diminish the liquidity of the market to rule out a large proportion of the transactions characteristic of Wall Street. The introduction of a substantial government transfer tax on all transactions might prove the most serviceable reform available, with a view to mitigating the predominance of speculation over enterprise in the United States (Keynes, 1936, 159–60.)

The same proposal has recently been elaborated by Tobin (1978), in the context of international financial transactions, in order 'to throw some sand in the wheels'. Such a tax, to be effective, should be an internationally agreed uniform tax, applied in proportion to the size of transactions involving conversions of one currency into another in order to raise the cost of short-run transactions relative to longer-run currency conversions and maturities. It should be applied not only to spot transactions but also to outright forwards, swaps, futures, and options involving foreign currency transactions. Interbank foreign exchange transactions can be exempted from such a tax as long as banks are discouraged from taking open positions in the ways described above. Such an agreement would be of unprecedented scope. Its benefits, however, would be fully commensurate with the effort required.[15]

There can be little doubt that restrictions on capital flows can be ineffective and even counterproductive if they are used as substitutes for exchange rate alignment and/or policy adjustment. However, as stressed above, regulations and restrictions regarding financial transactions and flows would need to complement appropriate policies rather than be a substitute for them, and would be used solely for the purpose of reducing the scope of markets to create autonomous disturbances.

[15] For a detailed examination see Ch 7.

Part II

Labour and Capital

4.   Employment and Unemployment, North and South

Ajit Singh and Ann Zammit[1]

A central and pressing economic problem today both in the developed and developing countries is that of unemployment and underemployment. This chapter proposes that the main focus of a new global development agenda for the 1990s should be the restoration of full employment in the North and the creation of adequate jobs in the South to meet the needs of its fast-growing labour force. Employment is not only important in itself. It is crucial because of its all-pervading comprehensive economic and social linkages. Unemployment leads to poverty, social degradation, and marginalization; history tells us that, if it reaches a high level, it often gives rise to social and political strife, with deleterious consequences.

In the 1990s, despite some changes for the better in some regions, large parts of the South are confronted by problems more difficult than before, because of the setbacks suffered by these countries during the 1980s. It is not necessary to catalogue these problems, many of which in any case are interrelated. Suffice it to say that in Latin America, after a sustained rise in the previous three decades, per capita incomes fell by 10 per cent in the 1980s. In Sub-Saharan Africa, per capita incomes fell on average by as much as 25 per cent during the same period, which has rightly been called the 'lost decade' for these two developing continents. Countries in both these regions are therefore faced not only with an enormous problem of unemployment and underemployment today, but with an even bigger potential challenge of providing employment opportunities for the expected rapid growth of their labour force.

However, it is not the South alone that is confronted with an employment problem today. Over the last decade or more, by post World War Two standards, the industrial countries of the North have been experiencing extremely high rates of unemployment. The workers, trade unionists, and politicians in these countries increasingly blame competition from cheap labour products from the developing economies for these job losses. Hence the growing populist demands for protection in one form or another

[1] An early draft of this chapter was prepared as a contribution to the work of the South Centre, Geneva, on 'An Agenda for Development' and on the Social Summit.

in many of these countries. Eradicating unemployment and creating adequate remunerative employment opportunities is therefore a common concern in both the North and the South. The main thesis of this chapter is that in an interdependent world economy the optimal solution to the employment and unemployment problem lies in cooperative action: both regions should follow 'positive sum' policies which help to create jobs in the North as well as in the South in a virtuous circle of cumulative causation. Indeed, not only are such cooperative policies optimal, they are in important ways the only ones which are feasible. In other words, neither the North nor the South can resolve this problem on its own.

The essential approach of this chapter is historical. It looks back to a previous era of North–South cooperation in the not too distant past—the Golden Age of capitalist development between 1950 and 1973—when countries in both regions prospered. Indeed during this period of high employment and growth for the world economy, the competitive game, not only between the North and the South but among nation states in general, was by and large played in a non-zero sum way. The chapter tries to draw lessons from this harmonious period of world economic development for the present.

1. THE DIMENSIONS OF THE EMPLOYMENT PROBLEM: SOUTH AND NORTH

The employment situation in the South, particularly in Latin America and Sub-Saharan Africa, is dire. There are not only current high rates of urban, especially youth and 'educated' unemployment,[2] but there is also the necessity of providing productive jobs for a labour force which is growing at approximately 3 per cent a year.[3] On the basis of past relationships between economic variables, to create jobs at this rate in order to meet the employment needs of new entrants to the labour force, the economies of these countries need to grow at a rate of about 6 per cent per annum.[4] If the cur-

---

[2] The recorded rates of unemployment in most developing countries tend to be relatively low. This is because in the virtual absence of a publicly provided social security system, people are obliged to engage in any economic activity, however non-remunerative and non-productive that may be. The problem of 'unemployment' in poor countries, therefore, manifests itself generally in the form of what Joan Robinson called 'disguised unemployment', or as 'underemployment'.

[3] The world labour force in 1993 is estimated to be 2.4 billion people, of whom 1.8 billion (75 per cent) are in developing countries. The United Nations estimates that the labour force in developing countries will in the foreseeable future grow at a rate of approximately 3% per annum. In Africa, the rate of labour force growth is expected to increase to 3.5% a year. (See UN, *World Social Report* (Geneva: 1993).)

[4] To illustrate, the annual rate of labour force growth in Mexico is about 3%. The long-term trend rate of growth of productivity in the period 1950–80 has also been about 3% a

rent high levels of unemployed and underemployed in these developing countries are also to be reduced, the growth rate will need to be higher still. Unfortunately, in the 'lost decade' of the 1980s, the rate of economic growth has been considerably less than is required: it has been only of the order of 2.1 per cent per annum in Sub-Saharan Africa and 1.6 per cent per annum in Latin America; (see Table 4.1).

Table 4.1. Growth performance in developing countries by category and region, 1965–80 and 1980–90

| | Average Annual Growth Rate of GDP (%) | |
	1965–80	1980–90
Low income economies	4.9	6.1
China	6.8	9.5
India	3.6	5.3
Other low income	4.8	3.9
Middle income economies	6.3	2.5
Sub-Saharan Africa	4.2	2.1
East Asia and Pacific	7.3	7.8
South Asia	3.6	5.2
Latin America and Caribbean	6.0	1.6

Notes: (a) The World Bank defines 'low income countries' as those with per capita income of $580 or less in 1989. Middle income countries are defined as those with income per capita of more than $580 and less than $6000.
(b) For the lists of countries included in each region, see the source listed below.
Source: World Bank, *World Development Report* 1992.

One outstanding success story for the South during the recent period has been the extremely good economic performance of the Asian countries, particularly those in East Asia, including China. In contrast with the Latin American and African countries which suffered economic collapse in the 1980s, the East as well as the South Asian countries either maintained their high previous momentum of economic growth or achieved a trend increase in it. The industrial revolution, which has been interrupted in Africa and Latin America, proceeded apace in these Asian countries, leading to

year. This means that GDP needs to grow at nearly 6% per annum in order just to provide jobs for the new entrants in the labour force. Similarly, the UN *World Social Report* notes that, since about one-half of all output accrues to labour, developing economies will need to grow at 6% a year, during the present decade, in order to absorb the growing labour force at current levels of income.

substantial creation of new jobs and higher real wages.[5] However, even these countries are faced potentially with a serious employment problem.

In countries like China and India, while agriculture accounts for a decreasing proportion of national output as they industrialize, the bulk of their population and labour force is still engaged in agriculture. The challenge in these countries is to provide adequate employment opportunities in industry and services as people leave the rural sector. Given the size of the rural population, this is an enormous task. The employment question is directly linked to that of the reduction of poverty. At the microeconomic level a reasonably remunerative job will keep a family out of poverty. At the macroeconomic level, the relationship between the two, even though indirect, is equally close. Just as the creation of sufficient employment opportunities requires a reasonable rate of economic growth, so does the eradication of poverty and meeting the minimum basic needs of the people.[6]

Although, at any one time, a redistribution of national output may enable a society to better meet the basic needs of its people, on a longer term basis such needs can only be met if there is an expansion of the national economy. Economic growth generates increased employment and household incomes; equally importantly, it increases government revenues, which may be spent on health, education, clean water supplies, and other basic needs of the people.[7]

---

[5] The South and East Asian countries recorded an increase of more than 50% in their per capita incomes in the 1980s. This compares, as noted earlier, with significant reductions in per capita incomes in Latin America and Sub-Saharan Africa in the 'lost decade'. There is a large literature on why the Asian countries succeeded and the Latin Americans so comprehensively failed in this period. For different views on this subject see among others, J. Sachs, 'External Debt and Macroeconomic Performance in Latin America and East Asia', *Brookings Papers on Economic Activity*, 2 (1985), World Bank, *The World Development Report* (New York: Oxford University Press, 1991); and *The East Asian Miracle: Economic Growth and Public Policy* (New York: Oxford University Press, 1993), A. Fishlow, 'Some Reflections on Comparative Latin American Economic Performance and Policy'; A. Hughes and A. Singh, 'The World Economic Slowdown and Asian and Latin American Economies', both in T. Banuri (ed.), *The Limits of Economic Liberalization* (Oxford: Clarendon, 1992); and A. Singh 'Asian Economic Success and Latin American Failure in the 1980s: New Analyses and Future Policy Implications', *International Review of Applied Economics*, Sept. 1993 (1993). The reasons for the economic failure in Sub-Saharan Africa are discussed in Singh, 'Manufacturing and De-Industrialization' in J. Eatwell, M. Milgate, and P. Newman (eds.), *The New Palgrave*, (London: Macmillan, 1987) and 'Global Economic Changes, Skills and International Competitiveness', *International Labour Review*, 133/2 (1994).

[6] For the relationship between employment, basic needs, poverty, and economic growth, see Singh, 'The "Basic Needs" Approach to Development vs The New International Economic Order: The Significance of Third World Industrialisation', *World Development* (1979), 7, 1992*b*). See also International Labour Organisation (ILO), *Employment Growth and Basic Needs: A One World Problem*, Geneva, 1976.

[7] In its influential 1976 report, the ILO estimated that even allowing for some redistribution of incomes, if the minimum basic needs of the poorest 20% of the Third World's population were to be met by the year 2000, their economies would have to grow at an annual average rate of 7 to 8% a year. These rates are not all that different from those required to create sufficient employment opportunities for the South's growing population. During the

Unemployment in the North

The European economies are today experiencing very high rates of unemployment. The current rates in leading economies like France, Italy, and the United Kingdom approximate 10 per cent of the labour force. In Spain and Finland, the unemployment rate is over 15 per cent. In Sweden, which maintained high levels of employment throughout the slow-growing 1980s, the rate of unemployment has increased in a very short period of time from 1.5 per cent of the labour force in 1990 to well over 10 per cent now. The United States has experienced somewhat lower unemployment than the European countries.[8] One reason for this is that the welfare provision in that country is not as extensive as that in Europe, so that many people are obliged to seek work even at non-remunerative wage levels. It is striking that, in the US economy, average real wages have hardly increased over the last twenty years.[9] Thus a large proportion of individuals and families are living below the poverty line. Hence the emphasis and the political compulsions of the present US administration are on creating remunerative jobs, not just any jobs.

2. THE EMPLOYMENT CHALLENGE IN ITS HISTORICAL CONTEXT

In the context of postwar economic history, the current high rates of unemployment in the North are a relatively recent phenomenon. During the 1950s and the 1960s, leading countries of the North not only enjoyed full employment but had overfull employment. In addition to being able to employ all their own people, these countries also provided jobs for additional labour from abroad. In countries like France and West Germany nearly 10 per cent of the labour force came from abroad. The contrast with the current employment situation could not be more striking.

The period 1950–73 has been aptly described as the Golden Age of the world economy. In the advanced economies during this period, there was a historically unprecedented expansion of production and consumption at a

last 15 years, those economies (mainly in Asia) that were able to achieve such high rates of growth have succeeded in significantly reducing poverty in their countries. On the other hand, low economic growth in the Latin American and African countries over the recent period has had a serious negative effect both on poverty and employment generation in these economies.

[8] Between 1983 and 1992, the average unemployment rate in France, Italy, and the UK was around 10% of the labour force. The corresponding figure for the USA for this decade was 6.7%. See Ch. 12.

[9] The average real compensation of the American worker in 1991 was only 6% higher than it had been in 1973. Moreover, compensation has risen only for the highly educated workers; the real wages of blue collar workers have fallen in most years since 1973. P. Krugman and R. Lawrence, 'Trade, Jobs, and Wages', NBER working paper 4478 (1993).

rate of nearly 5 per cent a year. This was accompanied by a huge increase in world trade, particularly in the export of manufactured products. The latter grew in volume terms at a very fast rate of nearly 10 per cent a year. Most developing countries also participated in and benefited from this worldwide prosperity. Many Asian and Latin American countries embarked on a veritable industrial revolution in these postwar decades.

The Golden Age of simultaneous prosperity for the North and the South evidently came to an end with the first oil shock in 1973. Since then, the rate of growth of GDP for OECD countries and the world as a whole has nearly halved. Significantly, the recorded rate during the last twenty years is much more in line with the long-term trend rate of growth of industrial countries in the hundred years before the Golden Age (Reynolds, 1983; World Bank, 1987). It is therefore not surprising to find the high rates of unemployment recently experienced by the OECD—rates which were unthinkable in the preceding period. It is for the same reason that for a large number of countries in the South, in contrast to the industrial revolution and significant rises in the average standard of living of the Golden Age, the last fifteen years have been marked by de-industrialization and considerable falls in per capita incomes. The end of the Golden Age has also coincided with a significant deceleration in the expansion of world trade in manufactures.

The central issue for the world community is whether such a dynamic period associated with fuller employment can be re-created. This hinges on understanding how this Golden Age of plenty of jobs and fast economic growth for an extended period of nearly a quarter of a century occurred and why it ended.

3. NATIONAL AND INTERNATIONAL INSTITUTIONAL ARRANGEMENTS

Considered purely in statistical terms, in the long history of economic development in industrial countries, the postwar quarter century of the Golden Age appears to be a historical aberration. Measured in terms of the rates of growth of output, productivity, and capital stock, the period 1950–73 in advanced economies as a whole unquestionably represents a highly distinct deviation from the long-term trend values of these variables over the last two centuries. (See Glyn, Hughes, Lipietz and Singh, 1990; Maddison, 1982).

Turning to economic analysis, detailed examination of the data show that the length, steadiness, speed, and spread of the Golden Age economic boom was such that they could not be accounted for by an accidental combination of favourable economic circumstances. Rather, the extraordinary economic performance of the industrial countries was brought about and sustained by a unique historical conjuncture which created a specific *economic regime*.[10] This regime, which differed in very important respects from the interwar pattern of development, made full employment of the labour force and full utilization of resources, a primary objective *inter alia* for governments to pursue.[11]

The most important macroeconomic characteristics of the Golden Age pattern of economic development were rapid and parallel growth of productivity and capital stock per worker, and parallel growth of real wages and productivity. The significance of these two relations is that they guarantee both a roughly constant profit rate and roughly equal growth of consumption and production, thus ratifying and maintaining the initial rate of accumulation. However, such a macroeconomic growth path could only be perpetuated if it were compatible with the behaviour of individual economic agents—firms, workers, and consumers. This compatibility in the Golden Age was ensured by a social consensus around institutional arrangements in respect of the setting of wages and prices, the distribution between wages and profits, and the state fiscal, credit, and welfare policies which guaranteed minimum living standards and which maintained aggregate demand. In the sphere of wage setting, for example, productivity wage bargaining, which flourished during this period, played a key role both in keeping a rough constancy of the share of wages and profits in the national product, and also in helping to provide an adequate rate of growth in consumer demand. Similarly, at the international level, under the leadership of a single hegemonic power, the USA, for much of this period, the global economic system functioned under stable monetary and trading arrangements.

[10] For reasons of space, what follows is necessarily a highly schematic and condensed account of the analysis of the large question: why did the Golden Age arise and why did it come to an end? This summary is based on A. Glyn, A. Hughes, A. Lipietz, and A. Singh, 'The Rise and Fall of the Golden Age' in S. Marglin and J. Schor (eds.), *The Golden Age of Capitalism* (Oxford: Clarendon Press, 1990), to which the reader is referred for a full discussion of these issues. For some alternative interpretations, see A. Maddison, *Phases of Capitalist Development* (Oxford: Oxford University Press, 1982); M. Bruno and J. Sachs, *Economics of Worldwide Stagflation* (Oxford: Blackwells, 1985); R. C. O. Matthews and A. Bowen, 'Keynesian and Other Explanations of Post-war Macro-economic Trends', paper prepared for Keynes General Theory After Fifty Years Conference held at the National Economic Development Office, Sept. 1987; C. Kindleberger, 'Why did the Golden Age Last so Long?' in A. Cairncross and F. Cairncross, *The Legacy of the Golden Age: The 1960s and their Economic Consequences* (London: Routledge, 1992).

[11] How this economic regime came to be established in the postwar period is a complex phenomenon which had a great deal to do with the contention between the liberal, free market capitalist world economic order led by the United States and the alternative, represented by the then triumphant Soviet Union. It will be recalled that at the end of the Second World War the Soviet model had important attractions for people in Western Europe. The country had just played a critical role in defeating fascism; the crimes of the Stalin era had not yet been revealed. Equally importantly, compared with the mass unemployment in the interwar period in the industrial countries, Soviet planning was regarded as having achieved full employment of resources. See further Glyn, Hughes, Lipietz and Singh, 'The Rise and Fall of the Golden Age'.

The erosion of the Golden Age began well before the oil price shock of 1973. Serious difficulties arose at the levels of both the national and the international regulatory regimes; these began to interact with each other in a cumulatively adverse way to the detriment of the system as a whole. The Bretton Woods monetary system broke down in the late 1960s, partly as a consequence of the success of the Golden Age itself—the rise of the Japanese, the West German, and other European countries in the international market place led to serious balance of payments problems for the USA, hitherto the lynchpin of the international system. There is also evidence of a productivity slow-down by the late 1960s in several leading industrial countries, which was not matched by a deceleration in the rate of growth of real wages, thus leading to a profit squeeze.

By the early 1970s, the Golden Age system was so fragile that it disintegrated under the impact of the two oil shocks, thus pushing the world economy into a period of prolonged slow growth which began in 1973. The social consensus of the Golden years, which was crucial to the functioning of the economic system as a whole, broke down. For a while, after the first oil shock, the governments of the OECD countries tried to restore the Golden Age institutional consensus, by following expansionary economic policies. But, since inflation could not be controlled, this attempt was finally abandoned in 1979. This abandonment was symbolized by the so-called 'Volcker shock' (named after the then Chairman of the US Federal Reserve, Paul Volcker). This resulted in the implementation of deeply contractionary monetary policies in the United States and these were subsequently widely imitated elsewhere, particularly in the UK. These policies led to a more than tenfold jump in real interest rates compared with the preceding period, and gave rise to a prolonged recession in the industrial countries.

The effects on the Third World countries of these measures was devastating. They were disadvantaged through the following main channels: a) a reduction in the demand for the South's products in the North; b) as a consequence, a big fall in commodity prices and adverse terms of trade; c) a big rise in debt service payments; d) a sudden and large fall in normal capital flows to the South, particularly to the African and Latin American economies. The net result has been a long economic crisis and the 'lost decade' of the 1980s for large parts of the South.

In the 1980s and into the 1990s, the leading OECD governments have been attempting to create a new economic system based on more free market principles, despite this not commanding any broad social consensus in these countries. In pursuit of this objective, there has been a widespread movement towards 'privatization', 'de-regulation', and the erosion of Golden Age arrangements with respect for example to wage bargaining and welfare state provision (with the professed aim of increasing labour market flexibility).

At one level this post-1980 development model has had some success—the most conspicuous being the sharp decline in the OECD rate of inflation. Instead of the 'stagflation' of the 1970s—i.e. low growth and high inflation—the 1980s and the 1990s so far have been characterized by low growth and low inflation. However, most OECD countries, especially in Western Europe, are suffering from very high rates of unemployment. There are also large payments imbalances among the leading countries as well as fragile financial markets. On present projections of leading international organizations, the prospects for an appreciable increase in rates of economic growth and for a substantial reduction in unemployment in the OECD economies, in the foreseeable future, are rather gloomy.[12]

However, notwithstanding the fall of the Golden Age and the consequent slow-down in the growth of world production and trade, it is important to appreciate that the world economy is far more integrated than ever before. If greater economic integration is supposed to lead to more efficient resource utilization and hence faster economic growth, as the Bretton Woods institutions contend, this clearly has not happened. Be that as it may, close international financial integration has been a particularly significant feature of the post-1973 world economy. Such integration has been brought about by the more or less complete abolition of exchange controls in leading industrial economies and the globalization of the stock markets. (Cosh, Hughes, and Singh, 1992).

4. THE THIRD WORLD INDUSTRIAL REVOLUTION

Prior to the economic crisis of the 1980s, the postwar era from 1950 to 1980 was also, in an important sense, a Golden Age of development for the poor countries of the world. During this period, developing countries on average made historically unprecedented economic and industrial progress. In the propitious circumstances following the end of the Second World War, many of these countries, particularly in Asia and Africa, began to carry out an industrial revolution—a revolution that they had been prevented from implementing fifty or a hundred years earlier, on account of the rather

---

[12] With respect to unemployment in Europe, J. H. Dreze and E. Malinvaud, 'Growth and Employment. The Scope of a European Initiative', mimeo (Louvain-le-Neuve and Paris, July 1993) observe that: 'The Annual Economic Report of the EEC for 1993 advocates a forecast of GDP growth for 1993 of less than 1%, with employment falling and unemployment rising to similar extents.' More significant perhaps is the medium-term assessment: 'Estimates of potential growth are always difficult to make, but it seems clear that without a significant break from recent trends that the Community economy can only be expected to return gradually to rates of growth of between 2 to 2.5%. These are barely sufficient to stabilise unemployment and do not open up any medium term prospect of significant reductions. Even if in 1995–6 growth were to return to rates of about 3%, as various medium-term forecasts suggest, unemployment could be still as high as 10 to 11%.'

different world economic and political conditions which then prevailed. Even developing countries in Sub-Saharan Africa, which started with extremely unfavourable initial conditions when colonial rule ended, managed to increase their share of world manufacturing production during the 1960s and the 1970s. More significantly, a group of Asian and Latin American nations—the so called NICs—were especially successful in the post World War II period in establishing technical, scientific, and industrial infrastructures; in training their labour forces, in creating managerial and organizational capacities; and in developing broad-based industrial structures. By the 1970s these countries were beginning to provide formidable competition to the rich industrial economies in a range of consumer and producer goods industries.

In statistical terms, the Third World's economic achievements of the three decades 1950–80 are a story without parallel in world development history. During this period, the South surpassed the eighty-year record of the North's nineteenth century (1820–1900) advance. The South did this in half the time, at twice the growth rates, and with five times the North's population in the nineteenth century (Patel, 1992). In addition to these economic gains, the Third World countries during this period also made extraordinary advances in the social fields of health and education. Consider for example literacy rates. The North's rates have been estimated to have averaged below 25 per cent in 1850 and below 50 per cent in 1900. The corresponding level of literacy in the South was about 30 per cent in 1950. By the 1980s, however, it had risen to 50 per cent in Africa, 70 per cent in Asia and 80 per cent in Latin America. More significantly, despite all the shortcomings both in the data and in the quality of education imparted in developing countries, the North–South educational gap narrowed spectacularly during these decades of relative prosperity.

Similarly this period witnessed vast improvements in public health and life expectancy in the South. Life expectancy rose from around forty years in 1950 to sixty years by the mid 1980s—in other words twenty years were added to the life of the average citizen of the South. Life expectancy for females increased even more than for males almost everywhere in the South.

5. DOES THE SOUTH'S INDUSTRIAL REVOLUTION CAUSE DE-INDUSTRIALIZATION IN THE NORTH?

The impressive industrialization of the Third World during its Golden Age raises the important question of whether it is responsible for de-industrialization and the rise in overall unemployment in the advanced countries. It is indeed true that during the last two decades manufactured exports from the South to the North have been rising at a fast rate.[13] It is also the case that in industrial countries the share of manufacturing output and employment, particularly the latter, has fallen substantially in the same period.[14] The salient analytical question is whether this is just a coincidence, or whether one has caused the other.

This is by no means a straightforward issue, since de-industrialization and the rise in overall unemployment in the industrial countries can be caused by a whole range of other factors as well. For example, a falling share of manufacturing employment in the labour force is a long-run phenomenon of economic development, which arises from technological change and the faster growth of productivity in manufacturing than in services. De-industrialization in this sense may simply be like de-ruralization (a falling share of agricultural employment) which has occurred in the course of this century in most advanced countries, without any necessarily negative economic connotations. Nevertheless, it is possible for de-industrialization in a particular country to occur at a rate that is much too rapid, so that the economy is prevented from achieving its full potential.[15]

In view of the complexity of the subject, there is no agreement in the literature on the appropriate theoretical or empirical models for analysing the impact of Third World competition on manufacturing output and employment in the North. There exist instead alternative paradigms, which lead to very different policy conclusions. According to the dominant neoclassical paradigm, trade does not cause unemployment (see, for example Dreze and Malinvaud, 1993). The observed de-industrialization in advanced countries is ascribed, in this doctrine, to the following two causes: (a) the long-run factors mentioned above which lead to a shift from manufacturing to service employment; (b) a shift in comparative advantage for a range of manufactured products from the North to the South. This leads to a temporary problem of structural adjustment for which the proper remedy is to reduce

[13] To illustrate, between 1965 and 1973, the rate of growth of manufacturing exports of the developed countries was much the same as that of the developing countries—about 10% p.a. at constant prices. Between 1973 and 1985, the former's exports grew only at 4.4% p.a., whilst the latter's increased at an incredible 12.3% p.a. Moreover, much the larger part of the Third World's manufactured exports go to the North. Further, there is evidence that the developing countries are exporting not only the traditional labour intensive and resource based products, but are also recording a very fast growth in the exports of a variety of products of capital goods industries. (World Bank, *World Development Report* (Washington DC., 1987); UNCTAD, Trade and Development Report (Geneva: United Nations, 1993)

[14] In the USA, manufacturing employment as a percentage of civilian employment has fallen from 24.2% in 1974 to 18% in 1990; in the UK the corresponding figures are 34.6 and 22.5%; in Japan 27.2 and 24.1% and in Germany 35.8 and 31.5% respectively. OECD, *Historical Statistics* (Paris: OECD, 1992).

[15] See A. Singh, 'UK Industry and the World Economy: A Case of Deindustrialization?' *Cambridge Journal of Economics* (June 1977); Sir A. Cairncross, 'What is De-Industrialisation', in F. Blackaby (ed.), *Deindustrialisation* (London: Heinemann Educational Books, 1979).

the rigidities in the North's labour markets rather than to call for protection or subsidies.[16]

Building on the work of Sayers and Kaldor, Singh (1987, 1989, 1990) put forward an alternative non-neoclassical conceptual framework for investigating this issue. In this framework, although the long-term factors of economic development do cause de-industrialization in advanced countries, trade can also significantly contribute to it and to overall unemployment. Singh advanced twin concepts of an 'efficient manufacturing sector' and that of 'long-term structural disequilibrium' for examining this issue for an advanced economy like the UK. His analysis suggests that industrial countries with 'inefficient manufacturing sectors' or those in 'long-term structural disequilibrium' can be seriously disadvantaged by trade (which could lead to speedier de-industrialization as well as to rising overall unemployment). In summary, in Singh's framework, the answer to the question whether, and to what extent, de-industrialization in an advanced economy is due to Third World competition in manufactures, requires the following chain of causation to be established: first, taking into account its interactions with the rest of the world, is the economy in 'long-term structural disequilibrium'?[17] Second, if so, is this disequilibrium due to trade in manufactures rather than, for example, to trade in services? And third, if the structural disequilibrium is, indeed, because of the trade in manufactures, is this due to competition with the Third World or with other advanced countries (for example, Japan)?

Singh's (1989) empirical analysis for the 1970s, showed that for an advanced industrial economy with an 'inefficient' manufacturing sector like the UK, trade in manufactures did lead to a *net* loss of jobs.[18] But importantly, the study also showed that it was not manufacturing trade with the Third World but rather with the other advanced countries which was the main cause of the disequilibrium. On the contrary, Singh estimated that at least in the 1970s, UK manufacturing trade with the newly industrializing

---

[16] This view is best expressed in M. Beenstock, *The World Economy in Transition* (London and Boston: Allen and Unwin, 1984) and in the recent American Express Gold Medal winning essay, R. Brown and D. Julius, 'Is Manufacturing Still Special in the New World Order?' The Amex Bank Review: 7, *Finance and the International Economy* (Oxford University Press, 1993).

[17] An advanced country like the UK is regarded as being in long-term structural disequilibrium if its manufacturing import and export propensities are such that the country is unable to achieve current account balance at a desired level of employment and a desired rate of growth of real wages. In this conceptualization, for an industrial country, manufacturing performance in the world economy is regarded as the key to the achievement of the desired current account balance (and hence the country's ability to reach its long term growth potential).

[18] 'Gross' job losses, however, can and often do cause enormous social distress even if there is equivalent employment created elsewhere. New service sector jobs often pay less and are less protected by union rights and other benefits than the manufacturing jobs that disappear. B. Bluestone and B. Harrison, *The De-Industrialization of America* (New York: Basic Books, 1982) called particular attention to this phenomenon.

countries, led to an increase in trade balance, and hence in total output. It probably also generated a small net rise in employment rather than a fall. However, the econometric analysis also showed that there was evidence that if British industry did not become more efficient, in the longer term Britain's trade with the NICs was likely to become as disequilibrating as that with the advanced countries.

In analysing the impact of Third World competition on advanced industrial economies as a whole, the important conceptual point in Singh's analysis was to distinguish between countries like the UK with 'inefficient' manufacturing sectors (which led to these economies being chronically balance-of-payments constrained at desired levels of output and employment) and those like Japan and West Germany with 'efficient' manufacturing industry (i.e. industry generates enough net exports to ensure the required current account balance at desired levels of employment or overall economic growth). Empirical evidence (see OECD, 1979) indicates that the North's trade balance in manufacturing with NICs was positive and it increased over the period 1970–7. This suggested that even if in some balance-of-payments constrained advanced countries, manufacturing trade with NICs had become disequilibrating in the 1970s, it was likely in general to have been a far smaller source of disequilibrium than the trade among the industrial countries themselves.

In the 1980s the situation has been rather different. There is, for example, evidence of significant job losses in the USA as a result of its manufacturing trade with developing countries. But, barring a few East Asian countries, as Marshall (1988) rightly pointed out, this fall in employment was due more to a loss of US exports than to a huge increase in imports. US merchandise exports to developing countries declined by 24.4 per cent in real terms between 1980 and 1985 compared with an 11.7 per cent reduction in total exports. This was, however, mainly due to 'import strangulation' in developing countries as a consequence of the debt crises (Singh, 1986; Khan and Knight, 1988). US exports to heavily indebted Latin American countries fell, for example, by 30.9 per cent during this period. On the other hand, job losses arising from US trade with an industrializing economy like Taiwan, which was running sizeable trade surpluses in the 1980s, was more likely due to its greater penetration of the US market. Taiwan was not subject to import compression arising from the debt crises in the way the Latin American countries were in the last decade.

To sum up, the evidence suggests that in the 1970s the North–South trade in manufacturing products did not in general lead to trade imbalances, or a net loss of either manufacturing or total output in the North; rather it provided a positive impulse to industrial development in the advanced countries. The main reason for this is that, although manufactured exports from the NICs to the North expanded very fast, the North's

exports to the South grew even faster in the 1970s. The developing countries need technology and capital goods from the advanced economies. The
NICs used the opportunity provided by easy availability of credit at almost
zero real interest rates in the mid 1970s to greatly increase their imports of
capital goods to accelerate their industrialization process. However, in the
1980s, as a consequence of the debt crisis, Latin American NICs became
severely balance-of-payments constrained and they were obliged to curtail
sharply their imports from industrial countries. Indeed, during much of the
1980s, the Latin American countries were running trade surpluses amounting to as much as 5 per cent of their GDP. They were obliged to do so in
order to pay debt service to the North's banks. As a consequence the
North–South trade in manufactures in the 1980s provided a negative
impulse for the Northern industrial economies.

This analysis suggests that in general, because of the very high propensity to import of the developing countries, North–South industrial trade
should not be disequilibrating for the North. It could, however, exacerbate
the existing disequilibrium between the strong and the weak industrial
countries. To illustrate, China today has a large trade surplus with the
United States, but an even larger deficit with Japan. Thus China's overall
trade with the North is not a source of disequilibrium. The basic problem
here is that, presumably because of the greater competitiveness of the
Japanese capital goods industry relative to that of the US, China exports
more (generally consumer goods) to the USA and imports more from
Japan (capital goods).[19]

6. MEETING THE NEW CHALLENGE

The second oil shock saw the final abandonment of what may be called the
Golden Age *pattern of development* (encompassing both the internal and
external rules of coordination of the economic system). It is beyond the
scope of this chapter to provide a full discussion of the emerging post-1979
pattern. However, it may be briefly recalled that at the international level,
instead of attempting to compensate for the deflationary effects of the 1979
oil price rise, restrictive monetary and fiscal policies were strongly

[19] There are other aspects of the impact of North–South manufacturing trade on the North's
economies. Specifically, it has been suggested that the stagnation and decline of real wages of
blue-collar workers in the USA and the growth in wage inequality between skilled and unskilled
workers in the recent period has been due to cheap labour imports from developing countries.
Krugman and Lawrence, 'Trade, Jobs, and Wages', NBER Working Paper no. 4478, (1993),
R. Freeman, 'Is Globalisation Impoverishing low skill American Workers', Harvard University
mimeo, (1993) and R. Lawrence and M. Slaughter, 'Trade and US Wages: Giant Sucking
Sound or Small Hiccup?', *Brooking Papers on Economic Activity: Microeconomics*, (1993) pro-
vide analysis and evidence against this thesis. For a different perspective, see A. Wood,
North–South Trade, Employment and Inequality (Oxford University Press, 1994).

reinforced in the USA and adopted by other main industrial countries. In an international economy, ever more closely linked by 'free' and gigantic capital movements, this resulted in the early 1980s in a 'beggar-my-neighbour' competitive deflation and a prolonged recession.

Although the retreat from the Golden Age institutional arrangements has inevitably occurred at different speeds in the various countries, there has broadly been a common overall pattern. The specific measures implemented for this purpose since 1980 have included: legislation to restrict the role of the unions (UK, Germany); abolishing norms of indexation (Italy); relaxing employment protection legislation (UK, France); relaxation of labour standards and restrictions on welfare provisions (in most countries); significant steps towards marketization and privatization (almost everywhere). Moreover, in the adoption of rules about monetary growth and public sector deficits in most countries, there has been an implicit abandonment of the full employment policies of the Golden Age. The countries of the South have also had to implement similar arrangements in order to meet the conditionalities of the Bretton Woods institutions.

For vast numbers of people in the South and in the North, the post-Golden Age economic era has been exceedingly bleak. In many countries in Africa and Latin America, real wages have fallen drastically by 50 per cent or more, and there have been vast cut-backs in employment and, instead of a continuing industrial revolution, there has been de-industrialization.

Similarly in the North, there has been an enormous increase in unemployment, cuts in social provision, and a much reduced quality of life for the bottom 30 per cent or so of the population. It is therefore not surprising that the new post Golden Age economic regime has still not gained widespread acceptability in the advanced countries. As noted earlier, the only major success which can be claimed for these policies is a fall in the rate of inflation in these economies. However, this 'victory' over inflation has come at an exceptionally high cost in terms of social justice and economic efficiency. The extension of the role of free markets in the name of efficiency has, paradoxically, generated massive inefficiency characterized by a huge underutilization of resources worldwide, not least human resources. Thus the average unemployment rate has gone up from 0.79 per cent of the labour force in West Germany during the Golden Age decade, 1964–73, to over 6 per cent in the recent decade, 1983–92. In France, the corresponding increase has been from 2.2 per cent to 9.7 per cent of the labour force, in the UK from 2.9 per cent to 9.8 per cent.[20]

It has been suggested by some that the present unemployment problems in the world economy, and particularly in the North, have been caused by

---

[20] See Ch. 12, Table 12.1.

the new technological revolution, based on information and communications technology. However, the evidence does not support this view, since what the world has witnessed in the post Golden Age period has not been a rise but rather a fall in the rate of growth of productivity. More extensive or faster technological change should lead to greater, rather than slower, growth of productivity. Indeed, if productivity growth had been as fast as during the Golden Age, the number of unemployed would have been far greater than they already are, given the slower rate of growth of production.[21] What this means is that the full potential of the new technology has not been realized.

The following comparison between the Golden Age and the post Golden Age periods is relevant to the question of the impact of competition from cheap labour products from the South on unemployment and real wages in the North: Krugman and Lawrence (1993) point out that, in 1990, US imports from low-wage countries, defined as countries with wage rates less than half the US level, were only 2.8 per cent of GDP. Such imports—using the same definition as before, i.e. countries paying less than half the US wage—were almost as large in 1960, 2 per cent of GDP. These imports at that time came from the then low-wage countries in Europe as well as from Japan. Yet during the Golden Age the average wage of the American worker more or less doubled, whilst, as noted before, it has hardly increased in the two decades since then. The average rate of unemployment in the USA between 1964 and 1973 was 4.5 per cent compared with 6.7 per cent between 1983 and 1992.

It is commonplace for international economic organizations to argue that the rise in unemployment in the 1980s, particularly in the European countries, has been due to labour market rigidities and the inflexibility of real wages.[22] Countries, not just in Europe but everywhere, are therefore urged to institute wage and labour market flexibility as the best way to reduce unemployment. The proposition in this form cannot withstand serious scrutiny. For example, in the 1980s, countries in Africa and Latin America have had massive cuts in real wages. Yet, instead of an increase, they have had a decrease in the level of employment. On the other hand in the Asian countries, real wages have risen at a fast rate and so has employment. Similarly, in the North, labour markets have been much more flexible in the 1980s than they were in the 1960s, yet the 1960s were characterized by full employment and the 1980s (and the 1990s) by large-scale unemployment. There is thus no reason to believe that further labour market flexibility in the North and in the South, as demanded under the current economic regime, will by itself give rise to adequate productive employment opportunities.

---

[21] See Ch. 12, and Singh, 'Global Economic Changes, Skills and International Competitiveness' *International Labour Review*, 133/2 (1994).
[22] See for example, IMF, *World Economic Outlook* (Washington D.C., Mar. 1994).

Clearly, the massive rise in unemployment and much reduced economic growth in the North in the post Golden Age era are not due to new technology, cheap labour competition from the South, or the domestic labour market conditions, but are essentially caused by a reduction in the trend rate of growth of world demand, compared with the earlier period. The change in the monetary and fiscal policy stance of the OECD governments, which put the fight against inflation as the primary objective of economic policy in the 1980s, has been a major factor in the reduced rate of growth of world demand. The latter needs to expand at the rate it did in the 1950s and the 1960s, if the world economy is to achieve sufficient growth to bring about full employment of material and human resources in the North and the South.

The South itself can take certain steps to improve the employment and poverty situation both through appropriate national policies and greater South–South cooperation. However, despite the increased economic strength of a number of developing countries, and in view of the great degree of North–South interdependence, the South also needs expansionary measures to be taken in the North. The North, in addition to taking its own measures to deal with its employment crisis, also needs a substantial improvement in the levels of employment and standards of living in the South. Not only does it require markets and outlets for investment, but development in the South would help reduce the flows of labour from the South searching for employment in the North. To advance on each of these fronts requires action on a third: North–South cooperation.

However, the demand constraint on world production is not technical: rather, the constraint is deeply institutional. It cannot simply be relaxed by the leading Northern governments changing their fiscal and monetary policies. A sustainable increase in the rate of growth of world demand will only be possible if the confrontational free market pattern of development of the 1980s is abandoned and replaced by more cooperative institutional arrangements involving workers, employers, and governments in the North as well as more cooperative relationships between the North and the South.

What would happen if such cooperative arrangements were not in place and the OECD governments followed expansionary policies in order to reduce unemployment, and the world rate of economic growth rose on a sustained basis to anywhere near the Golden Age levels? Most likely it would lead to increased labour strength and militancy in the North in pursuit of higher wages and better employment conditions, as well as to a sharp rise in world commodity prices, including oil.[23] This in turn would rekindle inflation and thwart the expansionary process.

[23] The sharp fall in real commodity prices in the 1980s was a primary factor in reducing the rate of inflation in industrial countries to a low level. For a discussion of the magnitude of this effect, with differing estimates, see W. Beckerman and T. Jenkinson, 'What Stopped

Thus growth rates approaching the Golden Age levels (the sort of level required to resolve unemployment problems), with low inflation, will only be feasible and sustainable if three basic conditions are fulfilled. First, a new institutional and behavioural framework is required internally within the North. And within the South, a major change in policy direction is generally required. On the global scale, a rather different system of international arrangements between the North and the South is necessary, involving, among other things, some scheme for orderly commodity price movements hitherto rejected by the leading OECD governments. Only if such a mutually cooperative pattern of development were instituted would the world be able to begin to meet the challenges of the 1990s and beyond. If this opportunity is missed, the prospects for employment, democracy, and social justice, and for political stability would not appear to be very strong.[24]

the Inflation? Unemployment or Commodity Prices?', *Economic Journal*, 96 (Mar. 1986) and C. Gilbert, 'Primary Commodity Prices and Inflation', *Oxford Review of Economic Policy*, (1990) 6, Winter.

[24] Moreover to be sustainable, such faster growth of world demand and production will have to pay full attention to ecological concerns. This will require the North to recognize the South's right to 'ecological space', in the sense of recognizing that, but for the South's underdevelopment, the current and looming environmental threats would be that much greater. The South's development cannot be prohibited on environmental grounds. Both North and South will need to economize on scarce materials, and increasingly produce products and introduce processes which do not damage the environment.

5. Globalization and Labour Standards

Werner Sengenberger and Frank Wilkinson

Markets and productive systems progressively move beyond national boundaries. The increasing importance of multinational enterprises, cross-national strategic alliances, transnational subcontracting and sourcing of production and services, and regional economic integration signal the trend towards an internationalized economy. By contrast, labour institutions and labour market regulation remain at the national or sub-national level and it is there that pay, employment rules, working conditions, occupational health and safety, and social security are determined.

The growing incongruity between the economic and the social space of organization creates a major challenge to economic, political, and social stability. As companies and capital move ever more freely to where they expect the best returns, and large enterprises grow increasingly powerful— with the sales of some of the giant corporations well exceeding the GNP of small nations—national governments and national labour organizations lose their regulative power over economic behaviour within their borders. The danger is that this loss of autonomy will throw national social 'models', and national systems of labour institutions, into international competition. This could provoke economic war, destructive social conflict, and a new upsurge of nationalism. But if properly handled, it could lead to new international accords, enhanced mutual understanding in a more closely integrated world, promote better resource utilization, and help resolve the growing world problems of poverty and environmental pollution.

To meet the challenge constructively, labour institutions will necessarily play a crucial role and, to be effective, labour organizations and labour market regulation need to be coextensive with the market. Otherwise, labour standards can be undercut and free riding encouraged. Fears of 'social dumping', as the trade unions call it, are being voiced in the European Union. While trade union organization and collective bargaining are still largely national, and progress towards the European Social Charter of Community-wide social standards is slow, economic integration moves much faster as rules and institutions inhibiting capital mobility and the free flow of trade are dismantled. However, the mismatch between the economic and social space in Europe is minor when compared with other world regions which are taking initiatives towards economic integration. In every one of these regions labour market organization far from matches even in a remote sense the degree of internationalization of production and trade relations.

This chapter will briefly consider the trend towards globalization before describing progress towards global labour standards. The third section will argue the economic, social, and political case for labour market regulation and the final section will outline institutional responses designed to reconcile labour policies with international integration.

1. THE INTERNATIONALIZATION OF THE ECONOMY

The driving force behind the internationalization of the economy are the multinational enterprises (MNEs). The importance of MNEs have increased dramatically over the past two decades in terms of their numbers—37,000 in 1992, their foreign investment—reaching a stock of $2000 billion in 1992, and their total sales outside their own country—$5500 in 1992 (UNCTAD, 1993). In the last three years of the 1980s alone, foreign direct investment (FDI) measured in 1980 dollars was more than 100 billion a year, ten times as much as it had been in the first three years of the 1970s. The MNEs account for the bulk of foreign direct investment by establishing facilities abroad, and a significant component of foreign trade is made up of trade between parents and subsidiaries of MNEs. In 1992 MNEs controlled about one third of the world's private productive assets (UNCTAD, 1993) so that, in a real sense, they have become the private regulators of borderless economies.

At the beginning of the 1980s MNEs employed at least sixty-five million workers worldwide, of whom forty-three million were in the countries where the parent enterprise was located. A further fifteen million were in industrialized countries and only seven million in developing countries (ILO, 1981). By the end of the 1980s the total of employment in MNEs was more than seventy millions (Parisotto, 1993). These figures say little, however, about the role played by MNEs in internationalization and globalization and how their competitive strategies have been changing. In the 1970s the multinationalization of manufacturing resulted from international subcontracting in search of lower labour costs increasing intra-industry trade, the international division of labour, and investment and technology links between countries of the North and the South. This phenomenon sparked a theory on the 'new international division of labour' (NIDL). It was argued that the existence of global capital markets and a reserve army of labour would generate a massive out-migration of capital, structural unemployment in the OECD countries, and exploitation of workers in the Third World (Fröbel et al., 1977).

In the 1980s, however, growth came to be driven by the spread of cost-reducing and quality-enhancing advancements in the electronics-based industries (semi-conductors, telecommunications, computers, consumer and industrial electronics) which transformed the production processes of other industries. Information could now be carried by electronic impulses around the globe in less than seconds, enabling and accelerating globalization. Moreover, the new technologies generated a new wave of automation and this put pressure on producers to cut fixed costs by boosting sales and broadening markets. The more labour-intensive operations started to be farmed out to a second tier of NICs, such as Thailand, Malaysia, and other Asian countries that offered even lower labour costs. At the same time, the shortening of product cycles, and the concomitant acceleration of product innovation, led MNEs to enter strategic alliances, often with their competitors from other regions, to share sharply rising R&D costs, pool resources, and gain better access to different technologies and markets. The linkages and inter-firm networks created by such inter-firm alliances and collaborative agreements primarily span the United States, Europe, and Japan and involve electronics, aerospace, pharmaceuticals, automobiles, and the electrical goods industry, in which product cycles are short and the shares of R&D in sales are high. The growing links between multinational companies has been accompanied by a growing vertical disintegration by large firms which began to retain in-house only those production stages essential for maintaining strategic control.

The rapid expansion of international investment and offshore markets, along with the assertive role played in it by corporate strategies of the MNCs, have led observers to speak of the 'globalization' of the economy. Globalization is seen as the third phase of cross-national economic integration going beyond international exchange of goods and services and foreign direct investment to all phases including conception, development, manufacturing, distribution, and consumption. Views on the consequences of these developments for global institutions vary. Many observers would not go as far as Petrella (1991) in envisaging the end of such institutions as the nation state, national currency, national economy, national bank, national postal services, national education, national culture, and their replacement by international institutions. However it is generally recognized that the interpenetration of markets, the generic nature of the new information technologies, the accelerated homogenization of consumer tastes, product standards, and production methods on a global scale, and mergers and acquisitions are leading to worldwide economic restructuring leaving large corporations less dependent on any one nation's economy. This tendency is seen as weakening the ability of the nation state to control the behaviour of major economic actors theoretically under its jurisdiction, and has pushed the boundaries of policy making into the sphere of the global rather than the national economy (OECD 1991).

Two major reservations to the globalization thesis should be noted. Firstly, it can be argued that the three economic superpowers, Japan, the United States, and Europe, with their satellites, shape the global economy, to the exclusion of the LDCs of the South. Growth in developing countries has been largely concentrated in a few countries such as the East Asian NICs, and the overriding event in the international economy in the past three decades has not been the rise of the developing world but the steadily increasing share of Japan in world production.

A second reservation to the globalization thesis is the observable trend towards economic 'regionalism'. Rather than an increasingly borderless worldwide economy, freer circulation of capital, goods, and labour is developing within regional groupings of countries, such as the Single European Market, the zone of the North American Free Trade Agreement, MER-COSUR in the Southern American zone, and the Japanese-led trading bloc in the Pacific Rim. Such regional integration could retard internationalization by protectionism.

2. LABOUR STANDARDS AS AN INSTRUMENT OF REGULATING INTERNATIONAL COMPETITION

Theoretically the internationalization of economies enhances global welfare. But this depends on the form competition takes. The more wages, hours, and other terms of employment vary for workers of comparable productivity, i.e. the more segmented the international labour market is, the more tempting it will be for firms to exploit these differences to gain competitive advantages and the greater will be the risk of a general downward slide in pay and working conditions.

The problems with trade in products and services that owe their competitiveness to low labour standards was recognized early in the course of economic integration, and repeatedly considered at the international level. As early as 1906 an international labour conference in Bern adopted a treaty, later ratified by twelve European countries, prohibiting the manufacture and trade of matches containing white phosphorus, a major cause of industrial diseases. More comprehensively, the international debate which culminated in the foundation of the Covenant of the League of Nations of 1919 resulted in the member states agreeing to endeavour to secure fair and humane conditions of labour, both at home and 'in all countries to which their commercial and industrial relations extend' (Treaty of Versailles, Part I, Art. 23(a)). This commitment was repeated in the Preamble of the Constitution of the ILO, founded in 1919, which states that 'the failure of any nation to adopt humane conditions of labour is an obstacle in the way of other nations which desire to improve the conditions in their own countries.' After the Second World War, in 1948, the United Nations Conference on Trade and Employment explicitly linked trade and labour standards in Article 7 of the founding charter of the proposed International Trade Organization. This initiative failed, due to the refusal of the US Government to ratify the constitution of the Organization because of the link it made between trade and labour standards. The compromise was GATT with much more limited objectives.

More recently, however, the USA has shifted its position and has begun to take account of the labour standards operating in the countries with which it has trading agreements. For example, in 1983, it was stipulated that before a Central American or Caribbean country could take advantage of provisions for duty-free admission to US markets it should be examined whether 'workers in such countries are afforded reasonable workplace conditions and enjoy the right to organize and bargain collectively'. Other similar pieces of US legislation followed. Recently, a panel of the Economic Policy Council of the UN Association of the USA viewed it necessary to make GATT the venue for imposing economic penalties on countries and industries not in compliance with labour standards and other international norms of trading conduct (Economic Policy Council of UNA/USA, 1991). The European Parliament also advocated trade-linked standards when in 1983 it called for a new GATT article requiring members to respect ILO conventions, and a social clause is being debated in connection with the completion of the Single European Market. As yet, the inclusion of a social clause has been limited to the agreement concluded by the USA, and a few international commodity agreements, such as those on rubber, sugar, and tin (for a full account, see Servais, 1989, and van Liemt, 1989), but there is no international consensus in favour of using GATT as a lever for labour standards. Attempts by the International Confederation of Free Trade Unions (ICFTU) and the International Metalworkers' Federation to raise the inclusion of a social clause in GATT based on ILO standards, first in the Tokyo Round, then in the Uruguay Round of negotiations, have failed. One major reason for this failure was the fear on the part of the governments of developing countries that the social clause would reduce their competitive advantage. They rejected the clause as 'disguised protectionism' on the part of rich industrialized countries. The proposal to include a social clause in the Lomé Convention (between the EC and the countries of Africa) also fell through.

The purpose of a social clause is to restrict imports of products originating in countries, industries, or firms where labour standards are inferior to certain minimum standards. Producers who do not comply with the minimum requirements must choose between an improvement in pay and working conditions, or running the risk of being confronted with increased barriers to trade. There is, however, to date no universal agreement on which labour standards should be included in a social clause. In this context, the most frequently cited conventions are:

- Freedom of Association (Convention No. 87)
- The Right to Organize and Bargain Collectively (Convention No. 98)
- Minimum Age for the Employment of Children (Convention No. 138)
- Freedom from Forced Labour (Convention Nos. 29 and 105)
- Freedom from Discrimination in Employment and Occupation (Convention No. 111)
- Equal Renumeration for Men and Women for Work of Equal Value (Convention No. 100)

These standards can be regarded as 'basic human rights' and, as such, fundamental to the ILO's core mandate. In addition, they are universal standards in the sense of being independent of a country's level of economic development.

In his report to the International Labour Conference in 1994, the Director General of the ILO proposed a policy framework within which a solution to the issue of trade and standards may be sought. Reaffirming the principle of multilateralism, voluntarism, and cooperation (rather than coercion), the ILO should not endeavour to legislate the equalization of labour costs across nations, but should expect countries to improve their labour protection from the additional wealth generated by the growth of trade. A quid pro quo between the North and the South could include the renunciation by the North of trade restrictions in return for the commitment by the South to make progress on the improvement of essential labour standards. For the latter the ILO could provide technical assistance, and financial assistance from international trade itself—for example, from a levy on exports (ILO, 1994).

However, despite being enshrined in international agreements and policy discussions at the highest level, labour standards have remained a battleground of controversial viewpoints and diverging interests. Substantial progress in advancing standards has been made, mainly in the years following the two world wars when the fresh memories of economic, social, and political catastrophes encouraged employers and workers to cooperate and induced governments to take greater responsibility and make greater commitments in the area of social and industrial policy. This 'new horizon' spirit was reflected in important enactments, both at national and international level, in labour policy. The period of 1919 to 1921 was one of heavy standard setting at the ILO, dealing with the long-standing demands by workers for the eight-hour day and the forty-eight-hour week, and conventions dealing with unemployment, night work by women and young persons, the minimum age for industrial employment, and the employment of women before and after confinement. Conventions 87 and 98 on the freedom of association, and the right to organize and bargain collectively, perhaps the most important conventions of all, were adopted in the aftermath of World War II.

By contrast, the 1980s was a decade of limited advancement, stagnation, and even retrogression in labour policy. Although the ILO had more member states than ever, the rate of ratification in this period was slow, and a number of countries, including such prime movers in the original proposals for international standards as Britain, denounced standards. It was a period of heightened international trade rivalry and increasingly global interdependence in which labour conditions and labour standards were increasingly thrown into competition. The growing problem of unemployment was attributed to market inflexibility and the policy emphasis shifted to the deregulation of markets and especially the labour market. The collapse of communism was interpreted by many as evidence against intervention into the economy and for the unimpeded market. All this created hard times for progress on labour standards despite growing unemployment, poverty, and associated social problems.

3. LABOUR STANDARDS AS A CONTESTED TERRAIN

Labour standards at the international level have traditionally been opposed by some countries on the grounds that they would handicap them on the international market by increasing their costs relative to other countries not covered by the common rule. Others, on the contrary, argued that international agreements to set standards would ensure that competition was not at the workers' expense and would in fact amount to a code of fair competition between employers and between countries.

Some critics, among them governments of developing countries, contend that trade-linked labour standards are a disguised form of protectionism on the part of the industrialized countries (Servais, 1989; van Liemt, 1989). They feel that linking labour standards to trade will in fact work against the very people it seeks to help by removing one of their few competitive advantages, such as low wages and low labour costs. If developing countries were forced, it is argued, to raise labour standards in order to secure trade agreements, they would erode their own competitiveness, lose the attraction for MNEs, and thus kill the goose which lays the golden eggs. The International Metalworkers' Federation has responded to this criticism by showing that its affiliate trade union organizations in developing countries, such as in South and East Asia, do not cling to such arguments and are generally in favour of trade-linked labour standards.

Objections raised in the 1980s against labour standards were primarily couched in economic terms. Academics and practitioners alike asserted that a trade-off exists between labour standards and economic development. From an orthodox theoretical perspective, labour standards and labour market regulation have been charged with constraining, or even impairing, economic growth, structural adjustment, and the expansion of employment in developing (see, e.g. World Bank, 1988) and advanced industrialized countries (for Germany, see Deregulierungskommission, 1991). This theoretical framework rests on the notion that wage inequality and differences in job opportunities reflect differences in labour quality and motivation. In such circumstances, it is argued, the imposition of labour and social standards designed to equalize wages and redistribute income by means of the tax and benefit system will reduce the incentives to the more productive whilst pricing the less productive from the labour market. Egalitarian policies are regarded as particularly counter-productive in developing countries where, it has been argued, any job under any conditions is better than no job (Fields, 1990), and in areas adjusting to high levels of unemployment from the effects of de-industrialization. In this latter case, what is prescribed is revision of the wage expectations of redundant workers downwards to reflect the obsolescence of their skills, as a prelude to economic recovery, and in these circumstances an important purpose of training programmes for the jobless has been to instil this realism (Mehaut, 1988; Villeval, 1988). The theme of the low quality of labour is echoed in the opposition to minimum wage legislation which, it is claimed, could have a devastating effect on the employment of less-skilled people which could only be avoided by the retraining of the low paid to raise their market price (Wilkinson, 1992). More generally, in the wake of the re-emergence of traditional free market economics as conventional economic wisdom, the direction of government policy in a growing number of developed and developing countries has been advised by the arguments that high unemployment and labour market inflexibility result from trade union and government regulation of the labour market, that social welfare is an important disincentive to labour market activity, and that the unemployment, low pay, poor working conditions, and casual employment of those trapped in the lower strata of the labour are to be explained by their low quality and weak labour market orientation (Deakin and Wilkinson, 1991).

4. THE CASE FOR LABOUR STANDARDS

The case for labour standards—universally applied equitable terms and conditions of employment—rests on the recognition that labour markets are deeply segmented by power relationships so, in the absence of countervailing regulation, labour is undervalued to varying degrees. Far from determining equal pay for work of equal value—Alfred Marshall's 'true' labour standards (1982, 588)—the institutions on the supply and the demand side of the labour markets operate so as to discriminate between claimants in the allocation of job opportunities and in doing so generate wage inequalities which bear little or no relationship to the value contribution of individual workers.

As early as the mid-eighteenth century, Adam Smith recognized that within the labour market employers had innate superiority over labour because of their greater resource endowment, their control over the means of production and subsistence, and, because they were fewer in number, the ease by which they colluded (Smith, 1986). Smith also commented on the greater success of capital than labour in securing political, legal, and popular support for its side in wage bargaining. Taking into account the enormous concentration of capital since Adam Smith's days, there is no reason for believing that his judgement about the relative power of capital has lost much of its force despite the growth of trade unions, the development of the welfare state, and the greater involvement of the state in the labour market. Then as now, however, the relative power of capital was redressed to a greater or lesser extent by, for example, labour organization, by company and labour legislation, by social security and taxation systems, and by economic policy. However, the extent of this varies widely both within and between countries.

Differences in economic and social advantage segment the labour supply, and the consequent inequalities are reinforced by the institutions of the labour market which regulate access to jobs and levels of pay.[1] The structuring of the labour force results from, amongst other things, inter- and intra- country, community and family differences in resource availability, expectations and knowledge of job opportunities.[2] As a result, individuals have different degrees of access to the socialization, educational, and training processes which, whatever their vocational content, provide credentials with high labour market status. Such tendencies create non-competing groups which widen the income and job opportunities of members and limit those of non-members (Levitan and Shapiro, 1987). These differences are reinforced by unequal distribution of domestic and other responsibilities, differences in state provision and regulation of labour markets, and by sexual, racial, and other forms of discrimination.[3]

---

[1] For discussion of this see F. Wilkinson, 'The Structuring of Economic and Social Deprivation and the Working of the Labour Market in Industrial Countries', *Labour and Society*, 16/2 (1991) of which the following is a summary.

[2] For a comprehensive discussion of the position of women in the labour market see Rubery (1992).

[3] Adam Smith recognized that income from other sources was a reason why an individual would accept low pay (A. Smith, *The Wealth of Nations* (London: Penguin, 1986), 219–21).

Within the labour market, professional associations, trade unions, and other formal and informal organizations and networks exercise control over entry to particular labour market segments and to training and other forms of in-market advancement. Labour market disadvantages such as sex, race, age, low social status, and poor educational achievement are exacerbated by the difficulties such groups experience in forming or joining effective in-market organizations. The hiring, training, and labour management policies of firms interrelate with supply-side factors in further differentiating job opportunities. Hiring rules adopted by firms rest on signals transmitted by social characteristics (age, sex, race, education and training qualifications, dress, deportment, etc.) which are only partially objectively based but which are taken to measure the relative worth of job applicants (Spence, 1973). The technical and organizational structure of the firm, the related systems of labour management and collective bargaining (or its absence) structure job opportunities within firms, and training and promotion policy regulate the allocation of workers within this internal labour market. Firms with a range of abilities to pay offer widely different levels of wages for comparable jobs so that promotion prospects—in terms of job content and/or pay—exist both within and between firms (Horrell, Rubery, and Burchell, 1989). Successful progression within this job structure enhances the labour market status of individuals whereas redundancy and other involuntary quits, periods out of the labour market for domestic reasons, and spells of unemployment have the opposite effect. Thus individuals' job prospects can be continuously modified from the supply side by their own employment experience, and from the demand side by such factors as plant closures, industrial restructuring, and changes in hiring and training rules adopted by employers.[4]

This structuring of relative opportunities is not confined to labour. Wide variations in the efficiency of machines and access to finance and other basic requirements structure capital into a hierarchy based on relative market power. Differences are buttressed and multiplied by the 'technical' advantages of the economies of scale and massed resources for research, development, and marketing, and by trade association, agreements, and laws which concentrate power in selected hands. Within this hierarchy of firms, subordinate relations develop. Large firms 'capture' their suppliers and can dictate the terms of trade. In the product market, the 'leaders' establish the ruling price to which the 'followers' must adjust. The factionalization of capital influences the demand for labour by ranking firms according to their ability to pay, and by providing the opportunity for firms to choose between centralizing and decentralizing production. In this way,

---

[4] For detailed analyses of the dynamic effects of industrial restructuring and changes in hiring, training, and other aspects of labour management on the supply and demand side of the labour market, see the collection of articles in *Labour and Society*, Oct. 1988.

powerful firms can vary demand for labour between the different segments so as to make the most effective use of the weakness of both disadvantaged labour and capital.

Economic orthodoxy has it that the market is the most reliable vehicle for ensuring that wages are proportional to labour productivity and for ensuring equal pay for work of equal value. This line is difficult to sustain in the face of wide variation in inter- and intra-class differences in bargaining power on both the supply and demand side of the labour market. The consequence is a deeply segmented labour market in which labour of comparable efficiency is available at different prices. Moreover, the more global the market becomes the wider will be the range of labour valuations. It also follows that the greater the disadvantage suffered in the labour market the greater will be the degree of labour undervaluation and, as the poor and unorganized are least powerful, the degree of undervaluation can be expected to be higher the lower the segment in the labour market.

Whether or not there is an 'ideally' efficient free market system has no direct bearing on the question in a world where the distribution of income and economic opportunities are largely determined by power relationships.[5] This does not mean, however, that allocative or any other form of efficiency should not be a policy objective, rather that, if such aims are to be achieved, regulation will be required to counteract inequalities in economic, social, political, or other sorts of power, the deployment of which frustrates efficiency objectives. The rest of this section considers the social and economic consequences of labour market inequalities and draws mainly on examples from Britain and the United States, the two industrial countries most actively involved in labour market deregulation and resisting the development of international labour standards.

The Undervaluation of Labour and Productive Efficiency

The availability of labour undervalued to varying degrees has important negative influences on productive efficiency by providing a means by which firms can compensate for organizational and other managerial inadequacies; delay the scrapping of obsolete capital equipment; and engage in destructive price competition. Employers can adjust their wage costs to their ability to pay by either shifting their demand for labour to a more disadvantaged segment of the labour market, or because their workers, trapped in their segment, are unable to resist wage reductions (Wilkinson, 1991). By being in a position to increase the degree of undervaluation of

---

[5] This is not to suggest that labour quality and compensating differentials and other explanations deployed by labour economists have no role in explaining wage variations, rather that there are more fundamental forces at work differentiating workers and their rewards.

the workers they employ, firms can avoid more radical remedies such as the restructuring of production, managerial reorganization, and the replacement of obsolete equipment. The absence of wage discipline means that technologically and managerially backward firms are difficult to dislodge, and helps prevent more innovative firms from expanding their share of the market. Moreover, the ability of workers in the more efficient firms to extract higher wages reduces profit expectations on new investments below what it would have been if the valuation of labour was equalized across firms. The overall result is a lower average level of productivity because of the extended tail of obsolete equipment and the slow rate of introduction of new techniques. Salter (1966, p. 153), writing about productivity and technical change, summed up the relationship between wages and the ability of individual firms to pay:

The argument that an industry cannot 'afford' higher wages is, in the long run, very dangerous. If it were accepted and wages were based on the 'capacity to pay', employment would be perpetuated (unless labour deserted them) in industries which should properly decline to make way for more vigorous industries. Equally dangerous is the argument that industries which are prosperous because of new techniques have 'the capacity to pay' high wages.

Price competition based on wage cutting also fosters obsolete product structures. Competition based on the development of new, and the modification of existing, products has the effect of continuously shifting product market boundaries. Failure by firms to respond traps them in declining market niches and, although they may remain viable by cutting labour costs and capturing a larger share of a reduced demand, this can only be a short-term expediency. The long term depends on product rather than price competition and this requires an emphasis on research and development, product design, and quality. But this is discouraged by low wage competition and its continuous downward pressure on profit margins which rules out long-term considerations and encourages cost paring which threatens quality standards. Moreover, as will be argued below, associated wage cutting has the effect of 'dishonouring' skilled work and driving skilled workers out of the industry. Destructive rivalry based on a downward spiral of wages and working conditions explains the competitive failure of such industries as jewellery in America (Scranton, 1991) and hosiery in Britain (Wilkinson and You, 1993). In both cases, the progressive degradation of products and the growing inability to compete in the quality end of the market played a central role in competitive failure.

The third detrimental effect on the long-term competitiveness of the availability of undervalued labour is the encouragement it gives to predatory capitalism. Predatory firms actively seek out profitable opportunities in the form of undervalued labour or ways to further undervalue labour.

One industrial example from Britain is contract cleaning. The proprietors of contract cleaning firms were centrally involved within the Conservative Party and government in promoting privatization (Ascher, 1987) and the removal of minimum wage protection from the employees of public sector contractors (Brosnan and Wilkinson, 1988). The ability to lower terms and conditions of employment has generated large cash flows and provided the financial resources for the large firms to consolidate control by buying up other companies (Ascher, 1987). This increased competitive pressure, combined with progressively more and more intrusive legislation by central government designed to oblige local government and other public agencies to privatize services and to drive down labour standards, has led to a general worsening of wages and working conditions—including those of direct employees, covered by collective agreements, who are obliged to compete with outside contractors for their own jobs (Brosnan and Wilkinson, 1988).

The scope for predatory capital is much wider in the USA where the federal law limits the ability of individual states to regulate corporations where labour standards vary between states, and where legislative changes and judicial judgements have made it increasingly easy to dislodge trade unions and to dismantle collective bargaining (Goodman, 1979). These developments have interacted with growing excess manufacturing capacity to provide the leverage for companies to make profits by specializing in extracting concessions from workers, locally based firms and from communities. This 'rent seeking' (Craypo and Nissen, 1993) has manifested itself in a progressive flight of capital from states with high levels of unionization and good labour standards to others with more repressive labour regimes with the effect of reducing wages and worsening conditions of work (Bluestone and Harrison, 1982; Harrison and Bluestone, 1988). Other devices have enabled corporations to evade their pension and other non-wage obligations to their workforces and to avoid their creditors (Ghilarducci, 1992).

Meanwhile, the control corporations exercise over jobs has enabled them to extract concessions on subsidies and tax abatements as communities threatened with growing unemployment have been thrown into competition with each other to attract relocating plants. In turn, this has created conflicts, which corporations have been able to turn to their advantage, between communities and organized trade unions whose attempts to maintain labour standards have been portrayed as a threat to local efforts to attract and keep jobs (Craypo and Nissen, 1993).

The emphasis on rent seeking rather than new wealth creation has redefined what constitutes enterprise in the US economy. There has been a rapid growth in legal and other forms of consultancy specializing in union busting and the degrading of wages and conditions of work. This purpose has been central in the reorganization of corporations to allow double breasting (the setting up of non-union subsidiaries as competitors to unionized plants) and the acquisition of foreign holdings for similar purposes (Birecree, 1994). Associations such as the Business Round Table have been formed specifically to counter organized labour and to lobby Congress for deregulation. These objectives have been furthered by an increasingly anti-labour bias in legislation and legal judgements. The intention to reduce terms and conditions of employment has been only too successful and from 1974 to 1990 real wages fell on average by 1.2 per cent per year.

However, this has done little to restore the competitiveness of the US economy which has continuously declined with a growing dependence on imported manufactured goods and a worsening balance of payments. The reason for this can be found in the failure of American industry to adopt the process and product innovation, reforms of organizational and management structures, and new forms of work organization necessary to respond to foreign competition based on quality and product variety (Magaziner and Reich, 1983; Hayes and Abernathy, 1985; Dertouzani, Lester, and Solow, 1990). Such long term strategies are precluded by the short-termism of predatory capital and the industrial disruption and uncertainty it engenders.

Labour Undervaluation and Worker Efficiency

Orthodox economists argue that low pay reflects low levels of productivity. When low pay and poor working conditions result from the undervaluation of labour the direction of causation runs in precisely the opposite direction. The previous section related this reversal to industrial performance, this section analyses the direct effect on workers. Sweatshop conditions and the hard driving associated with the absence of any effective employment rights or worker representation are directly detrimental to the health and general well-being of workers and hence to worker productivity in the long term (Haraszti, 1981). For example, in the US meat packing industry, a hazardous trade at the best of times, the speeding up of work and a failure to observe health and safety standards has radically increased the incidence of occupational disease and the accident rate. This, and the success of the leading firms in driving down pay, has so increased labour turnover that the workforce has become increasingly untrained and inexperienced and therefore more accident prone. As a result of these processes meat packing has regressed to the most dangerous industry in America (Craypo, 1994).

Low health and safety standards and the consequences of dangerous and unhealthy work environments have direct implications for work effort and productivity by increasing risk and uncertainty and time lost through injury. The more indirect and long-term consequences of overwork, injuries, and occupational diseases include worker debilitation and premature death, and the health care and other resources tied up in dealing with the consequences of the absence of effective health and safety at work (Shostak, 1980; Brodeur, 1985; Kazis and Grossman, 1982). The irony is that experience shows that standards directed against dangerous work practices and health hazards from the handling, production, and emission of poisonous substances generally results in directing technology in directions which are more efficient (Sengenberger, 1990). And even if that is not the case, as industry is responsible, and probably largely responsible, for polluting both the social and natural environment (with all the costs that entails) the workplace would seem to be the natural starting place for clean-up operations. But the absence of internationally (or even nationally) agreed and enforced health, safety, and environmental standards provides the opportunity for mobile capital to escape to where standards are low and hampers their enforcement where standards are high.

A second negative consequence of the absence of an effective floor of employment rights is the disincentive effect on worker performance of poor terms and conditions of employment and the denial of effective representation. Industrial efficiency requires worker cooperation but low pay, poor conditions, and harsh supervisory regimes are far from the best way of achieving this objective (Fox, 1974). In such circumstances, workers (and impartial observers) might conclude that it is legitimate for them to improve their lot by making the best use of the power they derive from their ability to withhold labour, and from the knowledge and experience acquired on the job. The resulting 'non-cooperation' might take a range of forms including workers keeping effort within prescribed limits, working closely to the 'rules' so as to resist any flexible use of their time, keeping managers uninformed of improvements to technology and working methods learned on the job, and pilfering or even sabotage. In effect, work effort (the avoidance of which might require more ingenuity and effort than the work itself) is adjusted downward to match the pay and conditions.[6]

A third important way by which the undervaluation of labour leads to its dissipation is the negative relationship between low pay and poor working conditions on the one hand and skill and training on the other. The orthodox explanation is that low pay is the result of a lack of training and skill and that an increase in pay will further discourage employers from providing training. But a closer examination again reveals a quite different

---

[6] For a graphic description of the ingenuity and effort put into disguising productive potential in the expectation that if these were revealed then piece rates would be cut, see A. Sillitoe, *Saturday Night and Sunday Morning* (New York: Knopf, 1959); for an East European example of different attitudes to work when not in an exploitative context see S. Haraszti, *The Worker in the Worker's State* (London: Penguin, 1981); see also S. Mathewson, *Restriction of Output Among Unorganised Workers* (New York: Viking Press, 1931), D. Montgomery, *Workers' Control in America* (New York: Cambridge University Press, 1979), M. Burawoy, *Manufacturing Consent: Changes in the Labour Process Under Monopoly Capitalism* (University of Chicago Press, 1979), and R. M. Pfeffer, *Working for Capitalism* (New York: Columbia University Press, 1979).

direction of causation. Firstly, low paying employers are the least likely to train. Inefficient, low payers require undervalued labour to subsidize poor management or keep obsolete equipment in production, and cannot afford to train except in the narrowest sense; the interests of predatory low payers are in exploiting human capital rather than creating it. Secondly, skill is to an important degree a social category, and jobs with poor terms and conditions of employment are unlikely to be afforded high status whatever their skill level. Moreover, status as well as the content of jobs will determine the willingness of individuals to acquire the necessary entry qualifications by undertaking education and training. The identification of particular jobs with socially deprived groups lowers the status of their skill and the training routes by which they are acquired. One of the effects of the process of de-industrialization in the UK, USA, France, and elsewhere has been a decline in levels of pay and conditions of work in industries directly affected and those into which the redundant workers from traditional industries have been crowded. This has led to a social reordering of jobs and this dynamic interrelationship contributes to the process of decline.[7]

Industrial failure creates conditions for social deskilling in four closely related ways. Rapid increases in unemployment weaken workers' resistance to employers' offensives against the terms and conditions of employment and traditional forms of control of skilled work. A second common response by firms to their declining fortunes is to cut back on training. This may take the form of a reduction of in-house training and/or a decline in support for external provision by training agencies so that the local infrastructure for skill generation is weakened. This, and the migration from the trade of workers in a position to do so, creates a skill shortage. The response to this, in the face of the decline in formal training, is the substitution of on-the-job instruction with a focus on a narrow range of specific skills to meet the firms' immediate needs. Consequently the skill content of jobs is diluted and this interacts with the deterioration in the terms and conditions of employment, and increasing pessimism about the future prospects of the industry, to discourage new entrants from traditional areas of recruitment (Wilkinson, 1992). Any subsequent relaxation of hiring standards to meet the labour shortage serves to reinforce further the social downgrading of the job. The response by governments to the twin problems of increasing unemployment and a growing skill shortage has been to institute new training schemes. Whatever the original intention, or indeed the quality of much of the training, these schemes acquire a reputation for disguising unemployment, creating new forms of cheap labour and for failing to provide adequate training. The general effect is therefore a down-

---

[7] See *Labour and Society* 16/2, 1991 and 13/4, 1988.

grading in labour market terms of the participants and the job areas at which the schemes are targeted. Individuals then become increasingly unwilling to take part in training programmes because of the knowledge that the time and effort spent is wasted, and individuals who have so trained tend to quit the resulting job at the earliest opportunity. A related problem is that the targeting of training at the unemployed to get them into jobs with low paying firms in need of undervalued labour to keep obsolete equipment in operation and outdated product lines profitable is a waste of training resources. Such firms need skills which are specific to outdated technology and are therefore effectively obsolete. The cumulative effect of low pay and poor working conditions and the policy responses by employers and the state is therefore to weaken the skill base—both in technical and social terms, to discourage individuals from undertaking training, and to misallocate training resources. In these circumstances, lack of demand for training rather than paucity of supply explains skill shortages.

These degenerative processes are by no means confined to failing firms or declining industries. In meat packing in the United States, the fastest growing firms have taken the lead in degrading their workforces, reducing skill levels, and downgrading training, and by doing so have undercut their competitors and forced their compliance with such practices (Craypo, 1993). In transport, a major growth industry, deregulation intensified competition and drove down wages and road-safety standards. The legislative response was to impose more stringent requirements for licensing truck drivers (Belzer, 1994) which necessitated higher skills and more expensive training. But lower wages and poorer working conditions have proved a disincentive and there is a growing shortage of skilled and competent drivers. Similarly, in construction, one of the success stories of the 1980s, the concerted efforts by employers to de-unionize and cut pay has exerted a parallel downward pressure on skills. Apprenticeship programmes, designed to provide general skills, have been increasingly replaced by non-union firms with on-the-job training and learning by experience, so that although labour has been cheapened it has also become partially deskilled and increasingly less efficient (Allen, 1994).

Labour Undervaluation, Consumption, and Growth

Inequality in income distribution resulting from the undervaluation of labour has a detrimental effect on both the level and structure of consumer demand. The undervaluation of labour produces a shortfall of income below productivity and leads to underconsumption. The surplus of income generated by labour undervaluation in the lower segments of the labour market is transferred to higher income receivers with high savings ratios, such that the average propensity to consume and hence, other things being equal, the level of aggregate demand can be expected to be lower the more undervalued is the labour force. The distribution of income also has impor-tant implications for the composition of consumption and related growth processes. At very low levels of income, food, fuel and light, and housing absorb a high proportion of income. As income grows, a higher and higher proportion is spent on mass-produced manufactured goods where wide markets give potential for rapid productivity growth, but beyond a certain point the emphasis shifts towards services and luxury goods where the potential for productivity increases is more limited. One expected effect of a growing undervaluation of labour, therefore, will be a decline in the demand for manufactured products compensated for, in part at least, by an increase in the demand for services as high incomes expand and as the price of services fall with the fall in the relative wages of low paid workers. However, for reasons outlined above, as less trickles down the income scale in the form of demand than trickles up in the form of income, the net effect of this will be a reduction in aggregate demand and hence unemployment. And this process will become cumulative if higher unemployment leads to a further undervaluation of low-paid labour.

By the same logic, a reverse causation can be expected from a reduction in the degree of undervaluation of labour and a more equal distribution of income. The demand for mass-produced products is higher as a proportion of income in the middle and lower ranges of the income distribution. Therefore, the more even the distribution of income, the greater is likely to be the demand for manufactured consumer goods and the greater will be the opportunities for product and process innovation, productivity gains, and hence further real income advance.[8] In turn, the broad consumer base and the encouragement it gives product and process development provides the platform for taking a lead in trade in income-elastic goods and to growth-led exports (Cripps and Tarling, 1973).

The Social and Political Case for Labour Standards

It is argued that, whatever the case for labour standards, countries with high unemployment and low incomes cannot afford them (Fields, 1990). In these circumstances, the absence of labour standards and laws restricting the activities of labour unions free employers to create jobs and this induces economic development. Evidence for this, it is further argued, is be found in the success of the export-led growth strategies of the fastest growing developing countries. It is maintained that in South Korea and other South East Asian countries growth based on low wages in labour-intensive indus-

---

[8] For detailed discussion of this, see F. Wilkinson, 'Real Wages, Effective Demand and Economic Development', *Cambridge Journal of Economics*, 12 (1988).

tries tightened the labour market, increased wages, and improved working conditions and, by doing so, induced changes in the industrial structure away from dependency on traditional goods. Therefore, it is argued that equitable labour standards are an output of development rather than an input (Fields, 1990). The validity or otherwise of these assertions is of crucial importance currently because of the threat of mass unemployment and escalating poverty in Eastern Europe following the collapse there of the Communist regimes.

The argument against a cheap labour strategy to induce export-led growth is that, at best, such a strategy is an economic dead-end and, at worst, it creates a socio-economic environment damaging to economic development. The income elasticity of demand for the products of traditional labour-intensive industries is low in developed countries and this limits the size and growth of the existing export markets. Therefore, whilst it may be possible for a single country or small group of countries to increase their share of the market at the expense of others, growth led by the export of such products cannot possibly be an effective strategy for all developing countries. This is particularly so because the strategy's dependence on keeping real incomes down amongst the poorest of the world's population restricts the growth of those markets where the highest demand for traditional products can be expected. One response by the most successful developing economies to such demand restrictions is policy-induced switches from traditional goods to, for example, electronic consumer goods, to which cheap labour employed in traditional industries can be switched (Grunwald and Flamm, 1985). However, as more and more countries have adopted this policy these markets have, in turn, become satiated and the successful developing countries have, in effect, exported their unemployment to advanced industrial economies. This has led to growing demands for trade protection and, from employers, an insistence on the relaxation of labour standards to improve their competitiveness. Governments have responded sympathetically to these latter demands in the alleged interest of creating employment and of encouraging inward investment. Therefore, a version of Gresham's law operates on a global scale with poor labour standards increasingly driving out the good with all that implies for increasing poverty, underconsumptionist tendencies and declining social conditions.

The inherent contradictions in the low labour standard route to economic progress is only too evident from the experience of the UK and the USA where the experimenting with unregulated markets has gone furthest and where, amongst advanced economies, industrial decline is most advanced. Despite a decade or more of labour market deregulation in these NDCs (newly de-industrializing countries) the balance of payments on the trade account is progressively worsening, the manufacturing base is shrinking, productive investment is declining, and income inequality, unemployment, and poverty are all on the increase. Moreover, consumption at the upper end of the income distribution generally has a greater foreign exchange content than that at the lower end both because of a higher level of consumption of imported luxury goods (Borooah, 1988) and more foreign travel. Thus, in the USA and Britain, the increasingly unequal distribution of income has compounded the negative consequences of deindustrialization on the balance of payments.

When interpreted as an example of the effective working of the market, evidence from South East Asia points in the opposite direction to that from the UK and USA (Fields, 1990). But closer examination of the experiences of South Korea and other successful developing economies reveals a set of causal relationships rather different to those of the market's invisible hand. There it was the strengthening of the hands of workers by industrialization and the demands they made for higher pay and improved working conditions which threatened the low pay/export-led growth strategy rather than any smooth working of market processes. Attempts to counter increased worker militancy by repression threatened the legitimacy of the government and induced policies designed to improve labour standards and to give greater scope for independent trade unionism (Lim, 1990; You, 1990; Amsden, 1989). Modifications to industrial policy also engineered major structural changes shifting the composition of exports towards skill- and capital-intensive products. In addition, the growth in real wages raised living standards, induced an increase in domestic demand, and reduced reliance on export-led growth (You, 1990). Labour standards have therefore made three important contributions to economic development in these countries: firstly, they have restricted recourse to counter-productive sweatshop competition; secondly, they have induced a switch to a development strategy based on product and process innovation and high quality production; and, thirdly, they have deepened the domestic market so that economic development is much less dependent on exporting at any cost. The consequent improvement in living standards has in turn made an important contribution to the easing of political and social tensions so that effective labour standards can be regarded as an essential ingredient of social as well as economic development. Such a transformation was facilitated by the rising quality of labour supply through educational and training policies which could explain why they continued to move so fast in spite of labour shortages and rising real wage levels (*Labour and Society*, 1988; Amjad and Mohanty, 1991; Lim and Tsui, 1991).

Nevertheless, during the 1980s the USA and UK achieved a certain political stability and a growth in employment which was cited as convincing evidence for the success of their economic labour market deregulation policies. But the growth in employment was largely accounted for by low paid, insecure jobs with poor working conditions whilst the political stability has been explained by the contribution the intensified exploitation of this growing 'underclass' has made to the 'contentment' of the more affluent members of society who wield electoral power (Galbraith, 1992). Galbraith's contented classes are those protected from the erosive effects of unregulated internal and international competition and the beneficiaries of regressive realignments of the tax benefit systems. They also include the managers and stockholders of the corporations whose interests are becoming increasingly internationalized and those whose interests lie in the stockmarkets and other global institutions. These enjoy high and growing incomes and in addition benefit from the low-paid service labour at home and the imports of cheap products from abroad. However, this is a very precarious equilibrium which is increasingly threatened by social instability resulting from unemployment, poverty, crime, and the effective exclusion of a growing proportion of the population from any meaningful economic or social prospects. It is also becoming increasingly clear that many of the previously protected white collar and managerial jobs are becoming exposed to international competition as computer programming and other high-tech jobs are subcontracted abroad and as corporate headquarters relocate internationally. The cumulative consequences of these processes can be expected to reduce the ratio of winners to losers and undermine the fragile political stability.

CONCLUSIONS: LABOUR STANDARDS AS POLITICAL, SOCIAL, AND ECONOMIC OPPORTUNITIES

The reality of labour markets is that power relations on both sides of the market determine job opportunities and levels of pay, with the result that a mismatch exists between labour input and reward which is tilted in favour of the more powerful. These inequalities structure the historical development of wages, prices, production, and consumption. The consequences of this are that operational, allocative, and dynamic inefficiencies are built into the use of resources and the path of economic development. This can only be made worse by the mobilization of the world's reserve army of labour and throwing it into competition with labour which, by democratic processes, has secured a greater degree of equality by establishing social and labour standards and the rights to independent representation in industrial relations. This is not to argue that the existing labour organizations and regulations are beyond reproach; they have too often acquired a narrow and parochial scope and by various forms of exclusions added their own contribution to inequality in economic and social opportunities. But this is an argument for the universalization of effective worker representation and labour market regulation rather than one for deregulation.

The evidence from the so-called 'social corporatist' nations of Northern Europe is that the existence of an institutionally determined, effective floor of rights to wages and conditions of work is an essential ingredient to sustained economic growth in *democratic* societies. In the decades following the Second World War, countries demonstrated how effective the taking of wages and conditions of work out of competition, the forestalling of destructive rivalry, and the setting of high social welfare, training, health and safety at work, and environmental standards could be in generating rapid and sustained levels of economic growth and high consumption. They demonstrated conclusively that egalitarianism was no obstacle to effective competition and that private affluence does not in any way require public squalor. The social democratic systems also proved more effective than other countries with less regulated labour markets and less well-developed labour standards in resolving the inflationary crisis of the 1970s and 1980s with a much lower cost in unemployment (Rowthorn, 1992; Rowthorn and Glyn, 1988; Bruno and Sachs, 1985; Calmfors and Driffill, 1988).

However, recent years have demonstrated the fragility of this combination of social and economic progress when it exists in only a small group of countries. Openness to the international economy where lower and less equitable labour standards prevails risks a flight by capital to evade regulation and the undermining of domestic standards by destructive competition from abroad. This in its turn reinforces the divisions between, on the one hand, the 'contented classes' who are protected from the forces of competition and/or who have a vested interest in globalization and, on the other, the victims of internationalization. The growing economic crisis has triggered political instability and progressive social degeneration in what previously were the most socially and politically stable countries.

It is of the greatest significance that the last serious attempt to construct a world economic order in which universal labour standards were seen as playing a central part was made by that generation that had lived through economic crises of the 1920s and 1930s and the world war that followed. They recognized the central necessity of the equitable treatment of labour at both national and international level in avoiding the economic, social, and political disaster they had just witnessed. However, they failed to put effective machinery into place and the world was lulled by a false sense of security in the 'golden age' into supposing that economic growth would solve the problems of endemic inequality in life chances. How short-sighted this was is increasingly apparent as the cumulative downward spiral gathers pace.

What was recognized in the 1940s was the vulnerability of democracy to mass impoverishment and the importance to democracy of regulatory systems designed to remove inequalities by reforming education, training, and social welfare and the establishment of high and common labour standards.

It was also recognized that effective procedures would need to be established so that the interests of all individuals and groups could be independently represented at all levels which influence job opportunities, terms and conditions of employment—in education and training systems, at the place of work, at the level of the industry, and the wider general labour market as well as in the legislative, judicial, and administrative processes at the national and international level.

The labour standards required are for *protection* to set minimum and maximum terms for the utilization of labour resources (e.g. minimum wages laws, maximum number of weekly hours, maximum noise levels, maximum weight carried by a worker, protection from toxic substances, etc.); standards of *participation* to regulate the collective organization of actors and the relations and forms of negotiation between them; standards of *promotion* to provide ways and means of support or promotion for particular courses of action or services (for example, public agencies for the placement and training of workers). To be effective the different categories of standards have to form a coherent, interactive, and mutually reinforcing package of intervention into the labour market (Sengenberger, 1994).

Labour standards therefore have an important role to play in stemming downward directed wage and price competition. They serve the more general interest through averting individual opportunistic action. Their importance lies in directing economic activities in such a way as to prevent 'destructive' competition and to promote a 'constructive' competitive regime. The *common standard* removes from the employer the possibility of seeking and gaining competitive advantage from paying substandard wages, and from the public and/or the state the opportunity to 'subsidize' firms that cannot pay a living wage (Marshall, 1988*a*). They act to oblige firms to be active and look for alternatives to low pay and poor working conditions, such as introducing product and process innovation to gain competitive advantage. In a market environment in which competition is based on process and product development, a low pay strategy designed to retain the profitability of increasingly obsolete equipment and product lines can bring only temporary respite. There is a limit to wage reductions even in the most segmented market, but no limit to cost reductions from technical improvements. Similarly, at some point a product becomes so obsolete that it cannot be sold at any price.

By obviating destructive competition, labour standards can also help to promote *cooperation* between firms in joint development, pooling and sharing of resources for gaining markets and improving performance, and for generating a political voice. Cooperation requires minimum levels of stability in social relations, security, and mutual trust. None of these is easy to secure on any broad scale unless there is some form of collective understanding that assures each competitor that undercutting wages and other destructive competition is not to be tolerated. But labour standards are also important in securing for workers fair standards of pay and working conditions, for guaranteeing their continuance, and for encouraging the cooperative relations with their employers now generally recognized as an essential ingredient for success in markets where product design, quality *and* price are all important. Policies designed to counter the undervaluation of labour also have the added demand side benefits of maintaining the pace of real wage advance in line with productivity increases thus generating sufficient demand to absorb full employment production.

It has to be recognized though that it may be impossible to establish common labour standards without regard to the different levels of productivity in different countries. This suggests a two-stage process whereby each government be required to introduce effective labour standards within their country followed by a staged progression to common international standards. It is essential, however, to support any policies aimed at equality in the labour market by complementary measures to ensure the successful redeployment of workers displaced by technical progress and changing consumer demand. This requires a full employment macroeconomic policy; effective, universal, and equitable social welfare provision; adequate and widely available facilities for retraining; the minimization of barriers to entry into different occupations; an effective strategy on working time, and a united international effort to level up the economic performance of developing countries. Such policies are required to maintain demand in the labour market and to reduce structural unemployment so as to prevent the establishment and growth of disadvantaged segments in the labour market. The latter poses a threat to employment and labour market stability by generating a more unequal distribution of income and increasing disadvantage and distress amongst the unemployed and those downgraded in the labour market. The consequent desperation will pressure the victims of this degrading process into accepting low wages and poor working conditions so that the effectiveness of labour market regulation will be undermined and labour standards elsewhere in the labour market threatened.[9] Thus, if the complementary objectives of social justice and economic progress are to be achieved, it is essential to regulate-out both the undervaluation of labour by employers and also the risk that poverty will expose workers to such exploitation.

[9] For discussion of this in the British context see S. Deakin and F. Wilkinson, *The Economics of Employment Rights*, London: Institute of Employment Rights, 1991.

6. Transnational Corporations and the Nation State

Richard Kozul-Wright[1]

The end of over a quarter century of growth and economic stability—appropriately christened a 'Golden Age'—has given way to a period of unstable growth, increased economic uncertainty, and widespread political instability. It has also seen the continuation and, in important respects, acceleration of a trend towards greater international specialization and economic integration that had already begun during the Golden Age. National states and labour movements, both important pillars of the Golden Age, have found it difficult to adapt to these changed circumstances. Their weakness contrasts, markedly, with the rising influence of transnational corporations (TNCs). This rise of the TNC, on many accounts, marks a transition from the Golden Age to a 'globalising age' (Dunning, 1994). In these accounts, the role of TNCs as long-standing organizers of a broad range of cross-border economic assets and activities has been transformed by new technologies and the relaxation of regulatory controls; free from their national setting and with a fully internalized governance structure these firms can now pursue global strategies of production, marketing, and profit seeking.[2]

Although there is disagreement over the extent to which the global age has already arrived, the basic philosophy—and the corresponding policy advice—underlying much of this analysis is that what is good for TNCs is

[1] Transnational Corporations Affairs Officer, Division on Transnational Corporations and Investment, UNCTAD, Geneva. The views expressed in this chapter represent those of the author and in no way reflect those that might be held by the United Nations Secretariat. The work for this chapter has been carried out as part of a larger project in collaboration with Karl P. Sauvant, UNCTAD and Professor Peter Dicken, Department of Geography, University of Manchester, UK.

[2] See S. Ghoshal, 'Global Strategy: An Organizing Framework', *Strategic Management Journal* (1987) 8; C. A. Bartlett and S. Ghoshal, *Managing across Borders: The Transnational Solution* (London: Hutchinson Business, 1989); C. Michalet, 'Global Competition and its Implications for Firms', *Technology and Productivity: The Challenge for Economic Policy* (Paris: OECD, 1989); K. Ohmae, *The Borderless World: Power and Strategy in the Interlinked Economy* (London: Collins, 1990); S. Reich, 'Roads to Follow: Regulating Direct Foreign Investment', *International Organization* (1989), 43; J. Dunning, 'The Theory of Transnational Corporations', *The United Nations Library on Transnational Corporations*, i, (London: Routledge, 1993). In one form or another, this perspective on the origins and growth of TNCs builds on the idea that the firm is a cost-effective response to market imperfections—the internalization thesis.

also good for national and regional economies and ultimately the world economy. With the pursuit of corporate goals unhindered by discontinuous political boundaries and organized national interests, TNCs emerge as the most efficient allocators of global resources and the implicit—and sometimes explicit—assumption that geography and history are increasingly irrelevant as determinants of economic performance reinforces a belief that the nation state is at best of marginal importance in today's world economy, more likely an obstacle to renewed growth and prosperity (O'Brien, 1992; Ohmae, 1990; Petrella, 1991).

This contrasts sharply with a view that the tendency of capitalist firms to expand across borders is part of a dynamic but also uneven and conflictual process of international production and competition in which large firms extend corporate rivalry to the regional and international levels in a constant search for market leadership and economic rents (Hymer and Rowthorn, 1970; Rowthorn, 1971; Hymer, 1976; Panić, 1988; Auerbach, 1988). In a prescient article written before the end of the Golden Age, Hymer and Rowthorn anticipated the globalization thesis, criticized its technological determinism, and outlined a different policy agenda to deal with the likely consequences and contradictions of accelerating international production (Hymer and Rowthorn, 1970, 83–7). The underlying philosophy of their approach was that, because the combined actions of TNCs are as likely to exaggerate differences and inequalities within and between regions as remove them, the full benefits of international integration require a complementary and robust framework of social agreements and constraints—including strong nation states—to resolve problems generated in production and to manage distributional conflicts.

This chapter draws on the second of these approaches to present an essentially historical perspective on the globalization process.[3] Although questioning the extent to which TNCs have *radically* transformed the world economy, it moves beyond the earlier work in this tradition in arguing that

---

[3] For perspectives on the globalization thesis see C. Kindelberger, 'The New Multinationalization of Business', *Asean Economic Bulletin* (1988) 5; Christopher Lorenz, 'The Transnational's Identity Crisis', *Financial Times*, 19 March 1993; A. Glyn and R. Sutcliffe, 'The New World Order: Global but Leaderless' in *Socialist Register*, 1992; P. Krugman, 'Competitiveness: A Dangerous Obsession', *Foreign Affairs* (1994), 2. It is worth stating at the outset, that orthodox economic analysis has always contained its own globalizing agenda. Under the umbrella of international trade theory, the potential gains from cross-border trade and factor mobility assume a world where the irregularities and idiosyncrasies of national firms and industries give way to ideal economic agents and perfectly functioning markets. It is, of course, a world in which the international activity of national firms is noticeable by its absence (S. Hymer, *The International Operations of National Firms: A Study of Direct Foreign Investment* (Cambridge, Mass.: MIT Press, 1976); Dunning, 1993*b*; S. Lall, 'Transnational Corporations and Economic Development', *The United Nations Library on Transnational Corporations*, ii (London: Routledge, 1993); P. Robson, 'Transnational Corporations and Regional Economic Integration', *The United Nations Library on Transnational Corporations*, xiii (London: Routledge, 1993)).

the expanding role of TNCs over the past fifty years describes an *evolution* from international production to integrated international production. This process is consistent with dynamic forces in the world economy. However, the re-emergence of a neo-liberal agenda accompanying the fall of the Golden Age, coupled with weakened national states, whilst reinforcing the economic advantages of individual TNCs, does not necessarily enhance the growth potential of a more integrated international production system. Considering the direction of international production over the last two decades, the chapter argues that an appropriate framework for regulating integrated international production will most likely, and most effectively, be constructed at the regional level.

1. GLOBALISATION: A LONG-TERM PERSPECTIVE

The origins of the modern world economy lie in the eighteenth century transition to an industrial world. This transition finally broke the predictable and essentially static relations common to agricultural production and introduced deep-seated changes in the organization of economic activity. The rise of the industrial enterprise provoked a continuous search for more effective ways of producing goods and services through the application of capital-intensive techniques and scientific knowledge, the novel use of natural resources, and the organization of longer production runs, resulting in a steadily increased scale of economic activity. Of equal importance, the simplification and standardization of industrial activities gave rise to an increasingly specialized division of labour and more complex linkages in the chain of production transforming raw materials into finished goods and services. These advantages of scale and specialization, as Adam Smith insisted, depend upon the size of the available market (Smith, 1986). But the process is cumulative and interdependent; expanding production, by enlarging the potential market, further reinforces the opportunities for specialization through a continual subdivision of industrial activities (Young, 1928). The structures and strategies of capitalist firms have been continuously shaped by these dynamic internal and external economies (Chandler, 1990; Teece, 1993).

Although the earliest stages of industrialization were confined to products manufactured, finished, and sold within national economies, the combined pressures to enlarge production, specialize activities, and seek markets quickly outgrew local conditions and larger domestic firms soon faced the choice of whether to compete internationally by extending production activities abroad through foreign direct investment (FDI) or to export from their domestic base. At the industry level, historical accident and cultural influences certainly appear to have played a far from marginal role in influencing this choice. Trial and error, routine and inertia, and above all the creation of an industrial and technological heritage have shaped particular patterns of expansion abroad (Porter, 1990). However, it is the constant pressure on firms to grow in size and remain industry leaders that provides the basic impulse, as well as the organizational capabilities, to extend economic activity abroad through foreign production facilities, jumping natural and artificial barriers to compete directly with domestic producers in the expectation that larger rents from firm-level advantages will offset the additional costs accompanying production in an unfamiliar environment.

But whether through increasing trade linkages or FDI, international economic integration is not a linear product of the actions of individual capitalist firms. The dynamic internal and external economies embodied in international production, because they involve powerful cumulative forces and externalities, also introduce significant discontinuities into the growth and integration processes (Kaldor, 1985). Existing advantages are reinforced and the resulting spatial distribution of economic activity is likely to exhibit strong divergences, leading to increasing inequalities within and between regions. Managing all the consequences of these dynamic forces is not within the capacity of firms, acting individually or collectively. Consequently, international economic integration has never been a spontaneous process but has depended on varying degrees of consensus, cooperation, and compliance to ensure that the short-term losses from integration do not outweigh the longer-term benefits; the internationalization of capitalism has always been a regulated process. Historically, the nation state has set the context in which the interdependence of national and international economic activities could be regulated. Governments have modified—indeed helped to *create or destroy*—comparative and competitive advantage (Scott, 1992; Chang and Kozul-Wright, 1994) and as *containers* of specific political, economic, social, cultural, and institutional attributes (Whitley, 1992*a,b*) have constantly influenced the pace and nature of international economic activity.

Two elements of regulated capitalism deserve particular attention in the context of the globalization pressures established by TNCs. First, whilst a range of national institutional arrangements are required to manage the conflicts arising from the process of international integration and to establish a working consensus (including at a minimum, appropriate wage-setting institutions, an effective fiscal authority, and a broad policy framework to facilitate adaptation to changing locational patterns of economic activity, new skills, and work organization), appropriate rules and regulations must also be established at the international level, and supervisory authorities created to ensure the process of international integration is managed effectively and conflicts among nations are resolved equitably. Ideally, the spread of TNCs needs to be matched by transnational state structures. However, because many of the features that make for successful states do not carry well across borders, the dynamic world of continuous but uneven change will involve an important, but unpredictable, role for bargaining processes between TNCs and various levels of political authority.

Second, an effective institutional environment to facilitate international activity must help reduce the costs of transacting and coordinating cross-border activity. Technological progress has had a pivotal role to play in this respect. But the creation of an international economic framework—particularly an international monetary framework—to facilitate and regulate cross-border flows of economic activity has played an equally important role. These developments do not, of themselves, cause international integration but, without the ability to shorten geographical distances and diminish financial uncertainly, it is clear that greater integration would not be possible (Panić, 1992; Dicken, 1992b). Historically, both technological progress and a functioning international order have depended upon the presence of a lead economy which, in turn, has become an important influence on the globalization process (Kindelberger, 1986; Abramovitz, 1989).

The conclusions from this, admittedly brief, discussion of the dynamics of capitalist expansion are not altogether surprising; in a world where history is continuously present in the contemporary structures and strategies of firms, where corporate rivalry is inherent in the dynamics of production and competition, and where the spatial distribution of economic activity reflects the complex interdependences of firms, states, and market exchanges, TNCs are not a neutral conduit for the efficient allocation of capital, technology, and know-how guided by an invisible hand. Equally, the growing importance of FDI, no more than expanding trade flows, does not harbour a global equilibrium path. Rather, globalization is a continuous process of extending interdependent cross-border linkages in production and exchange, pursued by firms, many of which by definition are transnational, with the aim of advancing their particular interests, and regulated by states (and other institutions) with the aim of ensuring the potential benefits are obtained by wider communities. The diversity of experiences that can emerge from this interaction of states, markets, and firms is apparent in earlier periods of international economic integration.

(i) 1870–1913: A 'Golden Age' of International Integration?

The period 1870–1913 is often presented as an exemplary episode of rapid economic progress and unprecedented international integration (Keynes, 1971; Henderson, 1992). An open regulatory framework prevailed: short-term and long-term capital movements were unsupervised; the transfer of profits was unhampered; the gold standard was at its height and encompassed almost all the major industrial countries by the period's close and most smaller agrarian nations (McKinnon, 1993, 3; Maddison, 1989; Morgenstern, 1959, 17); citizenship was freely granted to immigrants; and direct political influence over the allocation of resources was limited.[4] Technological progress reinforced openness and Britain's undisputed leadership role underpinned the international gold standard, upheld the virtues of free trade (both through access to its own domestic market and enforced openness accompanying colonial rule), and provided the complementary financial and commercial services (in part at the expense of its own manufacturing base).

Under these conditions, markets linked a growing share of world resources and output; exports outgrew domestic output in the core capitalist countries, and exports per capita rose not only in these countries but in a number of developing countries (most spectacularly in some Latin American countries),[5] and the migration of labour was unprecedented.[6] But the full extent and impact of international economic integration cannot be gauged independently of changes in production and the ability of states before the First World War to foster structural changes in economic activity (Lewis, 1978; Chandler, 1990). The capital intensity of new industrial techniques simultaneously pushed the industrial take-off beyond the domestic resources of most countries,[7] and added impetus to the search for a reliable supply of inputs and guaranteed markets. Correspondingly, long-term capital flows were the single most important element of this 'Golden

[4] There is not, however, a simple relation between expenditure figures and the state's role in economic development. Moreover, a comparison of state expenditure figures in 1913 for the most developed market economies already indicates considerable variation; see A. Maddison, 'Origins and Impact of the Welfare State, 1883–1983', *Banca Nazionale del Lavoro Quarterly Review*, Mar. 1984.

[5] Still, the international integration of product markets seems to have been slower than during the preceding 50 years, the combined result of rapid import substitution in industries, primarily textiles, with a previously high export ratio, and rising trade barriers. Although quantitative restrictions on trade were absent, tariff protection could be considerable, and were rising for most of this period, see P. Bairoch, *Economics and World History* (Brighton: Wheatsheaf, 1993).

[6] Between 1870 and 1915, 36 million people left Europe, two-thirds for the USA. But the process of labour migration was more widespread. Intra-continental migration was significant in Asia; on one estimate, the number of Chinese and Indian emigrants—predominantly to Burma, Ceylon, the Dutch East Indies, Thailand, and Malaysia—in this period exceeded European emigration (A. Lewis, *Growth and Fluctuations, 1870–1913* (London: George Allen and Unwin, 1978), 183–4). Intra-European migration also reached significant levels, with large numbers of migrants from Austria, Hungary, and Italy seeking (often temporary) work in France, Germany, and Switzerland (I. Ferenczi, *International Migration* (New York: National Bureau of Economic Research, 1929), 223–7). Even so, it is clear that economic circumstances dictated limited destinations.

[7] On one estimate, when the UK began to industrialize in the early 19th century, the required capital per worker was equivalent to 4–5 months' wages. By the time Hungary began to industrialize, at the end of the century, that figure had reached 42 months' wages; S. Pollard, *Peaceful Conquest: The Industrialization of Europe 1760–1790* (Cambridge: Cambridge University Press, 1981), 221.

Age' of increased international economic integration (Bloomfield, 1968, 1); the growth in long-term foreign investment exceeded both trade and output and, according to one estimate, the total stock of long-term foreign investment had, by 1914, reached $44 billion,[8] as much as one third taking the form of direct investment.[9]

Two very different development paths emerged from the interdependence of cross-border market and production linkages in the period prior to the First World War. On the one hand, for a large group of countries (and territories), international integration was the result of primary exports.[10] This was facilitated and reinforced by FDI, labour flows, and liberal commercial policies. International primary production was extensive—accounting for 55 per cent of the total stock of FDI in 1913—integrated through strong vertical linkages at the firm level, and complemented by FDI in transportation and trade (Dunning, 1983, 89). The gains from integration accrued to the capital-exporting (commodity-importing) countries but also to small local elites clustered around these capital-intensive growth poles. These conditions were usually reinforced by the absence of a strong developmental state. During this period, some of the largest recipients of FDI, such as China and India, experienced a period of 'de-industrialisation' and

[8] Of this, $18 billion was held by the UK, $9 billion by France, $6 billion by Germany, and $5.5 billion by Belgium. Of the total, $14 billion was invested in Europe, $10.5 billion in the USA and Canada, $8.5 billion in Latin America, and the balance in Asia and Africa. The historical evidence points to considerable integration of financial markets during this period; covariations and correlations in interest rates, exchange rates, and stock prices in leading markets were high and appear to be higher than during any subsequent period (O. Morgenstern, *International Financial Transactions and Business Cycles* (Princeton: Princeton University Press, 1959); R. Zevin, 'Are Financial Markets More Open? If so Why and With What Effects?', WIDER conference paper, 1988).

[9] By 1914, the stock of FDI, by one estimate, had reached $14 billion (Dunning, 1983). The leading home country was the UK which accounted for perhaps 45% of the total, with the USA responsible for perhaps another 20%. The USA was the single largest host country, but substantial FDI flows went to developing countries in Latin America, China, and the less industrialized regions of Europe. By 1914, according to some researchers, the majority of FDI stock was concentrated in developing countries (J. Dunning, 'Changes in the Level and Structure of International Production: The Last One Hundred Years', in M. Casson (ed.), *The Growth of International Business* (London: Allen and Unwin, 1983). However, even using simple GDP per capita figures, the distinction between developed and developing countries should be treated carefully for this period. Thus Latin America (the largest host region in 1914) includes Argentina with a GDP per capita greater than some of the Western European core economies and other countries, such as Chile and Mexico, with levels comparable to some of the industrializing European periphery, such as Czechoslovakia and Hungary. Moreover, much of the FDI stock located in Africa, Asia, and some parts of Latin America was the product of intra-colonial flows rather than inter-country flows. It is the case, however, that the share of FDI in overall foreign investment appears to have been larger in developing countries than previously assumed—one estimate puts the figure at anywhere between 44 and 66% of total foreign investment (Svedberg, 1978).

[10] According to Bairoch (1993), 69, primary goods accounted for more than 90% of Third World exports. Nearly half of all exports were food products and a further 28% were raw materials. Almost 100% of the raw materials produced were exported to developed countries.

other countries such as Russia, Austro-Hungary, and Latin America which were industrializing, in part through FDI, continued to fall behind the core economies (Bairoch, 1982, 1993). In many cases, this path was reinforced by colonial governance structures but even nominally independent domestic states were weakened by these international forces.

On the other hand, the preconditions for rapid industrialization were being successfully established—with the help of strong states—in a few core countries and behind rising tariff barriers (Bairoch, 1993, ch. 4).[11] Close complementarities between capital exporters (in search of profitable opportunities) and the capital-scarce countries (Panić, 1992, ch. 3) supported this industrialization drive through flows of long-term capital and labour. These were concentrated in a small group of newly industrializing countries in North America and Europe; in a number of these countries foreign investment represented a very high share of gross domestic fixed investment.[12] These investments were mainly in the form of bonds with very long maturities and went predominantly to public projects—such as railways—where they were often matched by large amounts of government assistance, (Panić, 1992, 97). Foreign direct investment in manufacturing—although small—by adding technological and managerial flows, reinforced the advantages of the late industrializers (Lewis, 1978, 177–8). However, these international production linkages were not strongly integrated and, even as technological progress was breaking down the spatial constraints on shallow integration in financial and labour markets, the expansion of production activities abroad was strongly influenced by geographical proximity.

(ii) International Economic Integration During the Golden Age

Between the beginning of the First World War and the end of the Second, many of the linkages established across the world economy over the preceding forty years were severed. Wartime controls persisted after 1918 and, although economic growth accelerated in the 1920s, the international financial system was marked by increased instability, the export of long-term capital from industrial countries slowed dramatically, and world trade failed to recover to its pre-war levels. The international economic order crumbled in 1929 with world recession and a retreat into national autarkic recovery strategies.

---

[11] It is worth adding that some of these countries, and most prominently the USA, were exporters of primary products. However, sustained growth was premised on achieving high rates of industrial growth.

[12] Between 1880–90 this share was 50.5% in Australia, 47% in Sweden and 12.6% in Italy; between 1901–10 it was 26.9% in Norway, and between 1911–13 it was 46.2% in Canada (M. Panić, *European Monetary Union: Lessons from the Classical Gold Standard* (London: Macmillan, 1992), 101).

The renewal of international market linkages—shallow integration—began in the 1950s under new international institutional frameworks and United States leadership. The United States assumed the mantle of free trade at the end of the war, but was flexible on the timetable adopted by other advanced economies;[13] under the General Agreement on Trade and Tariffs, the tariff on manufactured exports has steadily fallen from an average of around 40 per cent at the end of the war to under 4 per cent with the conclusion of the Uruguay Round. The United States was less flexible on the construction of an international monetary framework (see Chapter 2). However, the Bretton Woods institutions were nurtured through their infancy with the help of extensive foreign aid and overseas military expenditures (Glyn et al., 1990, 67) and domestic macroeconomic regimes maintained firm control of national economic management. For most of the Golden Age, international financial integration was subordinate to the successful adoption and implementation of national recovery and growth strategies.[14] Under these conditions and particularly because rapid economic growth, full employment, structural convergence, and equalization of incomes and demand patterns within and between industrial countries provided a particularly favourable economic environment (Chapter 2, this volume; Baumol, 1986; Dowrick and Nguyen, 1989; Dowrick and Gemmell, 1991), the process of shallow integration appears to have gone further, lasted longer, and involved more countries than before the First World War. The process was led by trade; trade integration surpassed the previous peak of 1913 sometime in the late 1960s (see Chapter 1) and only in the 1980s have rates of export growth dropped below those registered before the First World War (Table 6.1). The internationalization of financial markets began later and had to overcome tighter controls on the movement of capital. For much of this period, financial integration was tied to integration through trade and, only with the end of the Golden Age and the return to fixed exchange rates, were the constraints on financial flows more fully relaxed. Since the early 1970s, international banking has grown at about 20 per cent per year, considerably faster than world output, trade, and FDI (see Chapter 3).[15]

[13] As M. Panić, 'The State as an Agent of Change', WIDER Conference papers, 1993, 18, notes, the decision in the late 1940s by the United States to reduce import duties unilaterally was a reversal of its more traditional protectionist stance.

[14] Delayed structural changes from the interwar period and the potential to catch up with the technological leadership of the United States reinforced national growth strategies centred around the productivity bargain, Keynesian management, oligopolistic pricing, and the adoption of Fordist production techniques, see A. Glyn, A. Hughes, A. Lipietz, and A. Singh, 'The Rise and Fall of the Golden Age', in S. Marglin and J. Schor (eds.), The Golden Age of Capitalism (Oxford: Clarendon Press, 1990)

[15] Moreover, because the 1980s witnessed a significant shift in international financial intermediation from banking to security markets, this figure underestimates the internationalization of finance. The full extent of financial integration is still being debated by economists; see

Table 6.1. Growth of world trade and output, 1870–1990

Item	average annual percentage change					
	1870–1913[a]	1913–1950[a]	1950–1960	1960–1970	1970–1980	1980–1990
World trade	3.9	2.0	6.5	8.3	5.2	3.7
World GDP	2.5	1.0	4.2	5.3	3.6	2.8
Difference	1.4	1.0	2.3	3.0	1.6	0.9

Source: Maddison, 1989; World Bank, 1991; UNCTAD, Trade and Development Report, 1993.
Note: [a] Includes Australia, Austria, Belgium, Canada, Denmark, France, Finland, Germany, Japan, Italy, Netherlands, Norway, Sweden, Switzerland, United Kingdom, United States.

However, the globalization process that began during the Golden Age did not simply repeat the shallow market integration of the 1870–1913 period. In contrast to the earlier period, international labour flows have been far less significant and the geographical patterns of shallow integration have changed significantly. In particular, colonial trade linkages have been replaced by closer regional ties. These regional influences have been strongest between industrial nations at a similar level of development, led by Western Europe. But North and South America have begun to pursue more formal regional arrangements beyond the already strong links established between the United States and Canada. To date Asia—as would be expected—has the least integrated regional trading bloc. However, this region has shown particularly strong intra-regional linkages during the last few years and (as is true for all the regional blocs) trade linkages are much stronger than would be predicted if trade were proportional to the share of world output (Table 6.2).

Table 6.2. Trading neighbours: ratio of share of trade to partner's share of world output, 1989

	United States	Canada	Other Americas	Japan	Developing Asia	EC
United States	—	6.06	2.38	0.87	2.34	0.61
Canada	2.63	—	0.66	0.47	0.97	0.39
Other Americas	1.13	0.63	3.16	0.31	0.57	0.67
Japan	0.95	1.15	0.75	—	4.33	0.53
Developing Asia	0.73	0.62	0.43	1.26	4.83	0.54
EC	0.22	0.30	0.42	0.17	0.63	1.75

Source: Summers, 1991.

Zevin, 'Are Financial Markets More Open?'; M. Panić, The National Management of the International Economy (London: Macmillan, 1988); R. Roll, 'Price Volatility, International Market Links and their Implications for Regulatory Policies', Journal of Financial Sources Research (1989); 3; R. O'Brien, Global Financial Integration: The End of Geography (New York: Council on Foreign Relations Press, 1992).

But the greatest changes in globalization during the Golden Age were in international production. Foreign direct investment was, in fact, a relatively robust component of the international economy during the interwar period; between 1914 and 1938 the stock of outward FDI almost doubled, most of the increase occurring during the 1920s. But, more significantly, it saw the rise of the United States towards becoming the leading home country. Although the United Kingdom was still dominant in 1938, its share of the world FDI stock had fallen to under 40 per cent, whilst that of the United States was approaching 30 per cent (Dunning, 1983). Much of this expansion was in manufacturing affiliates in Europe (Auerbach, 1988, 240–2).

This process accelerated after the war as FDI by large United States manufacturing corporations extended domestic oligopolistic rivalry overseas in the search for market share (Hymer and Rowthorn, 1970). Scale advantages—an important determinant of overseas production—combined with a clear lead in the financial, technological, and organizational assets which underpin international competitiveness to give the initial impetus for the formation of foreign affiliates. Only a small number of firms from traditionally internationalized economies—such as the United Kingdom, the Netherlands, and Switzerland—could match the operations of United States TNCs. However, the leadership of firms from the United States was only temporary.

The international diffusion of mass production systems began informally soon after the war ended—with numerous productivity 'missions' to the United States—and, more formally, from the late 1950s, through FDI itself.[16] But by creating an environment favouring larger manufacturing firms, the national structures of the Golden Age themselves provided an important stimulus to international production. From the late 1960s, the cumulative impact of economic convergence, regional consolidation, industrial policies, mergers and acquisitions, and the growth and increasing sophistication of domestic markets in Europe and Japan laid the basis for the intensification of international competition through FDI.[17] This challenge, and the intensification of international rivalry, was already apparent by the late 1960s:

As the gap between Americans and non-Americans closes, the scope for catching up will, of course, diminish and the non-Americans will be increasingly forced to become innovators themselves and competition will become increasingly centred on advanced products ... the growing strength of European and Japanese capital,

[16] In the early 1950s, outward FDI from the USA was dominated by the oil giants. However, the convertibility of most European currencies in the late 1950s, allowing remuneration of profits in dollars, was an important stimulus for manufacturing FDI into Europe; see P. Auerbach, *Competition, The Economics of Industrial Change* (Oxford: Blackwell, 1988), 243.

[17] In 1966 over 60% of the firms included on the International Fortune 500 list were from the USA; by 1991 the figure had fallen to 31%. The corresponding figures for European firms were 28% and 34% and, for Japanese firms, 7% and 24%; OTA, 1993, 73.

caused by mergers and accumulation, together with the growing size and sophistication of their markets, suggests they will be able to mount an effective challenge in most, if not all, advanced products. (Rowthorn, 1971, 162.)

Macroeconomic constraints on the world trading system and rising wage pressures in Europe and Japan reinforced the trend to meet the challenge from United States TNCs through FDI, and an increasingly liberal environment allowed United States corporations to respond in kind, giving a further impulse to international production (Hymer and Rowthorn, 1970; UNCTC, 1988).

Under these pressures, FDI flows have increased steadily throughout the postwar period and more rapidly with the ending of the Golden Age. The stock of FDI rose from $67.7 billion in 1960 to $1,949 billion in 1992, a compound annual growth rate of over 11 per cent.[18] Much of this increase occurred during the 1980s—and coincided with a shift to FDI in services—with a corresponding increase in the relative importance of FDI flows vis-à-vis other international flows, particularly trade, as well as in relation to domestic economic activity—including domestic investment (Table 6.3 and 6.4). There has also been a shift in the geographical locus of international production. The dominance of the United Kingdom and North America as home and host regions, which has characterized international production

Table 6.3. Foreign-direct-investment flows as a share of gross domestic fixed capital formation, 1971–5 to 1986–9 (per cent)

	1971–75	1976–80	1981–85	1986–89
Developed countries	3.0	2.8	2.9	5.0
United States	0.9	2.0	3.0	6.7
United Kingdom	7.3	8.4	5.4	12.3
Japan	0.1	0.05	0.1	–0.01
Germany	2.1	0.8	0.6	1.2
France	1.8	1.9	2.0	3.8
Developing countries	5.5	4.7	4.2	6.0
Asia + Pacific	4.7	4.2	4.8	7.5
Latin America + Caribbean	5.7	3.2	3.5	4.0
Africa	5.9	6.3	3.7	7.7

Source: UN-TCMD, World Investment Report, 1992.

[18] By the early 1990s, there were some 37,000 TNCs worldwide. The number of those based in 14 major developed home countries more than tripled during the past two decades, from 7,000 in 1970 to nearly 24,000 in 1990 (UNCTAD, DTCI, 1993). The total number of foreign affiliates stands at 200,000, a dramatic acceleration over the 3,500 manufacturing affiliates established between 1946–61 (Dunning, 1983).

Table 6.4. Inward foreign direct investment stock as a share of gross domestic product, 1975–89 (per cent)

	1975	1980	1985	1989
Developed countries	6.0	5.5	7.1	9.6
United States	1.7	3.1	4.7	7.3
Japan	0.3	0.3	0.5	0.6
France	1.5	2.5	3.1	4.9
Italy	5.0	2.1	3.9	5.3
Netherlands	12.0	12.1	16.4	22.2
Developing countries	7.7	8.0	10.5	15.1
excluding Singapore and				
Hong Kong	5.0	4.8	5.4	6.1

Source: UN-TCMD, *World Investment Report*, 1992.

Table 6.5. Share of outward stock of foreign direct investment, selected countries, 1914–92 (per cent of world total)

	1914	1960	1978	1992
France	12.2	6.1	3.8	7.8
Germany	10.5	1.2	7.3	9.5
Japan	0.1	0.7	6.8	12.9
United Kingdom	45.5	16.2	12.9	13.3
United States	18.5	49.2	41.4	24.3

Source: Dunning, 1983; UNCTAD, DTCI, 1993.

for much of the past century, began to diminish, replaced by a Triad pattern of FDI, centred on Western Europe, North America, and (albeit less significantly) Japan (Table 6.5).

More significantly, the regionalization of trade flows appears to be increasingly complemented by the regionalization of FDI flows. Given the more complex motivations associated with FDI, one would expect FDI flows to be more variable than trade flows. However, countries are undertaking a disproportionate share of their investment with regional partners; Canada, for example, placed 71 per cent of its investment with the United States and Latin America. Italy placed 74 per cent of its investment in the

Table 6.6. The intensity[a] of outward foreign direct investment, 1990

	North America	Latin America	Europe	Africa	West Asia	South Asia	East Asia
North America	1.97	1.12	0.84	0.49	0.85	0.32	0.8
Europe	0.98	0.53	1.32	1.16	0.79	1.77	0.56
East Asia	1.28	1.09	0.5	1.10	1.12	0.28	1.94

Source: Petri, 1994.

Note: [a] The intensity coefficient is the ratio of partner b's share in country a's investment to the partner's share in all world investment.

European bloc (Petri, 1994). In general, intraregional investment intensities are higher than extraregional intensities (Table 6.6).[19]

For much of the Golden Age, globalization pressures through renewed international market and production linkages were a reflection of growth and convergence among the advanced capitalist economies under United States leadership and supported by strong national states willing to experiment with new ways of managing economic activity. Declining trade barriers and technological revolutions supported this trend, which has evolved furthest at the regional level. By contrast, for much of the Golden Age, and certainly compared with the pre First World War One period, the developing world has been outside this globalization trend. The breakup of the internationally integrated primary production bloc provided room for industrialization drives in many developing countries, and the diffusion of mass production was promoted through import-substitution industrialization. Tariff barriers and changing trade patterns weakened integration through trade, and efforts to launch industrialization coincided with a relatively diminished role for FDI. For most of this period, the ten leading host countries have accounted for upwards of two-thirds of the total to all developing countries and changes in the composition of these countries are largely explained by the fluctuating performance of certain oil-exporting countries such as Indonesia and Nigeria.[20] This changing position of developing countries within the globalization process coincided with three decades of unprecedented economic growth (see Chapter 4) and, from the 1970s, manufactured exports from the newly industrializing countries began to make significant inroads into developed country markets.

Beginning in the 1980s, many developing countries have adopted a more

---

[19] It is of some interest to note, in terms of possible future trends, that intensities are actually higher for North America and East Asia, than for Europe, and that FDI in these two regions is relatively more important than trade in cementing regional integration.

[20] The recent revival of FDI flows to developing countries has been accompanied by an increasingly skewed distribution; the 10 leading host developing countries accounting for 81% of the total compared to an average of 68% for 1981–91 (UNCTAD, DTCI, forthcoming).

open stance, including on FDI. In nominal terms, the stock of FDI in the developing world rose threefold and FDI inflows have been even more rapid during the 1990s. The experience of some countries in East Asia and Latin America suggests that FDI can finance a significant share of domestic capital formation. However, the transition to fuller participation in the international division of labour has proved difficult for many developing countries. Only a small number of developing countries have been able to integrate FDI with successful domestic industrialization strategies, notably Singapore and Hong Kong. But in others—South Korea and Taiwan—the graduation from import substitution to export-led growth owed less to FDI. Particularly in the latter cases, successful industrialization has also begun to give rise to a growing number of TNCs (UN, TCMD, 1993). Despite these different channels of reintegration in the globalization process, a new dynamic region with strong interdependent economic links is now clearly visible. Coinciding with the slow-down in productivity growth in the developed market economies, these developments have added new pressures to the globalization of economic activity in the post Golden Age period. Whilst international integration has also been pursued by many developing countries as a necessary condition for renewed growth, by contrast to the so-called 'miracle' economies of East Asia, the trends overwhelming developing countries—rapid liberalization, renewed FDI, and weakening states—share uncomfortable similarities with the lost decades of the late nineteenth and early twentieth centuries.[21]

2. INTEGRATED INTERNATIONAL PRODUCTION

Foreign direct investment has accelerated with the breakup of the Bretton Woods institutions; technological changes, particularly the new information technologies, and changes in economic policy, particularly more liberal FDI regimes, have been among the most commonly cited reasons. However, the fact that FDI data show a greater increase compared with domestic economic activity can be a misleading criterion of the extent of international production. FDI trends do not capture the full extent of international production. In many instances it records only the initial entry of a firm into a foreign location; subsequent expansions by affiliates often involve little or no FDI. But conversely, FDI is only one (indirect) measure of the internationalization of production; output, sales, employment, and

---

[21] However, the links between FDI and economic growth in developing countries still remains a contentious issue, see UN-TCMD, 1993; M. Blomstrom et al., 'What Explains Developing Country Growth?' NBER working paper no. 4132, Cambridge, Mass.: NBER, 1992; R. Singh, 'The Multinationals' Economic Penetration, Growth, Industrial Output and Domestic Savings in Developing Countries: Another Look', *Journal of Development Studies*, 25 Oct. 1988.

assets provide alternative measures; reliable and comprehensive longitudinal data on all these measures are scarce, but a careful study of international production over the post Second World War period (UNCTAD, DTCI, 1994), actually points to a deceleration of international production activities after the first oil shock, with little change since the late 1970s; essentially TNCs from Western Europe and notably Japan having compensated for the reduced pace of transnational activity originating from the traditional home economies, notably the United States. Shifts in the sectoral composition of FDI towards service activities, new modes of FDI such as mergers and acquisitions and joint ventures, and the different objectives of firms from new home countries imply that qualitative changes in international production are perhaps more important than quantitative changes. Perhaps more importantly, FDI data does not, of itself, say very much about the way in which TNCs are coordinating and integrating the various assets under their control. This issue is of particular importance given that TNCs tend to be large domestic firms with considerable economic power and strategic influence.

International production under the gold standard was quite integrated, albeit confined to the primary sector; as discussed earlier, the strength and scope of this bloc rested on vertical links within large primary producing TNCs and complementary investments in trade and transportation. The shift to FDI in manufacturing meant that, for most of the Golden Age, international production was less integrated. The international production of national firms assumed a clear division of tasks between parent company and foreign affiliates and the latter would either replicate in total the entire production activities of the parent (with the exception of more strategic planning decisions), thus performing all tasks necessary for servicing the host country and/or neighbouring markets, or undertake a limited range of activities in order to service the parent with specific components not available in the home country (UNCTAD, 1993b). Under these arrangements, production by the TNC was quite fragmented and the cross-border internalization of economic activity remained weak. However, the opportunity for greater specialization within manufacturing activities held out the possibility of a more complex international division of labour; the idea of a 'new international division of labour' emerging between low-wage production platforms and high-wage capital exporting regions, tightly coordinated through the TNC was an early (over)reaction to new possibilities in international production (see Fröbel et al., 1980). But many of the same pressures accelerating international production have begun to alter the nature of corporate strategy and the links between parent and affiliates.

Diminishing market barriers and the emergence of new home countries have meant many new firms entering international markets, expanding the scope of international competition, whilst new technologies have improved the search for locational advantages to complement those created by the firm, and made it possible to coordinate a larger number of cross-border activities more effectively. At the same time, slow productivity growth and global surplus capacity in many manufacturing industries has added to cost pressures. Together, these changes have initiated a period of corporate restructuring involving a number of elements, all of which point in the direction of integrated international production.

Organizational pressures, particularly through the influence of economies of scale, have continued to expand the horizons of TNCs. The rationalization of production activities can no longer be defined along strict national lines; merger and acquisition activity has offered quick access to needed assets almost anywhere in the world, subcontracting has expanded beyond the sourcing of the simplest inputs in low-cost regions to include a growing number of activities and locations, and automation processes are defined in relation to regional and global activities (van Liemt, 1992). Cost-competitiveness of standardized goods has also been transformed by the search for global products; the convergence of consumption patterns and falling transportation costs enable large oligopolistic firms—in such industries as automobiles, aerospace, and consumer goods—to combine economies of scale and the organization of low-cost suppliers on a worldwide basis with the desire to create a global market for a particular product range (Levy, 1993); global advertising and marketing strategies have reinforced the tendency to define competition at a 'global' level.

Simultaneously, transnational corporations have begun to shift their competitive strategy towards product differentiation, through product quality, design, and closer pre- and post-sales relationships. This switch from standardized goods and bulk production implies greater emphasis on improving the knowledge base of the firm, building an extensive communication network, linking with a sophisticated business infrastructure, and achieving 'synergic effects' from combining specialized and complementary knowledge across corporate activities (Michalet, 1989, 80); the effective management of an entire production chain spanning different national boundaries becomes a source of strong competitive advantage. In addition, closer links to science and technology have transformed the nature of competitiveness, from one based on given advantages and predictable firm behaviour, to one of continuous innovation and cooperative agreements among firms in search of complementary assets, increased speed of market entry, and risk sharing; this search, too, is becoming increasingly 'global' in scope and including an ever growing number of industries (Jacquemin, 1991).

Finally, these organizational and technological changes require considerable, but often quite uncertain, investments if firms are to maintain their particular advantages. These growing investment demands have added to the pressures for financial restructuring. One response, particularly in the face of the wider uncertainty accompanying financial deregulation, has been a greater reliance on internally generated profits. But the internationalization of financial markets has also opened up new financing opportunities by encouraging firms to source finance globally, and the development of international risk management has expanded within most TNCs.[22]

Under these various pressures, a new best-practice set of global rules for designers, engineers, entrepreneurs, managers, and marketing agents is emerging, whereby it is no longer appropriate to think of the TNC as a simple agglomeration of discrete units but as a collection of different economic activities—manufacturing, marketing and distribution, research and development, procurement, accounting and legal services, finance, etc.—which increasingly can be separated into finer and more standardized activities, and more precisely distributed across the corporate structure. The resulting product is thus a complicated bundle of inputs, produced in a variety of locations, assembled in host or home countries for sale in those countries or anywhere in the world. Technological changes have also enabled a more discrete separation of the production process, including the standardization of particular functions (Chesnais, 1988; Teece, 1993). Because, under such arrangements each element of the production chain is highly dependent upon all other elements within the system, information and coordination pressures are high. In this respect, advances in information technology have played a pivotal role in turning the potential for operating and effectively coordinating spatially dispersed functions into a reality for many TNCs and integrated international production seems to be replicating at the international level production relations that have already become established practice domestically. Essentially, integrated international production consists of a dynamic mixture of internalized and externalised activities coordinated within networks of firms across national boundaries.[23]

Given their already high degree of international production, manufacturing firms have often been the first to be re-engineered for integrated international production. High volume industries, such as automobiles and chemicals, have replaced the simple outsourcing of parts and components on a regional basis with a more intricate global integration of all the elements of their production chain, linked through new technological arrangements. The contrasting success of the 'world car' in the 1970s and the 1990s provides telling evidence of the advance in integrated international pro-

---

[22] Following financial markets, the financial function is perhaps the most global of all corporate functions. Transnational corporations not only can raise capital where it is cheapest but have themselves become important sources of funds (*The Economist*, 27 March 1993, 13).

[23] It is worth noting that similar strategies have existed in some industries on a local level for a much longer period, see M. Piore and C. Sabel, *The Second Industrial Divide*: *Possibilities for Prosperity* (New York: Basic Books, 1984).

duction (Done, 1994; UNCTAD, 1993*b*). But a number of more traditional industries, such as textiles and furniture, have responded to low-cost competition from developing countries by a similar functional breakdown and reintegration of their production chain, aimed at a higher value-added market.

But many—indeed most—TNCs combine both service and production functions, internalizing this traditional division within the boundaries of the firm (Reich, 1992). Service functions—such as advertising and marketing—have grown in importance within many primary and secondary industries. Most importantly, continuous innovation and technological leadership in establishing and maintaining international competitiveness reinforce the pivotal role of R&D activities in a more integrated international production system.[24]

These new strategies of complex integration at the production level require new relationships, both within and between firms; these relationships are at the centre of an emerging system of integrated international production. Although such networks are indeed primarily under the overall governance of TNCs, this need not necessarily mean that governance is implemented through direct ownership of productive assets. That is obviously true of intra-firm networks but the governance of inter-firm networks is based upon the power and ability to coordinate geographically and organizationally dispersed activities performed by independent and quasi-independent firms.

A first indicator of increased integration of TNC functions is the growth of *intra-firm trade* and, especially, the changing composition of such trade. In the early 1970s, intra-firm trade accounted for perhaps 20 per cent of world trade, by the early 1990s the figure was perhaps one third (UNCTAD, 1993*b*, 164–5). According to David Levy (1993), the absolute level of United States intra-firm trade has increased sharply in recent decades, although relative to overall trade there has been little change over the past decade. Still, by 1989, intra-firm trade represented one-third and over 40 per cent, respectively, of total United States exports and imports. The

---

[24] Transnational corporations tend to commit more resources to R&D than other firms and, although expenditures remain concentrated in the home base, there are signs of the increased decentralization of the R&D function (F. Chesnais, 'Multinational Enterprises and the International Diffusion of Technology' in G. Dosi, C. Freeman, R. Nelson, G. Silvenberg, and L. Soete, *Technical Change and Economic Theory* (London: Pinter Publishers, 1988); J. Howells, 'The Internationalization of R&D and the Development of Global Research Networks', *Regional Studies*, 18, 1990; P. Gugler and J. Dunning, 'Technology-Based Cross-Border Alliances' in C. Relik (ed.), *Multinational Strategic Alliances* (New York: International Business Press, 1993)). This is particularly true of TNCs from smaller European countries, more recently of TNCs from the USA. Total R&D expenditure in the USA rose by 14.4% between 1987 and 1990 but the international proportion of that R&D carried out by affiliates abroad rose by 73.7% (with a corresponding increase in the overall share from 12 to 18%), *US News and World Report*, Mar. 1993.

figure is similar for Japanese exports but considerably lower (under 30 per cent) for imports (Bonturi and Fukusaku, 1993).

But the most significant changes have been in the product composition of intra-firm trade. There has been a decline in the relative importance of intra-firm trade in natural resource-based commodities—consistent with broader trends in trade—and a growth of intra-firm trade in manufactured goods during the 1970s, particularly in medium to high technology industries that have undergone rationalization at the international level. This trend is reflected in a higher level of intra-firm imports for manufactures compared to other products (Levy, 1993, 35) and, as data covering Swedish manufacturing TNCs shows, a parallel increase in intra-firm intermediate exports during the past two decades (Andersson, et al., 1992). It is notable that the industries in which intra-firm trade is especially important include automobiles, household appliances, radio and television equipment, office machinery, instruments, and pharmaceuticals.

The question, of course, arises as to why intra-firm trade has not continued to increase in relative importance with the alleged growth in integrated international production. One reason may be the growth in intra-firm trade among affiliates (Levy, 1993, 34), but the main reason lies in a major shift which has been occurring in the extent to which various production activities are being externalized. Outsourcing has become an increasingly important practice in most industries as firms focus more closely on core activities and buy in various intermediate goods and services.

Such externalized relationships take many forms, of which international sourcing and collaborative ventures are the most significant. The international sourcing of inputs has grown steadily in all the advanced market economies (Table 6.7). In the case of international sourcing, the principal firm (normally a TNC) coordinates, and often effectively controls, the relationship with its suppliers. The key issue here is the trend, apparent in many industries, towards much closer, longer-term relationships between firms and their principal suppliers. In some cases, these suppliers are being given greater responsibility by TNCs for the quality and design of the sourced product and TNCs are increasingly committing know-how and resources to ensure these firms have the appropriate technology and capabilities to be effectively integrated with their own value chain (UNCTAD, DTCI, 1994a; van Liemt, 1992). As a result, in several industries including automobiles, the maker of preferred supplies is being reduced but the relationship between them and their customers is becoming functionally much closer. A complex, multi-tiered structure of supplier firms and subcontractors is emerging.

The last indicator of integrated international production in terms of networked relationships is the proliferation of alliances between firms for spe-

Table 6.7. Ratio of imported to domestic sourcing of intermediate inputs, selected countries

	Early 1970s	Mid/late 1970s	Mid 1980s
France	21	25	38
Germany	—	21	34
United Kingdom	16	32	37
Canada	34	37	50
United States	7	8	13
Japan	5	6	7

Source: Levy, 1993.

cific purposes. Although, as Charles Kindelberger (1988) rightly points out, collaborative ventures between firms are not a new phenomenon, what is new is their increased frequency and their centrality to many firms' strategies. As the costs of innovation have risen, as effective patent protection has shortened, and the product cycle accelerated, the urgency and costs of carrying out innovation activities has risen dramatically, as have the needs to enhance its direct commercial applicability. The rising costs of developing new products and processes and the need to respond more effectively to user and consumer needs have been among the most important reasons behind the growth of strategic alliances. Although alliances are common in many sectors, they are especially prevalent in such sectors as information technology, biotechnology, automobiles, new materials industries (Table 6.8). Essentially, these are sectors that are characterized by high entry costs, scale economies, rapidly changing technologies, and substantial operating risks (Morris and Heigert, 1987). Table 6.8 also shows the changing geographical pattern of strategic alliances between the USA and Europe, the USA and Japan, and between Europe and Japan and reveals that there is no single trend for alliances to become more important between pairs of countries.

Thus, one of the most distinctive features of the new pattern of deeper integration involves the increased use of cooperative arrangements between firms—transnational and domestic, large and small, public and private—to speed up market entry, gain access to technologies, and share financial risks. In contrast to FDI, joint venture, and mergers and acquisitions, strategic alliances do not imply equity involvement. Rather, they involve sharing complementary assets between firms, often firms competing in the same market, to gain first-mover advantages and secure longer-term stability. Although the evidence on strategic alliances is uneven, there has been a persistent upward trend since the early 1970s. According to one study, cooperative agreements between United States firms and foreign firms

Table 6.8. Growth in strategic alliance formation, 1980–9

	1980–4		1985–9		% change
	number	per cent	number	per cent	
Automobiles	26	100	79	100	203
USA–Europe	10	39	24	30	140
USA–Japan	10	39	39	49	290
Europe–Japan	6	23	16	20	167
Biotechnology	108	100	198	100	83
USA–Europe	58	54	124	63	114
USA–Japan	45	42	54	27	20
Europe–Japan	5	4	20	10	300
Information technology	348	100	445	100	28
USA–Europe	158	45	256	58	62
USA–Japan	133	38	132	30	–0.8
Europe–Japan	57	16	57	13	—
New material	63	100	115	100	83
USA–Europe	32	51	52	45	63
USA–Japan	16	25	40	35	150
Europe–Japan	15	24	23	20	53
Chemicals	103	100	80	100	–22
USA–Europe	54	52	31	39	–43
USA–Japan	28	27	35	44	25
Europe-Japan	21	20	14	17	–33

Source: Office of Technology Assessment (OTA), United States Congress (1993), FIG. 5.3.

outweigh the number of fully owned foreign affiliates by a factor of four (Gugler and Dunning, 1993, 124).

3. GLOBALIZATION, THE UNEVEN LANDSCAPE OF INTEGRATED INTERNATIONAL PRODUCTION AND THE NATION STATE

A combination of economic and political factors has, over the past fifty years, produced an unprecedented period of international economic integration. Although this process has usually been described as the (more or less successful) recovery and spread of shallow integration through increased market linkages (Henderson, 1992), the growing scope and changing nature of international production has been as significant a feature of integration during this period. Combining TNC assets both at home and abroad gives a better indication of the scope of international production; on one estimate, perhaps as much as one-third of world output is under the direct governance of TNCs (UNCTAD 1993*b*, 158). Estimates of employment by TNCs put the figure at 73 million jobs in parents and affiliates and although this represents only 2 to 3 per cent of the world's labour force, it constitutes about one-fifth of paid employment in non-agricultural activities in developed and developing countries (Parisotto, 1993). Correspondingly, the opportunity for specialization and trade within and between TNCs is extensive.

However, the extent of these changes in international production is not unprecedented; indeed, Table 6.9 suggests that on a world scale the stock of FDI has not yet passed the high point of 1914. Moreover, the rapid pace of international production during the second half of the 1980s was the outcome of very particular circumstances and proved unsustainable (UNCTAD, DTCI, ch. 4). It seems unlikely that the recovery of the leading capitalist economies will see a return to such activity at quite the pace. Finally, even among the core capitalist economies, there has been considerable variation in the internationalization of production; two of the most powerful industrial nations, Germany and Japan, whilst emerging as important home countries over the last two decades have remained far less significant host countries. Still, over the last decade, the international production activities of national firms have begun to exhibit a more integrated pattern; the data on intra-firm trade, international sourcing, and strategic alliances all suggest the emergence of industries which are *potentially* global in their operations.[25]

Given the dynamic processes behind integrated international production—including potential productivity gains at the firm level, the rising productivity of coordination accompanying the introduction of new technologies, and the growing importance of innovation in maintaining international competitiveness—the further spread of integrated international production can be expected as recovery returns to the major capitalist economies. More speculatively, these changes at the firm and industry levels anticipate a new growth dynamic in the world economy (Whadwhani and Shah, 1994; Oman, 1994); cross-national economies of scale, economies of scope, and organizational learning hold out the possibility of TNCs

---

[25] Any list of such industries would almost certainly include e.g. automobiles, microelectronics, information technology, consumer electronics, household appliances, office machinery, instruments, pharmaceuticals, telecommunications, together with a number of service industries including financial services. Examples of the same tendencies can be found in other industries which are not fully integrated internationally and which, overall, do not possess the attributes normally identified with 'global' industries. The textiles, apparel, and furniture industries each contain elements of integrated international production systems even though, overall, they are predominantly industries in which there is still a high degree of organizational fragmentation.

Table 6.9. The role of foreign direct investment in world economic activity, 1913–91

	1913	1960	1975	1980	1985	1991
World FDI stock as % of world output	9.0	4.4	4.5	4.7	5.4	7.2
World sales of foreign affiliates as % of world exports	—	84[b]	97[c]	99[d]	99[d]	122[d]
World FDI inflows as % of world output	—	0.3	0.3	0.4	0.4	0.7
World FDI inflows as % of world gross fixed capital formation	—	1.1	1.4	1.8	1.8	2.9

Sources: UNCTAD-DTC, databases and UN, DESIPA, database.
Notes: [a] estimate based on data from Dunning, 1983; Maddison, 1989; and Bairoch, forthcoming;
   [b] estimate based on US data;
   [c] estimate based on US and Japanese data;
   [d] estimate based on US, Japanese, and German data.

reproducing internationally developments already established at the local and national level, in such forms as industrial districts and in the longstanding practices of many Japanese companies (Piore and Sabel, 1984; Best, 1990).[26]

The spread and deepening of dynamic internal and external relations among a growing number of firms, both small and large, domestic and transnational, might be described as the emergence of an integrated international production system. But trends at the firm and industry levels do not, by themselves, amount to systemic change. This requires complementary developments in broader social, economic, and political arrangements. This is true for at least three reasons. First, any systemic transition is certain to generate structural imbalances and growing disparities which require a broadly favourable social and macroeconomic environment to ensure their effective management; the structural disturbances in the North resulting from the migration of labour-intensive jobs to some developing countries, recently analysed by Adrian Wood, can be seen as indicative of

---

[26] That industrial districts are based on small and medium-sized enterprises whose international expansion has been through exports, suggests that firm size is not the quintessential feature of these more dynamic systems. However, firm size would still appear to be of importance in the international dimension of industrial organization.

the difficult problems that must be managed in the transition to a more integrated international production system.[27] Second, and even assuming a relatively smooth transition period, in important respects a fully operating system of integrated international production will be more vulnerable to microeconomic and macroeconomic imbalances than was international production during the Golden Age. Not only does integrated international production generate many more linkages of both a vertical and horizontal nature (increasing the complexity of the international division of labour and its vulnerability to shocks), but the high degree of specialization implies that no firm or industry can be fully effective without relying on many other firms and industries within the system; under these circumstances, infra-structure needs, human resource requirements, and rates of investment are all likely to be particularly high (Oman, 1994, 65) and more intangible investments in building cooperative relations, trust, and loyalty will also be integral to this system. Finally, because the systemic interdependence of international production across national borders, including at a global level, would appear to link many more locations of varying efficiency and income levels, the pressures for conformity in a wide range of economic policy measures that have traditionally been under the independent control of national decision makers are likely to impose considerable convergence costs on some countries and regions.

Under all these circumstances, avoiding the danger of 'system frictions' will place burdens on the governance of international integration that go well beyond the capabilities of individual firms and some countries (Ostry, 1992). To date, the emergence of integrated international production has coincided with—and possibly reinforced—a neo-liberal policy agenda as the renewed vehicle of economic growth, job creation, and improved social welfare. The search for and removal of 'rigidities' and 'barriers' to market adjustment has been a defining characteristic of the policy agenda to emerge from the breakdown of the Bretton Woods institutions, and the goal of perfectly integrated markets for all goods, services, and factors of production, in turn, implies the entry and exit of economic agents into markets and production locations, unhindered by the discontinuities of political boundaries and regardless of their place of origin. In this world, the genuinely footloose TNC, willing to locate anywhere to ensure the highest returns, appears to define the ideal agent of resource allocation. Conversely, strong states are seen as an obstacle to renewed growth. But this conclusion is superficial. The presence of these firms, in itself, is testament to discontinuities in the economic environment and there can be no *a priori* reason for assuming that the activities of TNCs, any more than

---

[27] See A. Wood, *North–South Trade, Employment and Inequality: Changing Fortunes in a Skill-Driven World* (Oxford: Oxford University Press, 1994). The magnitude of this problem is contentious.

international trade, will by themselves remove inequalities between and within regions. In fact, and recalling the experience of many countries caught up in an earlier period of international production and liberalization during the period before the First World War, weak states are more likely to establish weak, and ultimately unsustainable, growth paths and reinforce global segmentation.

A comprehensive alternative to a liberal agenda for a more integrated world economy has yet to take shape. However, the appropriate starting-point is the lack of any spontaneous equilibrating forces in the contemporary world economy, and the recognition that appropriate state structures and new policy initiatives must be found to manage the conflicting interests under a more integrated international production system. Shallow integration—through the spread of market linkages—can perpetuate inequalities and aggravate instability across the world economy, but FDI flows can also either produce a more dispersed pattern of international production (as more factors come to influence the location of FDI and TNCs can more effectively assess and monitor the range of locational options) or a more concentrated pattern (if TNCs are attracted to areas with already established advantages). Most likely these two effects occur simultaneously and in a cumulative manner. Consequently, the challenge facing any new model of regulated capitalism must be to reinforce the dynamic features of integrated international production and to counteract the possibilities for segmentation and exclusion.

(i) Geography Still Matters

Contrary to a strongly determinist strand in much of the contemporary globalization literature, technological developments in transport and mass communications have not removed the influence of either time or space on international production—history and geography still matter. This is true first of all at the firm level. Transnational corporations originate in specific places and, through the influence of routine and inertia, carry with them acquired attributes; cultural familiarity is still a powerful determinant of location decisions in such areas as marketing and personnel management and psychological and sociological 'belonging' (Stopford and Strange, 1991, 233); company control through the board of directors still firmly rests with the nationals of the home country and political alliances are still predominantly with home country governments (Hu, 1992; Streeten, 1992). Moreover, and despite the growing number of TNCs from an increasing number of home countries, ownership and control of assets abroad is still highly concentrated; the hundred largest TNCs—ranked by size of foreign assets—account for about one third of the combined outward FDI of their home countries. These largest companies come from a small number of countries and tend to be overrepresented in certain industries, in particular, mining and petroleum, electronics and computers, automobiles and chemicals and pharmaceutical industries—on many accounts the most global industries (UNCTAD, DTCI, 1994; Ostry and Gestrin, 1994).

Certainly, the argument that TNCs have already become de-nationalized (Reich, 1992; Ohmae, 1990) is a partial interpretation of the real world. Indeed, it seems just as valid to ask why so many companies—including TNCs—remain rooted in their home base and major centres of investment (Hirst and Thompson, 1992, 368). In light of the earlier discussions, the answer is rather predictable; most firm- and industry-specific advantages remain tied to the regional and local levels, and concentration is still a persistent feature of the geography of production. Local and regional economies of agglomeration have not disappeared, and high productivity activities will continue to be attracted to locations with the right mix of complementary industries and skills. Thus, even as capital becomes more mobile, TNCs and their affiliates will continue to derive their competitive advantages, in part, from interacting with the local economy.[28] In this respect, recent technological changes have, if anything, reinforced the importance of location to many production tasks and, in some cases, rapid technological change, including organizational innovations, such as lean production, where trust and reliability are at a premium, appears to reinforce geographical differences (Levy, 1993; Krugman, 1993).

The strong pull of geography is also visible in the accelerated FDI flows over the past two decades. Market-seeking FDI—as in the steady increase of the United States as a host country and the more recent insurge of FDI into China—continues to be a major rationale for FDI. However, this traditional motivation is increasingly accompanied by, and reinforces, efforts to seek greater corporate efficiency. The interdependence of these factors lies behind the previously noted regionalization of FDI flows, particularly in Europe, where international economic integration and corporate restructuring have been strongly complementary processes (Oman, 1994; UNCTAD, 1993b). As Miċa Paniċ has noted in the context of the European Union—although the point is of more general application—under varying levels of efficiency and income and with constraints on the mobility of labour, FDI could be expected to assume a particularly important role in any successful regional integration process (Paniċ, 1993, 149). Certainly, during the 1980s, in part anticipating the completion of the Single Market, inflows into the European Union rose significantly, from an annual average of under 30 per cent of world inflows between 1982–1987 to 44 per cent

---

[28] A recent study by D. Wheeler and A. Mody, 'International Investment Location Decision: The Case of US Firms', *Journal of International Economics* (1992), 3, found that agglomeration economies were the main locational determinant of US investment in industrialized countries.

of world inflows between 1988–1992. Some of the peripheral economies—notably those in the Iberian Peninsula—have been particularly attractive locations.[29] However, the full effects of FDI flows cannot be anticipated in abstraction from the wider economic environment. To date, FDI has been as much a defensive response to international competition, through the introduction of rationalization and cost cutting measures, as part of a broader experiment in regional expansion, innovation, and renewed development (Grahl and Teague, 1989, 42). In this context, it is important to recognize that some of the poorer countries, notably Greece and Ireland, have had little success in attracting FDI,[30] and that, whilst the contribution of FDI to gross domestic capital formation is modest in most European countries—certainly compared to the share of long-term foreign capital in some of the successful late industrializers of the nineteenth and twentieth centuries—it is actually greatest in those countries where incomes are already high (Table 6.10) and tends to be concentrated in the wealthier locations within these countries (de Vet, 1993, 107–9).

If there is still considerable uncertainty surrounding developments in Europe, the links between FDI and broader global economic trends are, if

Table 6.10. Share of inward foreign direct investment to gross domestic capital formation, for members of the European Community, 1976–92

	1976–80	1981–85	1986–90	1991–92
United Kingdom	8.2	5.6	13.6	11.0
Ireland	6.9	4.1	1.1	1.3
Belgium/Luxembourg	5.8	7.3	15.3	17.8
Greece	6.5	7.2	7.9	8.4
Netherlands	4.5	6.1	11.6	8.8
Spain	3.2	5.5	9.0	7.3
France	2.0	2.0	3.7	7.1
Portugal	1.7	3.6	9.6	11.1
Italy	0.7	1.2	2.1	1.3
Germany	1.1	1.1	1.6	1.9
Denmark	0.3	0.9	2.7	5.8

Source: United Nations, World Investment Directory, Volume III, 1993 and UNCTAD, DTCI, 1994.

[29] Although Portugal's share of annual inflows into the European Union rose significantly between 1988–92, albeit from a very low figure between 1982–7, the annual inflows to Spain actually fell during the same period, as a share of total inflows.

[30] The current recession also suggests the vulnerability of these flows; the figures for both Spain and Portugal indicate a significantly declining share in 1991 and 1992; the sustainability of these flows is far from certain.

anything, far more discouraging. Integrated international production is emerging in a world economy which is being shaped by strong deflationary pressures and visible signs of divergence and, possibly, fragmentation. The trend share of world output produced by the developed countries which steadily declined until 1980—with a corresponding increase in the share of all developing country regions and the former socialist bloc—has, over the past decade, slowed and in some cases reversed (Table 6.11). Similarly, the share of world merchandise exports between 1982 and 1992 showed a spectacular rise in Asia, smaller increases for North America, the European Union, and Japan and declines in all other regions of the world economy (de Jonquières, 1994). Growing income inequalities within regions—including developed countries—has been a pervasive feature of the last two decades (EC, 1993a). Under these conditions, the objectives of the largest TNCs may increasingly diverge with national or regional objectives.

Table 6.11. The share of major regions in world production, 1967–89 (per cent; gross domestic product at 1980 purchasing power)

	1967	1973	1980	1986	1989
United States	25.7	22.8	20.9	20.9	20.8
Western Europe	25.9	25.3	23.9	22.4	22.2
Japan	5.6	7.0	7.2	7.5	7.8
Developing Asia (including China)	11.0	11.8	13.8	17.4	19.3
Latin America	7.1	7.7	8.8	8.0	7.5
Africa (except South Africa)	3.1	3.2	3.4	3.2	3.0
Rest of world	21.7	22.1	22.2	20.5	19.4

Source: G. van Liemt, 1993, *Industry on the Move*, Table 1.1. (Geneva, International Labour Office).

The conclusion of this section is perhaps rather predictable. To the extent that FDI is a key component of integrated international production, unevenness and exclusion are as likely to be characteristic features of its evolution as was the development of mass production in the late nineteenth and early twentieth centuries. In a world where geography still matters and market pressures cannot ensure a spontaneous process of growth and convergence, appropriate policy measures aimed at counteracting segmentation tendencies and ensuring fuller integration in the world economy will continue to be of importance to the emerging system of integrated international production.

*(ii) Governments Still Matter: The Domestic Management of Integrated
International Production*

For much of the past fifty years, the conditions and benefits of increased
integration and economic growth have been successfully organized and
managed by national governments. However, weakening national economic
sovereignty has been a decisive factor shaping international integration
over the last two decades. The reasons for this diminishing influence of the
state are undoubtedly complex but mounting international pressures have,
themselves, certainly played an important role. The internationalization of
financial markets—particularly following the move to floating exchange
rates—has reduced the efficacy of unilateral macroeconomic policies, both
Keynesian and monetarist. But the higher share of economic activity organized within the boundaries of TNCs and the growing interdependence of
trade, investment, and technology linkages has further compromised the
policy autonomy of most governments. The idea that market flexibility provides the only environment compatible with international competitiveness
has justified a further erosion of regulations on the scope of corporate activity through deregulation, trade union reform, tax reductions, and deflationary macroeconomic policies. Consistent with this agenda, attracting
FDI through lowering costs appears as a central component of renewed
growth and job creation. The lessons have been absorbed by many developing countries as well as the former centrally planned economies; their
efforts to seek closer links with the world economy through a liberal agenda
of expanded market-based linkages reverses the idea of a more managed
entry into the world economy in the expectation that increased international integration will, spontaneously, bring about recovery and growth.

But in a more integrated international economy where the exit option of
firms has been strengthened, there is no guarantee that measures to enhance
corporate profitability will produce tangible benefits to the national or
regional economy—what is good for firms need not be good for national
economies. Thus a policy of lower taxes may, as intended, increase the volume of savings and attract FDI, but the detrimental impact on government
revenues and the quality of essential services may just as rapidly undermine
longer-term locational attractiveness (Panić, 1993). Similar results have
been noted from financial liberalization (see Chapter 3) and labour market
deregulation (see Chapter 5). The danger of taking a complacent attitude
to the domestic effects of increased international production and deregulation is perhaps best illustrated by developments in some of the smaller open
economies of Western Europe, where a rapid and unregulated acceleration
in the international activity of national firms has, since the mid-1980s,
switched from complementing domestic economic activity to substituting

for that activity (Andersson, 1994; Pontusson, 1993). The conclusion of a recent study on the relocation of production by Swedish TNCs is worth repeating in full:

The results give strong evidence for a negative effect of production abroad on exports from a parent company. Increased production in affiliates is not able to attract enough intermediate goods from the parent to compensate for the substitution of finished goods. . . . Although no welfare analysis has been undertaken in this study, it is obvious that negative effects on home country exports may be unfavourable for social welfare in that economy. That is, what is good for firms is not necessarily good for their home country. (Svensson, 1993, 23.)

This conclusion does not only apply to countries in a more open world economy. It is also true that what is good for TNCs may not be good for a more integrated international production system either. Much of the new investment required to establish integrated international production is in capital intensive technologies, requires large research and development expenditures, and involves the simultaneous penetration of many markets to combat shortening product cycles. New investments are also required to modernize the organizational structure and skill profile of firms. Financial deregulation by adding to the attractiveness of shorter-term (and often more speculative) investment opportunities and having financing issues assume an unduly large significance in corporate planning (Volcker and Gyothen, 1992) can have an adverse effect on the long-term investment at the heart of integrated international production; the rising share of mergers and acquisitions in FDI—accounting for over 50 per cent of the increase in FDI during the second half of the 1980s—can, in part, be seen as indicative of this trend; the tendency—at least historically—for these acquired firms to be less integrated with the exiting operations of a TNC is indicative of the potential problems for more integrated international production (Andersson and Svensson, 1994). Similarly, although exchange rate volatility can generate greater FDI, its defensive use as a hedging device is likely to be accompanied by its suboptimal spatial allocation (UNCTAD, 1987, 89; Cushman, 1985).

Thus, simply removing market rigidities and extending shallow integration is as likely to induce defensive responses from TNCs to increased uncertainty and volatility through an exaggerated concern over financial liquidity, the transfer of economic risk and social costs to a growing periphery of small firms and workers, and a bias towards cost-saving innovation and technological change. A broad consensus model of socio-economic development, including an important role for state action, is needed to correct the danger that short-term options will compensate for corporate inefficiencies, delaying change, and actually obstructing more productive investment and innovative strategies.

It would thus appear that, in a more integrated international production system, government policies to sustain economic performance retain much of their relevance, even if their nature has changed. Still, in light of the weakened role of the state it is possible to talk of a *contemporary paradox of national policy making* in today's world economy. On the one hand, international linkages and interconnections have created a perception that effective national policies (and their implementation) for adapting to a more interdependent world economy have gained rather than declined in importance (Landesmann, 1986; Porter, 1990). On the other hand, these same pressures make the identification and targeting of purely national objectives increasingly complex and have narrowed the scope for independent action. But the limits on state action are neither unprecedented historically nor irreversible. Moreover, it is important to remember that many of the contemporary problems of domestic economic management are, to a large extent, a product of changing political sentiments and commitments aimed, explicitly, at weakening the economic role of the state (Chang and Rowthorn, forthcoming). However, if the combination of weak states and strong TNCs is unlikely to sustain economic growth under a more integrated international production system, then sooner or later measures must be found to strengthen the role of national states.

A drastic response to strengthen strategies of national management of integrated international production would be to impose controls and restrictions on inward and outward FDI. Such restrictions were a feature of a number of countries during the Golden Age (OTA, 1993, 68–9). However, this is neither a realistic nor a desirable option in today's world economy. For most nations, it is difficult to conceive a reduction in international economic integration without significant welfare losses. The structural, technological, and organizational changes accompanying integrated international production are part of the prerequisites for renewed real income growth and increased employment opportunities, and any effective economic strategy cannot isolate itself from the regulatory pressure of international markets. The liberalization of FDI frameworks is, in part, a reflection of this situation (UNCTAD, DTCI, 1994, ch. VII). But greater openness does not translate in a simple manner into rapid inflows, as the Japanese experience testifies. Institutional factors, other than legal obstacles, can act to limit FDI flows. This is particularly true of the links between finance and industry. In this respect, measures to strengthen the links between domestic industry and finance, along the lines of the Japanese or German models, may indirectly strengthen the role of domestic states *vis-à-vis* domestic and foreign TNCs.[31]

---

[31] The links between these institutional forms of protection and economic welfare are far more complex than most advocates of liberalization are willing to admit. In a recent article on the institutional obstacles to inward FDI in Japan, Robert Lawrence concludes that any

In any event, measures to attract FDI will be of limited success unless selective supply-side measures can be used to ensure that stronger links with international production are consistent with the continuous upgrading of domestic economic activity. In light of the pressures on the labour market from a more open economic environment and more mobile capital, and given the demands on human capital in a more integrated international production system, one area of government focus should undoubtedly be active labour market policies. Such policies must increasingly take into account the requirements of large TNCs—both domestic and foreign—but they must also ensure that some of the more vulnerable elements in the international network—such as subcontractors and suppliers of spare parts—are not excluded from the process of skill formation. But in the face of economic and information advantages acquired by TNCs and given the enhanced mobility of many of the productive assets under their control, an independent public agency will be required to acquire information on the activities of domestic and foreign TNCs, to monitor their activity, and to devise effective policy responses that maximize national advantages from participation in an integrated international production system. Although an appropriate policy response is no longer likely to target particular firms— domestic or foreign—strengthening development clusters or blocs will require the formulation of complementary trade, industrial, and technology policies.

But probably the greatest challenge facing this agency would be to find new ways to make TNCs more accountable. It would seem ironic, if the demise of unaccountable power structures under central planning were to further reinforce existing hierarchies within international production which shape the life opportunities and working experiences of an increasing number of people. In this context, such a government agency could perhaps use funds released from privatization programmes or the defence dividend to acquire shares in those international firms with the greatest influence over the future direction of economic activity.

(iii) Cooperation and Convergence: The International Management of Integrated International Production

A still valuable lesson of the Golden Age is that international economic integration can only be sustained under conditions of full employment, rapid growth, and convergence in incomes and demand patterns. Under these conditions, states can be relatively confident that they can strike the

such restriction 'reduces domestic competition and may reduce technology transfer to Japan. However, restrictions on FDI could also increase Japanese welfare (and reduce foreign welfare) if it shifts rents to Japanese-owned firms by forcing foreign firms to license their products, rather than enter the Japanese market directly.' Lawrence, 1992, 72.

right balance between any short-term costs arising from international integration and its longer-term benefits to domestic growth. The revival of the neo-liberal agenda has exaggerated the limits to state action on the independent pursuit of these conditions. However, given the diminished sovereignty that does accompany international integration, and in light of the paradox facing policy makers, many more issues of mutual interest to states must now be solved cooperatively (Panić, 1988; Ostry, 1990).

The need for a common framework for regulating international production was already recognized in the Havana Charter of 1948 that was to underpin the World Trade Organisation. This early effort foundered on a variety of disagreements among developed countries and, despite subsequent efforts to establish cross-border investment principles and codes of conduct for TNC behaviour, these have been strongly contested or lacking in regulatory bite. One recent assessment of these various efforts concludes '. . . the resulting international regulatory environment for transnational business threatens to become a morass of binding and non-binding partial instruments that overlap on some issues while leaving broad areas of FDI policy and transnational business activity uncovered by effective regulations or guidelines' (Kline, 1993, 158).

In light of the changes in international production, the challenge to find a more effective regulatory framework appears all the more urgent, given that cross-border activities now connect a growing number of locations with considerable variations in efficiency, income levels, and industrial and institutional histories. Efforts to ensure convergence must recreate the environment for catching up through rapid productivity growth. But collective agreement must now encompass such issues as labour standards, workplace conditions, welfare provisions, and support for technology programmes. Achieving convergence in these areas will almost certainly prove difficult given the importance of intangible institutional elements in which the potential for system frictions and conflict is particularly strong (Ostry, 1990; Hirst and Thompson, 1992). But avoiding the danger of competing on lower social conditions in response to short-term business criteria is in the interests of governments in developed, developing, and transition economies. The appropriate response can be no more technocratic than with more traditional international public goods. Certainly, Charles Kindelberger's conclusion that 'There needs to be positive leadership, backed by resources and a readiness to make some sacrifices in the international interest' (Kindelberger, 1986, 10), seems even more relevant in an integrated international production system. But leadership must be complemented by 'bargaining structures and attitudes conducive to reaching negotiated outcomes that avoid further segmentation, while accepting rapid structural and technological change and the advantages of a more open world economy' (van Liemt, 1992, 468). The basic challenge is that, in a world where some productive assets have become more mobile, the only effective response is for communities that rely upon more fixed assets to establish social cohesion, trust, and cooperation across domestic borders to provide them with the necessary bargaining leverage.

In current circumstances, and in light of previous efforts at regulating international production, it seems unlikely that appropriate leadership and bargaining structures will emerge at global level (see Chapter 2). Rather, the strengthening of regional economic integration, notably in Europe (with the completion of the Single European Market and the subsequent development of the European Union) and in North America (the Canada–United States Free Trade Agreement and the North American Free Trade Area involving Mexico as well as Canada), because it is consistent with trade and investment patterns, would appear a more appropriate arena for regulating integrated international production. To date regional integration has been narrowly conceived as a removal of regulatory barriers between member states to reduce costs and stimulate rationalization in enlarged markets. But different regulatory structures can build on the democratic and cooperative traditions located at the regional level. Already programmes to strengthen competitiveness and cooperation have been conceived at the regional level in Europe and elements of a transnational social policy have begun to address the imbalances and inequalities emerging between groups from increased integration. A more robust regional policy will also be needed—probably including the former planned economies—to prevent corporate restructuring from following a defensive and ultimately defeatist strategy of competing on the basis of low wages and minimal social protection. Although these measures are perhaps best illustrated in the European context, all regional groupings face similar problems.

However, it is almost certainly not the case that any effective regulatory framework for integrated international production will emerge exclusively from the collective actions of states. The growth of TNCs has shifted the balance of control over international trade and production, and one of the most significant developments of the period since the late 1960s has been for firms in industries such as textiles, clothing, and electronics to locate parts of their activities so as to utilize either low-cost or specifically skilled labour. In response to cost pressures from slower growth and increased competition, the options available to firms, and particularly the larger TNCs, have expanded further; the ability of firms to seek out appropriate pools of labour on a global scale has increased, including, over the last decade, the ability of large corporations to recreate diverse labour pools within their own home economies (and regions). Divergence and inequality is now emerging within the boundaries of corporate networks. These developments lie behind the trend towards more decentralized negotiating and bargaining structures in most developed market economies (van Liemt, 1992) and pose a major challenge to traditional trade union practices, undermining their bargaining power, and creating organizational asymmetries with management whose scope and actions more readily extend across national boundaries in search of increased flexibility.

Integration at the level of production requires greater stability, participation, and cooperation between management and labour. In this respect, labour movements need to turn their organizing efforts away from the immediate threat of relocation to the wider economic and social conditions for a more integrated international production system. Again, the regional setting, because of the greater degree of political and organizational familiarity across national labour movements, provides the most likely context in which to forge new strategies and strengthen cross-border solidarity. Already in Europe (and more tentatively in North America), trade unions have begun to explore cross-border collective bargaining issues within individual TNCs, through voluntary company councils. Perhaps more significantly, trade unions have been instrumental in the efforts to strengthen regional and social legislation in the European Union. The creation of European Works Councils in TNCs operating in the Union has been the most notable and successful initiative in this regard, combining a traditional trade union demand for greater participation in corporate decision-making with legislative bite through the European Commission (see Hall, 1992; Marginson, 1992).

Significantly, these measures have involved new alliances between trade unions, regional bureaucracies, and TNCs and there are other possibilities for more extensive collaboration in the context of integrated international production. Thus, to the extent that integrated international production will need expansionary measures to guarantee a more robust investment climate, this will almost certainly require a European-wide incomes policy that can only be delivered by a more encompassing trade union movement and supported by active labour market policies constructed at the regional level.[32]

CONCLUSION

Transnational corporations have accelerated the pace and changed the nature of international production over the postwar period. The steady growth of FDI and the production activities of foreign affiliates attest to this change. Deeper integration between economies during the past one or

---

[32] However, and despite the growing influence of large TNCs, employers remain quite fragmented and do not speak with a single cross-border voice. This organizational weakness on the employers' side also makes it difficult to organize consensus.

two decades reflects the intricate ways in which the various components of the world economy are being organized and geographically arranged by TNCs. The emergence of a new integrated international production system under the governance of TNCs in many economic sectors is now visible. But its incidence is uneven, is quite vulnerable to adverse shocks, and does not rule out exclusion.

The resurgence of a neo-liberal agenda, whilst enhancing the exit options of TNCs, is as likely to reinforce differences at the national and regional levels as improve the longer-term investment strategies required to ensure the full potential of integrated international production. But the institutional context to redress this balance is still missing. In part this reflects the weakening of nation states consistent with the goals of the neo-liberal agenda. But it also reflects the difficulties of establishing appropriate forms of international cooperation. But, with no clear leadership role emerging in the world economy, the danger is that many of the same forces of international integration will reinforce the defensive role of exit strategies. The prerequisite for new and more innovative strategies to manage integrated international production is stronger not weaker states, albeit in the context of regional groupings and including new alliances with labour movements and with TNCs.

7. International Capital Movements: Some Proposals for Reform[1]

Yılmaz Akyüz and Andrew Cornford

The recent trend towards liberalization of international capital movements in most parts of the world economy has been accompanied by growing agreement concerning the potential benefits of long-term international investment, so long as it is subject to certain restrictions and conditions. But there is no such consensus as to the benefits of short-term capital movements, even though these too are now increasingly covered by measures of liberalization. Policy makers' concerns regarding short-term capital movements derive mainly from the volatility of many of the transactions through which such movements are effected. Unless offsetting action is taken, this is easily translated into volatility of the exchange rate, asset prices and interest rates, foreign exchange reserves, and the supply of domestic financing. Therefore such movements are capable of exerting a powerful influence on the economy as a whole, including resource allocation, consumption, and investment.

The unfavourable effects of such volatility have been extensively analysed in the literature.[2] For example, volatility of exchange rates, asset prices, and interest rates tends to shorten time horizons for investment decisions, to raise transactions costs, and to increase firms' incentives to maintain higher mark-ups and greater financial reserves. Moreover volatility blurs the signals which the exchange rate should give for resource allocation. Volatility of interest rates and asset prices increases wealth holders' preferences for liquid as opposed to longer-term financial instruments, thus exerting upward pressure on long-term interest rates. The volatility of foreign exchange rates and of foreign exchange reserves tend to exert a deflationary impact on the world economy owing to the asymmetry in pressures for

[1] We are heavily indebted to Jan Kregel for lengthy discussions of this chapter's subject-matter. We are also grateful for the comments of an anonymous referee. But we are solely responsible for the views expressed and for any errors.

[2] For a survey of the literature see The UNCTAD secretariat, 'The exchange-rate system', sec. B, in *Compendium of Studies on International Monetary and Financial Issues for Developing Countries* (United Nations Publication, Sales No. E.87.II.D.3), and *Trade and Development Report, 1990* (United Nations Publication, Sales No. E.90 II.D.6), Part II, ch. I, secs. B and C.

adjustment on countries with weak currencies as opposed to those with strong ones. Protection against some of these unfavourable effects at a microeconomic level, particularly those of the volatility of exchange and interest rates, can now be purchased in the form of forward, futures, option, and swap contracts. However, such contracts still leave several risks uncovered, especially those faced by developing countries, and they can be expensive.[3] Moreover increased buying and selling of such contracts have opened up new opportunities for speculative profits and are thus capable of adding to the very volatility against which they afford protection.

Section 1 discusses different techniques and instruments for controlling international capital movements. Section 2 discusses different regimes, the focus being on those of the OECD and the European Union (EU). Section 3 takes up proposals for curbing speculative international capital movements. Since there is an extensive literature on the contribution of macroeconomic policies to this objective, greater detail is reserved for proposals for a tax on foreign exchange transactions, and for measures affecting banks' balance-sheet management designed to increase the costs of engaging in foreign exchange speculation.

1. POLICIES TOWARDS INTERNATIONAL CAPITAL MOVEMENTS

Broadly speaking, international capital movements involve changes in the claims of a country's residents on non-residents in the form of real capital assets and financial instruments. There is a close correspondence, for example, between the categories of claim included under this heading and the items other than reserve assets covered in the capital and financial account of the balance of payments.[4]

In the Articles of Agreement of the IMF there is no explicit listing of international capital transactions, which are defined as those other than current.[5] By contrast both the OECD Code of Liberalisation of Capital

---

[3] Concerning the coverage of such contracts, see e.g. *Trade and Development Report, 1988* (United Nations Publication, Sales No. E.88.II.D.8), Part I, ch. II, sec. D. The sale of the contracts just mentioned has been an important source of revenue to the financial sector.

[4] IMF, *Balance of Payments Manual*, 5th edn. (Washington, D.C.: IMF, 1993), ch. XVI.

[5] Article XXX(d) specifies that 'payments for current transactions means payments which are not for the purpose of transferring capital, and includes, without limitation: (1) all payments due in connection with foreign trade, other current business, including services, and normal short-term banking and credit facilities; (2) payments due as interest on loans and as net income from other investments; (3) payments of moderate amount for amortization of loans or for depreciation of direct investments; and (4) moderate remittances for family living expenses.' In cases where these guidelines are not sufficient for the purpose of classifying transactions as 'current' or 'capital', the Fund 'may, after consultation with the members concerned, determine whether certain specific transactions are to be considered current transactions or capital transactions'.

Movements and the EU Directives concerning capital movements provide detailed lists of capital transactions. Thus the 1992 edition of the OECD Code[6] lists direct investment, the liquidation of such investment, operations in real estate, operations in securities on capital markets, operations on money markets, operations in collective investment securities, operations in negotiable instruments and non-securitized claims not elsewhere specified, credits directly linked with international commercial transactions or with the rendering of international services, personal capital movements, financial credits and loans not elsewhere specified, sureties, guarantees and financial back-up facilities, the operation of deposit accounts, foreign exchange operations not elsewhere specified,[7] and disposal of non-resident owned blocked funds. As might be expected in view of the overlapping of the memberships of the EU and OECD, the list of international capital transactions specified in the annex on nomenclature of the EEC Council's 1988 Directive on capital movements[8] is similar (though not identical).

Controls on Capital Transactions

Controls on transactions involving inward and outward flows of capital can be imposed by governments to further several different objectives of economic policy. These include both longer-term objectives, typically related to national development, and those of macroeconomic policy. Controls under the first heading may be intended to ensure that capital owned by residents is invested locally, or that certain categories of economic activity are reserved partly or wholly for residents. Although the objectives of development policy are long-term, their achievement may require several different kinds of intervention in the financial system and thus may include shorter- as well as longer-term instruments and operations (including shorter-term international capital movements). Thus controls on capital flows imposed for macroeconomic reasons are often closely connected to other measures of monetary policy designed to influence holdings of short-term monetary and financial instruments. The objectives of such controls include the avoidance of unwanted appreciations or depreciations of the currency; reductions in the volatility of the exchange rate; and preventing domestic monetary or fiscal measures, directed at levels of investment or overall expenditure, from being undermined by offsetting inflows or outflows of external financing.

---

[6] *Code of Liberalisation of Capital Movements* (Paris: OECD, March 1992).

[7] Inclusion of foreign exchange operations here is a little surprising in the absence of further specification of the purpose for which such operations are carried out.

[8] Council Directive of 24 June 1988 for the implementation of Article 67 of the Treaty (88/361/EEC), reproduced in *Official Journal of the European Communities*, 31/L178, 8 July 1988, 5–18.

A large number of different measures are available to governments for controlling international capital movements, some of them with a broad incidence and others aimed at more narrowly defined sets of transactions.[9] In the case of outflows of foreign direct investment (FDI) or medium- and long-term portfolio investment the controls may take the form of licensing procedures, taxes imposed on purchases of securites abroad by residents, and two-tier exchange rates. Different variants of the latter measure have been used. The most common involves a more unfavourable rate for capital transactions.[10] Inflows of medium- and long-term portfolio investment may also be subject to licensing. Furthermore they may be limited by ceilings on levels of foreign ownership in some or all sectors (which may include reservation for investment by residents in certain cases). Access to foreign direct investors may be granted only on conditions designed to contribute to development or other national policy objectives.

Controls over short-term capital movements have to contend with the very large number of methods available to take advantage of opportunities for profit in the international markets for financial instruments. Amongst OECD countries such opportunities have progressively increased in response both to the liberalization of the international financial regime and, since the 1970s, to the proliferation of new financial techniques and instruments made possible by the rapid development of computer technology and electronic communications. Short-term capital movements are not necessarily effected via short-term financial instruments, since the profits which motivate such movements may be best achieved through transactions involving longer-term assets, as is often true if there are liquid secondary markets for such assets. Thus control of short-term movements may include techniques discussed above in the case of FDI and medium- and long-term portfolio investment. But it must also be directed at the many other ways in which individuals and enterprises lend, invest, borrow, or otherwise take financial positions at short term, with an actual or potential impact on the movements of funds between currencies.

[9] No attempt is made here at a complete classification of controls over international capital movements. For further discussion see e.g. R. W. Edwards, *International Monetary Collaboration* (Dobbs Ferry, New York: Transnational Publishers, 1985), 449–54; A. Watson and R. Altringham, *Treasury Management: International Banking Operations* (London: The Chartered Institute of Bankers, l986), ch. 7; and R. W. Mills, 'An evaluation of measures to influence volatile capital flows' and 'The regulation of short-term capital movements in major industrial countries', chs. 6 and 9 of A. K. Swoboda (ed.), *Capital Movements and their Control* (Leiden: A. W. Sijthoff, l976).

[10] A stringent variant was deployed by the South African government during much of the 1960s and 1970s with the objective of isolating the market for the country's securities among non-residents from that among residents (which, *inter alia*, made it less likely that declines in securities prices would be *accompanied by drains of foreign reserves*). This was achieved by restricting transactions by non-residents in South African securities to those with other non-residents (and sometimes also limiting transfers of its currency for capital transactions by non-residents to those made through the purchase and sale of such securities).

To some extent this objective can be met by controls on transactions which are clearly of a capital rather than a current nature such as the buying and selling of short-term financial instruments issued abroad. But in practice control of outward capital movements is likely to be impossible without recourse to more general measures of exchange control, many of which would also typically be part of a regime for restricting payments for current international transactions. These include the requirement for official permission to open foreign bank accounts, limitations on the size and use of currency holdings abroad, restrictions on the amount of foreign currency that can be taken abroad by travellers, and regulations concerning the physical export and import of bills of exchange, securities, insurance policies, and bank notes. Thus, countries which do not restrict payments for international current transactions have to frame their regimes of capital controls in such a way as to avoid impeding such transactions. This may entail measures designed to ensure that certain payments are indeed for purposes which can be classified as current and not capital transactions.[11]

Inward as well as outward capital movements can pose problems for macroeconomic management. Examples of measures directed at such movements since the 1950s as part of macroeconomic policy are provided mainly by European countries. But more recently there has also been recourse to them by developing countries subject to large capital inflows. Such measures include forbidding banks from paying interest on the deposits of non-residents or even requiring negative interest rates on such balances; limiting banks' liabilities denominated in foreign currencies; and the imposing of differentially high (and possibly non-interest-bearing) reserve requirements on increases in such liabilities or in banks' liabilities to non-residents. Special taxes may be levied on credits from abroad—a measure affecting non-financial as well as financial enterprises; and cash deposits with the central bank, equivalent to a certain proportion of foreign borrowing by non-financial enterprises, may be required, a measure pioneered by Germany in 1972 (the 'bardepot').

The response to unacceptably high capital inflows has also taken forms such as the encouragement of increased foreign investment by financial institutions and intervention in the forward exchange market to encourage short-term capital outflows. An alternative approach to controls and the encouragement of outflows is to attempt to check the inflows through changes in interest rates. However, in the face of capital movements with the potential for generating substantial fluctuations in exchange rates and thus large returns from shifting funds between currencies, the changes

---

[11] Foreign-exchange controls designed to obtain statistical data or to segregate capital from current transactions are consistent with IMF Article VIII which, as described below, is concerned with the elimination of restrictions on current transactions. Edwards, *International Monetary Collaboration*, 394.

would probably need to be very large, and might thus be in conflict with the achievement of other macroeconomic objectives.

2. REGIMES FOR INTERNATIONAL CAPITAL MOVEMENTS

There is considerable variation in countries' regimes for international capital movements. Amongst OECD countries the long-term tendency has been in the direction of liberalization, although periods of instability in international money markets have often led to widespread recourse to restrictions, subsequently relaxed as calmer conditions returned. The tendency towards liberalization accords with the thrust of the OECD Code of Liberalization of Capital Movements and the pertinent EEC Directives. Among developing countries controls over capital transactions remain the norm. During recent years there have been substantial changes in the regimes of some developing countries in Latin America and South and South-East Asia, the longer-term thrust of which has been in the direction of liberalization. However, more recently the governments of some of the countries in question have taken measures designed to restrain capital inflows owing to the problems caused by their rapid expansion.

Obligations regarding international capital transfers are included not only in agreements covering several countries (such as the OECD Code and the EEC Directives) but also in the North American Free Trade Agreement (NAFTA) and in Treaties of Friendship, Commerce, and Navigation (FCN Treaties). The latter typically include provisions relating to various rights of foreign direct investors such as those regarding entry for business and residence, the practice of professions, the acquisition of property, patents, taxes, the remittance of earnings and capital, competition from state-owned enterprises, and expropriation or nationalization.[12] For OECD countries, the provisions of such treaties as to capital transfers have been largely superseded by the multilateral agreements mentioned. In the case of FCN Treaties with a developing country as one of the parties, it is difficult to evaluate how far they have had effects on freedom for external payments going beyond those resulting from obligations undertaken *vis-à-vis* the IMF, but any such effects have probably been fairly limited.

In section VII of the Keynes Plan, 'Proposals for an International Clearing Union', which treats the control of international capital movements, attention is drawn to the importance '(a) of distinguishing long-term loans by creditor countries, which help to maintain equilibrium and develop the world's resources, from movements of funds out of debtor countries which lack the means to finance them; and (b) of controlling

---

[12] The relevant provisions of FCN Treaties are surveyed in F. A. Mann, *The Legal Aspect of Money* (Oxford: Clarendon Press, 1982), 524–30.

short-term speculative movements or flights of currency whether out of debtor countries or from one creditor country to another'. The dividing line between non-speculative and speculative movements of international financing is not easy to draw, and the quotation above is open to the criticism that it omits shorter-term financing arrangements related to international trade. Nevertheless, thinking like that in the quotation left an imprint on the IMF's Articles of Agreement, and some kind of assumptions about the dividing line have since been an explicit or implicit part of the continuing debate about the desirability of, and modalities for implementing, capital controls.

The EEC/EU Regime

Until the second stage of economic and monetary union comes into force, the main features of the regime for capital movements in EEC countries are those prescribed by the June 1988 Council Directive on the subject.[13] This represented a substantial movement towards complete liberalization in comparison with earlier directives since the beginning of the 1960s. The revisions of the Treaty of Rome agreed at Maastricht in December 1991 reinforce this tendency. With the inception of the third stage of economic and monetary union, the countries adopting a single currency will have no further need for a regime covering international capital movements between each other, but there will still be such movements between this bloc and the rest of the world.

The 1988 Directive abolishes restrictions on capital movements between residents of EU countries subject only to provisos concerning the right to control short-term movements during periods of financial strain and to take the measures necessary for the proper functioning of systems of taxation, prudential supervision, and the provision of information for administrative purposes, as well as for law enforcement more generally. Moreover, measures directed at the regulation of banks' liquidity are to be limited to what is required for domestic monetary policy (a provision which considerably limits, if it does not actually eliminate, such regulation as part of policy towards international capital movements). The Directive also states that EEC countries should endeavour to attain the same degree of liberalization of capital movements with third countries as with the other countries of the Community.

The Directive acknowledges that short-term international capital movements may seriously disrupt the conduct of monetary and exchange-rate policies, 'even when there is no appreciable divergence [between countries] in economic fundamentals'. In such circumstances countries affected may

---

[13] See footnote 7 above.

be authorized by the Commission to take protective measures with regard to a specified list of capital transactions.[14] In sufficiently urgent cases they are permitted to take such action unilaterally, while at the same time initiating consultation procedures with the Commission and other EU countries. The Directive also provides for action, taken after consultation with other member countries, to counteract the effects of monetary and financial disturbances resulting from large short-term capital movements to or from third countries.

Prior to the 1988 Directive, the EEC regime for capital movements had involved prescriptions which provided governments with greater leeway for restricting different categories of transaction. According to Article 67 of the Treaty of Rome, 'During the transitional period and to the extent necessary to ensure the proper functioning of the common market, Member States shall progressively abolish between themselves all restrictions on the movement of capital belonging to persons in Member States and any discrimination based on the nationality or on the place of residence of the parties or on the place where such capital is invested.' Article 73 permitted the introduction of capital controls in response to disturbances in the functioning of an EEC country's capital market due to international capital movements. Articles 108 and 109 authorized the use of protective measures more generally by countries experiencing serious balance-of-payments difficulties.

More detailed guidelines as to the implementation of the EEC regime regarding capital movements was contained in two Directives of 1960 and 1962. These Directives divided international capital transactions into four categories, corresponding to four lists, with different liberalization obligations applying to each. A Directive of March 1972 actually required that EEC countries should have available and be able to use certain instruments of monetary policy required for the control of international capital movements and for the neutralization of their effects on domestic liquidity. These instruments included the following: rules governing investments on the money market and payment of interest on deposits by non-residents; the regulation of loans and credits which were not related to commercial transactions or to provision of services and were granted by non-residents to residents; the regulation of the net external positions of credit institutions; and the fixing of minimum reserve ratios, in particular for the holdings of non-residents. This Directive, which was adopted during the period of intermittent turbulence on currency markets in the early 1970s, was repealed as part

[14] The capital transactions included in the list are operations in money-market instruments, operations in current and deposit accounts with financial institutions, operations in units of collective investment undertakings for investment in money-market instruments, short-term financial loans and credits, personal capital movements in the form of loans, the physical import and export of money-market instruments and means of payment, and other miscellaneous short-term capital movements.

of the 1988 Directive on international capital movements discussed above.

It is not clear precisely what status the 1988 Directive will have with the beginning of the second stage of economic and monetary union in 1994. The Maastricht Treaty replaces Articles 67 to 73 of the Treaty of Rome with new Articles 73a to 73g, whose prescription of freedom of capital movements is less qualified. Thus Article 73b states that 'Within the framework of provisions set out in this Chapter [on capital and payments] all restrictions on the movement of capital between Member States and between Member States and third countries shall be prohibited.' There continue to be provisos concerning disruptive capital movements both between EU member and third countries (Article 73f) and more generally (Articles 109h and109i, which reproduce much of the language on the same subject contained in Articles 108 and 109 of the Treaty of Rome).

Once the third stage of economic and monetary unions starts, the safeguards provided for in Articles 109h and 109i cease to apply to countries moving to a single currency (though they continue for countries with a derogation from this movement); only Article 73f, regarding disruptive capital movements between EU and non-EU countries, will remain in force: 'Where, in exceptional circumstances, movements of capital to or from third countries cause, or threaten to cause, serious difficulties for the operation of economic and monetary union, the Council, acting by a qualified majority on a proposal from the Commission and after consulting the ECB [European Central Bank], may take safeguard measures with regard to third countries for a period not exceeding six months if such measures are strictly necessary.' Thus the circumstances in which measures can be taken are carefully circumscribed and the measures themselves are limited in time.

Policy Responses in some Developing Countries

At the beginning of the 1990s, legal regimes for foreign portfolio investment in developing countries typically reflected longer-term objectives; but as some countries in South and South-East Asia and in Latin America are increasingly incorporated into the global network of financial markets, they have experienced sharp increases in capital inflows with the result that there have been shifts in the focus of concern among policy makers. On the scale recently witnessed, such capital inflows can exercise significant upward pressure on the recipient country's exchange rate with potentially unfavourable consequences for its competitiveness and ability to attract foreign direct investment in sectors producing tradable goods and services. The monetary authority may take offsetting action through purchases of foreign currency. But this will generally be accompanied either by a rise in the money supply or, if this is unwanted, by an increase in government debt, which will have an adverse impact on the country's fiscal balance to the extent that the interest payments on such debt exceed interest receipts on the additional foreign reserves. Moreover, policy makers are only too aware that to the extent that the capital inflows are in volatile forms, they are easily subject to reversal, which can substantially complicate macro-economic management and at worst threaten economic stability.[15]

As a result, several of the recipient countries have had recourse to measures to restrict inflows, which have included various degrees of direct control as well as changes in incentives. For example, minimum conditions have been laid down for external bond and equity issues (Chile); limits have been placed on banks' liabilities in foreign currencies (Mexico) or on their short-term obligations to non-residents (Indonesia); and a queuing system has been implemented to slow external borrowing by private firms (Indonesia). Actions to reduce the profitability of foreign borrowing have comprised the imposition of special reserve requirements on almost all capital inflows (Chile); reductions in the availability, and increases in the cost, of swap facilities at the central bank (Chile, Indonesia); restriction to assets with a relatively low return of the positions which banks can finance with liabilities denominated in foreign currencies (Mexico); and the levying of a stamp tax on foreign credits (Chile). Financial outflows have been encouraged through the relaxation of restrictions on foreign investment by individuals and institutions such as pension funds, and on capital repatriation by foreign firms (Chile, Thailand). Moreover, risks to foreign lenders and portfolio investors have been increased by a widening of the bands within which exchange rates are permitted to fluctuate (Chile, Mexico).

These measures are unlikely to presage an end to the long-term trend among developing countries towards greater financial openness. Indeed, this could be reinforced by new international agreements such as that eventually reached at the Uruguay Round negotiations on financial services[16] or those resulting from a possible extension of NAFTA to other countries in Latin America.[17] But the counterpart of greater openness is likely to be

[15] This and the following paragraph summarizes the more extensive discussion in *Trade and Development Report, 1992* (United Nations Publication, Sales No. E.92.II.D.7), Part II, Annex II, and *Trade and Development Report, 1993* (United Nations Publication, Sales No. E.93.II.D.10), Part I, ch. III, sec. D, and Part II, ch. III, sec. C.4. They also draw on S. Schadler, M. Carkovic, A. Bennett, and R. Kahn, 'Recent experiences with surges in capital inflows', *IMF Occasional Paper 108* (Washington, D.C.: IMF, Dec. 1993), ch. IV.

[16] That part of these negotiations involving agreement by countries on their commitments with regard to their markets in financial services has not yet been completed and is currently scheduled to end in 1995.

[17] The provisions of NAFTA include the progressive removal of restrictions on market access for foreign financial institutions. Subject to limited qualifications, they also eliminate restrictions on capital transfers (thus going beyond obligations under IMF Article VIII). While the latter provisions do not involve additional obligations for Mexico, the former will lead to an opening-up of the country's financial sector. But, for possible future members of an

frequent recourse to measures designed to restrain capital inflows—and not just, as in the past, to check capital outflows—when this is seen to be necessary for macroeconomic management or to avoid deteriorations of international competitiveness. In taking such measures, developing countries would be following precedents set by OECD countries during the last thirty years as they progressively liberalized their regimes for international capital flows.

3. SOME PROPOSALS CONCERNING INTERNATIONAL CAPITAL MOVEMENTS

The intensity of discussion concerning policy towards international capital movements tends to vary with the most recent experience of the size of the movements themselves, typically being greatest in the aftermath of periods of international monetary turbulence. For instance, there has been the sharpened awareness in some developing countries of the problems which can be caused by such movements and the resulting policy responses. There has also been a revival of debate about international action. This is associated more with the continuing volatility in the markets for OECD currencies, especially those of EU countries, a phenomenon which is none the less also important to developing countries for various reasons. Macroeconomic policy responses to international capital movements on the part of OECD countries have repercussions for developing ones. Moreover, as the global network of financial markets expands, any internationally agreed measures to deal with capital movements will be effective only if they include some developing as well as OECD countries in their scope.

The debate about control has been accompanied by few ripples in the overall trend of policy in OECD countries which is still in the direction of liberalization. In the EU, the monetary turmoil in the autumn of 1992 did lead to the temporary imposition of controls by Spain. These initially (on 24 September) took the form of the introduction of compensatory one-year, non-interest-bearing deposits at the Bank of Spain against increments in open positions in foreign currencies and in peseta-denominated lending to non-residents, and of a rise to 100 per cent in the reserve-requirement ratio for increases in the peseta-denominated liabilities of resident financial institutions *vis-à-vis* their branches, subsidiaries, or parent companies abroad. These measures were revoked on 5 October and replaced by the imposition of compulsory non-interest-bearing deposits against increases in peseta lending to non-residents through foreign exchange swaps. Elsewhere in the EU, there was a tightening of the administration of the existing controls on

extended NAFTA, analogous provisions might require liberalization of their existing regimes in both areas.

capital movements in Ireland and Portugal. However, the Spanish controls were abolished on 24 November, and remaining exchange controls in Ireland and Portugal were removed in December.

Another period of speculative pressures in the currency markets during the summer of 1993 led to a decision by EU finance ministers to increase the bands for currency fluctuations in the Exchange Rate Mechanism (ERM) to plus or minus 15 per cent around the central rate. (Implicit in this decision was rejection of recourse to measures controlling capital movements more directly.) However, the countries still belonging to the ERM have made at most limited use of the greater freedom for monetary policy provided by the widened bands and appear to be continuing to treat Germany as the point of reference in this regard.[18] Moreover, the provisions of the Maastricht Treaty concerning both capital movements and monetary union remain in place.

Recent debate has been concerned both with the narrower issue of the regime for exchange rates within the EU during the interim before monetary union, and with arrangements that would reduce the effects of speculative pressures on the currencies of other OECD countries. While monetary union itself would serve the purpose of eliminating problems due to the volatility of the relative exchange rates of participant countries' currencies, whether transition to it can be successfully managed without measures designed to control capital movements directly remains open to question. For the OECD as a whole, not to mention non-OECD countries, monetary union is not a feasible solution to problems caused by international capital movements. Some of the policy options discussed in this context would entail improved policy coordination or policy convergence. Others (which are the principal subject of the remainder of this chapter) would involve more direct intervention in the operations of actors in the currency markets. The latter proposals reflect the belief that the benefits of considerable freedom for capital movements overall can be maintained in a system where the disincentives to speculation are increased.

---

[18] As Sir Leon Brittan, EU Trade Commissioner, put it ('A Europe that deserves support', *Financial Times*, 29 March 1994), 'Far from exploiting their monetary freedom after the crisis, most EU countries have followed fiscal and monetary policies consistent with the approach laid down in Maastricht. In fact they have not used the greater freedom given to them by the wider band in the revised ERM.' Comparison of figures for the average values of ERM currencies in terms of the Deutschmark during periods before and after the widening of currency bands at the beginning of August 1993 are instructive as to the effects of these self-imposed limitations. On average, between the periods Jan.–July 1993 and Aug. 1993–Jan. 1994 the French franc depreciated 2.4% and the Belgian and Luxemburg franc 3.1%, while the Netherlands guilder actually appreciated 0.1%. The Irish pound was devalued within the ERM in Jan. 1993, and on average between Feb.–July 1993 and Aug. 1993–Jan. 1994 it depreciated 1.8%. The Spanish peseta and the Portuguese escudo were devalued in the ERM in May 1993, and on average between June–July 1993 and Aug. 1993–Jan. 1994 depreciated 4.8% and 6.1% respectively. (The series for ERM exchange rates are from Deutsche Bundesbank, *Monthly Report*, Feb. 1994, 92).

Monetary Union

Countries can avoid the problems caused by international capital markets by forming a monetary union, thus fixing their mutual exchange rates for good. As already indicated, this is the solution to which the EU remains committed under the Maastricht Treaty, although the recent monetary turbulence is likely to affect the timetable for its implementation, pushing it further into the future.[19] The establishment of the union will not eliminate capital movements among its member countries, but thereafter unfavourable consequences will have to be handled by means of policy instruments analogous to those available to national governments for off-setting the undesired effects of monetary movements between the constituent regions of their countries. The single currency of the monetary union can be expected to become one of the world's major currencies, and the union will incorporate a number of major financial centres. Thus periodic pressures on the single currency are likely as a result of capital movements between the union and outside countries. This possibility is acknowledged in the text of the Maastricht Treaty, which provides that safeguard measures (of a rather limited character) may be taken in circumstances where such capital movements are a source of serious difficulties for the operation of the union. This possibility also means that measures to restrain international capital movements will still be of interest to policy makers in EU countries of an eventual monetary union after it is in place.

During the transition to monetary union, the Maastricht Treaty provides member countries of the EU with rather greater latitude for action to deal with disruptive capital movements. But it is questionable whether the criteria of economic convergence, which must be met if countries are to qualify as members of the union, can be attained in the face of destabilizing capital movements through sole recourse to the traditional instruments of macroeconomic policy. Three of the convergence criteria relate to the stability of exchange rates, the permissible deviation of interest rates from a benchmark, and the avoidance of excessive government deficits.[20] The condition for qualification regarding exchange rates is that a country must have respected the normal fluctuations margins of the ERM (i.e. those of plus or minus 2.25 per cent around central rates) without severe tensions for at least two years. Moreover, it must not have devalued its bilateral central rate against any other EU member country's currency on its own initiative

[19] Under Article 109j of the Maastricht Treaty a decision on the establishment of monetary union may be taken as early as the end of 1996. The latest date envisaged for its establishment is the beginning of 1999.

[20] See Article 109j and Protocol on the Convergence Criteria referred to in Article 109j of the Treaty Establishing the European Community.

during the same period. As to interest rates, the condition is that a country must have had an average nominal long-term rate not exceeding by more than two percentage points that of, at most, the three member countries of the EU with the best performance in terms of price stability. Regarding government deficits there are two conditions (subject to certain qualifications), firstly, that the ratio of the planned or actual government deficit to GDP at market prices should not exceed 3 per cent and, secondly, that the ratio of government debt to GDP at market prices should not exceed 60 per cent.[21]

In the event of severe downward pressure on its exchange rate these convergence criteria may present an EU country with policy dilemmas. Its currency must be kept within the normal fluctuation margins, and devaluation of the central rate is excluded. However, raising short-term interest rates, a traditional policy response in such a situation, may result in failure to meet the convergence criterion for this variable if this step also leads to a sufficiently large rise in long-term interest rates. Moreover the rise in interest rates, through the resulting increase in the government's debt-service obligations and the deterioration in its fiscal balance due to deflation, may also threaten the country's ability to meet the convergence criterion regarding excessive deficits. On the other hand, repeated or extended recourse to Article 109i of the Maastricht Treaty, which during the transition to monetary union allows for action limited in scope and time to safeguard a country's external payments position, might well be considered a failure to avoid severe exchange-rate tensions and thus also to be contrary to the convergence criterion for the exchange rate. Thus success in the qualification process for membership of the monetary union might be possible only if a country were permanently to maintain measures to restrain speculative capital movements during the transition. At a minimum such success could well be facilitated by measures of this kind.

Macroeconomic Policies

Two much discussed approaches to reducing speculative international capital movements and the resulting disorder in currency markets would rely largely on macroeconomic policies. One approach, which has been espoused by the UNCTAD secretariat, would achieve this objective as one consequence of policies designed to achieve better management of global macroeconomic interdependence.[22] These policies would aim, not only at reducing the volatility of exchange and interest rates, but also at achieving

---

[21] Article 104c and Protocol on the Excessive Deficit Procedure.
[22] *Trade and Development Report, 1990* (United Nations Publication, Sales No. E.90.II.D.6), IX to XII and Part II, ch. I, sec. D.

a sustainable pattern among countries of external payments positions and the avoidance of inflationary or deflationary bias in the combined impact of policy stances. This approach would entail a commitment by governments to defend a publicly announced pattern of exchange rates which had been internationally agreed and which was compatible with high levels of activity and employment, together with strengthened multilateral surveillance of the policies of major OECD countries with the objective of ensuring their consistency with the targets set for major macroeconomic variables. The macroeconomic policies would be reinforced by more microeconomic tax and prudential measures intended to exert their influence at the level of transactions and the management of financial institutions (such as those discussed in the next section). This approach would entail more binding policy commitments and tighter surveillance than the series of agreements and declarations concerning policy coordination of the major industrial countries in 1985–7.[23] It would also require that more account be taken of the effects of policies on countries other than the major industrial ones, including developing ones.

Another approach, recently articulated in studies of international macroeconomic developments by the IMF and the OECD,[24] would give primacy, as a way of attaining currency stability to convergence of macroeconomic policies and economic performance in major OECD countries. The advantage of this approach according to its proponents is that it does not require the extensive policy coordination which recent experience shows to be a difficult goal to achieve. Proponents of this second approach are primarily concerned with setting targets for price stability and fiscal deficits; thinking along these lines underlies the convergence criteria under the Maastricht Treaty, which EU countries are to meet if they are to qualify for membership of the monetary union.

It is doubtful whether attempts by EU countries to achieve such convergence solely through reliance on the traditional instruments of macroeconomic policy are likely to succeed. Moreover it is difficult to conceive of extending to the United States, Japan, and Canada agreement on convergence targets similar to those in the Maastricht Treaty. Especially in conditions like the present of continuing stagnation or low economic growth in the OECD area, efforts to attain convergence targets that emphasize low inflation and fiscal equilibrium can be expected to be a source of global deflationary pressure.

As mentioned earlier, the more microeconomic measures for curbing cur-

---

[23] E.g. the Plaza Accord of Sept. 1985, the Tokyo Economic Declaration of May 1986, the Louvre Accord of Feb. 1987, and the Venice Economic Declaration of June 1987.

[24] See e.g. IMF, 'World Economic Outlook Interim Assessment January 1993', *World Economic and Financial Surveys* (Washington, D.C.: IMF, 1993), 19–27, and *OECD Economic Outlook*, 53, (Paris: OECD, June 1993), 31–6.

rency speculation which are the subject of the remainder of this chapter were proposed in outline by the UNCTAD secretariat in *Trade and Development Report, 1990* as the complement of the macroeconomic policies contained in its package for better management of global interdependence. Consideration of the microeconomic measures in isolation should not be taken to imply that effects which they might have on speculation would not be greatly strengthened by appropriate macroeconomic action. Nor should it be assumed that international agreement on the transactions-tax component of these measures would necessarily be easier than on the macroeconomic constituents of UNCTAD's proposed package, though in the case of the regulations concerning banks' exposure to foreign exchange risk, as is discussed below, progress towards such agreement has already been made. However, much less attention has been paid to such microeconomic measures in debate concerning global monetary stability. Moreover it can be argued that they would contribute to such stability under regimes for global macroeconomic policies different from that in the UNCTAD package.

A Tax on Foreign-Exchange Transactions

The proposal for a tax on foreign exchange transactions seems to draw its original inspiration from a passage in Keynes's *The General Theory of Employment, Interest and Money*, in which he suggested that the relatively lesser importance of speculative transactions in stocks in London than New York was due to the greater costs in the former, made up of the jobber's 'turn', high brokerage charges, and a heavy transfer tax. In this vein he went on to suggest, 'The introduction of a substantial Government transfer tax on all transactions might prove the most serviceable reform available, with a view to mitigating the predominance of speculation over enterprise in the United States.'[25] Since the late 1970s there has been a revival of interest in such a tax on transactions not only in stocks but also in foreign exchange.[26] However, the detailed discussion has been concerned mainly with the version for stocks.

[25] J. M. Keynes, *The General Theory of Employment, Interest and Money* (London: Macmillan, 1960), 160.

[26] A tax on transactions in stocks is discussed in a series of articles in *Journal of Financial Services Research*, 3, 1989: R. Roll, 'Price Volatility, International Market Links, and Their Implications for Regulatory Policies', esp. 233–4; S. A. Ross, 'Commentary: Using Tax Policy to Curb Speculative Short-Term Trading'; J. E. Stiglitz, 'Using Tax Policy to Curb Speculative Short-Term Trading'; and L. H. Summers and V. P. Summers, 'When Financial Markets Work Too Well: A Cautious Case for a Securities Transactions Tax' (275–85 of which deal fairly extensively with problems of implementing such a tax in practice). Without going into much detail James Tobin proposed a tax on foreign exchange transactions in his paper, 'A Proposal for International Monetary Reform', *The Eastern Economic Journal*, July/Oct. 1978, 155–9. See also D. Felix, 'Suggestions for International Collaboration to Reduce Destabilizing

The underlying motivation for a tax on foreign exchange transactions is the same as in Keynes's proposal, namely reduction of incentives to speculation. Proponents also believe that if the profitability of currency trading were reduced by such a tax, the activity would be the focus of less innovation as to new techniques and contracts (innovation which, they argue, is of limited benefit to society as a whole as opposed to the financial sector), and would attract fewer well-qualified people.[27] In the absence of experience as to a transactions tax's effectiveness in restraining speculation in the markets for widely used currencies of OECD countries (in contrast to those of certain developing ones), the attention which the proposal attracts is due to the lack of plausible alternative solutions to this problem which are not of an emergency character (once the reimposition of direct controls over capital movements is excluded).[28] However, even if adoption of the proposal led to a dampening of speculation, occasional periods of serious turbulence in currency markets could still be expected to occur, during which a transactions tax at the rate envisaged would not be effective in offsetting the short-term profits for traders successfully calling large movements in exchange rates.[29] During such periods, recourse to more draconian measures would often continue to be necessary.

There are several problems regarding the design and implementation of a foreign-exchange transactions tax. Perhaps most importantly, the tax would require agreement to impose it among all countries with significant financial centres. Otherwise, foreign exchange business would be transferred to those where the tax did not apply.[30] Such an agreement would

Effects of International Capital Mobility on the Developing Countries' in *International Monetary and Financial Issues for the 1990s. Research Papers for the Group of Twenty-Four. Vol. III* (New York: United Nations, 1993), 56–8, which is primarily concerned with the benefits of a foreign-exchange transactions tax for developing countries.

[27] This point is made for financial markets more generally by James Tobin in his Fred Hirsch Memorial Lecture, 'On the efficiency of the financial system', *Lloyds Bank Review*, 153, July 1984, 14–15.

[28] As two commentators on recent currency disorder in the EU put it, 'These measures have disadvantages. . . . But it is not enough for critics to point to their disadvantages. They must offer an alternative. And they must show that their alternative is feasible.' B. Eichengreen and C. Wyplosz, 'The Unstable EMS', *Brookings Papers on Economic Activity*, 1, 1993, 121.

[29] If transactions in such cases were undertaken in the expectation of profiting from a movement in exchange rates over the period of a month, for example, translation of the expected rate of profit to an annual basis would involve multiplication of the monthly figure by 12. Such a figure explains the exceptionally high interest rates, sometimes of several hundred % per annum, often used to defend currencies during exchange crises. Estimating the effect of the tax on the profitability of each such transaction would also require multiplication of the tax rate by 12. However, even so, a uniform tax of 1% of the value of transactions (Tobin's proposal) would usually offset only part of the expected movements in currency prices in the sort of situation being discussed here.

[30] An analogous argument has proved a telling political weapon in the hands of opponents of a transactions tax applying to the Chicago markets for commodity futures and other derivative contracts. D. Greising and L. Morse, *Brokers, Bagmen and Moles. Fraud and Corruption in the Chicago Futures Markets* (New York: John Wiley and Sons, 1991), 65–6 and 141.

have to cover not only OECD countries but also offshore financial centres. Moreover, as new financial centres emerge in developing countries, these too would have to be brought on board.

A second problem is which agents and transactions should be subject to the tax. With regard to the coverage of agents, it can be argued that a tax applying to banks as well as to non-financial actors in the currency markets would not only 'throw sand in the wheels of speculation' but also increase the costs to banks of operations necessary to the provision of a service required for the non-financial, non-speculative business of international trade and investment. Typically, banks undertake a number of other foreign exchange transactions among themselves for every one with a non-financial customer as part of the process of laying off the risks of assuming an open position and of price discovery.[31] As to the coverage of transactions the situation is complicated by the variety of different instruments available to economic actors for taking positions which involve current and future receipts and payments of foreign exchange.

Concerning arguments over the imposition of a foreign-exchange transactions tax on banks, various points should be considered. In the first place the fact that banks do provide the foreign-exchange service for international business is not a decisive argument in itself against subjecting them to a transactions tax. There is no a priori reason why any economic activity should be exempt from taxation in all circumstances, and postwar tariff-cutting exercises have greatly lowered taxes on international trade. Moreover, while non-banks have been a major source of speculative pressures in currency markets, banks also often assume open positions in these markets and their foreign-exchange trading can be an important source of profits (and of losses). Nevertheless, there are other proposals for reducing foreign-exchange speculation by banks less open to the objection that they raise the costs of services required by non-financial activities. Such measures involve regulations regarding banks' operations and the management of their balance sheets. If banks were exempted from the transactions tax and subjected to some alternative regime, there would need to be a definition of the institutions to which this exemption would apply. Such a definition is particularly important at a time when the distinction between banks in the traditional sense and other institutions providing various financial services is becoming less clear-cut. A solution to this problem would be to limit the number of institutions permitted under their charter to participate in the interbank market in foreign exchange, and to grant the exemption from the tax only to institutions having such permission.

As for the question of the transactions to which the tax should apply,

---

[31] Price discovery refers to the process whereby the prices of foreign exchange (or of other contracts in the markets for financial instruments and commodities) transmit information concerning the current consensus of opinion as to the relative strengths of supply and demand.

these should include not only spot and forward transactions and foreign-exchange swaps (which combine the two) but also other contracts involving the obligation or right to exchange currencies at a future date. Thus the tax should cover spot transactions, outright forwards, foreign-exchange swaps, futures, and options.[32] Each of the first four of these categories of transaction is obviously capable of moving spot or forward exchange rates. But it might be argued that trading foreign exchange options does not exert direct pressure in the currency markets, since the contracts in question only confer the right to buy or sell currencies at a pre-set exchange rate. However, if options were not covered by the tax, they could increasingly be used as a vehicle through which traders could put themselves in the position to make large speculative purchases and sales of currencies capable of causing significant movements of exchange rates.[33] Such considerations seem to argue for inclusion of options, when exercised, in the scope of the tax.

As already noted, positions in foreign exchange can be taken via several different financial instruments. However, even in the case of some not covered in the previous paragraph, the transactions which the instruments entail often require the exchange of currencies and would thus not escape the tax. For example, cross-currency swaps or cross-currency interest-rate

[32] In a spot transaction in foreign exchange the two parties agree to exchange two currencies within two business days. Forward transactions are of two kinds, outright forwards, and swaps. An outright forward transaction involves an agreement by two parties to exchange two currencies more than two business days hence. Maturities can vary from a few days to several months (or even, much less frequently, to more than a year). Foreign exchange swaps have two separate legs, one consisting of the sale or purchase of a foreign currency and the other of a repurchase or resale of the currency at a future date (thus reversing the first leg). The initial leg is usually a spot sale or purchase but can also refer to a future date, in which case the transaction is called a forward/forward. Many outright forwards involve non-financial customers on one side of the transaction, while swap transactions take place mainly between banks. The two legs of a swap are part of a single agreement and are priced accordingly, transaction costs being lower than for the corresponding spot and forward purchases or sales undertaken separately. (Other categories of swap, some of them relevant in the context of the proposal for a tax on foreign-exchange transactions, are described below.) Futures are exchange-traded contracts specifying delivery of currencies at a specified price at a future date. Both the amounts in the contract and the delivery dates are standardized. Options are contracts giving the purchaser the right (but without any obligation) to buy or sell a certain amount of currency in the future at a pre-set exchange rate. Options may be exchange-traded, in which case the contracts are standardized (as for futures); or they may be sold over-the-counter, in which case contracts can be customized. According to a recent survey of the Bank for International Settlements (*Central Bank Survey of Foreign Exchange Market Activity in April 1992* (Basle, March 1993), table V) spot transactions accounted for 47 to 49% of activity in the foreign exchange market (the share varying according to the basis of measurement), outright forwards for 6 to 7%, swaps for 39 to 40%, futures for 1%, and options for 4 to 5%.

[33] It is of some interest in this context that historically commodity options trading was on occasion accused of disrupting spot and futures markets in the same underlying product. This concern resulted in a ban on trading in several commodity options under the Commodity Exchange Act of 1936 in the United States. See e.g. the brief account in R. J. Teweles, C. V. Harlow, and H. L. Stone, *The Commodity Futures Game. Who Wins? Who Loses? Why?* (New York: McGraw-Hill Book Company, 1974), 228–9.

swaps[34] involve the swapping by two parties of streams of payments in different currencies. So long as such payments are not subject to complete netting, each involves an exchange of currencies and would be covered by the tax. But coverage would not necessarily apply to all the instruments which can serve as vehicles for taking positions in foreign currencies. For example, back-to-back and parallel loans[35] have long been used by companies to get round impediments to their access to a currency or regulations increasing its cost. Under such arrangements, one company lends its country's currency either to another company or to another company's subsidiary in return for an öffsetting loan in the borrower's currency for itself or one of its own subsidiaries. Such transactions do not require an exchange of currencies. However, they do not seem especially well suited to short-term speculation, in part because the agreements frequently contain topping-up clauses under which one party compensates the other for the effects of unfavourable movements in the exchange rate for the two currencies during the period of the loan.

The examples given here are far from exhaustive, and in the event that a tax on foreign exchange transactions were imposed, new instruments or contracts would be likely to be devised or existing ones to be adjusted with the objective of evading the tax or reducing the amounts paid. It would be difficult to design the tax in such a way that it contained safeguards against all such eventualities. A more reasonable approach would be to accept the need for alteration in the tax's design if the new or adjusted instruments seriously threatened its effectiveness.

Other problems, which are beyond the scope of this chapter, relate to the modalities of the tax. For example, the design of the tax would need to take account of several features of interbank transactions if these were to be subject to it. (Indeed, the resulting complications constitute a further argument for exempting interbank transactions in foreign exchange from the tax.) Moreover the modalities must include the valuation of different categories of transaction involving commitments to currency exchanges in the future as opposed to currently, and the timing of its payment in such cases—whether, for example, the payment of the tax should take place at the initial entry into the commitment or at maturity. Another question under this heading would be the treatment under the tax of netting arrangements

[34] Terminology is not uniform with regard to different categories of swap transaction. Cross-currency swaps sometimes refer to agreements to exchange two currencies at the current exchange rate and to reverse the transaction at a future date. But sometimes the term is also used in the case of transactions involving the swapping of the interest payments as well as the principal of loans denominated in different currencies. The latter transactions are also denoted as cross-currency interest rate swaps.

[35] Back-to-back and parallel loans were used e.g. by British and United States companies before 1979 to enable the former to avoid purchasing dollars for the financing of their United States subsidiaries at the less favourable exchange rate prevailing in the market for investment currency under the exchange controls of the United Kingdom.

which could be used to reduce the amount of currencies actually exchanged in the case of some transactions.[36] And so on.

Bank Regulation and Currency Trading

Among the alternatives to a foreign exchange transactions tax as a vehicle for reducing banks' participation in currency speculation, one would be the requirement to make non-interest-bearing deposits corresponding to increases in open positions in foreign exchange. Such a measure was deployed by the Spanish government in the autumn of 1992. Since it applies to balance-sheet positions, it can be imposed in such a way as to serve as a tax on speculation without being open to the objection that, through its incidence on individual interbank transactions, it raises banks' costs of providing a foreign exchange service for international trade and long-term international investment.

Another approach would be to impose capital charges on banks' open positions in foreign exchange. As in the case of the transactions tax, international agreement would be necessary on the adoption of the measure by all countries with significant banking centres, so as to avoid the danger that foreign exchange business would move to countries where the regulations did not apply. This approach has the advantage of relying on regulations analogous to those already proposed as part of the current initiative of the Basle Committee on Banking Supervision[37] concerning standards for the supervision of banks' market risks including those due to their positions in foreign exchange.[38] Although this initiative is more narrowly directed at objectives regarding the prudential supervision of banks, it would none the less cover the very transactions through which banks can engage in currency speculation.

The regulation of banks' foreign exchange exposure in the major OECD countries is far from uniform. The specification of the contents of such regulation in banking law is much more detailed in some of these countries than in others. However, even in the latter the supervisory authorities can generally be expected to subject banks' management of their foreign

---

[36] Under such arrangements payments between parties are made only of sums due after a mutual offsetting of obligations.

[37] The Basle Committee on Banking Supervision (originally named the Basle Committee on Banking Regulation and Supervisory Practices) was established in the mid-1970s to improve standards of supervision for international banks. Its member countries are Belgium, Canada, France, Germany, Italy, Japan, Luxembourg, Netherlands, Sweden, Switzerland, United Kingdom, and United States. The work of the Committee between its inception and mid-1992 is surveyed in Andrew Cornford, 'The Role of the Basle Committee on Banking Supervision in the Regulation of International Banking', *UNCTAD Discussion Paper No. 68* (Sept. 1993).

[38] The guidelines under discussion are set out in the paper, 'The Supervisory Treatment of Market Risks. Consultative Proposal by the Basle Committee on Banking Supervision' (Basle, Apr. 1993).

exchange exposure to careful scrutiny, whilst, in the former, supervision in practice may also include matters not expressly mentioned in the relevant legislation. This variation is illustrated in a recent survey of banking regulation in seven OECD countries,[39] which shows that in four of them (Germany, France, United Kingdom, and Japan), for example, explicit provisions of regulations as to foreign exchange exposure emphasize levels of capital required in relation to open positions, whilst in another (Canada) they specify the minimum ratio of liabilities to assets in Canadian dollars for the subsidiaries of foreign banks.

Formal regulations concerning foreign exchange exposure are frequently of a fairly aggregate character. Within the limits laid down in them, banks may thus be permitted to assume substantial net open positions for different currencies or for different maturities in a given currency. For example, a small net overall open position for a currency is compatible with much larger net open long and short positions for individual current and future months.[40] Thus a bank with a small net overall open position might none the less be susceptible to significant profits and losses in response to changes in relative forward exchange rates. Consequently, many banks adopt mismatch limits for internal use going beyond those specified in their countries' regulatory regimes.

The initiative of the Basle Committee is a response to this lack of uniformity. As in other areas of its work, the Committee's objectives are the establishment of minimum supervisory standards both for prudential reasons and to eliminate the unfair competitive advantages that may accrue to banks subject to laxer regulatory regimes. The emphasis of the Basle Committee on capital requirements against positions involving market risk rather than the prescription of limits on such positions reflects its preference for enabling banks to retain flexibility in their financial management by giving them the opportunity to allocate their capital amongst different activities on the basis of their assessment of profiles of risk and return. In the Committee's view this approach also gives banks additional incentives to use hedging techniques, while providing 'a prudent capital cushion' for possible losses. However, the Committee supports the use by supervisory

---

[39] I. Swary and B. Topf, *Global Financial Deregulation. Commercial Banking at the Crossroads* (Cambridge, Mass.: Blackwell Publishers, 1992), which includes country surveys of Canada, France, Germany, Japan, Switzerland, the United Kingdom, and the United States.

[40] This would be reflected in a bank's exchange ladder, a management tool which shows receipts and sales of a currency for the current and future months resulting from spot and future purchases and sales. Large net open, long or short positions for particular months, resulting from the excess of receipts over outgoings of the currency or vice versa, can to a significant extent offset each other across different maturities, thus giving a relatively small overall net open position. Profits and losses in response to movements of exchange rates are calculated by multiplying the net open position for each maturity by the appropriate new exchange rate. The detailed arithmetic is discussed e.g. in J. Walmsley, *The Foreign Exchange and Money Markets Guide* (New York: John Wiley and Sons, 1992), 439–42.

authorities of limits as well as capital requirements in banks' treatment of market risk if they consider that such additional controls are necessary.

The Basle Committee's proposal begins with a specification of methods for measuring banks' exposure due to different categories of currency transaction (as well as to transactions in precious metals, which it regards as closely related to those in foreign exchange). The actual capital requirements would be based on either of two alternative approaches. Under the first, 'the shorthand method', the requirement would be 8 per cent of a net open position consisting of the greater of the sum of short or long positions in different currencies plus the total of each net position (short or long) in precious metals, regardless of sign.[41] Under the second approach, 'the simulation method', the capital requirement would be set in relation to the worst or near-to-the worst loss which, it is estimated according to a simulation based on the behaviour of exchange rates during some past period, could result from a bank's foreign exchange exposure. The Committee proposes that the capital requirements should apply as at the close of each business day.[42]

This would still leave banks some leeway for speculation, and in the aftermath of the recent currency crises in the EU more stringent measures have been proposed. One idea is that the capital requirements should apply not just at the end of business days but also continuously throughout them.[43] In view of the difficulty of controlling exposure precisely from moment to moment, this proposal would mean that in practice banks would need to maintain levels of capital against their foreign exchange positions significantly in excess of prescribed minima.[44]

Continuously applied capital requirements would raise the cost to banks of functioning throughout the business day as market makers in foreign

[41] The same approach to the management of foreign exchange risk is included in the proposed Directive on capital adequacy for member countries of the EU. For the 1992 version of this proposed Directive see 'Amended Proposal for a Council Directive on Capital Adequacy of Investment Firms and Credit Institutions' (92/C50/05), reproduced in the *Official Journal of the European Communities*, 25 Feb. 1992.

[42] The Basle Committee draws attention in its consultative document to the opportunities for banks with entities in different time zones to engage in intra-group transactions designed to evade regulations limiting open positions in foreign exchange at the close of business. ('The Supervisory Treatment of Market Risks', para. 24.) Such opportunities accentuate the need for international agreement among countries with financial centres on the application of capital requirements against open foreign exchange positions. (Examples of the exploitation of such opportunities by a major international bank are given in R. Dale, *The Regulation of International Banking* (Cambridge: Woodhead-Faulkner, 1984), App. 2.)

[43] This proposal is attributed to Javier Alonso, an official of the Bank of Spain, in D. Shirreff, 'Can Anyone Tame the Currency Market', *Euromoney*, Sept. 1993, 60.

[44] The capital requirements for securities firms in the United States which apply on a continuous basis have this effect. E.g. at the end of 1986 16 such firms reported average net capital 7.3 times larger than minimum legal requirements. G. Haberman, 'Capital Requirements of Commercial and Investment Banks: Contrasts in Regulation', *Federal Reserve Bank of New York Quarterly Review*, Autumn 1987, 6.

exchange. Market makers are willing to buy and sell at quoted prices (a bid price for buying and an offer or asked price for selling), if necessary taking net long or short positions in a currency since orders to buy and sell are not continuously balancing. This function is generally credited with contributing to the smooth functioning of the currency markets, in particular by reducing the volatility of prices. If performance of the function were to become more costly as a result of continuously applied capital requirements, banks could be expected to increase their spreads between bid and offer prices, thus raising the costs of interbank foreign-exchange transactions (and by extension those of providing foreign exchange services to the non-financial sector). Without pertinent experience, the size of the latter increase is difficult to forecast but could be expected to be small in comparison to that which would result from the application of a transactions tax to interbank foreign exchange transactions as well as to those between banks and non-bank entities.

Other proposals intermediate between that of the Basle Committee and continuously applied capital requirements can also be envisaged. For example, banks could assume open positions within specified limits without becoming subject to such requirements. But agreement would probably be difficult on limits which provided banks with the desired degree of flexibility in their foreign exchange operations, while also effectively reducing speculation. Alternatively, it might be argued that consultations on the Basle Committee's initiative have their own momentum and would be greatly complicated by attempts to extend it so as to become a more stringent restraint on currency speculation. Then, if, after eventual experience of the application of the Basle Committee's initiative in practice, such restraint still seemed necessary, continuously applied capital requirements might contribute to achieving it.

Proposals and Existing Regimes

For developing countries, the main regime for international payments to which the great majority is subject is that of the IMF. The IMF's Articles of Agreement are concerned primarily with payments for current transactions, leaving governments great latitude regarding the regulation of international capital transactions. Thus measures such as those recently taken by developing countries are not in conflict with their international obligations, and this would equally be true of recourse by such countries to taxes or other measures for the purpose of restraining capital movements on a permanent or quasi-permanent basis rather than as a shorter-term response to external payments pressures.[45]

[45] Some of this freedom may be lost by Latin American countries which are covered by any eventual expanded version of the North Atlantic Free Trade Area (NAFTA). See note 32.

The obligations of OECD countries in this area are more constraining. The OECD Code of Liberalization of Capital Movements is incompatible with direct limitation or restriction of international capital movements except in circumstances covered by its provisions for derogations. Nevertheless, the Code seems compatible with measures designed to restrain capital transactions by broad, non-discriminatory increases in the costs of those engaging in them. This would appear to be true of both the transactions tax and the capital requirements against net open foreign exchange positions for banks described above. But the compatibility of the transactions tax with the obligations of EU countries under relevant Directives and the Maastricht Treaty is less assured. These obligations permit protective measures of a short-term nature in response to the disruptive effects of international capital movements in certain circumstances. But a transactions tax adopted on a more permanent basis, even though its incidence was non-discriminatory, might not be acceptable. As for capital requirements for banks' net open positions in foreign exchange, these are actually part of the EU's own programme for the harmonization of banking regulations in its member countries. Thus it seems reasonable also to assume that any eventual recourse to a more stringent version of such requirements to restrain currency speculation would be consistent with obligations under the 1988 Directive on capital movements and the Maastricht Treaty.

Part III

International Finance and Exchange Rate Policy

8. International Financial Markets and National Transmission Mechanisms

Laurence Harris

Fifty years ago, as the postwar period began, financial markets were weak and, above all, fragmented. The national financial systems of the large capitalist economies were relatively self-contained, separated by, among other things, foreign exchange controls, government restrictions on financial institutions' balance sheets, restrictions on competition, administered interest rates, and distinct fiscal and legal systems. The self-contained character of national financial systems (extending to their currency blocs in the case of the Sterling Area, Franc Zone) was the basis for the Keynesian demand management policies of national governments.

From the beginning, however, that fragmentation was being overcome partly by official policy (especially the moves to convertibility attempted as early as 1947) and partly by market forces, the growth of uncontrolled banking centres in Asia and elsewhere, which, through arbitrage between currency blocs, profited from gaps in exchange controls. The growth and transformation of Eurocurrency markets in the 1970s, and the demolition of national controls in the 1980s, dramatically accelerated the process by which financial markets in all major currencies and countries have become fully integrated with each other; a development strengthened by innovations in both information technology and financial instruments. That integration of financial markets across national boundaries is one pillar of the globalization of finance and, in contrast to the national system's Keynesianism has given rise to what Juliet Schor calls 'global neoclassicism'.[1]

The essence of 'global neoclassicism' is that financial globalization subordinates national economies to international markets, and one variant or another of that view commands wide support. A basic version is the principle of uncovered interest parity which anchors simple exchange rate and balance of payments models; it formalizes the casual understanding that interest rates in any one country more or less follow world rates, or follow interest rates in a lead country (the US, Germany, or Japan). In more wide-

---

[1] J. B. Schor, 'Introduction' in T. Banuri and J. B. Schor, *Financial Openness and National Autonomy: Opportunities and Constraints* (Oxford: Clarendon Press, 1992), 4.

ranging versions, the linkage between national and global conditions
extends beyond interest rates: 'Interest rates, profit rates, wage rates, and
commodity prices will equalize across borders. A country deviates from the
logic of the world market at its peril.'[2]

The globalization of finance, which increases the tendency towards equalization of rates of return on financial assets, is judged differently according
to the standpoint. From the global neoclassicism perspective, it is a wel-
come increase in the ability of markets to allocate capital efficiently; in theories of economic policy which give national states a role, it raises the
question of whether the state retains any power over domestic economic
policy;[3] from the point of view of financial markets and regulators, the
focus is on the risks for economic activity posed by the new systemic risks
of global financial markets. From any of those standpoints, the significance
of financial globalization lies in its potential impact upon real economic
activity. Surprisingly, however, the literature on the effect of financial globalization pays little attention to the transmission mechanism through which
its 'real economy' impact may be exerted.

In this chapter, I focus on the transmission mechanisms linking international financial markets to real economic activity and discuss their relevance for the question of how far financial globalization does prevent
national states from determining economic conditions. Focusing on three
elements in those links, I argue that the transmission mechanisms are complex and contain potentially weak links. Consequently, although the globalization of finance does restrict the national states' autonomy in policy,
they do retain considerable ability to influence the domestic economy
through their policy choices. That conclusion stands in contrast to an
extreme view which sees today's global financial markets as wholly determining conditions in each country. For the advocates of 'global neoclassicism' such determinism has underpinned the monetarist political evasion of
'there is no alternative'; for Keynesians the same determinism leads to pessimism or to proposals for direct controls as an all-or-nothing solution; and
from any perspective the idea that global financial markets reign supreme
implies that, as long as they do, there is no reason for citizens following an
economic calculus to vote for one party or another.

I begin by outlining the way in which the transmission mechanism
between financial and real variables is significant for understanding the
effect of globalization. The definition of the problem is followed by a discussion of evidence on one, frequently neglected element of the transmission mechanism, stock markets; to what extent and in what ways has

---

[2] Schor, 'Introduction', 4.
[3] T. Banuri and J. B. Schor, *Financial Openness and National Autonomy*; L. Harris,
'Financial Integration and Economic Policy in Europe' in F. Brouwer, V. Lintner, and M.
Newman, *Economic Policy Making and the European Union* (London: Federal Trust 1994).

financial globalization caused convergence in stock market behaviour? The next step is to consider the role of liquidity constraints and the impact integration of financial markets has on internationalization of real capital. Finally, I discuss the relationship between the financial system and investment in innovation, a question with enhanced importance because of innovation's importance for endogenous growth.

TRANSMISSION MECHANISMS

The proposition that globalization of finance makes countries subordinate to world markets implies convergence to world norms for financial variables; in the simplest case, a global monetarist model with fixed exchange rates, small open economies converge toward the world interest rate and inflation rate. Similarly, policies to manage exchange rates, whether loosely and temporarily as under the Louvre and Plaza Agreements, or more substantially as in European moves towards monetary unification, require prior convergence of the rate of growth of monetary aggregates and appropriate interest rate differentials. But an exclusive concentration on interest rates, the growth rate of the money supply, and the rate of inflation is a bankers' perspective; from a broader view we are concerned with the impact of those financial variables upon the real economy.

The analysis of that problem depends on the transmission mechanism linking international financial markets to real variables. The starting-point in open-economy macro theory is the simple link between world and domestic interest rates encapsulated in the uncovered interest parity condition:

$$r = r^* + \mathrm{E}(\mathrm{d}s/\mathrm{d}t)$$

where r is the domestic interest rate, r^* is the world rate (or the rate in a dominant currency), $(\mathrm{d}s/\mathrm{d}t)$ is the rate of change of the relevant exchange rate, and E is an expectations operator.

If we adopt the usual neoclassical-Keynesian synthesis assumptions, perfect substitutability between long government bonds and other public and private bonds means r is the representative interest rate which equals the cost of capital for private investors, and the rate of investment is determined by adjustment of the stock of real capital to equate r to the marginal product of capital. Investment is an inverse function of the domestic interest rate, r, and since r is determined by the world rate, r^* (given exchange rate expectations), investment, and hence the individual economy's rate of growth, is determined by the interest rate set on international financial markets. The more extreme versions of the proposition that financial globalization constrains national economies rest on a model of that type, but three of the simplifying assumptions underlying that transmission mechanism merit attention.

One is that firms' cost of capital can be reduced to the government bond yield, r. One difficulty with that assumption is that the interest rate equated to the global rate is a money market rate while the rate influencing investment is a long rate and, in the short run, their covariance may be low; indeed there are several historical examples of monetary policy based upon a belief in such short-term changes in the yield curve. But, putting that to one side, an alternative assumption is that equity yields, rather than bond yields, have a direct influence on investment and may systematically differ from bond yields. That is, if investment is a function of Tobin's q and if equity yields are not systematically related only to bond yields, global determination of r has no effect on investment and growth. By posing that alternative sharply it can be seen that a frequently neglected transmission mechanism should be investigated; the determination of domestic equity yields and prices by international equity markets as a result of financial globalization. I examine that type of transmission mechanism in the next section.

A second assumption of the simple model is that only the cost of capital determines investment and that it is independent of firms' capital structure. If, in reality, agency costs or other factors cause the Modigliani–Miller assumptions not to hold, or if there are liquidity constraints, the availability of different sources of finance, or in other words, quantity constraints on finance, have a direct influence on investment and we should consider whether the globalization of finance influences those quantities. I consider that question subsequently, and argue that the role global financial markets may play in such a transmission mechanism can, in principle, be either direct or indirect.

A third assumption is that growth is determined by physical investment with no technical change. However, in a growth model with endogenous technical change, the financial structure itself would have an influence on technical change, and globalization would only have an effect on growth if the transmission mechanism from global financial markets to real accumulation involves a relation between global markets and domestic financial systems' impact on innovation. In the penultimate section I consider the scope for national policy in a world of international financial markets and endogenous growth.

INTERNATIONAL LINKS BETWEEN STOCK MARKETS

During the 1980s, financial globalization has increased links between stock markets in different centres. The removal of capital account exchange controls led to international diversification of savings institutions' portfolios; competitive reforms of stock exchange dealing practices, such as the Big Bang reforms in London, were associated with expansion of foreign issues on the major markets; and the growth of new 'emerging markets' widened the range of markets in which funds invested. If, as a result, price movements in national stock markets follow a common international path, that international influence on the cost of domestic companies' equity finance may affect their investment, overriding the effects of national policy. Are national stock markets increasingly influenced by international stock market events?[4]

From everyday observation it is evident that stock markets in different countries are strongly linked. The fact that movements in equity prices in one market are often paralleled by movements elsewhere was illustrated most forcefully by the crash of October 1987 when the New York Stock Exchange, falling by 23 per cent in one day, was followed by extreme falls on stock markets around the world (as has been the February 1994 decline in Wall Street which was initiated by actual and expected rises in US interest rates). The Brady Commission's early report on the 1987 crash and the unsustainable boom that preceded it summarized a prevalent view of the causal role of international linkages between stock markets: 'investors made comparisons of valuations in different countries, often using higher valuations in other countries as justification for investing in lower valued markets. Consequently a process of ratcheting up among worldwide stock markets began to develop.'[5] But since casual observation also includes clear examples of weak linkages—for example, the large fall of the Japanese stock market in 1990 was not mirrored in the New York or London markets—the degree of linkage, and the channels through which it occurs, warrant further investigation.

A simple model for estimating the relation between a country's stock market and foreign markets is:

$$D (\ln x_t) = a_1 + a_2 D (\ln y_t) + e_t$$

where x_t and y_t are levels of stock price indexes in countries x and y, and D is a difference operator. Using daily data for 1980 to September 1987, one estimate of a_2 suggests that a 1 per cent change in the US index was associated with changes of 0.24 per cent to 0.33 per cent in Japan's, the UK's, and Germany's over the following twenty four hours.[6]

---

[4] The arguments in this section have benefited from research assistance by Purnima Roy and discussions with Graham Smith.

[5] Presidential Task Force on Market Mechanisms, *Report* (Washington DC: US Government Printers Office, Jan. 1988), 10.

[6] P. Bennett and J. Kelleher, 'The International Transmission of Stock Price Disruption in October 1987', *Federal Reserve Bank of New York Quarterly Review*, Summer 1988, 17–33, Table A4.

To distinguish international effects from domestic influences on stock markets, OLS estimates of the following simple model can be carried out:

$$\ln x_t = b_1 \ln N_t + b_2 \ln y_t + e_t$$

where N is a vector of domestic variables (such as output and labour market variables) representing 'fundamentals' in country x that should influence that country's stock prices. Using monthly data for the USA, Japan, Germany, and the UK, from 1967 to 1988, OLS estimates of this type of equation suggest significant positive values for b_2.[7]

Many writers report similarly that foreign stock market behaviour influences domestic stock markets[8] but the existence of such a relation itself is not very informative. To evaluate the impact of globalization on domestic markets we have to consider more specific questions.

One particularly relevant question is whether international links between stock markets increase the volatility of individual markets. Since Shiller's 'excess volatility' hypothesis that share prices are more volatile than would be warranted by economic 'fundamentals' is now well established for both the USA and UK[9] it is pertinent to consider whether excess volatility has been increased by globalization; has internationalization increased the tendency of stock markets to price equities in arbitrary ways? Several studies have found a positive relation between volatility in one market and another,[10] but that does not necessarily indicate a transmission of volatility that is 'unwarranted', for the volatility in foreign markets may convey information about foreign fundamentals that is relevant to domestic fundamentals. Remenola's attempts to separate such volatility from 'unwarranted' or 'excess' volatility, however, suggests that international links have, in some cases, increased the excess volatility of domestic markets; in terms of King and Whadwani's model, that implies that domestic investors believe they can obtain information about fundamentals from foreign stock

[7] Bennett and Kelleher, 'The International Transmission of Stock Price Disruption', Table B1.

[8] Bennett and Kelleher, 'The International Transmission of Stock Price Disruption'; G. P. Dwyer jun. and R. W. Hafer, 'Are National Stock Markets Linked?', *Federal Reserve Bank of St Louis*, Nov/Dec. 1988 3–14; G. M. von Furstenberg, and B. N. Jeon, 'International Stock Price Movements: Links and Messages', *Brookings Papers on Economic Activity* 1 (1989) 125–79; M. A. King, and S. Whadwani, 'Transmission of Volatility Between Stock Markets', *Review of Financial Studies* 3/1 (1990), 5–33; E. M. Remolona, 'Do International Reactions of Stock and Bond Markets reflect Macroeconomic Fundamentals?' *Federal Reserve Bank of New York Quarterly Review*, Autumn 1991, 1–13.

[9] J. Y. Campbell and R. J. Shiller, 'Cointegration and Tests of Present Value Models', *Journal of Political Economy* 95 (1987) 1062–88; J. M. Poterba and L. H. Summers, 'Mean Reversion in Stock Prices: Evidence and Implications', *Journal of Financial Economics* 22 (1988) 27–59; G. Buckley and I. Tonks, 'Are UK Stock Prices Excessively Volatile? Trading Rules and Variance Bound Tests', *Economic Journal* 99 (1989), 1083–98.

[10] Bennett and Kelleher, 'The International Transmission of Stock Price Disruption'; and King and Whadwani, 'Transmission of Volatility between Stock Markets'.

market prices, but either foreign price changes excessively reflect 'mistakes' or the way domestic investors interpret them is mistaken.

From the point of view of this chapter, the most important question about linkages between equity prices in different markets is whether they have changed over time in a way that reflects the set of institutional changes summarized by the term globalization. The mid 1980s was a period of fast change, marking the creation of today's internationally oriented equity trading and leading to a suspicion that the new internationalization accounted for the global character of the October 1987 crash. One measure of those institutional changes was the growth of equities traded daily on both their 'home' market and a 'foreign' market; the number of firms traded on that multimarket basis rose from 236 in 1984 to 493 in 1987.[11] Another measure is the value of purchases and sales of domestic equities by non-residents; between 1984 and 1987 such cross-border transactions in the US rose from $122bn to $482bn; in Japan from $78bn to $375bn; and in Germany from $12bn to $77bn.[12] Consequently, to examine the effect of such globalization upon the degree of linkage between different markets' price movements, we can take January 1985 as a dividing point and consider the estimates of the covariance of price indexes both before and after that date.

On Bennett and Kelleher's estimates (up to September 1987), the Tokyo and German index was more sensitive to the US index after January 1985 (and the USA became more sensitive to Japan). But the evidence for this link in the international transmission mechanism is not conclusive, for the sensitivity of the London market to the US (or to foreign markets in total) did not increase. A plausible hypothesis would be that London's openness had occurred earlier, for exchange controls on capital movements were removed in 1979, but the same authors estimate that the shift in sensitivity between the period before and after January 1979 was in the 'wrong' direction; using shift variables estimated by OLS, equity prices in London were considerably less sensitive to foreign markets' prices after January 1979 than before.[13]

The evidence reviewed here suggests that the simple notion of globalization of equity markets leading to domestic real investment being subordinated to international events is too simple. Even if real investment is a function of Tobin's q, increased internationalization of equity trading is not universally followed by increased covariance of price indexes (which affect q). That suggests the possibility that international covariance of indexes reflects, not so much the direct effect of internationalized trading itself, but,

[11] *Euromoney*, May 1987, 187–222.
[12] Bennett and Kelleher, 'The International Transmission of Stock Price Disruption', 22, Table 4.
[13] Ibid. 32–3 Tables B1 and B2.

instead, an indirect link, the internationalization of responses to simple signals. Foreign markets' price changes, whatever their basis, are increasingly taken as signals concerning what prices 'should' be on the domestic market. A case study of trading in the 1987 crash demonstrates that direct trading on foreign stock markets or in foreign stocks had low significance, but foreign price changes were taken as signals for price changes on domestic markets.[14]

That may contribute to markets' 'excess volatility' as some studies suggest, but what effect would it have on real economic activity? If that volatility, whatever its size, were around central values determined by 'fundamentals' it would raise the risk premia required by suppliers of equity finance in each country, but, since that leaves national differences between fundamentals unchanged and the pattern of risk premia changes is not predictable, there is no reason to think the effect of internationalization is to equalize q ratios in different countries. Alternatively, it is likely that equity price indexes are not determined by fundamentals, but, instead, as Robert Shiller argues with support from surveys, changes are due to 'spontaneous changes of public opinion. . . . People appear to react to price drops because they think the drops are evidence of market psychology'.[15] In that case, the herd- and casino-like aspects of stock markets also prevent us from expecting convergence of different countries' q coefficients on a central value determined by world conditions.

LIQUIDITY CONSTRAINTS AND THE TRANSMISSION MECHANISM

The transmission mechanisms discussed so far postulate effects of international markets on investment that work through cost of capital influences on real investment, but the relevance of stock market valuations is reduced by the evidence that low proportions of investment by UK and US firms are financed by new equity issues.[16] On the other hand, there is considerable evidence that investment is systematically related to quantity variables representing firms' internal funds or current cash flow.

The work of Kuh and Meyer more than thirty years ago was followed by numerous estimates of a positive relation between internal funds on

[14] R. Alderhold, C. Cumming, and A. Harwood, 'International Linkages among Equities Markets and the October 1987 Market Break', *Federal Reserve Bank of New York Quarterly Review*, Summer 1988, 34–46.

[15] R. Shiller, 'Comment' on von Furstenberg and Jeon, 'International Stock Price Movements', 173.

[16] C. Mayer, 'New Issues in Corporate Finance', *European Economic Review* 32/5 (1988) 1167–89; P. Srini Vasan, *Credit Rationing and Corporate Investment* (unpublished Ph.D., Harvard University, 1986).

investment, rationalized in terms of credit rationing.[17] The seminal 1988 study by Fazzari, Hubbard, and Petersen, using time-series and cross-section US data, demonstrates a positive relation between current cash flow and investment. The strength of the relationship is consistent with an explanation in terms of capital market imperfections (due to imperfect information or other causes) and varies according to the size and track record of the firm.[18] Similarly, using a panel of UK firms, Scaramozzino finds a relationship between cash flow and investment in a model which explains it in terms of investment irreversibility and a dividend payout constraint.[19]

Transmission mechanisms linking international financial markets to domestic real investment work through changes in prices affecting the cost of capital; by contrast a relationship between investment and corporations' internal funds implies no direct transmission mechanism. In a world where firms' investment is driven by internal funds, domestic conditions which affect investment have no direct pressure from financial markets. In a Kaleckian or Sraffian model, for example, the relative power of capital and labour—which may relate to monopoly power or to non-economic power—determine profit and wage shares and therefore affect firms' internal funds. Consequently internationalization of financial markets does not directly prevent countries from determining their own growth conditions.

However, in such a world, financial markets may have indirect effects on investment. One route can be that internationally motivated interest rate changes affect internal funds.[20] Another is that, if the relative power of labour reduces profit shares and profit rates below international rates, real capital resources can move abroad, arbitraging between different labour markets; for that to occur, international financial markets play an indirect 'facilitator' role, for the transfer of real capital resources occurs through financial transfers.

Since Feldstein and Horioka's 1980 article there has been considerable discussion of whether increased internationalization of financial markets has, in fact, been matched by increased capital mobility measured by real resource flows. Feldstein and Horioka's initial finding, that countries'

[17] E. Kuh and J. Meyer, 'Investment, Liquidity and Monetary Policy' in Commission on Money and Credit, *Impacts of Monetary Policy* (Englewood Cliffs NJ: Prentice Hall, 1963); W. H. L. Anderson, *Corporate Finance and Fixed Investment: An Econometric Study* (Cambridge: Harvard University Press, 1964); G. J. Anderson, 'A New Approach to the Empirical Investigation of Investment Expenditures', *Economic Journal* 91 (1988), 88–103; G. Meeks, 'Cash Flow and Investment' in W. E. Martin (ed.), *The Economics of the Profits Crisis* (London: HMSO 1981); M. Croasdale and L. Harris, 'Internal Funds and Investment' in L. Harris, J. Coakley, M. Croasdale, and T. Evans, *New Perspectives on the Financial System* (London: Croom Helm, 1988).

[18] S. Fazzari, R. G. Hubbard, and B. Petersen, 'Finance Constraints and Corporate Investment', *Brookings Papers on Economic Activity*, 1988, 141–95.

[19] P. Scaramozzino, 'Investment Irreversibility and Finance Constraints', mimeo 1994.

[20] Croasdale and Harris, 'Internal Funds and Investment'.

savings/income ratios are more strongly correlated with their investment/ income ratios than would be expected if capital were highly mobile, has proved remarkably robust.[21] Using the Feldstein–Horioka method with data for the most recent periods after financial deregulation suggests there has been a rise in international mobility of real capital, but there is not a simple link between internationalization of financial markets and mobility of real capital. Coakley, Kulasi, and Smith find a lower rate of growth of real mobility than would be expected; Sterne and Bayoumi find that increased real mobility follows a regional pattern and more work is required to link that pattern with patterns of financial integration before a strong connection is established.[22]

In sum, if real investment is determined by financial quantities such as firms' internal funds, the impact of global financial markets on domestic real capital formation is indirect. Their most important indirect role is as a channel for the export (or import) of real capital; a popular image is that they enable firms to close factories in one country if the share or rate of profit is too low and invest the proceeds in a production plant using cheaper or more efficient labour elsewhere. If that were the case, it would be a direct constraint on government policy and, indeed, recent British governments have justified policies which they believe will reduce labour costs (or, in the case of Britain's rejection of the Social Chapter, prevent them

[21] M. Feldstein and C. Horioka, 'Domestic Savings and International Capital Flows', *Economic Journal* 90/2 (1980); M. Feldstein, 'Domestic Saving and International Capital Movements in the Long Run and the Short Run', *European Economic Review* 21 (1983), 129–51; M. Feldstein and P. Bacchetta, 'National Saving and International Investment' in D. Bernheim and J. Shoven (eds.), *National Saving and Economic Performance* (Chicago, University of Chicago Press, 1991); T. Bayoumi, 'Saving Investment Correlations: Immobile Capital, Government Policy, or Endogenous Behaviour', *IMF Staff Papers*, June 1990, 360–87; J. Coakley, *Aspects of the Integration of International Financial Markets* (unpublished Ph.D., Open University, 1992); L. L. Tesar, 'Savings, Investment and International Capital Flows', *Journal of International Economics*, 31 (1991), 55–78; J. Coakley, F. Kulasi, and R. Smith, 'Savings, Investment, and Capital Mobility' (unpublished mimeo 1994). However, the last paper also shows that introducing the expected growth rate of output and the expected inflation rate as common-factor arguments in a regression of investment on savings leads to qualification of the Feldstein–Horioka results.

[22] T. Bayoumi, 'Saving Investment correlations; G. Sterne and T. Bayoumi, 'Regional Trading Blocs, Mobile Capital, and Exchange Rate Coordination', *Working Paper 12*, Bank of England Apr. 1993; Coakley, Kulasi, and Smith, 'Savings, Investment, and Capital Mobility'. Sterne and Bayoumi find that, within the eleven countries of the European Community (excluding Luxemburg) for the period 1986 to 1990, the relationship between a country's saving and its investment was not significantly different from zero, whereas for other European countries and non-European countries it remained positive. In other words, it appears that the increased integration of European financial markets was reflected in greater mobility of real capital resources. However, the interpretation of that result is not simple. Since a country's use of foreign saving is equivalent to its surplus or deficit on the current account of the balance of payments, the low ratio found for EC countries is equivalent to finding that EC countries with similar investment ratios were able to have different saving ratios, with resulting current account imbalances; and that may be attributable, for most of them, to their membership of the ERM rather than integration of capital markets as such.

rising) on the grounds that international capital mobility leaves no alternative. Mobility of real capital has increased in the late 1980s and early 1990s, but that cannot be attributed in a direct manner to the internationalization of financial markets. Moreover, measures of international mobility of real capital suggest it is relatively low between regions (such as flows between Europe and East Asia), even in recent years when barriers to financial investment have been abolished; they certainly do not warrant the conclusion that national governments' ability to influence domestic industrial conditions is abolished by financial integration.

FINANCIAL STRUCTURE AND TECHNICAL CHANGE

The general model implicit in most notions that financial integration constrains national economies, the model set out at the start of this chapter, assumes that growth is determined by the quantity of investment. However, 'endogenous growth' theories take a quite different approach by treating technological progress, which confers external as well as private benefits, as the driving force of continuous growth. The idea that internationalization of financial markets influences growth through a transmission mechanism involving interest rates or other measures of the cost of capital which, in turn, influence the amount of capital formation cannot be directly applied, since endogenous growth theory treats innovation as an economic activity in its own right instead of being exogenously determined and embodied in capital goods.[23] In the case of endogenous growth, we have to consider whether the internationalization of financial markets causes international links between variables which determine each country's technology thereby overriding national growth policies. I believe that in reality there are no clear links of that type.

Any such transmission mechanism has to work through financial markets. Since endogenous growth models treat innovation as an economic process determined by firms' maximising behaviour, in general-equilibrium versions of endogenous growth the cost of capital (or valuation of equity) on financial markets is an important element in determining the optimum amount of resources devoted to R&D.[24] In such a model, we may expect that international links between financial markets would affect different countries' R&D in similar directions if they lead to equalization of the cost of capital. Similarly, if financial markets do facilitate the international

[23] G. M. Grossman and E. Helpman, *Innovation and Growth in the Global Economy* (Cambridge, Mass.: MIT Press, 1992); M. Scott, *A New View of Economic Growth* (Oxford University Press, 1989).

[24] Grossman and Helpman, *Innovation and Growth in the Global Economy*, ch. 3.

mobility of real capital resources, that process could directly lead to convergence of technology.[25]

However, those models of financial markets are highly simplified and should be contrasted with theories of financial intermediation in a world of imperfect information and agency costs. Developments in finance theory over the past two decades have demonstrated that financial intermediaries can be understood as efficient devices for monitoring investment decisions, that they are possibly superior to financial markets for that purpose, and that the effectiveness of monitoring may depend on the debt–equity ratio.[26] In other words, the structure of a country's financial system can influence the productivity of the investment projects being financed as a result of the different types of monitoring and screening associated with different forms of finance. Similarly, the structure of the financial system can influence the success of investment in R&D projects,[27] the driving force in endogenous growth. Those views on the role of the financial system's structure have achieved popularity partly because at one level they have appeared to explain the high growth rates of Germany and Japan, economies with financial structures apparently different from British and North American types.[28]

Whether that empirical judgement is justified or not, the idea that financial structure influences the returns to investment in projects has a good theoretical basis in a world of imperfect information and agency costs, and it leads to different conclusions from models in which the only financial influence is through financial market prices. In this case, the internationalization of finance would only introduce a foreign influence to a country's level of R&D if it led to a change in the financial structure, and hence the whole process of monitoring and screening. In the stylized conception people have of the difference between US–UK and German-Japanese systems, an example of such an influence would be if internationalization led to the latter adopting 'short-termism' in their financing criteria.

There may, in fact, be some evidence of that. For example, the traditional structure of German finance was disturbed in 1993 when Daimler Benz

[25] G. Saint-Paul 'Technological Choice, Financial Markets, and Economic Development', *European Economic Review* 36 (1992), 763–81.

[26] D. Diamond, 'Financial Intermediation and Delegated Monitoring', *Review of Economic Studies*, 1984, 393–414; J. Stiglitz, 'Credit Markets and the Control of Capital', *Journal of Money Credit and Banking* 17/2 (1985), 133–52; Mayer, 'New Issues in Corporate Finance'; C. Mayer, 'The Assessment: Financial Systems and Corporate Investment', *Oxford Review of Economic Policy* 3/4 (1987).

[27] Y. Qian and C. Xu, 'Innovation and Financial Constraints in Centralized and Decentralized Economies', *Discussion Paper 109*, Centre for Economic Performance, Dec. 1992.

[28] J. Cable, 'Capital Market Information and Industrial Performance: The Role of West German Banks', *Economic Journal*, 95 (1985), 118–32; Mayer, 'The Assessment: Financial Systems and Corporate Investment'.

obtained a listing on the New York Stock Exchange. Such US listings have historically been shunned by German companies because they require a different shareholder–management relation than has prevailed in the German system; in particular, they involve greater public disclosure of information. Thus, the development of international links between equity markets can lead to changes in the structure of corporate finance relations. Nevertheless, given the complexity of the determinants of different countries' financial structures (including the historically determined roles of culture, social, and regional structures, the political and institutional system) the effect of internationalization on financial structures is likely to be a complex process and countries' financial systems may retain significant differences in their monitoring and evaluation of innovation; at present our knowledge of how financial systems and their monitoring roles develop is so limited that we cannot make any useful judgement about the result of internationalization.

NATIONAL AUTONOMY IN THE CONTEXT OF GLOBAL FINANCIAL MARKETS

In the previous sections I have considered whether the internationalization of finance constrains individual economies; does it prevent national states choosing any policy of their own? Examining the theoretical basis and the empirical evidence for different elements of the transmission mechanism through which that might occur suggests that the constraints imposed by internationalization of finance are not absolute. Since transmission mechanisms are complex, have weak links, and include links of which our knowledge is speculative, countries have considerable scope for divergent growth policies.

The conclusion has considerable significance for policy, particularly since political debates over economic policy are frequently characterized by claims that international integration leaves governments with no alternative but to follow the dictates of international markets. The weakness of the transmission mechanisms from international markets means that governments have considerable room for manoeuvre in determining a country's growth policies. For example, in a world where endogenous growth is driven by investment in knowledge and innovation, a government policy to alter the structure of the financial system in ways which promote the financing of such projects (or, for that matter, to alter the structure of training and education) would be significant and sustainable even if international financial markets do constrain what the central bank can do on interest rates.

That conclusion does not warrant complacency about the internationalization of financial markets. In the 1940s, Keynes sought to restore the power of governments and restrict the freedom of operation of financial markets partly because of the potential impact on economic stability of the latter's irrationality, and today's internationalized financial markets present the same problem in different ways. Although the core theories present these markets as ultimately anchored by fundamentals (even if subject to speculative bubbles), market traders' assumptions defining what those fundamentals are, or what signals measure them, can be arbitrary, and changes in those assumptions create great instability. The most significant source of irrationality and instability is the growth, especially since the late 1980s, of international markets in derivatives. Although derivatives are valued on the basis of theoretical models, their valuation for reporting purposes is contentious; they are the vehicle for highly levered trading; the impact of derivative trading on the prices of underlying securities is not well understood; and the existence of derivatives markets has strengthened the tendency of industrial and commercial corporations to seek (risky) profits through purely financial operations. Moreover, the impact internationalized financial markets and global institutions have on some countries is greater than others; developing countries frequently have no capacity to choose policies different from those required to maintain markets' 'confidence' however arbitrary the latter.

9. Derivatives—A Growing Threat To The International Financial System[1]

Ruth Kelly

On 4 February 1994, the world's financial markets were thrown into a frenzy. When the US Federal Reserve raised short-term interest rates—the first tightening for five years—the shock waves emanated across the industrialized world. A month later, the market was still nervous. The final straw was the announcement that the Bundesbank's key measure of money supply, M3, had grown by a freak 20 per cent in one month. The reaction was swift and brutal. On the trading floor of Liffe, the London futures[2] exchange, dealers were overwhelmed by orders. Prices crashed. By mid-morning, the London clearing houses responsible for settling futures trades, had called for members to put up £500 million of fresh collateral to cover their position—the largest call in the market's history. On that same day, trading on Liffe hit an all-time high of £300 billion—roughly equivalent to half of the UK's annual gross domestic product. Although the panic later subsided, all bets on further cuts in UK base rates were off. It was a near miss. Some analysts were predicting that further fallout in the bond market would trigger a rise in interest rates.

Paradoxically, both in the United States and in Europe the impact at the long end of the bond market was far more severe. In theory at least, a precautionary tightening of US monetary policy to stave off inflationary pressures should have reassured the markets, easing the pressure on long-term rates. Reality was somewhat different. Derivatives contracts had been used by bulls to punt billions of dollars into the bond markets, and the optimism was suddenly punctured. Long-bond yields shifted up 1.75 per cent, running counter to all the goals of the US Treasury. In the UK, for example, fixed rate mortgages were suddenly withdrawn and replaced a couple of days later with much less generous terms.

In the spring reporting season of the US commercial banks, a further impact of the bond market fallout was revealed. All reported declines in

---

[1] This chapter could not have been prepared without the assistance of Alistair Hudson at Goldman Sachs International.

[2] For a definition of 'futures' and other terminology used in this chapter please see the Glossary.

their trading revenues in the first quarter as a result of rising interest rates, which had damaged their bond and currency operations. Citicorp, for example, acknowledged that a large part of its losses came from derivatives and swaps trading on its own behalf rather than for clients. But a series of industrial clients such as Procter and Gamble were also knocked, taking a $157 million hit on a swap transaction. Waking up to the importance of financial derivatives, Mr Lloyd Bentsen, the US Treasury Secretary, suddenly announced that their use would be examined by the Group of Seven leading industrialized nations at their spring financial meetings.

Just eighteen months earlier, the international financial markets had wielded even more power over the-then UK Chancellor of the Exchequer, Norman Lamont, forcing him within a matter of hours to raise rates from 10 to 12 to 15 per cent before standing by helplessly as the pound tumbled out of the European exchange rate mechanism (ERM). In both the bond market crash and the breakup of the ERM, the blame was put squarely on leading financial players. Notoriously, George Soros's Quantum Fund was rumoured to have made $1 billion betting against the pound on Black Wednesday. In the spring of 1994, the growing might of these 'hedge' funds was once again thrust under the spotlight. As Gavyn Davies wrote in the *Independent* (28 March 1994):

These facts show how easily the financial markets can, if they choose, take domestic monetary conditions into their own hands, and out of the hands of the Chancellor. All that the Treasury can do in co-operation with the central bank is determine the spot rate (today's rate) of interest on very short-term assets, perhaps up to three months in duration at most. All other rates, now and in the future, may or may not be affected by the authorities' actions at the short end of the money markets—it depends on how the market reads the runes.

Both examples show that cash transactions in the foreign exchange market are no longer the only way financial markets can undermine exchange rate and interest rate policies. This chapter argues that the key to understanding the events of 16 September 1992, the subsequent breakup of the entire European exchange rate mechanism in August 1993, and the bond market crash in the spring of 1994 lies in an appreciation of the changing financial structures to which European economic policy in the 1980s itself gave rise—in particular, the reams of novel financial instruments spawned by the gradual abolition of exchange controls in member countries throughout the period.

If hedge funds became the natural scapegoat for governments embarrassed by policy failures, the fact is that they were the natural offshoot of a set of policies which provided fertile ground for the explosion of new financial instruments or 'derivatives'. And it was the growth of financial derivatives which made aggressive speculation against currencies cheaper and faster than had previously been possible, exacerbating the short-term bias of financial markets and undermining international policy coordination. Below, we argue that their increasing importance meant that the ERM was only able to survive under artificial conditions of what has been called 'perfect credibility', a condition in which member countries cannot be seen to contemplate exchange rate realignment. Once the financial markets began to reassess the prospects of currency realignments, the ERM was doomed.

Outside the ERM, the growth of financial derivatives continued unabated. And in conditions of floating exchange rates the financial markets also had the power to dictate economic policy, contributing to exchange rate and interest rate volatility. They also posed new systemic risks to the financial system—risks which were manifest in the international bond market crisis in the spring of 1994, when it became clear that banks and securities houses dealing with 'hedge' funds did not even clearly monitor their exposure to these high-risk products. An indication of just how far these markets have grown is the increase in the notional value—the underlying principal value used to calculate the cash flows resulting from derivative contracts—of outstanding exchange-traded and over-the-counter contracts. The notional value quintupled to an estimated $8 trillion at the end of 1991, from $1.6 trillion in 1987. That is equivalent to an increase from 35 per cent of US GDP to 140 per cent of US GDP. In 1994, those numbers are even greater.

The first section of this chapter examines how in the early 1970s a weakening of governmental control over financial markets proved a fertile seedbed of future instability in foreign exchange, bond, stock, and commodity markets. It argues that the explosion of financial derivatives has its roots in this period, but was fuelled by the policies of governments throughout the industrialized world over the last decade. The second section explores the risks posed by—and the benefits brought by—the new financial products, and looks particularly at the role of hedge funds in precipitating financial crises. The third section examines the threat of systemic risk to the financial system posed by the growth of derivative products. Finally, the last section of the chapter argues that policy should aim to reduce volatility in financial markets, by attempting to secure an international agreement to curb speculation. A national strategy should focus on limiting systemic risk, isolating those transactions used for speculation and those for hedging, and seeking to confine speculation to 'special purpose vehicles' (SPVs). By permitting speculation, but confining it to these SPVs, its deleterious effects could be mitigated, shielding vulnerable sectors of the economy from risk, making regulation more manageable, reducing the total volume of business, and helping prevent trading from moving offshore.

1. THE CHANGING LANDSCAPE

The seeds of the explosion of financial products were sown in the second half of the 1960s and the early 1970s when the Bretton Woods international system of managed exchange rates was still in place. Fluctuations in exchange rates became more and more pronounced, giving birth to increased opportunities for profit-making—a phenomenon which in turn exacerbated the swings in exchange rates. As these swings became more exaggerated, the corporate sector found itself in an ever-more volatile and unpredictable environment—and needed to insure itself against losses in the foreign exchange market. In the jargon, the corporate sector needed to 'hedge' risk. The necessity to insure against risk, led to greater and greater pressure for regulatory structures to be dismantled so that more hedging possibilities were opened up. This culminated in the demise of Bretton Woods in 1973, which ushered in a period of international floating exchange rates. As John Eatwell argues in Chapter 12, in the Bretton Woods era, the public sector assumed all foreign exchange risk, but the advent of freely floating exchange rates brought in its train the 'privatization' of risk, imposing substantial strains on the domestic and international banking systems.

As the International Monetary Fund (IMF) itself recognized, although derivatives can be used effectively to reduce the risk borne by individual agents, they cannot reduce the overall risk in the system but rather can 'only transform and re-allocate risk' (IMF *Survey*, 21 February 1994).

The United States was the first country to abandon capital controls, acting in 1974 soon after the official demise of Bretton Woods. It took another five years for Britain to follow suit, with Mrs Thatcher stripping away controls within months of assuming office in May 1979. In 1981, Germany and the Netherlands followed, while Denmark abandoned controls in 1988. Italy had a phased strategy, starting in 1988. The following year, France started to phase out its capital controls and, in 1990, the Benelux countries abandoned their dual exchange rate system. The remaining EMS countries set timetables, when they met in 1988, for the gradual abandonment of controls.

As the Mundell–Flemming model of exchange rates would predict, the stripping away of controls over capital movements meant that interest rates between different countries started to converge. At the same time, the abolition of controls on capital movements meant that institutional funds, such as pension funds, insurance companies, and life assurance funds, started to increase their overseas holdings of assets. Certainly, the experience of freely-moving capital after 1988 suggests that significant monetary policy autonomy was lost. Examination of onshore and offshore interest rates

during the early years of the ERM's operation shows that significant pre-
miums existed on interest rates in the Euromarkets, suggesting a significant
degree of national policy autonomy. These differentials melted away completely once exchange controls were lifted (see Artis, 1987).

After 1988, the only differences in interest rates which existed between
members of the ERM could be accounted for by differences in the markets'
perception as to how 'fixed' a particular exchange rate really was. In other
words, any differences in interest rate levels reflected the risk premia on the
currencies. That meant that the only way a weaker economy could reduce
its level of interest rates nearer to that in the leading economy—which in
the case of the ERM was Germany—was by reducing the risk premium,
that is, by enhancing the 'credibility' of its exchange rate level. Thus 'credibility' became all important—weaker economies realised that a loss of
credibility would force its interest rates higher, and force it into deflationary adjustment which could weaken its economy further.

This is why leading economists and politicians argued over the summer
of 1992 that any consideration of devaluation was fatal and that a devaluation of the pound would be counter-productive by forcing British interest
rates up, despite the fact that, in the event, UK interest rates actually fell
sharply after leaving the ERM. The paradox was due to 'credibility' being
not just about the direct effect of the value of the exchange rate on international competitiveness—it was also about the indirect effects that
exchange rates had on the level of interest rates. Higher interest rates in
weaker economies themselves jeopardized that economy's 'credibility'—by
deepening deflationary forces at the time Europe was entering a prolonged
period of recession, higher interest rates made the prospect of devaluation
more likely. It was a catch-22 situation.

In effect, any loss of credibility meant that devaluation became a self-
fulfilling prophecy. The result was that, for five years from 1987 onwards,
ERM currencies existed in a situation of almost-perfect credibility with no
realignments. Market participants focused on an imminent monetary union
in Europe and were willing to regard ERM member currencies as virtually
interchangeable. This meant that volatility increased between the currencies
of the ERM grid and the dollar and yen, and decreased between individual
ERM currencies. Hedging still assumed increasing importance for companies—the demand for, and consequent supply of, financial instruments bal-
looned out of all recognition.

The fatal result was that misalignments of real exchange rates became
more and more pronounced. In the summer of 1992, the 'no' vote in the
Danish referendum meant market participants reflected on the consequence
of the fact that monetary union was not a forgone conclusion and
reassessed the prospects of devaluation. The overvaluation of the lira and
pound was clear to most commentators. But the terror among European

governments at the prospect of a realignment after five years of tranquillity on the markets meant that, when European finance ministers gathered at Bath in the first week of September 1992, they could not agree to devaluing the Italian currency, so upsetting the fragile equilibrium which had been in place for five years. A few days later, the markets took the decision into their own hands: the lira was thrown out of its ERM band by speculators. Having smelt blood the markets were unstoppable. Within ten days, the pound was unceremoniously bundled out of the ERM.

The next phase has been described by some economic commentators as 'pathological' behaviour by the financial markets. Most people agreed that the franc/mark exchange rate was appropriately valued for competitiveness; the markets, however, focused on the fact that interest rates in France—and in most other ERM countries—were too high and that participation in the system meant that they could not be brought below the German interest rate floor. Unceremoniously, the franc was dumped in the summer of 1993, signalling the breakup of the entire mechanism. Almost a year later, the franc and the other ERM member currencies, apart from the pound, are back within their old narrow ERM bands. Interest rates, however, are much lower—mainly as a result of the gradual reduction of the discount rate in Germany as it came to terms with ever-deepening recession.

The second effect of the abolition of capital controls was the increasing internationalization of financial assets, which also exposed the international currency markets to sudden and dramatic shifts in and out of currencies. The abolition of exchange controls on capital permitted UK financial intermediaries to invest freely abroad in deposits, bonds, and shares, having a marked effect on the export of capital. In the first six months of 1980, for example, pension funds and insurance companies invested four times as much in overseas equities as they did in the first half of 1979.[3] This trend was fuelled by the growth of derivative products which opened up opportunities for funds to insure themselves against adverse movements in exchange rates by 'hedging'.

The result was stark. According to the IMF, cross-border equity holdings in the USA, Europe, and Japan increased from $800bn in 1986 to $1,300bn in 1991. In Europe, institutions invest about 20 per cent of their assets abroad while foreign investments of US and Japanese institutions generally range between 5 and 7 per cent. These holdings dwarf central bank reserves in size, making any large-scale reallocation a potential source of huge exchange rate instability. But it is only recently that pension funds have begun to exert their new power. The explosion of financial derivatives has allowed them to move quickly and relatively cheaply in and out of currencies and equities.

[3] See J. Coakley and L. Harris, 'Financial Globalisation and Deregulation', in J. Michie (ed.), *The Economic Legacy: 1979–1992* (London: Academic Press, 1992).

According to the IMF: 'Advances in the technology of financial transactions—ranging from back-office clearance and settlement to trading and information systems to settlements of payments—have reduced transaction costs to the point where they less and less serve as an impediment to rearranging portfolios when expectations change.' Moreover, the IMF report on international capital movements and the Dini report into financial derivatives from the Group of Thirty both predict that the trend to international portfolio diversification will keep growing. The IMF quotes research by InterSec Research Corporation, a company that tracks pension fund investments worldwide. This estimates that the share of foreign currency denominated assets in the portfolios of the world's 300 largest pension funds will increase from about 7 per cent at present to about 12 per cent by the middle of this decade. If true, global pension fund assets will rise to around $7,200bn by 1996, of which $880bn will be cross-border investments. US pension funds are projected to double the share of foreign securities in total assets to 10 per cent by the mid-1990s.

In addition, specialist managers are now managing currency as a separate asset class in itself, or managing the currency exposure of funds as a separate decision. This latter method of control, called currency overlay, makes it easier to separate currency management from that of the underlying assets. Mr Dirk Morris, of JP Morgan Investments, in London, says: 'The currency overlay business has grown from nothing four years ago to the management of somewhere between $15bn and $25bn today. And our own business has grown by 30 per cent over the past year.'[4] The next section of this chapter examines how derivatives can be used to move markets, triggering outflows from fund managers, and injecting an unprecedented degree of instability into the market—both on a day-to-day basis and from year to year.

2. THE ROLE OF HEDGE FUNDS IN PRECIPITATING FINANCIAL CRISES

When the Bretton Woods system broke up in 1971, no one realized how violent the swings in exchange rates would be under a floating rate system. The dollar–sterling rate swung by 30 per cent within a couple of years—and then swung back the other way. Now these wild swings have an added twist—the growth of derivatives trading has made them more sudden and more violent. Part of this increased volatility can be attributed to 'hedge funds', a particularly aggressive type of speculative investment vehicle that uses sophisticated hedging and leverage techniques to play in the financial

[4] Quoted in the *Financial Times*, 26 May 1993.

markets. Hedge funds are operated offshore 'so as to be exempt from most types of regulatory oversight and restraints' and have recently begun to play a major role in the international bond market.[5]

There are two main reasons which gives them much more financial clout than other funds of their size. First, they take highly leveraged positions in the market, that is, they borrow up to fifty times the amount of their capital from banks in order to take aggressive bets. Second, by using derivative products, the power of that money is magnified, because only a small fraction of the notional cost, or face value, of a derivative contract is needed up front. In other words, hedge funds can take huge bets in which way a market will move without putting up much of their own cash. If they get it right they can even reinvest the profits, helping to maintain the momentum of the original movement. The trouble comes when they get it wrong. Then they face 'margin calls'—that is, they are forced to put up more of their money because the contract becomes more expensive to deliver. They also face a tactical problem. They can hope for a change in the market or get out—knowing that in doing so they are adding to the selling pressure against their original positions and thus fuelling their losses.

This is where the use of technology, the cheapness of making transactions, and the power well-respected fund managers have over expectations' formation comes in. John Maynard Keynes pictured the operations of the speculative market in his *General Theory* when he likened it to a beauty contest. In the 1930s, a favourite British pastime was for readers of tabloid Sunday newspapers to rank pictures of young women in the order which they believed they would be ranked by a 'celebrity' panel. In other words, they won not by using any subjective judgement about the merits of the beauty queens but by guessing correctly who other people would choose. Imagine a situation in which the view of one of the celebrities leaked out—it would probably be sufficient for most of the readers to vote the same way. In the same manner, the key to playing the markets is not what the individual trader considers to be the virtues or otherwise of any particular policy, but what he or she believes everyone else in the market will think. In this context, hedge fund managers such as George Soros can provide a beacon in the dark around which other players can rally. If Mr Soros says publicly that he is going to bet against the franc—as he did in July 1993—the large fund managers have to protect the value of their portfolios. They change their asset allocation in accord with the Soros prediction that the franc will fall out of the ERM—and so make it self-fulfilling. As the IMF report puts it: 'While the hedge funds acted as market leaders, the real financial muscle was provided by insti-

---

[5] Quoted in the joint report on the Government Securities Market by US Department of Treasury, Securities, and Exchange Commission and Federal Reserve Board, January 1992.

tutional investors (mutual funds, pension funds, insurance companies) and by non-financial corporations.'[6]

Technical analysis of trading strategies can also play a role in exaggerating market movements. One fund manager who bases his strategy on reading charts says: 'If a market is rammed hard enough by hedge funds at strategic technical levels, a "domino" effect may occur in which a predetermined series of stop-loss orders will carry the market further and further down quickly precipitating those fund managers, who are geared up in a market moving quickly against them, to run for cover, irrespective of any arguments about "fundamentals".'[7] The result is that the underlying currency or stock rises further on a bull run than it otherwise would—and crashes further.

It is not just that movements in derivative markets can trigger copycat behaviour in other markets, however; they can also by their very nature feed through into greater volatility in the cash market. Again, take swaps: the opinions that the swaps markets forms about where interest rates are going to be between three months and thirty from now create speculative pressures on the currencies traded in the cash market. While any guess about interest rates in the UK thirty years from now is bound to be plucked out of the sky, traders do not concern themselves unduly on this front, knowing that they can always swap again to reverse any exposure. However, while the dealers can cover their bets, the level of the pound itself will be affected. A large swap transaction of this type that anticipates a volatile movement in the pound will affect the way in which the markets view UK interest rates and will therefore introduce volatility into the cash market. The next section of this chapter examines how the use of financial instruments also increases systemic risk in the financial system.

3. SYSTEMIC RISKS

If hedge funds can make spectacular gains, they can also make spectacular losses. Just ahead of the European bond crisis in February and March 1994, it was widely reported that George Soros had lost $600 million speculating against the yen. When the bond market crashed, concerns were triggered that, if hedge funds suffered heavy losses by playing the market the 'wrong' way, they could start to default on their bank loans—and that, if the funds could not settle their debts, that could spark a chain reaction affecting the whole financial system. In its report on hedge funds, the Bank of England noted that the 'sheer size' of the position taken by hedge funds

[6] *International Capital Markets, Part 1. Exchange Rate Management and International Capital Flows*, IMF, Aug. 1993.

[7] Michael Petley, managing director of ECU Fund Management talking to the *Guardian*.

raised concerns about systemic risk that these funds may introduce into the financial markets, adding, however, that 'regulators currently have little information that might help them assess the market impact of failure of a hedge fund or that would warn of an impending failure'.

And it is not just hedge funds that raise concerns about systemic risk; so do all derivative products. An examination of how hedging works illustrates the point. One way to view hedging is to see it as similar to betting on a two-horse race. You place a bet on the grey horse to win but you are worried that you will lose your stake if the brown horse wins. So you 'hedge' your risk by putting a bet on the brown horse that will just produce a large enough win to equal the cost of your stake of betting on the grey. Of course, financial markets are more complicated—but the principle is the same. A hedge is just a bet which reduces the risk of a bigger bet, and speculation is a bet which, in itself, simply hikes the stake on another bet. Swaps provide a useful illustration. Say a lender bets on UK base rates falling, and buys a swap to that effect. In order to insure themselves against losing all their money, they hedge their exposure—that is, they take out, say, an option which will pay out enough to cover the loss if UK base rates actually go up. The important difference between the experience of the financial markets and the two-horse analogy is the chain reaction which one hedging transaction can precipitate. This was vividly illustrated when the local authority, Hammersmith and Fulham, was censured for playing in the swap market—it did not swap once, but hundreds of times. The local authority had been seeking to speculate on interest rate movements by entering into a series of swap transactions. When the initial bets went wrong, the authority entered into more and more until it was unable to meet the interest payments it was required to make. It started off betting the wrong way—and ended up entering into 500 separate transactions like a gambler on a losing streak.

As the IMF notes: 'derivative instruments tend to strengthen linkages between market segments and between individual financial institutions in ways which are difficult to identify or quantify. Consequently, disruptions or increased uncertainty in one market may now be more likely to spill over into other derivatives markets and into cash markets.'[8]

Systemic risk—the threat to the smooth functioning of the entire financial system—is therefore much increased by this myriad of interlinkages between derivative products and the institutions trading in them. It can be sparked off by any of three occurrences: the default of a major player, a large market movement which wipes out a trader, and the inability to match obligations and receipts of market participants. To understand each of the three types of risk it is first necessary to distinguish between deriva-

---

[8] IMF, *International Capital Markets, Part 1*.

tives, which are traded on exchanges—usually standardized products, subject to the regulations which the exchange imposes—and derivatives which are tailor-made for individual requirements and traded off-exchange or 'over-the-counter' (OTC).

The design of markets for exchange-traded derivatives controls and eliminates credit risk. For instance, credit exposures can be easily monitored on exchanges because there is a near-continuous market for the contracts. This allows the exchanges to ensure that all exposures are 'marking-to-market' at the end of each day—that means the value of products is calculated after each trading session taking into account the market movement during the day. Exchanges also protect against credit risk by acting in collaboration with clearing houses, which allow all private risks to be pooled centrally. The effect is that the exchange itself is the counterparty to transactions, not the individual trader.

The real growth in derivative markets over the past few years, however, has occurred not so much in exchange-traded products, but in OTC contracts which are far more prone to credit risk. The total value of the market rose from $500 billion in 1986 to $4,449 billion in 1991—an increase of 790 per cent. Exchange rate instruments grew slightly less fast, from $583 billion in 1986 to $3,518 billion in 1991—an increase of 503 per cent. And the fact that these obligations are held off-balance-sheet means that creditors (whether trade creditors or banks) do not know of the other party's exposure. If a party cannot pay its obligations under one transaction, it will mean that it cannot pay its obligations under any of its other transactions: the complex house of cards starts to crumble.

The second type of risk—market risk—is the danger that a sharp change in the price of an underlying security or stock will feed through more violently to the price of the derivative contract. In the derivatives market there is a real danger of this being exaggerated by the matrix pattern that the need to hedge produces. As the IMF admits, hedging operations: 'can raise credit risk because they involve taking new positions rather than unwinding existing ones.'

The third danger comes from an illiquid market—the risk that a transaction cannot be arranged at the prevailing market price. The markets for over-the-counter products are less liquid than the more homogeneous markets for exchange-traded products. Dealers with uncovered OTC positions will try to cover them either by taking offsetting positions in an exchange-traded instrument or by synthesizing such a position through 'dynamic hedging', a process which often mandates either the sale of an underlying security when its price falls or its purchase when its price rises. The problem is that these mandated transactions can trigger an avalanche of purchase or sale orders into a relatively illiquid market for the underlying security. In times of crisis, 'the resulting illiquidity may even violate the assumptions underlying the models used to construct these portfolios at precisely the time when the hedges are most needed.'[9]

The next section of this chapter examines the different institutions involved in the derivatives market and argues that a regulatory strategy should aim to secure international agreement for curbs on the overall size of the market in derivative products by increasing capital adequacy requirements for banks and margin requirements for traders. In the absence of such international agreement, however, the regulatory authority should try to prevent increasing the cost of trading unilaterally, so avoiding a rush to offshore hedge funds. It should try to ensure the market has sufficient liquidity, while attempting to isolate and control the 'speculative' use of derivative instruments. This could be done by prescribing politically high-risk institutions from any involvement in the market, other than 'hedging' activities.

4. THE APPROACH TO REGULATION

Regulation of derivatives markets has to occur on two fronts—nationally, through the control of systemic risk; and, internationally, by raising the cost of trading in derivative products. The first part of this section examines how to tackle systemic risk and isolate vulnerable groups in the economy from the effects of engaging in risky speculation.

The National Agenda for Regulation: Channelling All Trading Through Clearing Houses

Systemic risk threatens the whole financial infrastructure of the economy—interest rates, mortgage rates, insurance premia, and the value of personal and corporate pensions—as well as threatening the possibility that large companies will go out of business. The major risks, however, could be contained by the creation of a clearing house system. This would pool the risk of market participants, standardize products, and prescribe certain institutions from involving themselves in speculative activities in the ordinary course of their business. Product standardization also has the added advantage of helping investors to understand better some of the risks involved in particular instruments.[10]

Once products were standardized, a clearing house—regulated by the Bank of England—could act as a repository for all the risks in the market. Only larger financial institutions—deemed to be highly creditworthy and

---

[9] IMF, *International Capital Markets, Part 1.*
[10] Exchanges such as Liffe already use some of these techniques to control credit risk.

capable of assuming risk—would be clearing members. Other—'ordinary'—members would be granted trading rights according to their experience and credit rating. At the moment, traders on an exchange deliver deal tickets by computer to the central exchange system—so it would be easy for that computer system to ensure that those conditions for trading were always met. At the end of the day, the clearing house would 'novate'—transfer and renew—contracts, and match all the receipt and payment obligations of its members. Because the clearing house has taken the obligation on each side of the trade, they should, at the end of the day, cancel out.

There also needs to be a centrally controlled system of marking-to-market, the process in which the central exchange calculate the value of its members' exposures, as the present system is wholly inadequate. At the moment, the amounts made are compared with daily market movements on a three-month swap, and neither party can calculate accurately the amount that they will or will not receive at the end of the three-month period. The process does not compute the cost of undertaking the transaction and the cost of hedging against the exposure. Nor is it a factor in the level of risk involved and the completeness of the hedge. Next, more vulnerable parties—companies, insurance funds, pensions funds, and building societies—should be prevented from speculating as part of their ordinary business activities. They should not be allowed to become involved in derivatives that are not covered by exchanges and clearing houses, and should only be permitted to hedge.

Nor is this difficult. The Bank of England at present operates by requiring that there is a conceptual distinction drawn between 'structural' and 'dealing' positions with reference to foreign exchange risk. The structural side relates to those foreign exchange dealings which have to do with the intrinsic business of the entity, whereas the dealing side is to do with those transactions which are entered into purely with an eye to financial gain in themselves. It would be relatively simple to extend this distinction to all derivative activity.

Undoubtedly, however, 'prescribed' institutions would want to speculate and the problem is that if only hedging is permitted they will turn to more aggressive offshore hedge funds to meet their demands, making the problem even worse. So rather than ban speculation by these institutions altogether, the second-best solution is to allow 'controlled' speculation in specially established Special Purpose Vehicles. These SPVs would need to have credit ratings of AA or better and would need to be separately capitalized from the rest of the group. On disclosing their results into the group accounts, the extent to which the market moves are profitable would be revealed. But no matter how great the losses, the institutions themselves would be shielded from risk.

Further measures would also be needed to ensure that only those who can deal with the risks are allowed to play in the markets. One way this could be done is by increasing prudential capital requirements. There are various ways this could be done—tightening up requirements regarding absolute levels of capital held in deposit accounts, making insurance against speculative losses compulsory, or insisting on government guarantees for depositors—and the aim should be, not to establish a capital adequacy norm at an absolute amount of equity, but rather to operate by means of financial ratios which indicate the entities' ability to meet their obligations. The ratio would require that the level of exposure to the selected markets would not exceed the pre-decided amount. Rather than rely solely on capital adequacy, which, to some extent, can be avoided by 'fiddling' the books, more collateral should be deposited with newly created clearing houses to ensure it has access to a sufficient margin to cover any losses caused by insolvency.

Vitally important is that the whole process is opened up to scrutiny. The markets need to know about the exposure of the counterparties with which they are dealing: trade creditors need to know whether the company they are supplying can meet its obligations; and banks need to know more about the risks involved in the companies to which they are lending money. Accountancy rules must be altered so that companies are required to publish their interest rate and other derivative strategies—and the derivative contracts entered into, and the gains/losses that result, must be made visible on the balance sheet as unrealized assets or liabilities of the company.

International Action

Once speculation is controlled in special purpose vehicles, the next step would be to seek international agreement to increase the cost of trading. Old-fashioned capital controls have been made obsolete in large market-orientated foreign exchange centres. But this section argues that a two-pronged approach could be taken once international agreement was secured—a tax on foreign exchange transactions, and increased capital adequacy and margin requirements on derivatives' trading in SPVs.

First, some of the strategies which have been outlined above to control systemic risk on a national level could be strengthened on an international basis to improve the regulation of OTC products and, eventually, to reduce the overall size of the derivatives' market. The Basle-based Bank for International Settlements is already drawing up plans for incorporating market risk, previously excluded from discussion, into the international definitions for capital adequacy. We need to build on this work, bringing all regulators together in an umbrella organisation to establish common standards across banks, securities houses, and all institutions trading in derivative products. There should be common accounting and disclosure rules, as well as trading standards.

Henry Kaufman in the United States has suggested a new international institution which could serve as a focal point for regulatory harmonization.[11] Called the Board of Overseers of Major International Institutions and Markets, it would consist of central bankers, other governmental agencies, and have some private sector members. It could set acceptable minimum capital requirements for all major institutions in the business, and establish uniform trading, reporting, and disclosure standards for open credit markets. It could also monitor the performance of institutions and markets under its jurisdiction.

There are already some signs of progress. In March 1994, the US Commodity and Futures Trading Commission joined forces with the Securities and Exchange Commission and the UK Securities and Investment Board to discuss regulation of derivatives markets. The meeting resulted in a seven-point plan designed to enhance information-sharing between regulators, to promote the use of legally enforceable netting of claims where one counterpart had gone bust, and proposed a clearing house for OTC derivatives. The SIB said it hoped this Anglo-American agreement would be followed by further global link-ups on the supervision of OTC products.

A priority should be to work towards the official registering of all transactions: on- and off-exchange. The difficulties of this move are often exaggerated, considering the fact that there are at most three or four computer systems used for deal-making in each sector of the market. Currency transactions, for example, are carried out in one of three systems: Reuters, the business information group; Minex, a Japanese company; and EBS, launched last year by a consortium bringing together the major foreign exchange banks and the electronic information group, Quotron. Reuters has more than 19,000 terminals worldwide and estimates that over 50 per cent of all foreign exchange transactions are carried out on its system. Similarly, Bloomberg monopolizes equities trading. Most traders automatically register all transactions made already; the only step necessary for a regulatory body to take would be to standardize recording procedures across exchanges and OTC products, in collaboration with the systems-makers.

Once prudential controls were established across international boundaries, the next stage of regulation should focus on stabilizing the economic environment by reducing the overall volume of business conducted in currency and derivative markets. One possibility is that an international body should introduce a transactions tax on foreign exchange dealing, changing

---

[11] See 'Financial Derivatives in a Rapidly Changing World'. Talk delivered to the City of London Conference on Derivatives, Skinners' Hall, 14 October 1993.

the bias of dealing away from the short-term and towards the longer-term. This chapter will not enter into the detailed arguments concerning the desirability or feasibility of a transactions tax which has been discussed at length elsewhere.[12] It merely notes that, once all transactions were officially registered, it would be relatively straightforward to implement a tax on each transaction. In addition, a distinction could be made between deals which are related to underlying trade and those which are not, subjecting only the latter to the tax.

In derivative markets, the same effect could be obtained by raising the price of trading—in the jargon 'internalizing the externality', that is, making the individual price of trading better reflect the social costs of trading. The attack should take place on two fronts—capital adequacy requirements for institutions and higher margin requirements for individuals. These determine the effective price at which trading takes place and hence they determine the leverage a trader can control, that is, the volume of speculative activity. Both margin requirements and capital adequacy ratios act as a tax on trading.[13]

In addition, circuit-breakers—price halts and trading limits—could also be used to inject a degree of rationality into the system. Already used effectively on Wall Street and in the Paris bourse to shut down trading at times of crisis, they are a recognition of the fact that no system is able to cope with the volume of selling and no amount of liquidity can forestall the gridlock when panic occurs. They provide a much-needed breathing space for potential buyers to assess the market and rework their portfolios. These measures should also make it more costly for institutional investors to reallocate their portfolios for short-term reasons, and remove that bias from their decision-making.

CONCLUSION

The experience of the ERM crisis in 1992–3 and the bond market crash in 1994 underline how government policies can be undermined by financial markets, and, in particular, by the use of derivative products. It has now become imperative that action is taken—on both the national and international level—to regulate derivative markets. First, nationally, the price of derivative products needs to better reflect the systemic risks involved in trading these instruments. To a large extent, this could be done by requir-

---

[12] See e.g. the discussion in R. Kelly, 'A Framework for European Exchange Rates in the 1990s', ch. 14 of J. Michie and J. Grieve Smith (eds.), *Unemployment in Europe* (London: Academic Press, 1994), and the further references given there.

[13] It should be possible to design a system so that it is equally costly to deal indirectly in derivatives or directly in the underlying cash markets.

ing any speculation by institutional funds or the corporate sector to be undertaken in special purpose vehicles on a regulated exchange. Clearing houses need to be established for the purpose. On the international front, the cost of trading in derivatives needs to be raised to curb both hedging and speculative transactions. A new international regulatory agency needs to be established for this purpose, and it should also be charged with setting common standards for accountancy, exposure, and trading.

GLOSSARY

capital adequacy The amount of capital an institution has to set aside in order to assume a certain degree of risk in the markets.

clearing house This is a corporation created by the market, but regulated by the Bank of England, that acts as a central repository for all the risks in the market. It has large financial institutions as clearing members and these deal with smaller financial institutions and with companies who want to use the market. The clearing members pool all the risks owed, matching all the receipts and obligations at the end of each trading session.

derivatives These are financial tools derived from other financial products, such as equities and currencies. The most common of these are futures, swaps, and options, although warrants and swaptions are growing in importance. The derivatives market aims to enable participants to manage their exposure to the risk of movements in interest rates, equities, and currencies.

forward A forward is a promise to supply a particular commodity or security at a set price on a set date in the future.

future A forward contract traded on an exchange.

hedge funds The term hedge fund does not have a precise definition, but the Bank of England accords them the following status: 'a cadre of private investment partnerships that are engaged in active trading and arbitrage of a range of different securities and commodities'. It adds that they are usually operated offshore (or in the USA) so as to be exempt from most types of regulatory oversight and restraint, are highly leveraged, and mainly use the derivatives markets.

hedging This can be seen as a form of insurance against risk. You take out a bet which will pay off if events don't turn out in your favour. For example, if you expect base rates to fall and buy a swap to that effect, you would hedge this by buying another type of product that would pay out enough to cover your losses if base rates actually rise. The current tax authorities' official statement of practice states that 'the intention of the taxpayer in entering into the transaction is of considerable importance'. A transaction is regarded as a hedge if the transaction is economically appropriate to the reduction in the risk of the underlying transaction and if the price fluctuations of the options and futures are directly and demonstrably related to the fluctuations in value or composition of the underlying transaction, asset, or portfolio at the time the hedging transaction is initiated.

leverage   This is the ability to use borrowed funds to bet much larger amounts of money than the trader actually possesses. A hedge fund for example can sometimes borrow up to fifty times the value of his portfolio from a bank to place a bet. That means if the bet proves to be correct, much greater sums are made. Equally, the reverse can happen and huge losses can be incurred.

liquidity   This is the ability to match obligations with the ability to pay. Derivative markets add to the pool of liquidity as well as adding speculative obligations.

margin   This is the amount of collateral a trader has to put upfront before undertaking a deal.

marking to market   This is the system of calculating profit. The amount made during the day is measured against the movement in the overall market.

netting   Under many systems of law, an insolvent company will be entitled to receive all moneys owed to it, but not to pay any moneys out. An alternative is to enforce all of the obligations so that the net amount is paid to the party who is owed it. This is called netting.

options   An option is a contract which gives the buyer the right to buy—or sell—a product at a particular date in the future at a particular price. For example, an option can be a cheap way of guaranteeing the price of a share. Take ICI shares: if these are trading at 500 pence in May 1994, the buyer of an option might want to acquire the ability to be sold a specific number of ICI shares at 600 pence each on 1 November 1994. If ICI shares are trading at 600 pence each on that date, then the option offers the prospect of instant profits for the buyer. This option, and the rights under it, can be traded.

speculation   The speculator takes a view about what is going to happen to the price of a currency, equity, or derivative instrument, and wants to place a bet on being proved correct.

swaps   A swap is simply an exchange of the rate of interest that one borrower is being charged by a lender with that of another borrower. Typically, companies swap floating rate debt for fixed rate debt or vice versa, and a fee is charged. A swap can have a speculative nature: a borrower bets on whether interest rates are going up or down. If they think the cost of borrowing is going to fall, floating rate debt will be the better alternative. Alternatively, the prospect of rising interest rates will probably make a borrower want to switch into fixed rate debt. The problem comes when interest rates start to move in the opposite direction to the prediction of the borrower. In that case, they may find themselves trapped in a costly debt situation—and be forced to take out another swap to bet the other way. In this way, one flawed swap can trigger a whole loop of transactions.

swaptions   This is an option to buy or cancel a swap at some point in the future.

warrants   A warrant is a particular type of option: an obligation on the part of the issuer to provide a predetermined number of a particular type of share to the investor at the time specified by the warrant.

10. Managing the Exchange Rate System

Gerald Holtham

The current system of floating exchange rates between major currencies with intermittant 'management' by central banks has many critics. Yet the Bretton Woods adjustable peg system operated in a world of extensive capital controls and the overwhelming dominance in the system of a single power and currency, the United States and its dollar. Neither of those two conditions now applies. Capital markets are increasingly open and, while the USA retains hegemony, two other currencies, the Deutschmark and the yen, are important centres of regional currency blocs and are willingly held by money managers internationally. Is there a feasible alternative to the *status quo*?

Bretton Woods broke down after the dollar changed from being a hard currency to a relatively weak one as a result of US financial policy during the late 1960s. The more recent experiment in adjustable peg rates, the European Exchange Rate Mechanism, broke down when the hegemonic central bank was perceived by the markets as operating too tight a monetary policy for many of the adherents of the system. The experience convinced many people that an adjustable peg system cannot operate in current conditions and only a single currency can eliminate exchange rate fluctuations. Various schemes for a world central bank have been put forward from time to time. Keynes's original blueprint for Bretton Woods envisaged a more powerful body than the IMF with the right to issue a world reserve currency 'bancor'.[1] That may have been possible in the capitalist world of 1945 but the Americans themselves rejected the suggestion. There is even less political enthusiasm for it at present and in the current multi-polar system it looks utopian. Any reform of the system must be more incremental.

Most suggestions for reform take the form of countries cooperating, with or without supranational insitutions, to limit or manage the flexibility of exchange rates. Two broadly separate sets of reasons can be advanced for seeking to manage exchange rates; they appeal to (i) the effects on government policy and (ii) the effects on the market and individual behaviour.

---

[1] J. M. Keynes, *Proposals for an International Clearing Union*, Cmnd 6437, 1943.

(I)   THE EFFECT ON PUBLIC POLICY

Floating rates present the possibility of competitive policy whereby countries become involved in a zero-sum game, seeking, for example, competitive depreciations or appreciations of their currencies. The first-best solution to this problem is international policy coordination but many (for example Oudiz and Sachs) have speculated that managing exchange rates could be a second-best, eliminating grosser forms of policy competition, or could provide a focus for coordination that might otherwise be too diffuse.[2] Logically the argument is plausible but work by Hughes Hallett, Holtham, and Hutson has shown severe limitations in practice. Model simulations suggest that a 'sensible' path for exchange rates, not an arbitrary one, must be selected if the benefits of avoiding competitive policy are not to be outweighed for any given country by the loss of a policy instrument. Moreover the identification of such a path and securing agreement on it are not trivial problems.[3]

Even if such a path is identified, it does not make sense to have an absolute target which ignores policy trade-offs. Some flexibility is required. The rigidity of ERM rates after German reunification may be seen as an example of problems stemming from an absolutist approach in the face of systematic shocks.

Another argument for fixing is that a fixed rate may be the kind of quasi-binding commitment that helps policy to be credibly 'time-consistent', improving private sector expectations. The notion of 'credibility' has become so fashionable that this idea has given birth to a large literature on the theoretical advantages of combining policy coordination with 'pre-commitment'. The evidence, however, appears to be that this concentration is out of proportion to the empirical importance of credibility or institutional changes aimed at achieving it. That importance appears easy to overstate.

Nonetheless, there is no doubt that international financial markets can react violently to changes of policy and this is a potentially powerful influence on government policies. The question of the appropriate division of power between democratically elected governments and markets remains relevant. How far should the interests of savers and rentiers, as expressed in financial markets, dominate or constrain governments supposedly acting in the interest of their constituents in general? The issue has not generally

    [2] G. Oudiz and J. Sachs, 'Macroeconomic Policy Co-ordination Among the Industrial Economies', *Brookings Papers on Economic Activity*, 1 (1984), 1–64.
    [3] A. Hughes Hallet, G. Holtham, and G. Hutson, 'Exchange-rate Targeting As Surrogate International Co-operation', in M. Miller, B. Eichengreen, and R. Portes (eds.), *Blueprints for Exchange Rate Management* (CEPR/Academic Press, London, 1989).

been put in that way by the economic literature which has been more concerned with principal/agent problems in which governments might fail to
represent the interests of their electorates through preoccupation with the
interests of politicians and bureaucrats. Putting the matter as voters versus
wealth-holders rather than politicians versus the voters turns the spotlight
on private behaviour.

(II) THE EFFECT ON MARKET BEHAVIOUR

Attempts to influence private sector behaviour depend on the notion that
uncontrolled asset markets display excess volatility and/or medium-term
swings unrelated to economic fundamentals and foreign exchange markets
simply provide an example of that. This view used to be severely contested
by many academic economists wedded to the efficient market hypothesis
but the balance of academic opinion appears to have shifted. An important
corollary is that institutional changes or central bank intervention in the
foreign exchange market could reduce exchange rate volatility—without a
compensating increase in volatility elsewhere in the system.

Studies of the ERM, for example, found that while exchange rate volatility dropped after the system was introduced, so did the volatility of interest rates in those countries taking part, compared both with their own
previous history and with similar countries outside. This was first shown in
'City' research by Holtham, Keating, and Spencer and then in academic
research by Artis and Taylor.[4] It was not attributable to exchange controls
since the findings were true of offshore 'Euro' rates. More recently, Flood
and Rose have shown that while fixed rates are less volatile than floating
rates, the volatility of 'fundamental' determinants of exchange rates, including money stocks and interest rates, does not differ much across exchange
rate regimes.[5] A successful fixed rate system therefore suppresses exchange
rate volatility without cost.

An important question is whether this excess volatility has any significant
deleterious effects on economic activity. Suprisingly perhaps, the evidence
is that there are no perceptible effects on trade volumes or their growth.
Paul Krugman asserts two other costs, however.[6] One is that the problem
of noise/signal extraction means that trade prices respond less to changes
in exchange rates when the latter are volatile. The response of product-

[4] M. P. Taylor and M. J. Artis, 'What has the European Monetary System Achieved?' in
Bank of England Discussion Paper 31, Mar., 1988.
[5] R. P. Flood, and A. K. Rose, 'Fixing Exchange Rates: A Volatile Quest for
Fundamentals', London School of Economics Financial Markets Group Discussion Paper
163, 1994.
[6] P. Krugman, 'The Case for Stabilizing Exchange Rates', *Oxford Review of Economic
Policy* 5/3, Autumn 1989.

market participants to real factors which affect the exchange rate, and should alter their behaviour, is therefore attenuated. A second cost is that international companies have an incentive to maintain spare capacity in a world of capricious exchange rate swings so that they can vary the source of production according to temporary exchange rate movements. That is wasteful from a social viewpoint.

The final indictment of unmanaged floating exchange rate markets therefore reads as follows: they obscure relative price changes impeding resource allocation; they encourage wasteful excess capacity; they place in the hands of some private agents considerable power to influence government policy that many think excessive (others on the political right, however, regard any private restraint on government power as salutary).

Notably, one criticism of floating rates has been winnowed by events; in the 1970s it was common to contrast the inflationary bias of floating rates with the supposed deflationary bias of fixed rates (the latter bias was what Keynes's bancor was supposed to eliminate). As noted above, however, Bretton Woods broke down because many countries considered it had become too inflationary, though the ERM did fall apart for the opposite reason. The absence of fixed parities among the dollar, yen, and Deutschmark has not prevented a global disinflation in the 1980s and research has not found that this proceeded significantly more quickly in the ERM than elsewhere. What emerges is that for an adjustable peg system to survive there has to be a consensus on policy among the participants. If there is a hegemonic monetary authority (which has always been the case), the others must be willing to follow its lead. Moreover in a free-capital system, the markets must be persuaded that they will continue to do so, if trouble is to be avoided.

ADJUSTABLE PEGS OR TARGET ZONES ARE DIFFICULT TO MAINTAIN

Because freely floating rates are an imperfect system, it does not follow a better one can be found. The two alternatives (excluding a world money) are an adjustable peg system or a target zone system. Hybrids, combining both features, are, of course, possible. Target zones have become fashionable because a line of theorizing, pioneered by Krugman, showed how the existence of a credible zone could reduce volatility without cost.[7]

The recent experience of ERM has eliminated much optimism. The main criticism of managed systems now is that they cannot be maintained in conjunction with open capital markets. Bretton Woods and ERM were

[7] ——, 'Target Zones and Exchange Rate Dynamics', NBER Working Paper, 2481, June, 1988.

founded; both thrived for some fourteen years and then fell apart. Both systems were founded on a policy consensus and foundered when that began to fray. In 1971, both France and Germany considered US policy to be inflationary; as that perception spread there was a flight to gold. The ERM was founded on a shared determination to give priority in macroeconomic policy-setting to fighting inflation.

The ERM breakdown was different from its predecessor in that the policy consensus did not break down, although it came under strain as inflation was low everywhere, while unemployment mounted. The view that macroeconomic policy was impotent to affect activity and employment over all but the shortest run survived among European policy makers and protected the system. What broke down was market confidence that they would continue to think like that.

The speculation that ensued was different from the textbook, economic theoretic phenomenon described in the 'speculative attack' literature. In theory an attack arises when a country is following unsustainable policies which will eventually exhaust foreign exchange reserves. The attack merely accelerates that event.[8] In the case of ERM, no country was evidently following a financially unsustainable policy. The markets judged that some countries' policies would be politically unsustainable because they would result in 'excessive' deflation. The attack then forced up interest rates in those countries, making the deflation worse. Governments which were genuinely ready to persist with 10 per cent interest rates and a fixed parity were forced by the market to instead raise interest rates much higher. That did indeed make the prospective deflation really intolerable and a currency depreciation followed. The speculation was destabilizing in that it changed a situation that would have continued unchanged in the absence of the speculation and self-fulfilling in that it brought about that which it expected. Governments were not allowed to pursue the policies they had—rightly or wrongly—chosen.

There are reasons to think that such 'self-fulfilling' speculative attacks will be relatively rare. Often governments will intend to do what the market suspects them of. If they do not, why, in general, should large numbers of non-colluding market participants come to share the same suspicion? Indeed, the current fashion in economic theorizing, to assume that everyone knows all they need to know to pursue their self-interest via rational calculation, blinded economists to the possibility of destabilizing self-fulfilling speculation. After all, if everyone knows everything, or at least can quote correct odds on the probability of all possible events, markets would 'know' governments were sincere and would not speculate! None the less,

---

[8] P. Krugman, 'A Model of Balance of Payments Crises', *Journal of Money Credit and Banking*, 11/3, 1979.

though rare, such attacks are manifestly possible and any viable system has to have a protection against them.

The requirements for an operational fixed rate or fixed zone system are therefore heavy: a consensus on monetary policy and either utter credibility of that consensus or some mechanism to defend against destabilizing, self-fulfilling speculative attack.

A POOR SOLUTION: 'SAND IN THE WHEELS'

Because many doubt whether such conditions can be fulfilled, they argue for the reimposition of exchange controls or taxation of foreign exchange transactions in order to inhibit the international flow of finance—putting sand in the wheels.

These proposals, however, raise other difficulties. Firstly, unless exceptionally well designed, they could inhibit international financial investment flows or trade finance. One of the features of the period after liberalization has been larger currrent account deficits or surpluses than at any time since the nineteenth century. That reflects an ability to finance investment or government expenditure by drawing on the savings of other countries to a greater extent than previously possible. An OECD study has shown a diminishing correlation between domestic saving and investment since the end of the 1960s.[9] In principle that ought to be a good thing, at least potentially raising rates of return to saving and investment around the world. The attempt to distinguish investment from speculation is likely to prove a nightmare but, anyway, misses the point. Some speculation is not at all destabilizing; indeed it is benign, even necessary.

Some flows, and much volatility of exchange rates, have not been 'excessive' but an appropriate response to government policies. Administrative or fiscal controls would throw out the proverbial baby with her bath-water by inhibiting stabilizing as well as destabilizing speculation. Given the existence of a J-curve in the response of the current account to exchange rate changes, any exchange rate driven wholly or largely by the current account (the situation in the absence of capital flows), is subject to unstable oscillations. Some speculative capital flows are necessary for stability. The efforts by companies engaged in trade to hedge against foreign exchange losses are another, wholly legitimate, form of speculation.

Those objections can be illustrated by the experience of floating exchange rates in the past two decades. Exchange rate volatility can be related to the brutality of discordant policy moves, and exchange rate instability has

[9] A. Dean, M. Durand, J. Fallon, and P. Hoeller, 'Savings Trends and Behaviour in OECD Countries', OECD Department of Economics Working Paper, 67, 1989.

increased in cases where capital flows have been impeded. The impediment was not created by government but the effect is the same in any case.

A GLANCE AT HISTORY

Table 10.1 shows the level, standard deviation, and coefficient of variation of the real (i.e. inflation-adjusted) yen/dollar and Deutschmark/dollar exchange rates over the past three decades. High coefficients of variation, around 20 per cent, in the 1970s and 1980s have fallen to under 10 per cent in the 1990s. In the last five years, the fluctuations of the dollar against the Deutschmark have been less than the wide bands of the current ERM and much less than the proposed width of target zones proposed by Williamson and others. Similar results apply to nominal exchange rates and to the volatility of monthly changes in exchange rates. The annual volatility of DM/\$ (defined as the standard deviation of monthly percentage changes multiplied by $\sqrt{12}$) has fallen from 2 in the 1970s to 1.5 in the 1980s to 0.3 in the 1990s.

Table 10.1. Real currency volatility

		1970s	1980s	1990s
Real Yen/US\$	Mean	245.6	195.6	148.5
	SD	58.5	38.8	14.1
	CoV	0.24	0.20	0.09
Real DM/US\$	Mean	1.97	2.25	1.84
	SD	0.34	0.40	0.09
	CoV	0.17	0.18	0.05

Real exchange rate indexed on 1985 nominal exchange rate and relative prices.
Coefficient of variations = Standard Deviation/Mean.

The drop in volatility is entirely owing to changes in objective conditions and in government policy. Evidently the 1970s were a period of very high and variable inflation rates that differed considerably across countries. Sharp movements in nominal exchange rates were therefore to be expected. Interestingly, these failed, in general, to stabilize real exchange rates. If that is a cost of inflation, it is unclear that it is possible, or wise, to eliminate it by controlling exchange rate movements rather than by taking it into consideration when determining inflation targets.

The 1980s were a period of wildly different fiscal policies in major countries that led to large changes and differences in real interest rates and ultimately to large current account imbalances that fed back on exchange rates. Table 10.2 shows cyclically adjusted budget balances as a percentage of GNP/GDP and Table 10.3 shows current account balances.[10]

Expansionary fiscal policy in the United States coincided with restrictive policies in Germany and Japan leading to higher US growth rates and interest rates and a rising dollar, particularly against the Deutschmark. This development through 1982 and 1983 led to a speculative bubble in 1984 when the dollar became detached from all attempts at fundamental explanation even *ex post*. However, the trouble was initiated by discordant policy. That policy then led to current account imbalances that threatened to lead to unsustainable foreign debt positions and the bubble burst and the dollar fell substantially for several years. Impeding capital flows might have stabilized exchange rates but at the cost of less trade; with less foreign borrowing, the Americans could not have imported so much. That would have resulted in more inflation in the United States and more deflation in Japan and Germany. There is no evident advantage in such an outcome.

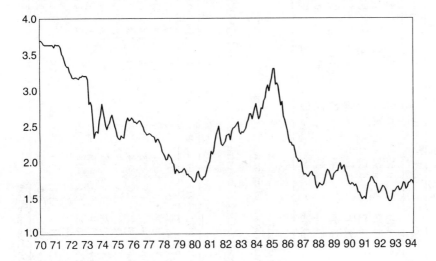

Fig. 10.1 DM/US$ exchange rate

Subsequently, as the figures show, the exchange rates have been quieter, despite German unification in 1989 leading to a large shift in German fiscal policy. That did trigger a Deutschmark appreciation of some 25 per cent, relatively modest in the circumstances, and there was no speculative bubble. The outcome was superior to events within the ERM where the

[10] G. Holtham, 'World Current Account Balances', *Oxford Review of Economic Policy*, 6/3, Autumn.

Table 10.2. Cyclically adjusted budget balances[a] (changes as a percentage of GNP/GDP)[b]

	1979	1980	1981	1982	1983	1984	1985	1986	1987	1988	1989
United States	0.26	-1.01	0.60	-1.31	-0.11	-0.11	-0.87	-0.29	0.49	-0.01	0.27
Japan	0.56	0.19	0.92	0.46	0.51	1.72	1.09	0.14	1.67	—	0.06
Germany	-0.57	-0.32	0.55	2.47	2.38	0.72	0.85	-0.47	-0.61	-0.30	1.65
France	1.63	1.05	-1.19	-0.36	-0.19	1.33	0.26	0.27	0.87	0.35	-0.19
Italy	0.41	1.56	-2.40	0.56	1.08	-0.79	-0.96	1.43	0.92	0.69	0.10
United Kingdom	0.94	0.52	2.67	1.38	-0.20	-0.37	1.32	0.41	0.24	0.99	-0.19
Canada	0.68	-0.84	1.36	-2.17	-0.12	0.14	-0.86	0.59	0.60	0.98	-0.97

Source: Holtham, 1990.

Notes: [a] Based on a moving benchmark.
[b] A positive figure indicates a lower deficit or a higher surplus.

Table 10.3. Current balances of OECD countries as a percentage of GNP/GDP surplus (+) or deficit (−) as a percentage of nominal GNP/GDP

	1971	1972	1973	1974	1975	1976	1977	1978	1979	1980	1981	1982	1983	1984	1985	1986	1987	1988
United States*	-0.1	-0.5	0.5	0.1	1.1	0.2	-0.7	-0.7	—	0.1	0.3	-0.2	-1.3	-2.8	-2.8	-3.1	-3.2	-2.6
Japan*	2.5	2.2	—	-0.1	-0.1	0.7	1.6	1.7	-0.9	-1.0	0.4	0.6	1.8	2.8	3.7	4.4	3.6	2.8
Germany*	0.4	0.5	1.5	2.8	1.0	0.8	0.8	1.4	-0.7	-1.7	-0.5	0.8	0.8	1.6	2.6	4.4	4.0	4.0
France	0.3	0.1	0.6	-1.4	0.8	-1.0	-0.1	1.4	0.9	-0.6	-0.8	-2.2	-0.9	-0.2	-0.1	0.3	-0.5	-0.4
Italy	1.3	1.5	-1.5	-4.3	-0.3	-1.3	1.0	2.1	1.6	-2.2	-2.2	-1.5	0.4	-0.6	-0.9	0.4	-0.2	-0.7
United Kingdom	1.9	0.3	-1.3	-3.8	-1.4	-0.8	-0.1	0.6	-0.3	1.4	2.7	1.7	1.3	0.6	0.9	—	-0.7	-3.1
Canada	0.4	-0.3	0.2	-0.9	-2.7	-2.1	-2.0	-2.0	-1.7	-0.4	-1.7	0.8	0.8	0.6	-0.4	-2.1	-1.7	-1.7
Total of the above countries	0.5	0.2	0.3	-0.4	0.5	—	—	0.4	-0.2	-0.5	0.1	—	-0.2	-0.8	-0.6	-0.1	-0.3	-0.3
Total of the smaller OECD countries	-0.2	1.1	1.1	-2.0	-1.5	-2.0	-2.3	-0.9	-1.5	-2.8	-2.2	-1.9	-0.8	-0.3	-0.3	-0.3	-0.5	-0.4
Total OECD	0.4	0.3	0.4	-0.7	0.1	-0.3	-0.4	0.2	-0.4	-0.9	-0.3	-0.3	-0.3	-0.7	-0.6	-0.1	-0.3	-0.4

Source: OECD, *Economic Outlook*, 46, December 1989.

Notes: *Percentage of GNP.

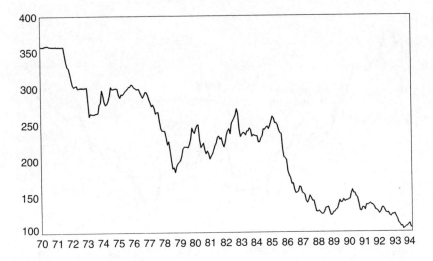

Fig. 10.2 Yen/US$ exchange rate

need for a real Deutschmark appreciation was not recognized by countries besotted with the need to maintain 'credibility' in the fight against inflation.

However, while volatility has fallen, it has done so much more in the case of the Deutschmark than in the case of the yen. As Table 10.1 shows, the coefficient of variation of the yen/dollar remains nearly twice as high as that of the Deutschmark/dollar. Moreover, that measure understates the difference between the currencies because the yen/dollar has also been the object of more central bank intervention than has the Deutschmark/dollar in the recent past. The reason for the difference is that the latter is much more sensitive to relative interest rates, driving short-run capital flows, than is the latter. This is indicated in Figures 10.3 and 10.4, showing the association of the two exchange rates with real short-term interest differentials and in Figures 10.5 and 10.6 showing the influence of the bilateral current accounts of Germany and Japan with the United States. The greater importance of interest rates for the Deutschmark and the current account for the yen is evident.

The lower elasticity of short-term Japanese capital flows is not evidently caused by government action but that is not relevant. Any attempt to tax or regulate such flows would have a similar result. A consequence of that lower elasticity is that the currency is driven more by the current account. As the charts show, that results in an oscillation in both the currency and the current balance, which is quite possibly explosive. An appreciation of the yen increases the Japanese current account surplus because of its effect on trade prices—the so-called J-curve. This increase in the surplus propels

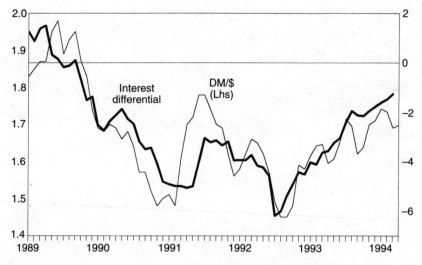

Fig. 10.3 DM/US$ and real three-month interest differential

the yen higher, causing another increase in the current account. Eventually, after a period of years, the effect on trade volumes overtakes the overlapping J-curves and begins to reduce the current account. After another lag, the yen begins to depreciate and the process goes into reverse.

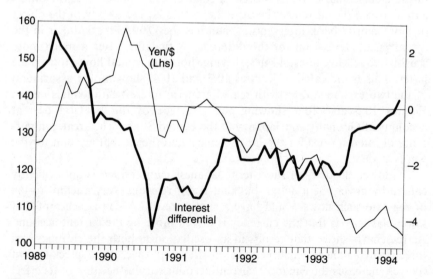

Fig. 10.4 Yen/US$ and real three-month interest differential

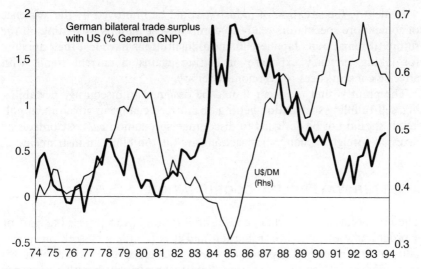

Fig. 10.5   DM/US$ and bilateral trade surplus

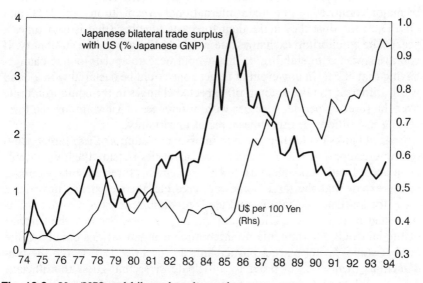

Fig. 10.6   Yen/US$ and bilateral trade surplus

Evidently, the situation of industry would be improved by the existence of some more speculators ready to damp the oscillations by betting on the future turning-point. Japanese financial institutions have lost their appetite for taking currency exposure or betting against a current trend, with adverse consequences for economic welfare.

The point is that a system should be designed to discourage destabilizing, self-fulfilling speculation betting on a forced change in government policy. It should not be designed to discourage speculation *per se*. Controls or taxes on foreign exchange transactions are far too blunt an instrument.

A BETTER WAY: POLICY COORDINATION

The first point is that exchange rate stabilization has to proceed as part of a programme of policy coordination and it is pointless to seek more stability than various policy positions warrant. One approach would be to set target zones between the currencies of major countries or blocs whose monetary and fiscal policies are substantially independent. The width of the target zone would reflect the disparity of policy and the expected change in the 'equilibrium' exchange rate, conditional on stated policies being followed.

There is a great deal of obscuranticism about the determination of exchange rates. Pure prediction is very difficult but there is substantial consensus on what determines equilibrium exchange rates on stated conditions. A requirement would be projection of implied 'equilibrium' exchange rates of major countries by the main international organizations, the IMF and OECD, at the time they make their forecasts together (that is four times a year). The equilibrium exchange rate would not in general be stationary. If countries wished to stabilize it, they would need to specify policy changes having that effect. In any event, a target zone could be declared with a band width sufficient to take account of: expected changes in the equilibrium rate over the forecast period, together with differences of view among the forecasting institutions or other measures of uncertainty.

Central banks could then agree to intervene to support these target zones on the presumption that movements of currencies outside them would not be in accord with fundamentals. Such a system has three advantages. First, to the extent that the target zones are credible, their existence provides a focus for market expectations and tends to stabilize market movements, as suggested in the academic literature on target zones. Second, the forecast of fundamental determinants by international organizations could acquire market value, giving market participants an incentive to research the fundamentals themselves in order to anticipate or second-guess the officials. This would tend to concentrate resources on forecasting fundamentals rather than simply trying to guess or assess what other market participants will do, on the lines of Keynes's beauty contest analogy. At the moment, long-run research has only limited value to market participants if they are unclear whether the long-run fundamentals will prove relevant over their planning or trading horizon. It pays to be cleverer than the rest of the market but not much cleverer, otherwise you can go broke waiting to be vindicated. Multiple market equilibria are surely possible depending on the amount of information on fundamentals that market participants have judged it worthwhile to collect at any time. From a social point of view, there is probably an excess of resources devoted to monitoring market gossip at any time and a shortage devoted to genuine research. The public interest is probably served by having financial markets in 'high-information' rather than 'low-information' equilibrium. This proposal might tend to increase the amount of privately generated research and information in the market.[11] Third, the provision of quasi-independent forecasts of fundamentals would prevent governments setting arbitrary target zones and to the extent that they were concerned about exchange rates, would provide pressure for policy coordination or 'horse-trading' over policy.

This proposal is modest enough. In fact, it could frequently be the case that policy or analytical disagreements would be so great that the agreed target zones would stretch beyond the normal range of variation of the currencies in question. In that case, the system would do little good but no harm either.

Adjustable Pegs Based on Close Policy Coordination

Some countries may be more ambitious and seek tighter control of exchange rates, being substantially agreed on macroeconomic policies. An adjustable peg system then becomes possible—except for the risk of destabilizing speculation. I believe there are two requirements to obviate that risk. One is a strong consensus on policy with a committed hegemony. The second is the existence of clear rules for when parity changes should occur. The ERM failed because it lacked both those requirements.

It is sometimes argued that central banks or monetary authorities cannot cope with unregulated capital markets because the latter deploy many times more funds in a week than the total of central bank reserves. The premise is true but irrelevant and the assertion is simply mistaken. The point is that currency speculators have to buy some currency whenever they are selling another. If they are speculating against fixed parities, it follows

[11] G. Holtham, 'Foreign Exchange Markets and Target Zones', *Oxford Review of Economic Policy*, 5/3, Autumn, 1989.

they are buying one of the currencies in the fixed rate system. The central bank which controls that currency does not need reserves; it can simply provide unlimited amounts of its own currency to meet the speculative demand. It is impossible to run the Bank of Japan out of yen or the Bundesbank out of Deutschmarks.

The only limitation on this central bank response is that officials may share the fears of the speculators; they may be concerned that other currencies are overvalued or that others' policies are inflationary (and inflation could then be imported through massive unlimited intervention pushing up the domestic money supply). Furthermore they may fear that while others' policies are sound, the speculators are correct in thinking them politically unsustainable. If a central bank prints enormous sums of money to buy foreign currency (incidentally sterilizing any effect on domestic money-market interest rates) and then the foreign government changes policy and depreciates after all, the central bank will incur a currency loss. When it buys back its own currency with the newly acquired foreign currency reserves, it will leave domestic currency in the system because the reserves have lost value. That is potentially inflationary. If, on the other hand, the speculators are wrong, they will have to close their positions at an unchanged parity. The increase in domestic currency caused by the central bank intervention is then fully and harmlessly reversed.

To reduce the risks, the adjustable peg system needs a set of agreed indicators for policy and for the sustainablility of existing parities. The unconditional commitment that was a feature of the ERM, that central banks would intervene to protect parity limits, would be made conditional. A central bank whose currency was being bought would have no obligation to support another currency unless the indicators indicated it was sustainable and its government's policy was in accord with agreed indicators. If those conditions were met, however, it would intervene literally without limit. Such a system is neither necessarily deflationary, as the ERM turned out to be, nor necessarily inflationary (as Keynes's bancor system might well have been in practice). The overall stance would depend on the consensus involved. Inevitably, initiative lies in the hands of the monetary authority with the strongest currency. Its policy stance must be broadly acceptable to other countries if the system is to survive but would be subject to modification if it were forced to intervene to support other countries whose indicators were in order.

If the indicators were publicly known, much speculation would be eliminated. It was never credible that the Bundesbank would increase German M3 enormously to support another ERM currency, irrespective of the policies being followed elsewhere. It is more credible that a central bank would agree to expand money supply to support another currency, the stock of which was growing very slowly. In effect, the existence of indicators puts central banks in the system in the position of jointly targeting a range of indicators covering all the countries concerned. Of course not all speculation would be eliminated. If a country were meeting the stated conditions for support but only just, markets could speculate that soon the conditions would cease to be met and so on. Nonetheless if speculation were restricted to such marginal cases it would be an advance and close coordination should enable central banks to deal even with those.

The ultimate source of the ERM's instability was the incredibility of the Bundesbank's commitment to fixed parities, irrespective of the effects on domestic money supply. If one could imagine a situation in which the credibility of the Bundesbank's commitment to a parity was complete, it is evident that there would be no crisis and no instability. The essential step in achieving that, paradoxically, is to relieve the central bank with the strongest currency of the unconditional necessity to intervene when a currency is in trouble. It is precisely because the commitment is unconditional that it is incredible.

Rules of the Game

The basic requirement for an adjustable peg, therefore, is devising, negotiating, and agreeing a set of conditions which any currency must fulfil in order to qualify for unlimited support from the system's reserve bank—the one whose currency happens to be strongest. The conditions must be such as to persuade the reserve bank that speculation against the currency is not based on fundamentals and can be resisted. Even the conditional commitment necessarily entails that the reserve bank cannot control its money supply on a day-to-day or week-to-week basis. The conditions should mean, however, that departure of the money supply from target will be temporary and non-inflationary.

What of currencies that do not meet the conditions? The answer clearly is that, if subjected to speculative attack, they must devalue. The adjustable peg adjusts—along, no doubt, with other policies—until the conditions are met.

Conditions for Intervention

It is possible to argue that the indicators with which the reserve bank should concern itself are monetary indicators. After all, what does it matter if the current account is in deficit and inflation is high if monetary policy is restrictive? Eventually that restriction will slow inflation and rectify the current account. Yet, evidently, things do not work like that. The UK's monetary policy was as restrictive as anyone could wish in September 1992;

interest rates were high, the yield curve was inverse, money growth was
slowing rapidly—to the point where the monetarists were shrieking for
lower interest rates—and inflation itself was falling. Speculation arose
because the markets did not think this policy would lead to a rapid decline
in UK prices and a restoration of UK competitiveness and output. They
believed it would lead to a prolongation of recession or slump, leading
eventually to the policy being abandoned. The market thought real activity variables, not prices, would do much of the adjustment and in a politically intolerable way. That means that purely monetary conditions will not
do for a currency to qualify for reserve bank support. Monetary indicators
are necessary but not sufficient.

Implicitly, what everyone recognizes is that certain imbalances may be so
great that their rectification requires larger relative price changes than can
easily be achieved without changing the nominal exchange rate. The effort
to bring about those changed relative prices at a constant nominal exchange
rate will, in reality, entail such severe disruption to economic activity and
such consequent hardship to many voters, that it is politically unsustainable as well as being severely sub-optimal.

Monetary Indicators

Both monetary policy and other indicators will be necessary for the
adjustable peg system. There are periods of instability in the relation
between money and nominal GDP, so it would be as well to supplement
monetary aggregates with other indicators of monetary stance. Real short-
term interest rates and the yield curve are two such. Other indicators of
incipient inflationary pressure are available, notably certain prices that
tend to lead the general price level, such as asset prices, equities, and
property.

Real Indicators

A key indicator will be a cyclically adjusted measure of the current account.
As a country's level of activity rises or falls relative to that of trading partners, its current account moves into or out of deficit. This purely cyclical
movement can be measured approximately and the current account can be
corrected for it. The remaining or 'structural' current balance then becomes
a relevant indicator. There is no need to take it too seriously. Balance of
payments statistics are notoriously unreliable; indeed there is a large deficit
in the global sum of national balances of payments, which should be iden-
tically zero, indicating an error in the data. A deficit of, say, 3 per cent of
GDP, cyclically adjusted, might, however be prima-facie evidence of a

problem. It should be looked at in conjunction with the accumulated level of foreign debt (the sum of past current account deficits).

Another, more forward-looking, indicator of external competitivity is the prices of goods that are traded internationally, relative to their prices in other countries. If these prices are out of line, it is likely that trade will deteriorate even if currently in balance. This should at best, though, be a supplementary or tie-break indicator because measures of relative goods prices are extremely treacherous. Who is to say that similar goods are really similar to consumers? Attempts to establish that a law of one price prevails for traded goods have failed. The OECD publishes 'Purchasing Power Parities' (PPPs) or measures of difference in price level among countries. When these are used to calculate 'equilibrium' exchange rates, an exercise followed by a number of commercial companies, they produce implausible results. Even floating exchange rates show no tendency to revert to the calculated equilibrium. PPPs have a role but it is limited.

So far, none of the indicators is likely to cause any great problems in principle. All the difficulties would come in deciding on appropriate target levels and on relative weights, should the indicators point in different directions. Yet it would be necessary to be as explicit as possible on all these things for two reasons: first, to limit the scope for invidious exercises of judgement by the reserve bank, although these cannot be entirely eliminated; second, so that the reserve bank's decision will generally be predictable by the market.

One, much more difficult, consideration remains. Take the case of Ireland, which was forced into a devaluation in 1992 and refused convincing Bundesbank support, although it had a current account surplus as well as adequately tight money. If the Bundesbank was correct to cut Ireland adrift, its action could be justified only on the grounds that the effect on real activity made the Irish exchange rate policy unsustainable. In other words, an implicit judgement about the real economy and the limits of political toleration was involved.

If both the Bundesbank and the markets acted on such considerations, they are undeniably relevant to the rules of the game of an adjustable rate system. Yet they raise peculiar difficulties. How can a foreign central bank judge the limits of political tolerance and the politically acceptable better than politicians, whose careers depend on that judgement? A government with an 'overvalued' exchange rate can generally prevent the overvaluation showing up in a balance of payments deficit by following a very deflationary fiscal policy. That reduces absorption in the economy, almost certainly at the cost of high unemployment. Unemployment then becomes the only obvious indicator that the exchange rate is overvalued. The markets can look at the unemployment and conclude that a devaluation is in order and they can speculate that the government will eventually have one. That describes the situation of the French franc in 1993. Should the reserve bank therefore take account of unemployment rates in deciding whether a currency should be supported? If unemployment rates, why not opinion polls of government popularity? The market certainly takes account of those too.

It may well be in reality that no agreement could be secured on an 'activity variable' like unemployment being used as a condition for exchange rate support. If the current fashion for making central banks 'independent' and telling them to target only inflation or monetary variables spreads, the position will become even more difficult. How can a central bank be forbidden to take account of real domestic variables when setting domestic policy and yet be required to consider foreign activity? This suggests that close coordination of policies internationally, a precondition for managing exchange rates, requires equally close coordination of monetary and fiscal policies within each country and the practice of using all policy instruments to address all policy objectives together.

A compromise might be to introduce such an activity variable but to give it very wide bands. For example, unemployment or bankruptcies would have to have risen say three percentage points relative to a trend level within a limited time period, say eighteen months, before being regarded as relevant.

Double Jeopardy

Finally, consider the situation where a currency is not in accordance with the conditions and devalues. Evidently, the effect of a devaluation and of any accompanying policy changes will take time to have their effect. A current account imbalance, for example, is often worsened for a year or more by devaluation. Generally markets are aware of these lags and do not drive a currency ever lower while the lags work through. Nonetheless, a currency cannot be left without formal underpinning indefinitely. The conditions must include a 'no double jeopardy' clause. Once a currency has undergone an agreed realignment, it automatically becomes in good order and is subject to unlimited support for an agreed period—say six months. Thereafter, if it is still not in accord with conditions, its support may be withdrawn. Such a rule would have the effect of turning the system into a crawling peg arrangement for currencies where a fixed peg is not appropriate or defensible, with adjustment each six months. Forward markets and interest differentials would adapt to that situation.

CONCLUSION

There is no point in attempting to fix exchange rates in the absence of a degree of international policy consultation and coordination. The extent of ambition in fixing rates should depend on the degree of possible policy coordination. Given some readiness to coordinate, exchange rates are a reasonable focus for attention in that their management can discipline both governments and market expectations. It is tempting to seek to tax or constrain makets to reduce exchange rate volatility and make governments' task easier, but there are unresolved difficulties in any such attempt, notably that exchange rate stability depends on the existence of speculation. Not all speculation is stabilizing, by any means, but some speculation is necessary (not sufficient!) for stability.

An adjustable peg system requires a high degree of policy consensus to operate and perhaps requires a committed hegemony. It also requires clear rules and criteria on when parity realignments should be carried through. Even then, central banks might have to 'play poker' with the markets, to an extent which they normally avoid, to prevent recurrent bouts of destabilizing speculation seeking to change government policy. The monetary authority whose currency is in demand in a speculative attack must be prepared to see very large, though short-lived, fluctuations in domestic money supply as it accommodates temporary surges in speculative demand.

11. Lessons of Exchange Rate Targeting[1]

Mike Artis

A wide variety of exchange rate targeting practices have been operated in the last decade and a half. This fact, together with the range of outcomes we can observe, ought to enable us to draw some conclusions about best practice for particular circumstances and objectives. The chapter is structured as follows. In the section immediately following, we discuss the numerous forms exchange rate targeting may take and the variety of objectives and motivations lying behind these alternatives. Then, in section 2, we turn to discuss three recent episodes of exchange rate targeting. These correspond to: the Plaza Accord episode; UK practice with respect to exchange rate targeting in the 1980s; and the ERM experience. In section 3, we attempt to draw some conclusions. It is fashionable to argue that experience suggests that only two alternatives are viable—freely flexible exchange rates or completely fixed exchange rates (as in monetary union). Our argument will be that this dichotomy is too stark and that intermediate positions are possible. However, the force behind the dichotomy is the respect that must be given to speculative capital movements. Any claims to detect sustainable intermediate positions must incorporate some means of coping with speculative pressures.

1. FORMS AND OBJECTIVES OF EXCHANGE RATE TARGETING

Exchange rate targeting comes in several forms. Perhaps the weakest is to be identified with the presence of the exchange rate—along with other ultimate and intermediate variables—in the objective function of the policy authorities of a country. This means that the exchange rate 'matters', but it may not matter much and need not produce any central-rate-and-bands formula, whether publicly announced or 'secret'. At the other end of the spectrum is the fully-fledged exchange rate *system*, where a group of countries agree together to target their bilateral exchange rates within certain pre-announced bands around agreed central rates.

[1] The author acknowledges support from the Leverhulme Foundation through a grant administered by the CEPR.

A prior question in all this is the distinction between *real* and *nominal* exchange rates. In practice, exchange rate targeting almost invariably takes a formally nominal form; but it may be (explicitly or implicitly) agreed that the nominal central rate should be periodically revised to take account of relative inflation. An objective of *real* exchange rate targeting is explicit in Williamson's 'blueprint' (Williamson, 1985*a*) and implicit in the Plaza Accord episode. Exchange rate targets are usually announced in terms of a central rate, or set of central rates, with bands of fluctuation of pre-agreed size; this is the 'hard' version. In the 'soft' version, the central rate is simply a target and the bands are not binding—they are 'soft' barriers. The advantage claimed for the former is that, if credible, the announced bands attract supportive speculation (the 'target zone' literature (e.g. Krugman (1991) is based on this point). The advantage claimed for the latter, soft, version is precisely that when the system may not be credible and speculation may be destabilizing, the softness of the band removes the 'one-way bet' that is liable to induce overwhelming speculation. A third important distinction is that between exchange rate targeting taking place within a system and that based on a 'go-it-alone' individual country initiative.

A variety of objectives can be seen as motivating exchange rate targeting. A concern for competitiveness underlies real exchange rate targeting: and whilst this may have a mercantilist inspiration, this is by no means always so. In fact, a desire to protect the achievements of the global trading system has been seen as a motivation for the phase of exchange rate management inaugurated by the Plaza Accord (e.g., Kenen, 1989); more generally, it can be argued that a system of trade arrangements requires some assurance that it will not be undermined by real exchange rate misalignments that will give rise to demands for the imposition or reimposition of trade barriers. Williamson's (1985*b*) 'instruments and assignments' account of the Bretton Woods arrangements observes this point, which must also hold for the European Monetary System. Just as the need to preserve competitiveness from arbitrary shifts in exchange rates may call for a system response, so also may considerations of competitiveness lead an individual country to intervene to prevent or dampen what is seen as an undue appreciation of the currency. Vaubel (1980), for example, has spoken of an 'implicit emergency clause' under which a country which is normally devoted to the pursuit of monetary targets will abandon these in favour of exchange rate stabilization when there is a strong enough appreciation. In these circumstances it will normally be possible to argue that the counter-inflationary objectives of the money supply targeting will be easily met.

The second main objective of exchange rate targeting has indeed been that of inflation control. Two main arguments have been used in this connection. The literature on policy choice under uncertainty elevated a robustness criterion as a guide to best choice (see e.g. Pohl, 1993). In a standard model of this type, the objective function of the authorities could be satisfied in a number of alternative—and under deterministic conditions—precisely equivalent ways. An exchange rate path would be the dual of a money supply path, for example. In the presence of stochastic shocks, however, the duality would be broken. In the presence of instability in money demand, for example, the choice of an exchange rate target would force the money supply to accommodate the shocks, and so provide a superior solution to following a money supply target itself. In general, however, which policy regime the robustness criterion will favour will depend on the objective function facing the authorities and the likely size and duration of the shocks: the argument happened to favour exchange rate targeting in the eighties because of the widespread perception then that money demand functions were unstable.

There was a second reason why exchange rate targeting came into favour as a counter-inflationary instrument in the 1980s, however, associated with the popularity of the Barro–Gordon 'reputational model' of policy (Barro and Gordon, 1981). In the model, the key to counter-inflationary success lies in commitment and reputation. Considerations of which instruments are the right ones and whether there are problems of control are set on one side in this analysis. Part of the argument in favour of an exchange rate target in this context will be that the exchange rate is highly visible and continuously observable, so that it is easy to monitor the commitment of the authorities if that commitment is made to an exchange rate. (By contrast money supply observations are infrequent, lagged and subject to 'special factor' explanations which may be interpreted as chicanery.) In the context of the European Monetary System—or more properly, its Exchange Rate Mechanism—exchange rate targeting became associated with the idea that this was a way in which countries other than Germany could 'import the Bundesbank's reputation'. Targeting the exchange rate within the ERM had added value over go-it-alone targeting in this context: a participating country was taking on a commitment to external actors and risking a loss of face in the event of failure, which would provide added credibility to the commitment in the eyes of domestic agents; and the credibility of the system itself would assist the realization of the commitment.

A final objective of exchange rate targeting, which is relevant to European conditions, is that it may be seen as a 'dress rehearsal' or 'proving ground' for full monetary union.

2. EPISODES OF EXCHANGE RATE TARGETING

I now turn to consider three recent exchange rate targeting episodes which exemplify the various forms and objectives summarized above. The first of

these is the Plaza Accord episode; the second is UK experience before joining the ERM; and the third is the experience of the ERM itself.

The Plaza Accord

The so-called Plaza Accord of the G5 launched in September 1985 was
aimed at securing a controlled decline of the dollar and the restoration of
American competitiveness. Both features were desired—i.e., a decline in the
dollar, but one that avoided the contingency of the 'hard landing.'[2]
Although the episode encouraged the belief that a new phase of sustained
global economic cooperation and policy coordination was at hand, the
rationale offered by Peter Kenen (1989) seems the more compelling. Kenen
described the episode as a 'one-off' exercise in 'regime preservation'. His
interpretation was that the misalignment of the dollar was threatening the
maintenance of liberal trading arrangements in the world as evidenced in
the accumulation of protectionist bills placed before the US Congress; it
was therefore necessary to secure agreement to let the dollar fall. Kenen's
suggestion that the Accord and what followed were motivated by what was
essentially a single and limited objective helps explain the short life of the
new arrangements. More generally, analyses of international policy coordination (e.g., Artis and Ostry, 1986) tend to stress the costs of continuous
cooperation and suggest a bias in the direction of limited-objective
episodes.
     Implicit in the process set up at the Plaza were assumptions that nomi-
nal exchange rate changes lead reliably to real rate changes, that intervention in foreign exchange markets 'works', and that the authorities have
adequate policy instruments to target exchange rates with at least some
degree of success. One of the themes of the Plaza process was that fiscal
policy changes would be involved, a reining-back of the US budget deficit
being complemented by fiscal expansion elsewhere. The precise exchange
rate targets and the size of tolerated deviations from them were not
announced at the time. The account by Funabashi (1989), however, supplies a good deal of ex-post detail about the negotiations associated with
the Plaza process.

---

[2] The 'hard landing' scenario was described in detail by S. Marris, 'Deficits and the Dollar:
The World Economy at Risk', *Policy Analyses in International Economics*, 14 (Washington
DC: Institute for International Economics, 1985) who has subsequently (S. Marris, 'Why No
Hard Landing?' in C. F. Bergsten (ed.), *International Adjustment and Financing: The Lessons
of 1985–1991* (Washington DC: Institute for International Economics, 1991)) argued that part
of his purpose in doing so was to lend force to the call for the kind of cooperation that ensued
with the Plaza process.

Chronology

Funabashi points out that the Plaza Accord was anticipated by a G5 meeting in January 1985, which led to substantial foreign exchange market intervention in February of that year. The dollar had already begun to depreciate well before the Plaza meeting in September of that year; but the communiqué issued after that meeting noted that 'some further orderly appreciation of the main non-dollar currencies against the dollar is desirable.' According to Funabashi's account, the order of magnitude upon which the meeting agreed for the further appreciation of the non-dollar currencies was in the range 10–12 per cent—an amount already achieved by the end of October! The same account notes that although shares in foreign exchange market intervention between the participant countries were clearly agreed, there was no clear decision on the coordination of monetary policy. However, in the markets, 'the agreement was interpreted as having eliminated the likelihood that the Federal Reserve Board would tighten reserve conditions in response to rapid monetary growth.' There was a G5 meeting in London in January 1986 to take stock of developments since the Summer and coordinated interest rate cuts were accomplished in the wake of the oil price declines in March 1986. From this point on, the implications for monetary policy began to be felt more strongly, especially in the two main countries concerned—Japan and Germany, the former reluctantly acquiescent and the latter resistant to the demands falling upon them. By the Tokyo Summit in May 1986, the dollar had fallen considerably. The scope of the coordination exercise was increased significantly, involving a G7-wide 'indicators' exercise and a discussion of exchange rate targets. At the same time, a more focused G2 (USA–Japan) effort was under way, involving the Baker–Miyazawa agreement of October 1986 and, in January 1987, 'reverse intervention', in which the Federal Reserve intervened to sell yen as the dollar had by that time fallen strongly against it.

At the Louvre meeting in February 1987, the participating countries agreed that the fall in the dollar had been accomplished and defined the new task, in the words of the communiqué, as that of stabilizing rates 'around the current levels'. According to Funabashi's account, there was a serious discussion at this time of a formal 'target zone' arrangement, with an 'inner band' of +/– 2.25 per cent and an outer one at +/– 5 per cent.

The worldwide stock market crash in October 1987 seems effectively to have marked the public end of the Plaza 'episode', partly because, in terms of timing, difficulties with the coordination process seemed themselves responsible for the Crash, partly because the Crash focused different concerns. Whilst the objectives of coordination were reaffirmed in a soothing communiqué in December following the Crash, and concerted intervention has continued to take place at intervals subsequently, the public perception is that the distinctive G5 endeavour ended at about this time.

Was the Outcome as Desired?

Viewed as an exercise to restore American competitiveness and to reduce the US balance of payments deficit without the trauma of a 'dollar crash', the episode might well be taken to have been a successful example of policy coordination. Figures 11.1 and 11.2 show, respectively, that the depreciation of the real US dollar effective rate since 1985—however measured—has been substantial, and that there has been, subsequently, a clear turn-round in the US balance of payments deficit with corresponding changes in the external accounts of Germany and Japan. Earlier impatience with the slowness of the turn-round has been revealed for what it was— impatience. In substantial degree, the contributions to Bergsten's (1991) review of the period suggest that the basic theory of international adjustment has survived well.[3] However, it is less than clear how much of what is satisfactory about the outcome should be attributed to the Plaza process itself, rather than to other factors. There is the point that the dollar was already falling, ahead of the Plaza agreement itself, and in fact had gone the whole distance initially desired within a month of that agreement. There were substantial shocks during the period—the fall in oil prices in 1986, the stock-market crash, German reunification. And there are some doubts about the way in which the process was made effective.

INSTRUMENTS AND IMPLICATIONS FOR MONETARY POLICY

The rhetoric of the Plaza process laid great emphasis on the *combined* use of three instruments of policy—intervention in the foreign exchange markets, monetary policy and, fiscal policy. One seemingly very important finding to emerge from recent studies (see Catte *et al.* 1992) of the Plaza episode is the significance attached to foreign exchange market intervention. Prior to this, the conventional wisdom of academics was that intervention *per se*—i.e. sterilized intervention—could not be important, except for any

---

[3] Cf. the concluding remarks in Bergsten, *International Adjustment and Financing* by Paul Krugman who notes *inter alia* that 'The general verdict, then, must be that the international adjustment process has worked, in both meaningful senses: that is, it has worked acceptably, and it has worked about the way conventional wisdom thought it would.' This comment implies that the literature on 'pricing to market' and hysteresis effects, to which Krugman himself so notably contributed (e.g., R. Baldwin and P. Krugman, 'Persistent Trade Effects of Large Exchange Rate Shocks', *Quarterly Journal of Economics*, 104, Nov. 1989) may have less to contribute to an understanding of the adjustment process in the 1980s than appeared at first sight.

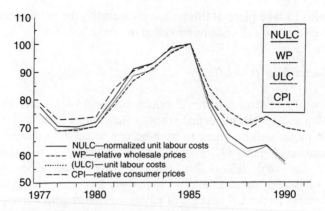

Fig. 11.1 Real US$ depreciation from 1985, various measures
Key: NULC = normalized unit labour costs (ULC)
      WP   = relative wholesale prices
      CPI   = relative consumer prices
Source: International Financial Statistics.

signals it might convey about monetary policy (i.e. about unsterilized intervention), a caveat that came to be treated as rather unimportant. This followed from the demonstration (e.g. Obstfeld, 1983) that, if assets of different currencies of denomination are perfect substitutes, then sterilized intervention could not change the exchange rate, and from a general presumption that 'perfect substitutability' would not be a bad characterization

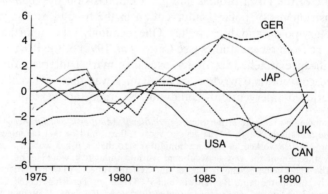

Fig. 11.2 Current account balance as % GDP: US, Japan, Germany
Source: International Financial Statistics.

of G5 currency-denominated assets. Mussa (1981) supplied the qualification about the possible signalling role of intervention. At the same time the Jurgensen Report (1983), which was inspired by the Versailles Summit, conveyed a similar message to policymakers. By contrast, the more recent studies of intervention suggest that, since 1984, all but one of the major turning-points in the trajectory of the dollar exchange rate coincide with episodes of intervention, and that over half of the episodes of concerted intervention (involving at least two of the G3) since 1984 were definitely successful, with the remainder registering temporary success. As Williamson (1993) notes, this 'new view' of the effectiveness of intervention sits better with theories that give much room in short-run exchange rate determination to fads and bubbles, than with theories which emphasize the fundamentals; for, in the former case, it is possible to argue that the markets have very little to go on and thus may be 'given a steer' by official intervention. It would also be wise to concede, though, that studies of this period are as yet few and do not amount to a consensus (e.g., the study by Kaminsky and Lewis (1993) arrives at fundamentally pessimistic conclusions about the usefulness of intervention: although intervention has information content, these authors find that the signal is actually *perverse*).

Nevertheless, sterilized intervention was not sufficiently effective to avoid pressures arising on monetary policy.[4] Among the criticisms of this policy episode are in fact the following points: that fiscal policy was relatively unresponsive to the demands of coordination, putting 'too much' of the burden on monetary policy; that the distribution of this burden was essentially decided in the interests of the United States; and that overall monetary policy was probably too lax, prolonging the life of the global stock market 'bull run' and making inevitable at some point a stock market crash of the kind that did in fact eventuate. The crux of the argument is the following simple point. The proximate determination of the exchange rate is a function of *relative* interest rates; to ensure that the dollar fell, but not too fast, US rates needed only to lie below rates in Germany and Japan by a judicious margin. But this does not determine the *absolute* level of interest rates, which in fact was left to the United States. For domestic reasons, the United States wished to see low interest rates at home; it left it to other countries to determine the exchange rate. Funabashi's comment is very revealing in this regard. Commenting on US policy through 1986, he says 'The Fed used monetary policy to stimulate the US economy or at least to keep it buoyant but it did not burden monetary policy with exchange rate management. Instead it used coordination of monetary policies—more accurately, the monetary policies of others—to keep the dollar from

---

[4] To the extent that the intervention works because it is a signal of future monetary policy it is not going to be a complete substitute for such policy. If the signalling is to be credible it will have to be followed up by the actions that it foreshadows.

dropping precipitously.' (P. 57.) It is arguable that the absolute level of interest rates to which this led, at least in Japan, was undesirably low, prolonging the overvaluation of the stock market. Also, it seems that it was conflict with Germany over the level of interest rates (with Germany's policy concerns pointing to higher levels than implied by US policy concerns) that led, proximately, to the Crash.

UK EXPERIENCE WITH EXCHANGE RATE TARGETING

Considering the way in which the decade began, the UK was to accumulate a surprisingly substantial amount of exchange rate targeting experience during the 1980s. Mrs Thatcher's first administration confirmed the Callaghan government's rejection of membership of the ERM for the (different but technically correct) reason that exchange rate targeting would be incompatible with money supply targeting. The government formally unveiled its framework for counter-inflationary policy (the Medium Term Financial Strategy or MTFS) in 1980. The centre-piece of the MTFS was a pre-announced four-year plan for the medium-term reduction of the growth rate of the money supply, on the sterling M3 definition (a broad definition). Alongside the medium-term trajectory for declining monetary growth was placed a plan for the steady reduction over the same period of the ratio of the PSBR to GDP. The exchange rate was 'assumed to be determined by market forces' (*Financial Statement and Budget Report*, 1980). The description of the MTFS referred to the primacy of the money supply objective and also argued that the out-turn for unemployment would depend *inter alia* upon the expectations of those involved in the bargaining process. But it was hoped that the public commitment to the MTFS would influence those expectations. Inputs from both 'Friedmanian monetarism' and the 'New Classical Macroeconomics' can be recognized by the ideologically sensitive economist in the statement of the MTFS. It was certainly new.

In the letter, the MTFS, as originally projected, was to be a distinct and definite failure. That is, the monetary growth targets for sterling M3 were substantially and persistently overrun. In response, the strategy was reformulated; initially, both narrower (M1) and broader (PSL2) monetary aggregates were added to sterling M3 in the expression of four-year forward rates of decelerating monetary growth; in 1984 these were excluded and M0 was added. After 1987, sterling M3 was omitted altogether. Most important of all, the exchange rate was introduced as a conditioning factor in the response to an overrun of the monetary target.

This was made quite clear in the 1982 restatement of the MTFS: 'External or domestic developments that change the relationship between the domestic money supply and the exchange rate may . . . disturb the link between money and prices. Such changes cannot readily be taken into account in setting monetary targets. But they are a reason why the Government considers it appropriate to look at the exchange rate in monitoring domestic monetary conditions and in taking decisions about policy.' It is clear, too, that this practice, of conditionalizing the response to a target overrun on the exchange rate, preceded the formal acknowledgement of it. In other words, the inflexibility proclaimed as a virtue of the original MTFS ('there would be no question of departing from the money supply policy, which is essential to the success of any anti-inflationary strategy') gave way under the pressure of events, fairly quickly, to a more pragmatic policy.[5] Among the events in question was a large appreciation of the exchange rate, and a huge and very rapid increase in the numbers unemployed.

The unravelling of the MTFS into a more pragmatic policy in which the exchange rate figured prominently was associated with a shift of emphasis for all but some formal purposes (including the annual restatement of the MTFS) away from monetary aggregates towards interest rates. 'The' interest rate became identified as a monetary 'fine-tuner'; at the same time, the theme set for fiscal policy by the initial statement of the MTFS was maintained, so that with some exceptions the goals by which fiscal instruments were set continued to be medium term in character. A popular characterization of this policy stance was that the Chancellor of the Exchequer was engaged in a game of 'one club golf'. A diagrammatic characterization, due to Walter Eltis, appears in Figure 11.3. The figure, in interest rate exchange rate space, describes an iso-inflation schedule labelled PP and a foreign exchange market equilibrium schedule FF. High interest rates coexist with an appreciated exchange rate. Low interest rates imply devaluation. The exchange rate is measured as the sterling price of foreign currency. Hence FF slopes down from left to right. The implicit horizon is quite short run. A depreciation in the exchange rate and a fall in the nominal interest rate both raise inflation. Hence PP slopes up from left to right; points to the right of and below PP are points of 'excess inflation' whilst points to the left and above indicate points of 'excess deflation'. The authorities use their single instrument, the interest rate, to react to changes in the exchange rate (as FF shifts), with a view to maintaining their inflation target. With no constraints on the exchange rate, this one-target, one-instrument policy can

---

[5] Indeed it was already evident to observers that the policy was compromised as early as the summer of 1980, when short-term interest rates were lowered despite an overrun of the monetary target. From his vantage point in the Bank of England, J. S. Fforde, 'Setting Monetary Objectives', *Bank of England Quarterly Bulletin*, 23 (1983) subsequently noted of this episode that 'it had to be judged that the performance of M3 required interpretation in the light of other indicators, including the exchange rate . . .'

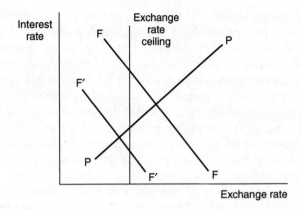

Fig. 11.3 Eltis's interest rate/exchange rate diagram

in principle maintain inflation on target. Clearly, with a constraint on the exchange rate, this will no longer be possible; a situation of Tinbergian instrument deficiency ensues. The exchange rate objective creates the need for an additional instrument or else the abandonment, temporarily, of the inflation target.

This dilemma became obvious in the next policy phase to ensue, which was marked by Chancellor Lawson's decision to 'shadow the Deutschmark'. This policy was inaugurated in the wake of the Louvre Accord in 1987. Without ever being announced as official policy the authorities nevertheless allowed it to become clear that they were pursuing a policy of targeting the Deutschmark exchange rate with a ceiling of three Deutschmarks to the pound. This policy may have been an attempt to demonstrate that joining the ERM in a formal way would be an entirely feasible—even easy—matter, and may have seemed to be a natural progression from the pragmatic policy described above. Whatever the motivation for its introduction, it was abandoned after about twelve months. During the currency of this policy phase, it became clear that the interest rate was being held down by the exchange rate commitment to levels below those indicated as desirable on domestic grounds—as simple manipulation of Figure 11.3 shows would ensue, should the FF schedule shift to the left sufficiently far (say to F^1F^1) as to intersect with PP at a point to the left of the upper exchange rate limit.

After this episode, monetary policy reverted for a time to its erstwhile more pragmatic stance, with the emphasis on interest rate increases to contain inflation. Then, in October 1990, the British government decided formally to participate in the Exchange Rate Mechanism of the European Monetary System. Perhaps reflecting experience in the 'shadowing' period, the 1991 restatement of the MTFS stated that 'There may be occasions when tensions arise between domestic conditions and ERM obligations, with domestic conditions pointing to interest rate levels either higher or lower than those indicated by ERM obligations [but] Any loss of discretion to respond to domestic monetary conditions is likely to be more than compensated for by the improved market confidence and reduced inflationary expectations that the ERM commitment is bringing about . . .'

Up to this point, then, it is possible to describe the decade as a whole as one in which, for the UK, there occurred a definite policy switch, away from an attempt to control inflation through adherence to an *internal* standard (afforded by money supply control) to an attempt to control inflation via adherence to an *external* standard (the rate of exchange of the pound sterling to the Deutschmark). This switch can be described as a decision to import the monetary policy of a country which has been markedly more successful than the UK in keeping inflation down. But, as it proved, it was not long before the British authorities reverted once again to an internal standard, this time not expressed in terms of a monetary target but in terms of a direct inflation target.[6] After the events culminating in 'Black Wednesday' (16 September 1992), after which sterling was floated, the British government declared an objective of controlling inflation in the retail price index excluding mortgage interest payments (RPIX) within a range of 1–4 per cent. The Bank of England, unprecedently, was given powers to monitor the pursuit of this target in published reports.[7]

THE ERM EXPERIENCE

This is not the place to provide a lengthy analysis of the ERM experience. The most salient features of that experience can be summarized in five points as follows.

(i) The dominant rationale that has been given for the ERM has been that of counter-inflationary policy. Until the 1992 crisis, the ERM appeared to have been markedly successful in reducing exchange rate volatility, though less successful in preventing real exchange rate misalignment (Artis and Taylor, 1994). (ii) The counter-inflationary effect of the ERM, however, remained 'unproven'. Whilst inflation in ERM countries fell during the 1980s and converged on the lower rates enjoyed in Germany, it has proved difficult to obtain any undisputed estimate of a beneficial 'ERM' effect. It may be that the ERM allowed inflation to be reduced more rapidly and more sustainably than would otherwise have been possible; but it is not

---

[6] Although, as during the period of adherence to the ERM, ranges for M0 continued to be announced, these had long since been regarded as secondary to the main target.

[7] The first of these appeared in February 1993.

clear that the unemployment and output costs (as opposed, perhaps, to other political costs) of this reduction in inflation have been any less than they would have been had inflation been reduced outside the ERM framework. (iii) Whilst the early phase of the ERM was accompanied by the maintenance of exchange controls over capital flows, from about 1985 onwards, these were gradually removed under the 'Single Market' legislation. The exact contribution of these controls to stability remains in doubt. The most positive case is that they contained speculation long enough so that the authorities could maintain control of the realignment process. Realignments helped to reduce the extent of misalignment in real exchange rates, although, owing to the counter-inflationary bias in the process, this was less than complete. (iv) From about 1987 onwards, the ERM experienced a period of very marked stability, with no full realignment until the crisis of 1992. Whilst this seemed initially an unsustainable phase (dubbed a situation of 'excess credibility' by Giavazzi and Spaventa, 1990), it persisted through 1992. When the crisis finally came, it was *not* signalled far in advance by the markets (Rose and Svensson, 1994). (v) The ERM crises of 1992 and 1993 have been given a variety of explanations. The chief contenders are: (a) misalignment in real exchange rates (Spain, Italy, UK); (b) 'domino' effects (as the devaluation of one currency put similar pressure on other currencies—the pound sterling on the Irish pound and so on); (c) policy cycle mismatch, specifically the maintenance by Germany of high interest rates to cope with unification-induced inflation, alongside a perceived need for reductions in interest rates in partner countries.

According to some analyses (such as Eichengreen and Wyplosz, 1993), the critical feature was the adverse (Denmark) or lukewarm (France) referenda on the Maastricht Treaty. These results were considered as revealing a lack of commitment to current exchange rates and an unwillingness to endure the rigours of the policy cycle mismatch at unchanged exchange rates. In the version favoured by Eichengreen and Wyplosz, the speculation would be self-fulfilling. Forcing abandonment of the ERM parities would release countries to reappraise their policies and to reduce interest rates. The 'fundamentals' would thereby shift, justifying *ex post* the speculation. This does not seem to have been borne out in the aftermath of the 1993 crisis. The countries concerned did *not* take advantage of the new wider ($\pm$ 15 per cent) bands, which were hastily improvised to maintain the letter of the ERM and the spirit of floating, to reduce interest rates. In fact, by December 1993, the exchange rates of the crisis-hit countries were all back within, or close to, the floor of the previous narrow band. Expectations were not self-fulfilling. The fact that the central exchange rates of the 1993 crisis participants were considered to be at their 'medium-run' fundamental values and that those rates were all but reinstated within six months of the crisis makes the speculation appear to be a 'nuisance', not revelatory of anything. (By contrast, the 1992 crises might be said to have 'revealed' the unsustainable positions of, at least, the UK and Italy—perhaps also Spain.)

The ERM episode has particular importance because of the provisions of the Maastricht Treaty. That Treaty requires that participants in Monetary Union should during Stage Two have accumulated at least two years' experience in the 'normal bands' of the ERM 'without severe tension' and without initiating devaluation. 'Normal' here means the ± 2¼ per cent bands, not the 'temporary and expedient' ± 15 per cent bands. The most obvious rationale for the inclusion of this ERM criterion among the set of convergence criteria for monetary union is that it provides a 'proving ground'. By going through a phase of narrow bands ERM, participant countries would experience 'monetary disarmament'. It would be the closest experience to full monetary union that could be devised. Can this convergence criterion be preserved in the aftermath of the 1993 crisis? If not, the crisis would not only have disrupted the ERM; it might also have made progress to EMU infeasible. It is tempting to suggest that the countries could simply reinterpret the 'normal' band to be the wider ± 15 per cent band and so avoid the danger of a repetition of the crisis. If, however, this is not feasible, a re-narrowing of the bands would still be possible if (a) there is policy symmetry, (b) consensus on the correctness of central exchange rates, and (c) as a longstop, agreement on indefinite intervention obligations. Provisions (a) and (b) should remove the provocation for a speculative raid; but, in case of doubt, provision (c) would make such a raid pointless. In such a setting, it could be argued that the proving-ground criterion could correctly be realized. In the conditions that would otherwise rule, the 'proving ground' is in fact likely to be unreasonably biased against the weak currency country. In the face of a suspicion about the sustainability of a parity, it is not enough for the weak country to maintain interest rates at the level prevailing in the strong currency country (higher, as these might be, than those desired on domestic grounds in the weak currency country). Interest rates in the weak currency country must in addition embody a devaluation premium.

It must seem reasonably clear that condition (c)—indefinite intervention obligations—is only likely to be committed to in circumstances in which there is wide agreement (and, especially, agreement by the hard currency country) that the prevailing central exchange rates and policies of the participating countries are sustainable. Such a set of conditions might be realizable if there were at the same time clear agreement that progress to full monetary union is desirable—and indeed all but assured.

LESSONS

What lessons can be drawn for exchange rate targeting from the experience recounted above? On the whole, I believe they are rather discomforting. Two positive points do, however, stand out and we might as well begin with these.

First, it appears that concerted foreign exchange intervention 'works'— or, rather, can work—in the right conditions. Studies of intervention operations in support of post Plaza Accord agreements seem to show this. Williamson has long drawn attention to the possibility that foreign exchange market conditions could actually provide just the setting in which a 'steer' can effectively be given by the authorities. His point is that the short-run equilibrium of the foreign exchange market is almost neutral. Expectations are dominant. Intervention can provide a signal of where the exchange rate will be, and provided that the signal appears to be an agreed one, speculative forces will reinforce it. If, on the other hand, there appears to be a lack of agreement among the relevant authorities or a suspicion that current agreement is only temporary, then speculation will not be stabilizing.

A second and related point is that, if exchange rate targeting is required as a prelude to, or transition towards, monetary union, then it is feasible: the conditions are that it must appear that the transition to full monetary union will occur at current exchange rates and that the authorities are prepared to commit to this, if necessary, by promising unlimited intervention in the transition. Once again, a high degree of policy symmetry and cooperation is implicit, suggesting that the circumstances of a transition to full monetary union should be propitious. (However, it bears repeating that there seem no compelling reasons why participant countries could not graduate directly to European Monetary Union from the present wide ± 15 per cent bands.)

These points aside, the cumulative experience of the 1980s may appear to provide poor support for exchange rate targeting. The ERM crises of 1992 and 1993 leave the impression that, however successful exchange rate targeting may have been in earlier years, the markets henceforth will arbitrarily test (and can always win in doing so) any firm commitment on exchange rate bands that may be announced. Exchange controls aside, the only 'solution' would appear to be for central banks to acquire more reserves by being able to call on unlimited intervention from the issuer of the strong currency. Yet it is hard to see that such a promise can be forthcoming outside a context in which a strong political commitment exists— as it may in specific circumstances, such as those surrounding the passage to full monetary union.

It may be that the position is less stark than this. The long period of stability in the ERM, which led directly to the 'bootstraps' view, celebrated in the target zone literature, appears to suggest that speculation can reinforce exchange rate commitments in conditions which fall at least some way short of those just described as necessary. It may be that 'short-termism' in the foreign exchange markets will permit exchange rate stability in the presence of policies that are incompatible only in the long run. But even this tolerance has a destructive implication for exchange rate targeting undertaken to 'force the pace' on inflation control. Since such a policy is unlikely to be instantly effective, it is liable to produce a competitive (real exchange rate) misalignment and thus to open up the prospect in the longer run of a corrective nominal depreciation. The policy may thus be said to contain the seeds of its own destruction. In this sense, the biggest casualty of the ERM crises was the 'monetarist' view that it was sensible to 'force the pace' on convergence by adopting fixed exchange rates in advance of the convergence that would naturally support such exchange rate stability.

The safest kind of exchange rate targeting, therefore, would appear to be real exchange rate targeting with soft bands. Intervention can help to sustain such a system, and the benefits of greater stability in competitiveness seem obvious. The weakness is that, for some countries, this implies a loss of 'nominal discipline' which needs to be supplied by some other means.[8]

---

[8] Note that a real exchange rate system need not be seen as merely accommodating of inflation. In such a system, a depreciation could still be associated, if desired, with a pre-set tightening of counter-inflationary policy.

Part IV

The Role of Government:
National and International

12.   The International Origins of Unemployment

John Eatwell

In all G7 countries, long-term trends in unemployment since the War show a distinct break around 1970. The increase in unemployment has been greatest in the major countries of the European Union, with Western Germany experiencing an almost eight-fold increase (from a very low base). Of the major European countries, only Italy had a relatively small proportionate increase in unemployment, but this was from what was, for the 1960s, a high base. Canada and the USA, both relatively high unemployment countries in the 1960s, have also suffered 'only' 50 per cent and 130 per cent increases in average levels of unemployment. Japan's experience is exceptional, having very low unemployment in the 1960s, and from that low base suffering 'only' a 120 per cent increase.

Table 12.1.   Unemployment[a] in the G7, 1964–73 and 1983–92

	A. 1964–73	B. 1983–92	B/A[b]
West Germany	0.79	6.03	7.63
France	2.23	9.70	4.35
Italy	5.48	10.13	1.85
UK	2.94	9.79	3.33
USA	4.46	6.69	1.50
Canada	4.23	9.64	2.28
Japan	1.22	2.71	2.22

Source: OECD main economic indicators.

Note: [a] annual standardized unemployment rates as % of the labour force, averaged for each 10 year period.

[b] Ratio of unemployment rate 1983–92 to unemployment rate 1964–73.

The economic disruption visited upon the 1970s by oil price shocks, together with the deflationary measures taken by G7 governments in reaction to the oil price rise, might be thought to be the source of the deterioration in G7 economic performance.[1] But as unemployment has persisted

---

[1] The OECD estimated that 20% of the loss in OECD real income was due to the terms of trade effect of the oil price rise, and 80% due to the concerted deflation of the Western economies.

into the 1990s, this explanation has become less and less convincing. Not only had the Western economies absorbed similar rises in raw material prices at the time of the Korean War without similar slow-down, but also the new high trend levels of unemployment were not notably affected by the collapse in oil prices and other commodity prices in 1986. It is these high trend levels of unemployment which underpin the yet higher unemployment figures produced by the early 1990s 'slow-down' in the G7 economies. That unemployment cannot possibly be considered to be purely cyclical. It is a combination of long-term trends and the cyclical factors associated with current recessions in Europe and Japan. Indeed, it may well be that the current recession is simply another step-up in the long-term trend of rising unemployment. This suggests that unemployment in the G7 today cannot be tackled by standard counter-cyclical policies. A new approach is required.

The commonality of the unemployment experience throughout the G7, outweighing the particular economic fortunes of individual countries, is especially striking. The particular circumstances of each country and policies which are peculiar to one country or group of countries will, of course, affect the distribution of unemployment between them. But the common experience suggests that some of the fundamental causes of high unemployment are to be found in factors which affect all G7 countries in a broadly similar manner, rather than in the individual circumstances of each country. So a constructive approach to tackling the G7 increase in unemployment requires the identification of the common factors underlying that increase. Likely candidates for a common source of increased unemployment are (i) the rate of technological change; (ii) the structural changes in world trading relationships which are associated with the increasing mobility of capital and the rapid growth of Third World manufactured exports, particularly from China and the Pacific Rim; and (iii) changes in the international financial environment and consequential changes in the macroeconomic policies of the G7 countries.

THE PACE OF TECHNOLOGICAL CHANGE

It has been a common view since the early nineteenth century that technological change is a threat to jobs. In the 1950s and 1960s, 'automation' was regarded as the key menace. In the 1970s and 1980s, the impact of information technologies and electronics has often been cited as potentially job destroying. Whatever technological changes may have done to the *composition* of employment, there is no evidence that the speed of technological change lies behind the growth in unemployment throughout the G7. If it did, then there should have been an acceleration of productivity growth in the 1980s and 1990s as new techniques sharply reduced the labour input required per unit output. In fact the reverse has occurred. There has been a sharp slow-down in productivity growth, a slow-down that has been greatest in Japan, and least in the USA and the UK (in both of which productivity growth was relatively low in the earlier period). Indeed, the slow-down in productivity growth has everywhere been greater than the slow-down in the overall growth of demand, which means that low productivity growth has contributed to the creation (or at least the preservation) of jobs, rather than their destruction.

Table 12.2. Overall productivity growth: GDP per person employed

	A. 1961–70	B. 1981–90	B/A[a]
West Germany	4.3	1.9	0.45
France	5.0	2.0	0.40
Italy	6.2	1.9	0.31
UK	3.3	2.0	0.60
USA	1.9	1.1	0.58
Japan	9.1	3.0	0.33

Source: European economy, annual economic reports.
Note: [a] Ratio of productivity growth 1981–90 to productivity growth 1961–70.

In each of the G7 countries, the slow-down in productivity growth has been less pronounced in manufacturing than in the economy as a whole. In so far as the growth of demand for manufactures has also slowed, the relative buoyancy of manufacturing productivity growth has resulted in substantial job losses in manufacturing, notably in the UK. An exception to the general trend has been manufacturing employment in Germany, which toward the end of the 1980s had resumed a (slight) rising trend, though this has been overwhelmed by the recent recession.

The loss of jobs in manufacturing has been exacerbated by a change in the relationship between the growth of demand and the growth of jobs. In the 1960s, growing demand was associated with increasing jobs. In the 1980s, growing demand has been satisfied (even more than satisfied) by productivity growth, and jobs have been lost. It is not clear to what extent the failure of manufacturing to create jobs as in the past is due to the slow-down of demand, and to what extent it is the result of a change in the relationship between the rate of growth of demand and the rate of technical progress. Whatever might be the case, it seems likely that a higher rate of growth of demand for manufactures, although it would probably bring

Table 12.3. Manufacturing productivity growth in the G7

	A. 1964–73	B. 1983–92	B/A[a]
West Germany	4.0	2.4	0.60
France	5.3	2.6	0.49
Italy	5.1	2.6	0.51
UK	4.2	3.6	0.85
USA	3.1	2.8	0.90
Canada	4.0	2.6	0.65
Japan	9.6	5.7	0.59

Source: OECD main economic indicators.
Note: [a] Ratio of manufacturing productivity growth 1983–92 to manufacturing productivity growth 1964–73.

with it a high rate of productivity growth too, would at least stem the loss of jobs. And there is certainly a potential for a higher growth of demand for manufactures. Even in the most advanced of the G7 countries, there are substantial proportions of the population who do not have access to the number and quality of manufactured goods which their fellow citizens regard as necessary to sustain a normal standard of living.

STRUCTURAL CHANGES IN THE WORLD ECONOMY

An issue of growing importance is whether the rise in competition from the newly industrializing countries, particularly those on the Pacific Rim, will jeopardize job creation in the traded goods sectors of the G7 countries. The possibility of securing full employment by a higher growth of domestic demand will be significantly diminished if the competitive strengths of G7 industry are overcome by the potent combination of low Third World wages and ever more mobile capital.

There has been a distinct acceleration of the penetration of developing country manufactures into G7 markets. In 1968, just 1 per cent of G7 domestic demand for manufactures was satisfied by imports from the Third World. By 1980, developing countries' market share had risen to 2 per cent; by 1988 to 3.1 per cent; by 1993 to 4 per cent. Developing countries' manufactures now account for 10 per cent of G7 manufactured imports. Competition from the Third World certainly leads to a loss of jobs in particular sectors (typically low-skill tradables), either directly, due to loss of markets, or indirectly, as innovation in response to Third World competition leads to the adoption of less labour-intensive techniques, particularly low skill intensive techniques.[2]

But if, despite these sectoral effects, the overall balance of trade is unchanged, there will be no net effect on aggregate demand. Whether there is any impact on the overall relationship between aggregate demand and employment depends on the structure of demand in the economy, including demand for non-tradables, and the pace and content of technological change in the production of tradables and non-tradables. In fact, leaving aside the impact of the oil price rises, there has tended to be a *surplus* in the balance of trade between the G7 and the more dynamic of the Third World countries. Indeed these countries are typically the fastest growing markets in the world. This was particularly true in the 1970s. Since then, overall G7 trade has moved closer to general balance with this group of countries, and this deteriorating trend may well result in a G7 deficit in the 1990s.

As far as technological change is concerned, there seems to be no significant difference in the rates of technological change as between those sectors which have been most affected by competition from the Third World, and those which have not. Of far greater importance as far as the impact of technological change on employment is concerned, has been the high rate of growth of productivity in services in the European Union, compared with the low rate of productivity growth in those same sectors in the United States.

The impact of low wage competition from the newly industrializing countries is not dissimilar from the competition which the northern European countries experienced form southern Europe in the late 1950s. That competition, which resulted, for example, in the growth of Italy's share of world manufactured trade from less than 2 per cent to over 6 per cent in twenty years, did not result in unemployment in northern Europe. On the contrary, throughout the period in which competition was most intense northern Europe suffered from a labour shortage, with about 10 per cent of the labour force in West Germany and France being immigrants. The structural changes associated with the development of Italy took place in the context of generally high growth rates. The structural adjustments heralded by the rapid growth of manufactured exports from the developing countries appear all the more threatening because of persistent slow growth in the G7.

If in the 1990s competition from the newly industrializing countries does result in increasing deficits with the G7, then they could be dealt with (to some extent) by the traditional method of changing the exchange rate between surplus and deficit countries. The effectiveness of exchange rate

[2] See A. Wood, *North–South Trade, Employment and Inequality: Changing Fortunes in a Skill-Driven World*, Clarendon Press, Oxford, 1994.

changes will, of course, be limited if the penetration of G7 markets were due to the technological superiority of the imports. For example, the impact of Korean steel on the US market is typically attributed to technological superiority of the product in an industry in which labour costs are a very low proportion of total costs. Whatever the character of Third World competition might be, the continued growth and prosperity of the G7 rests on maintaining its technological vitality, both in the quality of research and innovation, and in the quality of the labour force.

CHANGES IN THE INTERNATIONAL FINANCIAL ENVIRONMENT

The key to understanding the growth in unemployment throughout the G7 would, therefore, appear to be the third common element, the slow-down in the trend rate of growth of demand. This slow-down occurs around 1970, and has persisted ever since.

The *persistence* of the slow growth of demand into the 1990s seems to have been predominantly caused by the change in the structure of international financial relationships, and the consequent impact on the structure of domestic macroeconomic policies.[3]

Two fundamental institutional changes mark a clear break in the international environment: first, the collapse of the Bretton Woods fixed

Table 12.4. Growth of real GDP—the 'Slow-down'

	A. 1964–73	B. 1983–92	B/A[a]
West Germany	4.5	2.9	0.64
France	5.3	2.2	0.42
Italy	5.0	2.4	0.48
UK	3.3	2.3	0.69
USA	4.0	2.9	0.72
Canada	5.6	2.8	0.50
Japan	9.6	4.0	0.42

Source: OECD main economic indicators.
Note: [a] Ratio of growth in real GDP 1983–92 to real GDP 1964–73.

[3] The slow-down has also been attributed to a number of other factors, including the growing profit squeeze at the end of the 1960s, the exhaustion of easy opportunities for technological 'catching up' with the United States, and, of course, the impact on the growth of demand of the rise in raw material prices, particularly oil prices. But none of these seems to be an adequate explanation for the *persistence* of the slow growth of demand into the 1990s. These factors are reviewed in the essay by A. Glyn, A. Hughes, A. Lipietz, and A. Singh entitled 'The Rise and Fall of the Golden Age', in S. Marglin and J. Schor (eds.), *The Golden Age of Capitalism: Reinterpreting the Postwar Experience* (Oxford: Clarendon Press, 1990).

exchange rates in the early 1970s which resulted in the 1970s and 1980s being an era of floating rates; second, the replacement of the regulated financial markets of the 1960s by the deregulated global markets of the eighties. There has been extensive analysis of the inability of the post Bretton Woods trading and payments system to deal with international trading imbalances other than by deflation and growing unemployment in weaker countries—a deflationary impulse which has proved contagious. Less attention has been paid to the fact that this deflationary pressure is reinforced by the deregulation of global markets and the huge growth in short-term capital flows.

Financial markets are today dominated by short-term flows which seek to profit from changes in asset prices—in other words, from speculation. The growth in the scale of speculation, relative to other transactions, has been particularly marked in the foreign exchange markets over the past twenty years. It is estimated that, in 1971, just before the collapse of the Bretton Woods fixed exchange rate system, about 90 per cent of all foreign exchange transactions were for the finance of trade and long-term invest-ment, and only about 10 per cent were speculative. Today, those percent-ages are reversed, with well over 90 per cent of all transactions being speculative. Daily speculative flows now regularly exceed the combined for-eign exchange reserves of all the G7 governments. The explosive growth of short-term speculative flows originated in a powerful combination of the carrot of profit and the stick of financial risk.

To an important extent, speculation is an inevitable outcome of the aban-donment of fixed rates. Under the Bretton Woods system, there was little profit to be had in speculation, since currencies moved only in very tight bands, apart, that is, from the very occasional change in parity. Indeed the Bretton Woods system provided quite remarkable stability. For example, the core currencies of the European Monetary System, locked together in the 1980s in the ERM, enjoyed *greater* stability in relation to one another during the Bretton Woods era than they have been able to achieve since. In the face of Bretton Woods stability it was not worthwhile maintaining the large scale currency dealing facilities with which we are familiar today— even if the contemporary regulatory structures had not placed significant barriers in the path of short-term capital flows. However, once Bretton Woods had collapsed and significant fluctuations became commonplace, then opportunities for profit proliferated, regulatory structures which inhibit flows of capital were challenged as 'inefficient' and 'against the national interest', and the infrastructure of speculation was constructed. The Bretton Woods system was finally abandoned in 1973. The USA announced the elimination of all capital controls in January 1974.

The incentive to deregulate international capital flows, which was created by the abandonment of fixed rates, was decisively reinforced by the need to hedge against the costs which fluctuating exchange rates imposed upon the private sector. Under the Bretton Woods system, foreign exchange risk was borne by the public sector. With that system's collapse, foreign exchange risk was privatized. This privatization of risk imposed substantial strains on the domestic and international banking systems. The need to absorb and cover foreign exchange risk demanded the creation of new financial instruments, which in turn required the removal of many of the regulatory barriers which limited the possibilities of laying off risk, and a restructuring of financial institutions.

So, combined with other, domestic, pressures for the removal of financial controls, the collapse of Bretton Woods was a significant factor driving the worldwide deregulation of financial systems. Exchange controls were abolished. Domestic restrictions on cross-market access for financial institutions were scrapped. Quantitative controls on the growth of credit were eliminated, and monetary policy was now conducted predominantly through management of short-term interest rates. A global market in monetary instruments was created.

Today the sheer scale of speculative flows can easily overwhelm any government's foreign exchange reserves. The ease of moving money from one currency to another, together with the ease of borrowing for speculative purposes, means that enormous sums can be shifted across the exchanges—especially for short periods of time. Prior to the September 1992 run on sterling, the British government boasted of a $15 billion support facility it had negotiated in Deutschmarks, to be used to defend the parity of the pound. Yet that sum would in due course be matched by the sales of sterling by just one prominent player in the foreign exchange markets.

The overwhelming scale of such potential flows means that governments must today, as never before, keep a careful eye on the need to maintain market 'credibility'. Credibility has become the keystone of policy making in the nineties. A credible government is a government which pursues a policy which is 'market friendly'; that is, a policy which is in accordance with what the markets believe to be 'sound'. Particularly favoured are measures designed to meet a 'prudent' predetermined monetary target, such as maintaining a given exchange rate parity, or a given growth rate of the money supply. Governments which fail to pursue 'sound' and 'prudent' policies are forced to pay a premium on the interest costs of financing their programmes. Severe loss of credibility will lead to a financial crisis.

The determination of what is credible, and how governments lose credibility, is a product of the way that speculative markets actually work. In his *General Theory*, John Maynard Keynes likened the operations of a speculative market to a beauty contest. He was not referring to a 1930s equivalent of the Miss World contest. He had in mind a competition which was then popular in the British tabloid Sunday newspapers in which readers were asked to rank pictures of young women in the order which they believed they would be ranked by a 'celebrity panel'. So in order to win, the player should not express his or her own preferences, but the preferences he or she believed were held by the panel. In the same way, the key to playing the markets is not what the individual investor considers to be the virtues or otherwise of any particular policy, but what he or she believes everyone else in the market will think.

Since the markets are driven by average opinion about what average opinion will be, an enormous premium is placed on any information or signals which might provide a guide to the swings in average opinion and as to how average opinion will react to changing events. These signals have to be simple and clear-cut. Sophisticated multi-dimensional interpretations of the economic data would not provide a clear lead. So the money markets and foreign exchange markets become dominated by simple slogans—larger fiscal deficits lead to higher interest rates, an increased money supply results in higher inflation, public expenditure bad, private expenditure good—even when those slogans are persistently refuted by events. To these simplistic rules of the game there is added a demand for governments to publish their own financial targets, to show that their policy is couched within a firm financial framework. The main purpose of insisting on this government commitment to financial targeting is to aid average opinion in guessing how average opinion will expect the government to respond to changing economic circumstances, and how average opinion will react when the government fails to meet its goals.

The demands of credibility have imposed broadly deflationary macroeconomic strategies on the G7. In the 1960s, the managed international financial framework permitted expansionary, full employment policies which were contagious both domestically, encouraging private investment, and internationally, underwriting the growth of world trade. In the 1980s, the deregulated financial framework has encouraged policies which elevate financial stability above employment; this has ratcheted up real interest rates, which have in turn reduced domestic investment and slowed the growth of world trade.

Financial instability has a severe impact on the ability of companies to invest with confidence, and indeed, on their ability to survive. The globalization of financial markets has meant that, whereas international disequilibria may, in the past, have been manifest in exchange rate movements, today they have an impact on interest rates in domestic money markets. The instability of local interest rates means that international financial pressures are felt by small and medium sized firms operating in the home market, and not only by large companies operating internationally. Instability has a further negative effect on policy. It severely reduces the scope of the fiscal cooperation which G7 countries so desperately need to engineer a concerted attack on unemployment. With exchange rates fluctuating, the distribution of the gains of such a concerted strategy is highly uncertain. But if the 'pay-off' is unknown, it is difficult for governments to commit themselves to a cooperative strategy, particularly when that strategy carries the risk of loss of credibility.

A FULL EMPLOYMENT STRATEGY FOR THE G7?

The 'Golden Age' of full employment was a product of a particular combination of international relationships—a combination which collapsed in the early 1970s. Much of the rise in G7 unemployment since then can be attributed to that collapse. If this argument is correct, then the pursuit of a full employment policy must involve *either* withdrawing from the international pressures which create unemployment (the 'war' or 'siege' economy solution) *or* the creation of an international environment which replicates the expansionary framework of Bretton Woods. Simply to pose the issue indicates the scale of the task. However, there is no intrinsic reason why the G7 should not be able to create a new international regime which would underwrite national full employment policies.

'Back to Bretton Woods' is not a feasible proposition. The Bretton Woods system rested upon the economic dominance of the United States. That economic dominance produced a worldwide desire for dollar reserves, and the consequent ability to fund international imbalances by flows of US capital. Bretton Woods was not a multilateral system. It was USA-led, and was therefore incapable of dealing with the imbalances caused by the relative economic decline of the USA itself.

Neither of the two other dominant economies in the G7, Germany and Japan, occupies a position comparable to that occupied by the USA in the immediate postwar period. Leaving aside the temporary impact of reunification, Germany has run a large and persistent current account surplus for the past thirty years. But long-term capital flows out of Germany have never been sufficient to fund the counterpart deficits in other countries, in the way that US capital flows did in comparable circumstances. As far as Japan is concerned, the yen has not achieved the role in international trade played by the dollar even today, especially in third party transactions. Whilst Japanese exports amount to 16 per cent of total G7 exports, only 7.5 per cent of G7 exports are invoiced in yen. By contrast, 42 per cent of G7 exports are invoiced in dollars, even though the USA is the source of only 21 per cent of those exports.

So a 'new Bretton Woods' must be a genuine multilateral arrangement, forged out of the current G7, dominated by the leaders of the world's three main currency blocks, Germany, Japan, and the USA. At the core of that new system should be a renewed commitment to securing the currency stability which is necessary to underwrite the international cooperation needed to avert worldwide recession. The present, largely ceremonial, summits of the G7 would need to be replaced with meetings which actually dealt with substantive issues. A permanent secretariat should be created with the skills and authority to manage the international payments system.

It is often argued that a new stable currency system is simply not feasible in a world of deregulated finance linked by the modern technology of the money markets. This argument fails to take into account the fact that fluctuating rates are themselves the motive force behind the very existence of a large-scale speculative infrastructure. Moreover, whilst the speculators may be able to borrow very large sums for short periods of time, the central banks, as the creators of currencies, can, collectively, provide indefinitely large sums for just as long. New cooperation between the major central banks, and the creation of new techniques of domestic monetary control (and 'sterilisation') are vital if stability is to be restored.

It will not, of course, be possible to create a new stable system if there are persistent trade imbalances between the G7 which are not funded by long-term capital flows. Today, the fundamental imbalance is between the USA and Japan. European Community trade is broadly balanced—and has been for more than the past decade. The yen losses suffered on Japanese financial investments in the USA, combined with current difficulties in the Japanese financial sector, both suggest that financing a persistent US deficit is going to prove more difficult in the nineties than it did in the eighties. Sustained growth and expanding trade will therefore require action to correct the trade imbalance between the USA and Japan. The alternative is either persistent instability or the stability of permanent recession.

A G7 agreement to buttress economic policy coordination with a framework of stable exchange rates must be reinforced by action to monitor and perhaps regulate short-term international capital flows. Attempting to maintain stability in international currency markets under the current deregulated regime is like trying to cross an uneven field carrying a large volume of water in a shallow pan. It would be much easier if the pan contained a number of baffles to prevent all the water slopping in unison from side to side. Financial baffles are needed to slow down the rush of short-term capital from one currency to another.

The technical problems involved in creating suitable baffles in the international financial markets are typically overrated. The fact that trading today is typically by electronic transfer makes effective monitoring easier than ever before, and, with international agreement, it would not be too difficult to link the legal right to trade to the requirement to accept appropriate monitoring. Effective monitoring is the starting-point of effective

management. Both will only be possible if there is full and consistent cooperation amongst the G7 countries, in the pursuit of agreed objectives.

A FULL EMPLOYMENT STRATEGY FOR THE EU

The European Union forms a quasi-closed economy. The proportion of
foreign trade in EU GDP is slightly lower than the proportion of foreign
trade in the GDP of either the USA or Japan. Moreover, the EU external
account is typically in balance and much more stable that the current
account balances of either the USA or Japan, or indeed the member states.
This suggests that there is considerable potential for the EU to pursue a
'domestic' full employment strategy, whatever happens in the rest of the
G7. Unfortunately, the EU does not possess the institutions capable of pursuing such a strategy: monetary coordination is highly imperfect, and, in so
far as it exists at all, dominated by the domestic concerns of the
Bundesbank; fiscal coordination is non-existent.

It is difficult to envisage effective policy coordination in the near future.
The current exchange rate regime, in which several currencies, notably the
pound, are floating against the Deutschmark, means that estimation of the
national pay-off from any coordinated fiscal expansion is virtually impossible. Any country which devalued during the expansion would 'steal' jobs
from the others. An exchange rate regime which, by its very nature, creates

Table 12.5. Current account balance as a proportion of GDP

	European Union Countries	Germany	France	UK	US	Japan
1981	−0.8	−0.8	−0.8	2.5	0.2	0.4
1982	−0.7	0.5	−2.2	1.5	−0.3	0.6
1983	0.0	0.6	−0.9	1.1	−1.5	1.8
1984	0.3	1.0	−0.2	0.4	−2.9	2.8
1985	0.7	2.1	0.1	1.1	−3.1	3.7
1986	1.7	4.4	0.3	—	−3.5	4.3
1987	1.0	4.1	−0.6	−1.0	−3.6	3.7
1988	0.4	4.2	0.5	−3.6	−2.6	3.3
1989	0.1	4.9	−0.6	−4.4	−2.0	2.2
1990	−0.2	3.2	−1.3	−3.1	−1.7	1.3
1991	−1.0	−1.2	−0.6	−1.1	−0.1	2.2
1992	−0.9	−1.3	0.3	−2.1	−1.0	3.2
Average	—	1.8	−0.5	−0.7	−1.8	2.5
Variance	0.6	4.9	0.5	4.4	1.6	1.5

Source: Eurostat.

an environment in which member states *compete* over the allocation of employment between them is hardly conducive to fiscal policy coordination.

Moreover, the persistent EU external balance is a less secure foundation for coordinated fiscal expansion than might at first be supposed. The overall external balance is the result of netting out third party transactions. But in the coordinated expansion, the relationships with third parties will contribute to the pattern of surpluses and deficits. The UK for example might maintain a balance with EU partners, but suffer a severe deficit with non-EU countries, the counterpart of which might be a German surplus with non-EU countries. The EU as a whole would stay in balance, but the UK deficit might then force abandonment of its part of the growth strategy, bringing down the entire, interdependent effort. So policy coordination is made difficult within the EU, simply because member states have substantial trading relationships with economies which are not part of the coordination process, and the surpluses of one member state are not available to fund the deficits of another.

These factors are just some of the difficulties involved in creating an effective coordinated fiscal expansion.[4] Yet, given the high level of interdependence which has developed between the EU economies (about one in five of all jobs in the UK are directly dependent on demand from other EU economies), some structure of institutions which permits coordination, of monetary *and* fiscal policies, must be devised if the EU is not to suffer permanently high levels of unemployment.

This will require the creation of an entirely new institutional framework, not previously encountered in the history of modern capitalism. The Bretton Woods era was not a period of policy coordination. The fixed exchange rate system was buttressed by strict capital controls and by active trade policies, against which the dominant economic power, the United States, did not retaliate.[5] Individual countries were therefore able, within bounds, to pursue national economic objectives. That these added up to a reasonably coherent set of international growth rates is to a substantial degree attributable to the combination of managed trade and a persistent US deficit on combined current and long-term capital account which sustained the growth of world demand. The sustained high levels of employment were the result of the resultant structure of national policies: interdependent, yes; coordinated, no.

---

[4] The problem is surveyed in my article, 'The Coordination of Macroeconomic Policy in the European Community', ch. 13 of *Unemployment in Europe*, J. Michie and J. Grieve Smith (eds.), Academic Press, 1994.

[5] For a full account of the trade policies of this era, particularly the 'management' of trade by Germany, France, and Japan, and the response of the United States, see A. Shonfield, *Modern Capitalism*, Oxford University Press, 1965.

A similar reliance on national policies was the basis of the recovery from the recession of the 1930s. The recovery heralded by abandonment of the Gold Standard, and the successive devaluation of currencies against gold, was not due so much to the devaluations (after all it was not possible for all countries to devalue against each other, and the countries which did not devalue were not big enough relative to the world economy to act as deficit-absorbing engines of world demand). It was instead due to the adoption of national expansionary policies—notably cheap money policies, fortified by capital and trade controls, once the need to maintain the monetary ortho-doxy of the gold standard had been abandoned.[6]

These issues were not addressed in the Maastricht Treaty at all. The Treaty embodies the implicit assumption that monetary stability is all that is required for full employment to be restored.

UK POLICIES FOR FULL EMPLOYMENT

The international dimensions of the unemployment problem in the 1990s do not rule out unilateral action by the UK, even within the structure of the current trading and financial system. Quite simply, that will involve improving the competitive position of the UK so that more demand stays at home, and more demand is attracted from abroad. In the medium term, superior competitiveness will be necessary to ward off any jobs threat from the newly industrializing countries.

The economic state of Britain today is historically unprecedented. Never in modern times has this country faced a situation in which unemployment is due, quite simply, to an inability to produce enough of the goods that people want to buy. In the past, even in the 1930s, an increase in demand, as a result of increased spending either by the Government or by the pri-vate sector, would result in jobs being created predominantly in Britain.

This is not the situation today. Any expansion of demand today will lead to a rapid growth in imports: i.e. an export of jobs. This would not matter were there increased exports to match the growing imports, provide jobs in the export industries, and create a firm base for expanding jobs in other sec-tors too. Sadly that is not the case. The economy simply does not have enough competitive capacity to produce the goods for the home market nor for exports which would allow Britain to sustain a full employment level of demand, or anything like it. If there were full employment, the volume of imports would be so great, the borrowing to pay for them so enormous,

---

[6] See P. Temin, *Lessons from the Great Depression*, MIT Press, Cambridge, Mass., 1989; and the chapter entitled 'Depression and Recovery, Lessons from the Interwar Period', by M. Kitson and J. Michie in *Unemployment in Europe*.

that the economy would soon be crushed under the weight of unmanageable foreign debts.

That is the core of Britain's employment problem: not enough competitive capacity. And most important of all, not enough people with the skills to compete in the modern global economy, and the opportunity to use those skills with the latest techniques, producing the latest products. It is skills that really matter today. In a global economy where techniques and capital are more mobile than ever, and markets are truly international, what distinguishes a national economy are the skills and talents of its people. If those skills and talents—everything from management techniques, to handicrafts, to computer sciences, to electrical engineering, to design—are neglected then a country first loses its competitive edge, and then slips into a decline characterized by growing trend unemployment.

If this analysis is correct, then the attack on the problem of unemployment will require a significant rebalancing of the UK economy, with an increased share of total resources being devoted to investment in capacity, in people, in research, and in other aspects of competitiveness, including design. This poses a number of major problems for economic policy. Private sector investment will only increase to the extent required if there is a prospect of sales and profit, i.e. if there is expanding demand. There is therefore a chicken and egg problem: the ability to sustain a higher growth of demand requires competitive capacity; investment in competitive capacity requires a high growth of demand. It is likely, therefore, that the necessary rebalancing will require the public sector to play a role, taking the intertemporal risk which the private sector is not capable of carrying, perhaps in some innovative public–private sector partnerships.

Rebalancing the economy also means that consumption grows more slowly that output as a whole. It is the purpose of the Chancellor's recent tax increases to achieve this goal. If the reduction in consumption were to be accompanied by increased investment, then there would be considerable pressure on money wages to restore real income lost in higher taxes. Unfortunately, this second vital component of an effective recovery strategy is missing from the Government's programme.

Part of the process of rebalancing might be aided by a more aggressive exchange rate policy. But this is not a substitute for an investment strategy. Everything else being equal, too high an exchange rate will make British goods uncompetitive at home and abroad. Equally, even if products are old-fashioned and techniques out of date, a massive devaluation may lead to some sales—there is a market for Lada cars. But unless British industry is competitive, and competitiveness is maintained over time, then no level of the exchange rate is sustainable in the medium to long run. The pound has been continuously devalued against the Deutschmark for the past thirty years, with no obvious improvement in Britain's relative economic strength *vis-à-vis* Germany. Of course, it may be argued that Britain would be a lot worse off if the pound had not been devalued (going back to the eleven Deutschmark pound of the early 1960s doesn't bear thinking about). But that is to miss the point. The failure to invest, to train, to innovate on anything like the scale of Germany has not been disguised or overcome by devaluation. An economic policy which relies on continuous devaluation alone to overcome structural deficiencies is a sticking-plaster policy, incapable of tackling the real problem of productive capacity, and therefore incapable of sustaining full employment.

FULL EMPLOYMENT

The rise in unemployment in the 1980s and 1990s is predominantly a macroeconomic failure. It arises from the inability to adapt the institutions and tools of macroeconomic policy to structural changes in the global economy, most especially structural changes within and between the G7 countries themselves. The lessons which should be drawn from the experience of the 'Golden Age' are that sustained full employment is possible, is highly efficient (associated as it is with high productivity growth and low inflation), and requires an institutional framework within which expansionary policies may be consistently pursued and sustained. The Golden Age also teaches us that the simplistic attribution of unemployment to microeconomic factors is likely to be not only misleading, but positively harmful if policies to enhance the 'flexibility' of markets are divorced from the appropriate expansionary macroeconomic context.

13. A Programme For Reform

John Grieve Smith

The Bretton Woods agreement created both a new set of international financial institutions and for the first time a formal framework of rules governing exchange rates and international payments. The agreement, largely a creation of Maynard Keynes and Harry White, was originally conceived as part of a wide-ranging vision of how the postwar economic system might work, including a liberal regime for trade and tariffs, and measures to stabilize commodity prices. It was designed to overcome both the problems experienced in the interwar period with the breakup of the Gold Standard and the rise of mass unemployment, and those emerging from the Second World War, in particular restrictions on trade and payments and the dollar shortage. The rules were intended first to encourage a speedy, but orderly, dismantling of wartime restrictions on imports and movement to currency convertibility, and then to establish, as a permanent regime, a liberal system of trade and payments and fixed exchange rates which would be compatible with the pursuit of full employment. The operation of the international payment system was to be supervised by the International Monetary Fund controlled by the leading Allied Powers with a system of weighted voting ensuring a dominant voice for the USA.

Compatibility of a fixed exchange rate regime with full employment meant avoiding a situation whereby countries in balance of payments deficit, or whose exchange rates came under pressure, automatically had to deflate to the point where they would no longer enjoy full employment. To this end, the system provided that exchange rates could be changed where there was agreed to be a structural imbalance in a country's balance of payments (rather than excessive demand). It also in principle accepted that creditor as well as debtor countries had an obligation to ensure the necessary adjustments: the scarce currency clause (although never in the event invoked) would have allowed debtor countries to discriminate against a persistent creditor. Subject to these provisos, however, it was basic to the system that demand management was the normal means to be employed to remedy short-term imbalances. The underlying assumption was that, with exchange rates fixed at appropriate levels, such imbalances reflected excessive demand in the debtor countries or (in principle at any rate) deficient demand in creditor countries.

As operated by the IMF, this system had an inevitably deflationary bias because it was bound to be asymmetrical, with virtually all the pressure

being put on those in deficit to deflate. This was partly due to the fundamental fact that deficits can put direct financial pressure on countries who
incur them (and thus put them in the hands of the IMF), whereas those in
surplus are liable to no such pressure. Also with full employment generally
prevailing and the USA the main creditor, there was no general case for
pressing creditors to increase demand. By the standards of the 1980s and
1990s, however, the deflationary aspects of the system which concerned
many of us at the time now appear less significant.

The breakup of the Bretton Woods fixed exchange rate system seems to
reflect two main factors, both of which have also been fundamental causes
of the collapse of the ERM. The first is the difficulty of getting intergovernmental agreement on changes in rates when the existing structure is no
longer appropriate. The second is the growth of mobile financial capital
and the increasing importance of capital movements in determining or
putting pressure on exchange rates. To these might be added a fashion cycle
in which fixed and floating rates tend to alternate as the disadvantages of
either system lead to a reaction against it.

The Bretton Woods fixed exchange rate phase was one in which fiscal
policy tended to take precedence over monetary policy as the major instrument of macroeconomic policy. The growth of mobile capital and the
switch to floating rates during the 1970s increased the importance of interest rate policy as a means of influencing exchange rates, and then by the
1980s the rise of monetarism was making changes in interest rates the only
fashionable instrument of macroeconomic control. This has led in the 1990s
to the practical dilemma that an interest rate policy that may be appropriate for exchange rate purposes may be inappropriate for the needs of the
domestic economy (as in the case of the UK while it was in the ERM) or
vice versa (as in the case of Germany). A further related change is that
interest rate policy, like exchange rate policy, has increasingly become a
matter of international concern, leaving fiscal policy as the instrument over
which national governments have most effective control.

In order to assess the shortcomings, or merits of the present 'system' (if
it can be dignified as such), it is first necessary to postulate the objectives
of any international exchange and payments system. In the broadest terms
it should facilitate worldwide growth of output and living standards; to
which should be added a distributional objective in that the fruits of growth
should in some sense be 'fairly' distributed between countries; or in more
practical terms, the abolition of underemployment, poverty, disease, and
political autocracy in the poorer countries should rank highly in comparison with further increases in living standards in the richest countries.

FULL EMPLOYMENT

The architects of the Bretton Woods agreement recognized that an essential element in fostering world prosperity must be the maintenance of full employment in the industrialized countries. Not only would the industrialized countries themselves benefit from avoiding the waste and suffering of mass unemployment, but the less developed countries would also gain from the increasing demand for their commodities and manufactured goods. This remains equally true today. Emphasizing the need for full employment and steady growth should not be regarded as a selfish objective of the industrialized countries, but as a key part of any strategy for worldwide growth. There is a similar common interest in minimizing fluctuations in industrial activity and thus avoiding violent swings in commodity prices which can harm both the industrialized countries and primary producers.

The shift in the emphasis of macroeconomic policy during the late 1970s and early 1980s towards combating inflation rather than maintaining full employment represented a watershed in postwar economic history. Fear of inflation, the dominance of monetarist thinking, and the evidence that governments could still be re-elected despite the re-emergence of mass unemployment meant that by the 1980s the pursuit of full employment had been effectively abandoned. Not only had the fixed exchange rate mechanism established at Bretton Woods broken down, but the world economy had reverted to the pre-war state of chronic mass unemployment which most of us believed to have been banished for good. At the same time, the prevalence of monetarist and free market thinking among the political leadership of the industrial nations effectively ruled out any major structural reforms in the management of the world economy.

Both the policy assumptions and the mechanics of the world monetary system have acquired a deflationary bias. This is not a simple matter of floating or fixed exchange rates. The fixed rate system in the ERM had as strong, or stronger, deflationary pressures as the floating regime which replaced it. On the other hand, the floating rate regime in the world as a whole also has a deflationary bias because the growth of mobile financial capital puts pressure on governments to follow 'orthodox' (i.e. pre-Keynesian) policies. Until the emergence of the Clinton administration as spokesman for growth, summit meetings and gatherings of finance ministers and the pronouncements of the OECD and the IMF have tended to reinforce these tendencies.

The first essential for a restoration of full employment is a sea change in political and economic thinking. This may now be starting. Japan has been following Keynesian fiscal policies for some time. The Clinton administration is taking a more expansionary line than its predecessor. The European Union is becoming concerned about the political and economic dangers of mass unemployment, even though most of the remedies being put forward are wide of the mark. As I have argued elsewhere (Grieve Smith, 1994a), the key to expansion and reducing unemployment in the EU is fiscal policy; and, because they are so interdependent, the members need to adopt coordinated expansionary policies. This will both ensure that such measures are more effective and reduce the danger to the balance of payments of one country expanding on its own.

On a wider front, the EU as a whole, North America, and Japan are not so interdependent as the individual EU members. Nevertheless, coordinated expansion by the main industrial areas would not only benefit each other, but also the rest of the world. If Europe were to adopt a more expansionary stance, the three major players (Japan, the USA, and the EU) would then all be moving in the right direction. This is the most urgent need facing the world economy today and would not of itself necessitate any change in the formal structure of world payments. A great deal has been written about the refinements of macroeconomic policy coordination; but the problem today is not so much to get everyone marching in step, as to ensure that we are all at least going in the right direction.

THE MOVEMENT OF CAPITAL

The diffusion of technology and the pace of development are closely dependent on the international movement of capital and aid. With the growth of multinational companies, direct investment has become increasingly important, both through the construction of plant and through the purchase of existing firms or property. In addition, in the grey area between direct and purely financial investment, the purchase of shares with or without the immediate achievement of majority control may have longer-term industrial consequences.

In devising a contemporary concept of how the world economy should operate, it is important to consider both the actual and desirable movement of long-term capital and aid between countries or areas. At one time it seemed natural to work on a tacit model whereby the leading industrial country or countries, starting with the UK in the nineteenth century, and in the early postwar period the USA, had a substantial balance of payments surplus and invested heavily in less developed countries (as well as in other industrialized countries). The emergence of Japan as a major creditor, with the USA in chronic deficit and Western Europe generally more or less in balance, has shattered that model, as has the varying experience of the rest of the world. In addition, the growth of financial capital movements has meant that the pattern of capital flows in total may differ markedly from that of productive investment on its own.

The historic model of more advanced industrial countries with balance of payments surpluses investing in, or granting aid to, less developed countries provided a means of enabling the latter to catch up. This depended, of course, on their loans being at reasonably low rates of interest—the reliance on the international banking system to recycle the OPEC surpluses to developing countries provoked a catastrophic debt crisis when interest rates rose. Nevertheless, in seeking a desirable and sustainable pattern of payments surpluses and deficits and the associated flows of long-term investment, it seems reasonable to assume that the richer countries should be in surplus, or at least balance. The fact that an advanced country like the USA may have highly developed financial markets and also be an attractive area for direct investment means that industrial pre-eminence is no longer necessarily synonymous with being a net exporter of capital. But both the long-term future of the USA itself, and the interests of the rest of the world, suggest that this should be the appropriate policy objective.

If, however, the USA were in fact to revert to being a rich country in surplus, its role as the main provider of international currency reserves would no longer be tenable. The beneficial effects to the world economy of the USA swinging from surplus to deficit, thus ending the dollar shortage and providing a plentiful supply of dollars, the main reserve currency, have gone largely unrecognized. The simple-minded foreign critics of the US deficit should think themselves lucky that it remains so substantial, especially as long as there are no signs of the Japanese surplus declining to a similar extent. Indeed, unless the USA could improve its balance of payments solely at the expense of the Japanese, what would happen to the rest of us? While the reduction of the Japanese surplus might be regarded as desirable irrespective of who are the gainers, the reduction of the US deficit cannot be regarded as desirable without consideration of whose balance of payments would deteriorate as a consequence.

The history of the postwar period demonstrates that it is very much easier to operate a system in which the country providing the main reserve currency is in deficit rather than surplus, as with the dollar. Then other countries' desire to increase their reserves with the growth of trade (and the increasing need to be able to counteract short-term capital movements) can be met by their holding increasing amounts of the reserve currency, thus helping to finance that country's deficit. But if the yen were to become the main reserve currency and Japan were to remain in surplus, there might well be a shortage of reserve currency. There would then be a need to increase world liquidity, in the sense of the supply of reserve currency, by increases in Special Drawing Rights or other means.

THE SURPLUS PROBLEM

Although it is healthy to consider the problems of debtor and surplus countries in general terms, at any particular period of history these problems are specific to particular countries or groups of countries. In the immediate aftermath of war, the USA was the major creditor and the scarce currency clause was aimed at the dollar. It is interesting, however, that the clause emanated from Harry White, not Keynes, and was put forward by the Americans. Keynes's proposals for an International Clearing Union prior to Bretton Woods were designed so far as possible to introduce symmetrical penalties on both creditors and debtors: 'creditor' or 'debtor' status reflected a country's overall balance including capital movements. Keynes, however, envisaged permanent control of capital movements to avoid speculative movements. Thus a creditor was conceived as a country whose current surplus was not fully offset by the permitted outflow of capital. The sanctions against creditors were therefore not necessarily designed to get them to reduce their current surpluses; they could equally well be regarded as putting pressure on them to lend more.[1]

The provisions for dealing with creditors, which would obviously raise sensitive issues with the Americans, were revised several times in the course of discussions within the Treasury and with the Bank of England and other departments. In the final version published as a White Paper in April 1943, there was no longer any compulsion on creditors to revalue their currency as there had been in the earlier drafts. The idea of confiscating surpluses in excess of quotas had also been dropped. But the provisions for charging interest on surpluses remained: 1 per cent per annum on surpluses (and deficits) over one quarter of quotas and 2 per cent on the excess over one-half of quotas. In addition, a country whose credit balance had exceeded one-half of its quota for at least a year would have to discuss means of getting back into equilibrium with the Bank—although it would 'retain the ultimate decision in its own hands'. Measures to be discussed included the expansion of domestic demand, revaluation, and international development loans.

Today the major imbalances are those of Japan and the US. Over the five years 1988–92 the Japanese current surplus averaged $73 billion a year, but little over half of this was offset by direct investment and aid which averaged $34 billion and $5 billion a year respectively. In the same period the US current deficit averaged $79 billion; in addition US official aid aver-

[1] See D. E. Moggridge, *Maynard Keynes: An Economist's Biography*, (ch. 26) (London: Routledge, 1992); A. van Dormael, *Bretton Woods: Birth of a Monetary System*, (London, Macmillan, 1978); J. M. Keynes, *The Collected Writings of John Maynard Keynes*, xxv, (London: Macmillan, 1980).

aged $17 billion but the net inflow of direct investment from all sources was only $11 billion a year (which was more than accounted for by an average net inflow of $13 billion from Japan).

The fact that so much of the problem revolves around these two major countries should make it easer in a way to resolve, because any bilateral action is likely to work in the desired direction from a world point of view. It also makes it easier to see the basic industrial and technological factors involved and not overrate the effectiveness of any change in exchange rates. But it does mean that Japan as the major creditor nation must play a much larger part than it has hitherto in any rethinking of international payments arrangements. It is remarkable how little attention has been paid to the Japanese perspective, reflecting perhaps the Japanese reluctance to assume the full role of a major international power.

Nevertheless, although the surplus problem is at present largely specific to Japan, any new approach should consider the introduction of general sanctions or pressures on countries whose surpluses exceed the outflow of productive capital to the rest of the world. These new measures should either exert pressure to reduce the current surplus or facilitate its translation into productive investment and aid to the remainder of the world, particularly the poorest parts of it. One solution would be to lay down that a specified proportion of any country's current surplus should be deposited either with the IBRD (or a new financing institution) with a minimal return: for example, indexed against price increases but with a zero real rate of interest. These deposits would then be used to finance long-term 'soft' loans on favourable terms to developing countries.

The surplus problem is linked to the objective of increasing and stabilizing the flow of capital and aid to the Third World, and avoiding the re-emergence of the type of debt problems that were experienced in the 1980s with the consequent series of write-offs and rescheduling. Leaving the OPEC surpluses to be recycled to developing countries by the banking system turned out to be a major disaster, aggravated by the subsequent rise in interest rates (which was itself a consequence of the inflationary effects of the oil price boom). While the OPEC experience may seem a unique event, there will no doubt be other unforeseen scenarios where a *laissez-faire* approach may be equally disastrous. The basic need is to increase very substantially the proportion of capital movements to the Third World going through publicly owned international institutions, on terms that do not favour richer creditors and will not impoverish poorer debtors.

Two of the original purposes of the International Bank, set out in Article 1 of the Agreement (Bretton Woods, 1944) were:

'To promote private foreign investment by means of guarantees or participation in loans and other investments made by private investors; and when private capital is not available on reasonable terms, to supplement private investment by providing,

on suitable conditions, finance for productive purposes out of its own capital, funds
raised by it and its other resources.'

'To promote the long-range balanced growth of international trade and the maintenance of equilibrium in balances of payments by encouraging international investment for the development of the productive resources of members, thereby assisting
in raising productivity, the standard of living and conditions of labour in their territories.'

This reflected the implicit view that there should be a rational pattern of
long-term investment both between industrialized countries, and from
industrialized to developing countries, and that the network of countries'
balance of payments surpluses and deficits should be consistent with these
movements. It also saw the Bank as a rather more wide-ranging guardian
of such movements than it has actually become.

A WORLD PAYMENTS STRATEGY

A long-term strategy for world payments is needed to formulate a coherent approach to the movement of productive investment, the problems of
world liquidity, and a consistent exchange rate policy. If exchange rates are
a major determinant of trade balances, any targeted pattern of rates should
depend on the pattern of surpluses and deficits that it is desired to
achieve—at least as between the major countries or groupings. Exchange
rates will not in themselves, of course, necessarily bring about such a pattern. There may, for example, be no yen/dollar rate which will bring about
the desired adjustment in the Japanese/US imbalance.[2] But there is little
sense in trying to determine a reasonable target for such a rate without at
the same time having in mind a desired outcome in balance of payments
terms. Moreover, if we are to achieve full employment and eschew the use
of deflationary policies to remedy balance of payments deficits, exchange
rate policy must be used as the main macroeconomic instrument for adjusting trade balances and directed towards balance of payments objectives.

The difficulty in getting agreement between the major players on
exchange rates is partly the complex interaction of exchange rate changes
and partly the problem (hardly as yet explored) of providing a rational set
of objectives in terms of a desired and sustainable worldwide pattern of surpluses and deficits. It is sometimes argued that any attempt to postulate

---

[2] The IMF suggests, however, that there is some evidence that the yen's sustained appreciation beginning in mid-1985 did have a significant effect on its trade balance (*World
Economic Outlook*, Feb. 1994). Between 1986 and 1991, Japan's export volume growth was
only 2.75% a year compared with the industrial country average of 5% and US export growth
of 10%. Japan's import volume growth during this period averaged 8.5% a year compared with
the industrial country average of 6.25% and the US average of 4%.

consistent balance of payments objectives is unnecessary and futile on the grounds that a market mechanism is available to perform the reconciliation task.[3] But that is merely to say that, in the event, different countries' surpluses and deficits must cancel out. It is, however, only by clarifying some form of *target* pattern of surpluses and deficits that there is any rational basis for setting actual exchange rates or adopting other measures to influence the pattern of world payments. Foreign exchange markets left to themselves do not necessarily lead to anything like a desired pattern. Nor can the problems of imbalance be resolved solely by domestic demand management, save at the expense of massive unemployment in the deficit countries. As regards the USA in particular, it is one thing to say that if an increase in competitiveness *led* to an improvement in the US trade balance, this would necessitate an increase in domestic saving (i.e. a decrease in the fiscal deficit)—this need involve no change in employment. It is quite another to imply that a decrease in the US fiscal deficit would of itself automatically improve the trade deficit. Without an increase in competitiveness as a result of a change in the exchange rate, or improved industrial efficiency, deflationary fiscal measures would only achieve such an improvement at the expense of a multiple decline in employment.

The task for an international secretariat of analysing the existing and potential pattern of world payments in this way to devise strategic objectives may seem formidable, but it is analogous to the task facing the planning function in a large multinational company. The fundamental problem is not analytical, but political. The multinational has an overarching managerial structure and can take decisions. The nation states have as yet to take decisions by negotiation and agreement. One of the fundamental problems of any new settlement is thus to devise a system capable of reaching the necessary decisions, and, conversely, not trying to implement a system which requires decisions which the political structure is incapable of making (a recent example being the failure to agree on a general adjustment of exchange rates within the ERM). The first essential, therefore, is to concentrate the power of decision making into a relatively small number of hands. This was much easier in 1944 than it is today: at any rate as far as formal structures are concerned, for instance in the United Nations. Informal structures such as the G7 can be kept relatively small, but they are undemocratic in the sense that the interests of other countries remain

---

[3] E.g. in a detailed discussion of the problem of setting a coordinated set of targets for surpluses and deficits, Polak argues that it is impractical and reconciliation is best left to the market. (J. J. Polak, 'Comment on Andrew Crockett, The Role of International Institutions in Surveillance and Policy Coordination', in *Macro-Economic Policies in an Interdependent World*, ed. R. C. Bryant, D. A. Currie, J. A. Frenkel, P. R. Masson, and R. Pentes, Brookings (CEPR, IMF, 1989). See also 'The Theory and Practice of International Policy Coordination: Does Coordination Pay?' D. A. Currie, G. Holtham, and A. Hughes Hallett, in the same volume.)

unrepresented. This has led to the suggestion that the UN should have an economic equivalent of the Security Council, which in many ways has been remarkably successful in the political field (Stewart, 1994).

INSTITUTIONAL REFORM

With the ending of the Bretton Woods fixed exchange rate system, the Fund has become largely isolated from the affairs of the industrialized countries and increasingly concerned with giving assistance to developing countries, including more recently the countries formerly behind the Iron Curtain.[4] The Fund is thus tending to operate increasingly in what was formerly the Bank's territory. International financial policy, in so far as it exists, emanates from the G5, now the G7 Group. The OECD has no real operational role but survives as a research secretariat and the club with the widest membership of industrialized countries. The less developed countries look to the UN and its agencies for consideration of the policy issues in which they are mainly concerned. A fundamental external review of this institutional framework is long overdue.

The Bretton Woods institutions were originally set up under the auspices of the UN, although they have always tended to operate separately from it. Any rationalization of existing organizations should bring them under the UN umbrella. But this must be done in such a way as to create an overall supervising body sufficiently small, but representative, to be effective. This problem will be eased in so far as regional groupings of countries develop. The EU is at the moment a unique case, but over the years other looser groups may well develop.

The degree to which any international system should operate (a) automatically under preordained rules or (b) in an *ad hoc* or discretionary manner, depends on the extent to which international (or more accurately supranational) decision taking is practical. The less effective such decision taking, the greater the need to provide some degree of automaticity. There is thus a need to consider the possible creation of new international decision-making machinery hand in hand with any new framework of rules and objectives.

---

[4] For discussions of the present role of the Fund see A. Crockett, 'The Role of International Institutions in Surveillance and Policy Coordination', in Bryant, *Macro-Economic Policies in an Interdependent World*; C. D. Finch, 'IMF Surveillance and the G24', *International Monetary and Financial Issues for the 1990s* II, UNCTAD, 1993; Overseas Development Council, *Pulling Together: the IMF in a Multipolar World*, Washington D.C., 1989.

A NEW EXCHANGE RATE REGIME

To make the achievement of full employment a key objective in any new structure for world payments (as it originally was in Bretton Woods), we must find ways of obviating the adoption of deflationary demand policies to remedy balance of payments deficits or exchange rate crises. This means that the system must: (a) avoid exchange rates being determined by short-term capital movements rather than basic trade objectives; (b) ensure that rates can be adjusted as changing economic circumstances require (e.g. trade performance and relative inflation rates); whilst (c) avoiding speculative exchange rate crises.

As far as the exchange rate regime itself is concerned, any new agreement must in my view be based on a scheme for managed rates but one which is more flexible than the Bretton Woods or ERM. 'Some critics of exchange rate agreements argue that there is no reason to suppose that policymakers can take a better long-run view of exchange rates than the market. The difficulty with this view is that the foreign market is dominated by short-run speculation, including beliefs about what monetary authorities will do next. This short-run focus is due partly to the fact that, in a world of volatile exchange rates, the premium is in assessing short-run market developments, not longer-run trends. Given that larger and volatile funds are driven by expectations, fundamentals work slowly and feebly.' (Currie, Holtham, and Hughes Hallett, 1989.)

An important part of the case against free floating and the consequent instability is that it is increasingly inappropriate in a world of international industrial investment by multinationals and growing trade interdependence. Exchange rate instability prejudices the rationality of any investment decisions either in plant, or in sales and distribution networks. Moreover, as Krugman has pointed out, the more unstable rates are, the less effective they are as an economic instrument in influencing industrial decisions.[5] With a high degree of instability only large changes in rates tend to have any effect on firms' strategies.

On the other hand a 'fixed' rate system is vulnerable to disruptive macroeconomic effects of exchange rate crises and the deflationary bias they impose on monetary and fiscal policies. These stem from the inability of countries to make changes in their rates until they are forced upon them by a crisis. There are two possible approaches to remedying this defect. One is

[5] P. R. Krugman, *Exchange Instability*, Cambridge Mass., MIT Press, 1989. Krugman's theoretical exposition, based on a sunk costs model, reinforces my own experience in the steel industry that decisions to invest (or not to invest) in either plant, distributive facilities, or sales organizations in other countries depend heavily on confidence in the robustness of any exchange rate assumptions, in particular that current rates will remain unchanged for the foreseeable future.

to try to make international decision making on rates more effective. The difficulties of reaching such decisions by intergovernmental consultation has not yet been thoroughly analysed. It involves the directly conflicting trade interests of a shift in parity between two countries, the susceptibility of governments to pressure from financial institutions, and, not least, the need for finance ministers to deny that any change (particularly a devaluation) will take place until it has done so—as a consequence, for a finance minister to devalue is virtually equivalent to committing political suicide, a very important practical factor. It is difficult, however, to see any international body having the political power to dominate such decision making: although, if the Governors of a world central bank were to indicate that they envisaged such and such changes in rates, it would have a very powerful effect. (The corresponding problem in the case of the European Union has driven me to conclude that a European Federal government is needed to operate the ERM satisfactorily: Grieve Smith, 1994b.) The intrinsic difficulties of international decision making on exchange rates has long been recognized. Harry White's original proposals envisaged that an international monetary fund would have to have the authority to determine exchange rates (van Dormael, 1978). Before that, Lionel Robbins writing on the Economic Aspects of Federalism in 1940 envisaged the continued existence of separate currencies within a Federation, at any rate for an initial period, but with the important proviso that exchange rate policy should be determined by the Federal, not national, authorities (Robbins, 1940). Four decades later, but before the EMS had collapsed, Kenen wrote: 'Decisions about central rates must be made by governments, and unanimity must be the rule, as it is in the EMS. Passivity is out of date and supranationality is out of reach.' (Kenen, 1988.)

In trying to evolve an exchange rate regime which would avoid the more obvious and serious drawbacks of either the original Bretton Woods system or free floating, the Williamson target zone proposals (Williamson and Miller, 1987; Williamson, 1991) are still a valuable starting-point. Williamson envisages the establishment of target zones $\pm x$ per cent of a parity value fixed in real terms. Parity values would be automatically adjusted to allow for movements in relative prices. Thus there would be a degree of automaticity, in that nominal rates would be adjusted to allow for different rates of inflation. Adjustments in real rates to allow for changing circumstances would, however, still require conscious decision. But if the target zones were sufficiently wide (say ± 5 to 10 per cent), the new parity could still be within the target zone. Thus changes could be made in parities without large overnight changes in the actual rates, so avoiding the sort of one-way option for speculators that has been a feature of the Bretton Woods and ERM regimes.

Such a system would still be completely discretionary. A variant, however, would be to introduce some form of 'crawling peg' mechanism whereby parities would be automatically adjusted at the end of a period to, for example, the average actual rate in the period or the end part of it. The borders of the target zone would be automatically adjusted with the change in parity. Such a system would give more weight to market forces and might be less vulnerable to the build-up of speculative pressure. But by the same token it would be more influenced by short-term capital movements and less by fundamental trade objectives.

One consequence of the Williamson proposals would be that there would be stronger and more automatic pressure for interest rates in different countries to reflect their differing rates of inflation. On the other hand there might be less cause for differences to arise from expectations of changes in real exchange rates.

Williamson sees interest rates as the prime instrument for influencing exchange rates, and fiscal policy as the instrument for affecting domestic demand, and I would agree with this. The loss of freedom to tailor interest rates to the internal needs of the economy is an almost inevitable result of any managed system of exchange rates, unless special tax measures could be adopted to avoid this. But, in so far as a relatively high rate of inflation will automatically mean a declining exchange rate, it will also lead to relatively high interest rates: to this extent the Williamson scheme would mean that domestic interest rates would at least reflect differing inflationary situations.

Williamson's Blueprint formalizes an important *de facto* feature of world monetary policy by stating that the average level of world (real) interest rates should reflect the aggregate state of demand in the participating countries. (Williamson expresses his country and world targets for demand management in terms of nominal demand but this is not to my mind an essential or desirable feature of his proposed exchange rate mechanism.) Clearly the more closely national interest rates are linked to each other, the more important it becomes to gear their general level to the needs of the world economy. This is partly a matter of international cooperation and partly a matter of ensuring that the system does not have a bias in the wrong direction. In a period of prolonged recession, there is a need to keep world interest rates as low as possible, partly as a direct stimulus and partly to ease the cost of government borrowing. But apart from the needs of demand management, the experience of the 1980s also illustrates the need to avoid high interest rates penalizing countries dependent on international loans for development. It is perhaps fortunate that, although Germany has temporarily since unification become an influence for keeping interest rates up, the two most powerful industrial countries, the USA and Japan, are both traditionally low interest countries.

The target zone idea does seem to be a reasonable intermediate solution, avoiding the extremes of fixed or free floating rates. However, in determining rates, Williamson's 'fundamental equilibrium exchange rate (FEER)' concept needs to be conceived in terms of formulating a worldwide international payments strategy rather than a series of country by country calculations. Williamson goes part way to meeting this by envisaging that, instead of aiming at situations where everyone is in balance, account should be taken of the expected flow of long-term investment. This still leaves unanswered, however, the difficult, but fundamental, question of whether the existing flow of long-term investment is desirable or sustainable. (Indeed such flows are partly a reflection of existing exchange rates. Japanese multinationals might invest more abroad if the yen appreciated further and home production was less competitive.) Williamson partly recognizes the problem by asking whether the individual current accounts of individual countries in Europe sum up to a figure that the rest of the world will find sustainable. I would suggest that any worldwide system must be based on a view of target surpluses and deficits, and corresponding capital movements between the main participating groups. The most important thing about any exchange rate regime is to have the 'right' exchange rates, in that they are appropriate to the circumstances of the day. If they are not, they are either vulnerable to speculation or damaging if they survive. Britain's entry to the ERM at too high a rate was a prime example.

CURRENCY SPECULATION

An essential condition for the successful operation of any new exchange rate system must be to put the international financial markets in their proper place—that is as instruments for facilitating international trade and payments and the flow of productive investment, not (as at present) potentially dominant forces in their own right and major sources of instability. This was recognized in the Bretton Woods provisions permitting the control of capital movements. The subsequent abolition of virtually all such controls in the major industrial countries in the intended interests of efficiency has created the enormous problems described by Ruth Kelly and others (see Chapter 9).

International capital markets are not exercising the function of channelling investment efficiently between countries. Movements of capital involving real resources are swamped by purely financial transactions that are speculative in the sense that major investment funds are now held in whatever currency and country has the best short-term prospects and are subject to transfer by instant decision. The problem is to prevent these transactions, rather than trade payments or real investment, dominating the determination of exchange rates.

Following its historic tendency to sacrifice the interests of industry to those of the City, the UK has been in the forefront of this movement. In North America, where there is traditionally more suspicion of the financial fraternity, the reaction may already have set in. The General Accounting Office has recently published a report advocating tighter regulation of the derivative markets. Any reversion to the previous system of controls, which permitted some transactions and forbade others, now seems difficult to envisage. The two most promising lines of attack seem to be the possible taxation of foreign exchange transactions and the regulation of financial institutions and markets in such a way as to reduce the magnitude of speculative transactions, e.g. by increasing margin requirements. To be effective such measures might require foreign exchange transactions to be concentrated in the hands of recognized financial institutions subject to national and/or international regulatory standards. But there is no reason why such regulation should interfere with the efficient operation of foreign exchange markets. This is a highly difficult and complex question and the first need is to establish a general climate of opinion in which unregulated speculation is no longer taken for granted.

Whatever can be done to limit speculative capital movements, they may still remain a problem. We should therefore also consider strengthening the international banking arrangements to counter them. At the moment the key factor is central bank cooperation, and (as we have seen recently in the ERM) its effectiveness depends crucially on the commitment of the key players to maintaining a given pattern of rates. Central bank action needs to be reinforced by the operations of a reformed IMF or world central bank, with massive resources under its control and with a clearly defined duty to operate to support agreed exchange rate targets.

I have said nothing about the problems of world liquidity, in the sense of ensuring adequate exchange reserves. Liquidity in this sense was originally conceived in terms of means of financing temporary current deficits. Today the more acute problem is the different one of the resources needed to resist speculation against parities which should be an international, rather than national concern. But it could reappear as a problem if the yen were to supplant the dollar as the prime reserve currency, and the extension of Special Drawing Rights (SDRs) with the IMF would then be a major issue. It is frequently suggested that additional SDRs should be introduced to transfer real resources to less developed countries. Advocates of this proposal see it as a means of increasing world liquidity as well as achieving such a transfer. Issuing the corresponding amount of bonds and compelling the industrialized countries to hold them would equally well satisfy the first objective, of central banks, hence leading to a general expansion of credit. But I would favour keeping separate the problem of world liquidity and the transfer of real resources. The high profile role of the

Fund in providing finance to the Third World is already a source of con-
fusion between short- and long-term problems.

COMMODITY POLICY

Commodity prices are a key link between the economies of the industrialized countries and the developing world, and their instability is deleterious
to both sides. The unprecedented boom in commodity prices in the early
1970s was an important catalyst in accelerating worldwide inflation. Non-
oil commodity prices as measured by the *Economist* index rose by more
than 65 per cent in 1973, the largest year-on-year rise ever recorded, steeper
even than in the Korean rearmament boom. By the time they reached their
peak in 1974, world commodity prices (excluding oil) had more than doubled. Oil prices quadrupled. The resulting inflationary impact on industrialized countries was a key factor in shifting their macroeconomic policies
away from the maintenance of full employment in the interests of curbing
inflation. The consequent slow-down in the growth of output contributed
to the decline in real prices of many primary commodities in the 1980s
(Maizels, 1994). The balance of payments surpluses of the OPEC countries
became a major factor in the world economy, and higher interest rates
accentuated developing countries' debt problems.

Greater stability of commodity prices would be a major benefit to both
primary producers and the industrialized world. But the economic climate
of the 1980s has led to the abandonment of postwar buffer stock schemes
and a free market approach of letting the fluctuations take their course. It
is sometimes suggested that new financial derivatives might be used to
dampen down such fluctuations, but experience of derivative markets indicates that they are more likely to be a source of further instability, particularly if speculative activity spills over from financial to commodity
markets. Instability in commodity markets is thus a further problem to be
tackled in the 1990s.

SUMMARY OF ISSUES

In the half-century since Bretton Woods, international economic cooperation has declined, partly because of the growth of monetarism and extreme
free market theories which see no role for economic management by
national governments, let alone on a wider international scale, and partly
because of the increasing practical difficulties of cooperation as the postwar political hegemony of the Allied Powers declined. Since the end of the
war the Bretton Woods system of fixed rates has given way to a general

reversion to floating rates; global movements of financial capital rather than payments for trade now dominate foreign exchange markets; and the growing dependence of developing countries on private investment, together with the rise and fall of the OPEC countries' balance of payments surpluses, has created a series of problems not catered for in the postwar economic blueprint. The related issues which now need to be addressed may be summarized as follows:

1. A fundamental review is required of the existing international economic agencies, some at least of which have outlived their original functions and usefulness. A new structure is required both for intergovernmental decision making and for the relevant executive agencies. The immense professional resources scattered across existing organizations need to be rationalized into an effective economic secretariat to service a world economic 'cabinet' and forum under the aegis of the UN.

2. Careful analysis is needed of the evolving pattern of current surpluses and deficits and flows of 'productive' capital (private or official) and aid. An integrated world economic strategy is required in which the net flow of productive capital will be directed towards the most pressing needs of the developing and ex-Communist world, and exchange rates will reflect the need to establish a pattern of trade surpluses and deficits consistent with these movements.

3. The axis of any effective strategy must be a resolution of the Japanese and US surplus and deficit positions. It is essential therefore that Japan should play a key role in the formulation of any new arrangements.

4. A new exchange rate regime needs to be devised which will attempt to remedy the drawbacks experienced both with fixed and floating rates. In particular, the practical problems of target zones, with or without an automatic crawling peg mechanism, need further detailed examination, including the effects on interest rate differentials.

5. Speculative capital movements between countries and between currencies are now a normal part of every investment portfolio, but their negative effects outweigh their economic usefulness. Any new exchange rate regime needs to be accompanied by measures to curb speculation. The two most obvious instruments for this purpose are taxation and the regulation of financial institutions. This would probably require exchange rate transactions to be limited to regulated financial institutions, but there is no reason why this should interfere with the efficient operation of foreign exchange markets.

6. The IMF should play an active part in coordinating central banks' action to maintain the agreed pattern of exchange rates in the face of speculative pressure and should have access to additional resources to deploy in the market itself.

7. There is a longer-term need to consider the problems of world liquidity if the US dollar deficit no longer fills countries' growing needs for a reserve currency. Under existing institutional arrangements these needs might be met by a substantial increase in Special Drawing Rights.

8. The recycling of the OPEC surpluses through the banking system in the late 1970s and early 1980s and the consequent debt crisis illustrate the fallacy of assuming that private financial institutions and capital markets on their own will provide an adequate and stable flow of investment funds to developing countries. An overall strategy for the provision of development capital and aid to the Third World and the former Communist countries is needed, together with a fundamental review of the role and structure of international institutions to make effective the original Bretton Woods concept of the World Bank's role in this field.

9. There are already strong pressures on countries in deficit to reduce their deficits. There are no corresponding pressures on surplus countries either to reduce their surpluses or to ensure that they reflect a corresponding movement of long-term investment funds rather than the acquisition of financial assets. Consideration should be given to the possibility of raising further development capital by requiring countries to deposit a specified proportion of their surpluses with the IBRD or a new financial institution for lending to developing countries.

10. The industrialized countries have taken little interest recently in commodity policy, but fluctuations in world commodity prices (including oil) remain a potential destabilizing factor for both suppliers and consumers.

The most immediate need, however, is to recognize once again the importance of full employment and steady growth in the industrialized countries for the world economy as a whole, and for those countries to agree to follow policies directed to these ends. This does not in itself require any change in the formal system of world payments but is a key prerequisite for building any new structure on sound foundations.

14. A Postscript

Will Hutton

It is plain that the current international financial and trading system creates such enormous concentrations of private power, volatility of market behaviour, and economic illogicalities that remedies are required. But it is equally plain that the current system has developed because there is neither a global hegemony who could police a more disciplined order nor sufficient political will to delegate authority to a supranational authority which might do it instead. To echo the First World War song, we're here because we're here because we're here.

Thus any discussion of a new Bretton Woods or a more powerful World Trading Organization sits poised between the hopes that economic rationality must push the world in this direction and a cold-blooded recognition that states are simply not prepared to give up the degree of sovereignty that any such order implies. Bretton Woods was, in truth, an extension of the US domestic financial system to the world, and the attempts at building an enlightened world financial government were compromised even in the exceptional circumstances of the early postwar period. As Mića Panić says, to imagine a parallel initiative today is crying for the moon.

Worse, there is as yet no intellectual agreement on the principles around which such an order might be based. John Grieve Smith argues that any new exchange rate regime, crawling peg or semi-fixed parities alike, will require measures to curb speculation—and Ruth Kelly in her chapter sets out some of the options to contain the growth and speculative power of the derivative markets. But even in a book written by broadly like-minded people there are dissenters. Gerry Holtham dismisses the idea as unworkable and economically irrational; governments need the capital flows, even if speculative, to finance their large trade and public deficits—and instead argues for the more minimalist adjustable peg system, and leaving capital flows well alone.

But even if the reformers can agree a common front, there remains the formidable intellectual opposition of the free market theorists allied with the financial and trading interests for whom the current order provides an excellent living. No bond dealer of an international investment house or treasurer of a multinational is yet persuaded that the current financial order is either unstable or economically inefficient—and the howls of protest at the modest proposals of the US General Accounting Office to require more capital adequacy of the participants in the derivatives markets are tribute to the likely scale of the opposition if more full-blooded re-regulation was proposed.

Equally there is an argument that without a global hegemony the current system is the least bad. World trade does rise year by year, and, even though there is a trend to manage trade, at the same time industrialized countries are sufficiently open for the East Asian tigers and some Latin American countries to have successfully organized an export-led growth strategy around access to their markets. At the same time, the global capital market may produce a bias to disinflationary macroeconomic policies, but there are signs that the volatility of currencies is reducing—and the pool of capital has proved beneficial to developing and developed countries alike. It may not be perfect, but it functions. Equally, the powerful differences between the capitalist structures of North America, Japan and East Asia, and Western Europe make it almost impossible to find common ground over the rules of the international game. Japan and East Asia, with their high savings, outproduce and outinvest both Western Europe and North America—setting up a pattern of trade and capital flows that are almost impossible to manage and of their nature highly destabilizing.

The bilateral trade surplus that Japan has run with the USA for more than fifteen years, for example, has fundamental roots in the structures of the two countries' capitalisms. The relationship-based, long-termist capitalism of Japan is not merely highly productive, it has an inbuilt bias against openness because foreigners necessarily cannot join the same intimate relationships on which much of Japanese capitalism depends. Thus Japan, as Richard Kozul-Wright shows in Chapter 6, has extraordinarily low inward-direct-investment ratios and import penetration by comparison with other developed economies. It has hardly shared in the internationalization of the world economy over the last decade at all—at least if inward direct investment is used as a proxy.

Thus a highly competitive export sector combines with low import penetration to set in train Japan's trade surpluses. As long as the Japanese financial system was prepared to export capital, buying US debt during the 1980s, the outflows offset the trade surpluses and checked the upward movement of the yen. But the huge capital losses on the Japanese portfolio of dollar assets have stemmed the flow, and now the two countries are faced with their imbalances with no offsetting capital flows. The sharp rise in the yen and the fall in the US bond market are the consequences— imposing less competitiveness on Japan and more saving on the USA.

This may be uncomfortable for both countries but it is at least a means of imposing adjustment. The high Japanese yen is at last forcing an opening of the Japanese market because imports are supercompetitive, runs the argument, and even the Japanese economic machine is incapable of continuing to penetrate export markets with the yen under a hundred against the dollar. At the same time, if the US cannot grow at low interest rates because its domestic savings are inadequate, then higher long-term bond yields may be a means of jacking up domestic savings rates.

Such runs the apologist's argument. Moreover, the openness of the world economy and the global capital markets are increasingly seen as public goods by the less developed countries—who are anxious, as Ajit Singh and Ann Zammit argue in Chapter 4, to dispel what they see as a myth that competition from low cost Third World countries has contributed to the collapse of demand in the industrialized world for unskilled adult male labour. The volume of low cost imports is just too small to be blamed. We have been trying to encourage development for four decades, and if the current structures foster it then that too is an advantage that should not be lightly thrown away.

And yet. And yet. The difference in the capitalist structures between East Asia, Europe, and North America are so profound that it is likely that they will survive the attempts by the markets to organize adjustments by price changes. Indeed, Japan and East Asia on some measures already enjoy a collective GDP higher than Western Europe and North America, and are beginning to become less dependent on the American market. In 1975, 40 per cent of East Asian exports went to the USA and less than 20 per cent was intra East Asian trade; in 1995 the proportions will be reversed.

The dynamism and savings of this part of the globe will be decisive in the evolution of the global economy. Their high investment rates produce a rate of productivity and innovation with which European and American producers cannot compete, and access to East Asian markets, notwithstanding currency appreciation, will remain structurally difficult—even while their own economies remain open. The asymmetry in trade relations will become impossible to manage, and it is likely that both Europe and North America will become more protectionist. The European Union and North America Free Trade Agreement are in this respect forerunners of a more general trend.

Nor will it be easy to channel savings into Europe and America whose currencies will be in danger of constant depreciation against the emerging hard currencies of East Asia. Certainly it is likely that the process will be characterized by intermittent crashes, such as that in the world bond market in the first half of 1994, if it continues at all.

But of more general concern is the emerging veto the capital markets have over the economic sovereignty of all states. With international bank lending now twice the level of world trade and non-residents holding approaching a quarter of OECD government debt, the view that the markets have of the soundness of any one state's macroeconomic policy is pivotal to its sustainability. If the markets decide that they do not like what they see, then they retain the right of exit; and simultaneous exit can so destabilize the pattern of exchange rates and interest rates that macroeconomic policies are set to avoid this happening. In other words, everybody is concerned to minimize budget deficits and enlarge the market sector of the economy; that is what the capital markets approve.

Although Laurence Harris argues persuasively that states retain autonomy of action and that the power of the markets to force convergent economic policy is overstated, in a sense that is not the key point. From wherever they start, all countries have moved to accent price stability, the importance of inward investment, market-friendly microeconomic policies, and so on. When the African National Congress, the New Zealand Labour Party, and Forza Italia are all pursuing economic policies that are recognizably similar, even academic theorists have to pause and concede that, whatever the econometrics suggest, something important is happening to the wider framework of economic policy.

In particular, there is an inbuilt bias to prefer the values of finance over those of production and employment. This, coupled with the intense competition from the less developed world and East Asia, is the proximate cause of the unemployment in Europe and the low wages in the USA. It may be that low cost competition is still small in volume, but it is growing explosively, and producers in the mature industrialized countries are either giving ground before the challenge or anticipating it by moving away from labour-intensive production. The stone in my shoe may be small—but it still makes me walk differently. Low cost competition from labour-intensive processes is certainly making the industrialized world produce differently.

All this implies unemployment, and the case for new rules to manage the global economy is that, without the reassertion of the values of production over those of finance, the world will retreat from its current trade openness as the forces of protection mount—to the detriment of all. Countries need to be empowered to challenge the capital markets' preferences and organize more expansionary macroeconomic policies in order to keep their borders open; without them they will be forced into protectionist blocs.

But political realities will out. The most likely outcome is not the kind of genuine global initiative proposed by John Grieve Smith, but the hardening of the world into regional blocs in which some measure of policy autonomy is regained. Indeed, it may be easier within Europe or North America to organize the currency arrangements, capital transfers to less developed countries, and orderly patterns of economic adjustment than globally. Nor need this be a destructive outcome. So far, countries have avoided the competitive devaluation and protectionism of the 1930s despite the currency volatility and unemployment, and it may be that the best building bricks of a new world order will lie within the great regional trading blocs—as long as they retain the same willingness to abjure from 1930s-type behaviour in their inter-bloc behaviour.

That is not to deny the force of the arguments for reinventing a contemporary Bretton Woods. If the world could agree a more rational system of organizing its currency arrangements and capital flows, in the process reasserting the interests of production over finance, there would be more jobs and social cohesion. That alone justifies the case for keeping the flame of reform alive—even if high hopes have to be qualified by recognition of political realities.

BIBLIOGRAPHY

ABBEGLEN, J. (1994), *Sea Change*, New York: Free Press.

ABRAMOVITZ, M. (1989), *Thinking About Growth*, Cambridge: Cambridge University Press.

AKYÜZ, Y. (1993), 'Maastricht and Fiscal Retrenchment in Europe', *UNCTAD Discussion Paper*, no. 66, Aug.

ALDERHOLD, R., CUMMING, C., and HARWOOD, A. (1988), 'International Linkages among Equities Markets and the October 1987 Market Break', *Federal Reserve Bank of New York Quarterly Review*, Summer, 34–46.

ALLEN, S. G. (1994), 'Developments in Collective Bargaining in Construction in the 1980s and 1990s', *Contemporary Collective Bargaining in the Private Sector*, Ithaca, New York: ILR Press.

AMJAD, R. and MOHANTY, M. (1991), 'Industrial Restructuring and Implications for Human Resource Development in Asea', Asian HRD Networking Paper, ILO-ARTEP, New Delhi.

AMSDEN, A. (1989), *Asia's Next Giant: South Korea and Late Industrialisation*, Oxford: Oxford University Press.

ANDERSON, G. J. (1988), 'A New Approach to the Empirical Investigation of Investment Expenditures', *Economic Journal*, 91: 88–103.

ANDERSON, K. and NORHEIM, H. (1993), 'History, Geography and Regional Economic Integration', in Anderson, K. and Blackhurst, R., *Regional Integration and The Global Trading System*, Hemel Hempstead: Harvester Wheatsheaf.

ANDERSON, W. H. L. (1964), *Corporate Finance and Fixed Investment: An Econometric Study*, Cambridge, Mass.: Harvard University Press.

ANDERSSON, T. (1994), 'Foreign Direct Investment and Employment in Sweden', mimeo, Stockholm IUI.

—— et al. (1993), *Den laga vagen*, Stockholm: IUI.

—— and Svensson, R. (1994), 'Reconsidering the Choice between Takeover and Greenfield Operations', *Scandinavian Journal of Economics*, forthcoming.

ARGY, V. (1981), *The Postwar International Money Crisis—An Analysis*, London: Allen and Unwin.

ARMSTRONG, P., Glyn, A. and Harrison, J. (1991), *Capitalism Since 1945*, Oxford: Blackwell.

ARRIGHI, G. (1993), 'The Three Hegemonies of Historical Capitalism', Ch. 5 of Iivonen, I. (ed.), *The Future of the Nation State in Europe*, Aldershot: Edward Elgar.

ARTIS, M. J. (1987), 'Exchange Controls and the EMS', *European Economy*.

—— and Ostry, S. (1986), 'Monetary and Exchange Rate Targets: A Case for Conditionalising', *Oxford Economic Papers* (Suppl.), 33: 176–200.

—— and Taylor, M. P. (1989), *Memorandum of Evidence on International Monetary Coordination*, London: House of Commons Treasury and Civil Service Committee.

—— —— (1994), 'The Stabilizing Effect of the ERM on Exchange Rates and Interest Rates', *IMF Staff Papers*, Mar.

ASCHER, K. (1987), *The Politics of Privatisation: Contracting Out Public Services*, London: Macmillan.

AUERBACH, P. (1988), *Competition, The Economics of Industrial Change*, Oxford: Blackwell.

BAIROCH, P. (1976), *Commerce Exterieur et Dévélopment Economique de L'Europe au XIX Siécle*, Paris, Ecole des Hautes Etudes et Sciences Sociales.

—— (1982), 'International Industrialization Levels from 1750 to 1980', *Journal of European Economic History*, 11: 269–310.

—— (1993), *Economics and World History*, Brighton: Wheatsheaf.

BALDWIN, R. and KRUGMAN, P. (1989), 'Persistent Trade Effects of Large Exchange Rate Shocks', *Quarterly Journal of Economics*, 104, Nov., 635–54.

BANURI, T. and SCHOR, J. B. (1992), *Financial Openness and National Autonomy: Opportunities and Constraints*, Oxford: Clarendon Press.

BARRO, R. J. and GORDON, D. F. (1981), 'Rules, Discretion and Reputation in a Model of Monetary Policy', *Journal of Monetary Economics*, 12: 101–21.

BARTLETT, C. A. and GHOSHAL, S. (1989), *Managing Across Borders: The Transnational Solution*, London: Hutchinson Business.

BAUMOL, W. (1986), 'Productivity Growth, Convergence and Welfare: What the Long-Run Data Show', *American Economic Review*, 76: 275–85.

—— BLACKMAN, S. A. B. and WOLFF, E. N. (1989), *Productivity and American Leadership: The Long View*, Cambridge, Mass.: The MIT Press.

BAYOUMI, T. (1990), 'Saving Investment Correlations: Immobile Capital, Government Policy, or Endogenous Behaviour', *IMF Staff Papers*, June, 360–87.

—— and Eichengreen, B. (1994), 'Monetary and Exchange Rate Arrangements for NAFTA', *Journal of Development Economics*, 43/1.

BECKERMAN, W. and JENKINSON, T. (1986), 'What Stopped the Inflation? Unemployment or Commodity Prices?', *Economic Journal*, 96: Mar., 39–54.

BEENSTOCK, M. (1984), *The World Economy In Transition*, London and Boston: Allen and Unwin.

BELZER, M. H. (1994), 'The Motor Carrier Industry: Truckers and Teamsters under Siege', *Contemporary Collective Bargaining in the Private Sector*, Ithaca, New York: ILR Press.

BENNETT, P. and KELLEHER, J. (1988), 'The International Transmission of Stock Price Disruption in October 1987', *Federal Reserve Bank of New York Quarterly Review*, Summer, 17–33.

BERGSTEN, C. F. (1991) *International Adjustment and Financing: The Lessons of 1985–1991*, Washington DC: Institute for International Economics.

BEST, M. (1990), *The New Competition*, Cambridge: Polity Press.

BHAGWATI, J. (1993), 'Regionalism and Multilateralism: An Overview', ch. 2 of de Melo, J. and Panagariya, A. (eds.), *New Dimensions in Regional Integration*, Cambridge: Cambridge University Press.

—— and Irwin, D. (1987), 'The Return of the Reciprocitarians; US Trade Policy Today', *The World Economy*, 10/2: 109–30.

BIRECREE, A. M. (1994), *A Structural Analysis of the Recent Growth of Fragmented Bargaining in Soft Coal*, Department of Economics, Radford University, unpublished.

BLACKABY, F. (ed.) (1979), *Deindustrialisation*, London: Heinemann Educational Books.

BLOMSTROM, M., *et al.* (1992), 'What Explains Developing Country Growth?' National Bureau of Economic Research, Working Paper Series, no. 4132, Cambridge, Mass.: NBER.

BLOOM, D. and BRENDER, A. (1993), 'Labour and the Emerging World Economy', NBER, Working Paper Series, no. 4266, Cambridge, Mass.: NBER.

BLOOMFIELD, A. (1963), *Short-Term Capital Movements Under the Pre-1914 Gold Standard*, Princeton: Princeton University Press.

—— (1968), *Patterns of Fluctuation in International Investment Before 1914*, Princeton: Princeton University Press.

BLUESTONE, B. and HARRISON, B. (1982), *The De-Industrialization of America*. New York: Basic Books.

BONTURI, M. and FUKUSAKU, K. (1993), 'Globalisation and Intra-Firm Trade: An Empirical Note', *OECD Economic Studies*, Spring.

BORDO, M. D. (1992), 'Gold Standard: Theory', in Newman, P., Milgate, M., and Eatwell, J. (eds.), *The New Palgrave Dictionary of Money and Finance*, 2, London and Basingstoke: Macmillan.

—— and EICHENGREEN, B. (eds.) (1993), *A Retrospective on the Bretton Woods System: Lessons for International Monetary Reform*, London: University of Chicago Press.

—— and SCHWARTZ, A. J. (1984), *A Retrospective on the Classical Gold Standard, 1821–1931*, NBER Conference Volume, Chicago: University of Chicago Press.

BOROOAH, V. (1988), 'Income Distribution, Consumption Patterns and Economic Outcomes in the United Kingdom', *Contributions to Political Economy*, 7.

Bretton Woods (1944), 'Articles of Agreement of the International Bank for Reconstruction and Development', *Proceedings and Documents of United Nations Monetary and Financial Conference*.

BRODEUR, P. (1985). *Outrageous Misconduct: The Asbestos Industry on Trial*, New York: Pantheon.

BROOKS, H. E. and GUILE, B. R. (1987), *Technology and Global Industries: Companies and Nations in the World Economy*, Washington D.C.: National Academy Press.

BROSNAN, P. and WILKINSON, F. (1988), 'A National Minimum Wage and Economic Efficiency', *Contributions to Political Economy*, 7.

BROWN, R., and JULIUS, D. (1993), 'Is Manufacturing Still Special in the New World Order?', The Amex Bank Review: 7, *Finance and the International Economy*, Oxford: Oxford University Press.

BRUNO, M. and SACHS, J. (1985), *Economics of Worldwide Stagflation*, Oxford: Blackwell.

BRYANT, R. (1980), *Money and Monetary Policy in Interdependent Nations*, Washington, DC: The Brookings Institution.

—— (1987), *International Financial Intermediation*, Washington, DC: The Brookings Institution.

—— CURRIE, D. A., FRENKEL, J. A., MASSON, P. R., and PORTES, R. (eds.), (1989) *Macro-Economic Policies in an Interdependent World*, Brookings (CEPR, IMF).

BUCKLEY, G. and TONKS, I. (1989), 'Are UK Stock Prices Excessively Volatile? Trading Rules and Variance Bound Tests', *Economic Journal*, 99: 1083–98.

BURAWOY, M. (1979), *Manufacturing Consent: Changes in the Labour Process Under Monopoly Capitalism*, Chicago: University of Chicago Press.

CABLE, J. (1985), 'Capital Market Information and Industrial Performance: The Role of West German Banks', *Economic Journal*, 95: 118–32.

CAIRNCROSS, Sir A. (1979), 'What is De-Industrialisation?', in Blackaby (ed.), *Deindustrialisation*, London: Heinemann Educational Books..

CALMFORS, L., and Driffill, J. (1988), 'Centralisation of Wage Bargaining', *Economic Policy*, Apr.

Cambridge Economic Policy Group (CEPG) (1979), *Economic Policy Review*, Department of Applied Economics, Cambridge.

CAMPBELL, D. (1993), 'The Globalizing Firm and Labour Institutions', in Bailey, P., Parisotto, A. and Renshaw, G. (eds.), *Multinationals and Employment: The Global Economy of the 1990s*. Geneva: ILO.

CAMPBELL, J. Y. and SHILLER, R. J. (1987), 'Cointegration and Tests of Present Value Models', *Journal of Political Economy*, 95: 1062–88.

CATTE, P., GALLI, G. and REBBECHINI, S. (1992), 'Concerted Interventions and the Dollar: An Analysis of Daily Data', mimeo, Banca d'Italia.

CHANDLER, A. (1990), *Economies of Scale and Scope*, Cambridge, Mass.: Harvard University Press.

CHANG, H.-J. and KOZUL-WRIGHT, R. (1994), 'Comparing National Systems of Entrepreneurship', *Journal of Development Studies*.

—— and ROWTHORN, R. E. (eds.) (forthcoming), *The Role of the State in Economic Change*, Oxford: Oxford University Press.

CHESNAIS, F. (1988), 'Multinational Enterprises and the International Diffusion of Technology', Dosi, G., Freeman, C., Nelson, R., Silverberg, G., and Soete, L., *Technical Change and Economic Theory*, London: Pinter Publishers.

COAKLEY, J. (1992), *Aspects of the Integration of International Financial Markets*, Unpublished PhD, Open University.

—— and Harris, L. (1992), 'Financial Globalisation and Deregulation', in Michie, J. (ed.), *The Economic Legacy: 1979–1992*, London: Academic Press.

—— KULASI, F., and SMITH, R. (1994), 'Savings, Investment, and Capital Mobility', mimeo.

Commission of the European Communities (CEC) (1993a), *Employment in Europe, 1993*, COM(93) 314, Luxembourg: Office of Official Publications of the European Communities.

—— (1993b), *Green Paper—European Social Policy*, COM(93) 551, Luxembourg: Office of Official Publications of the European Communities.

CORNFORD, A. (1993a), 'Some Implications for Banking of the Draft General Agreement on Trade in Services of December 1991', UNCTAD Review, No. 4.

—— (1993b), 'The Role of the Basle Committee on Banking Supervision in the Regulation of International Banking', *UNCTAD Discussion Paper*, no. 68, Sept.

CORRIGAN, E. G. (1989), 'A Perspective on Recent Financial Disruptions', *Federal Reserve Bank of New York Quarterly Review*, 14/4 (Winter).

COSH A. D., HUGHES, A., and SINGH, A. (1992), 'Openness, Financial Innovation, Changing Patterns of Ownership, and the Structure of the Financial Markets', in

Banuri, T. and Schor, J. B. (eds.), *Financial Openness and National Autonomy*, Oxford: Clarendon, 19–42.

CRAYPO, C. (1994), 'Meatpacking', in Voos, P. (ed.), *Contemporary Collective Bargaining in the Private Sector*, Ithaca, New York: ILR Press.

—— and NISSEN, B. (1993), *Grand Designs: The Impact of Corporate Strategies on Workers, Unions and Communities*, Ithaca, New York: ILR Press.

CRIPPS, T. F. and TARLING, R. J. (1973), *Growth in Advanced Capitalist Economies 1950 to 1970*, Cambridge: Cambridge University Press.

CROASDALE, M. and Harris, L. (1988), 'Internal Funds and Investment', in Harris, L., Coakley, J., Croasdale, M., and Evans, T., *New Perspectives on the Financial System*, London: Croom Helm.

CROCKETT, A. (1989), 'The Role of International Institutions in Surveillance and Policy Coordination', in Bryant, R. C. *et al.* (eds.), *Macro-Economic Policies in an Interdependent World*.

CURRIE, D. A., HOLTHAM, G., and HUGHES HALLETT, A. (1989), 'The Theory and Practice of International Policy Coordination: Does Coordination Pay?', in Bryant, R. C. *et al.* (eds.), *Macro-Economic Policies in an Interdependent World*.

CUSHMAN, D. (1985), 'Real Exchange Rate Risk, Expectations and the Level of Direct Investment', *Review of Economics and Statistics*, 67, May.

DALE, R. (1984), *The Regulation of International Banking*, Cambridge: Woodhead-Faulkner.

DE JONQUIERES, G. (1994), 'Mood Swings and Trade Winds', *Financial Times*, 8 April, 13.

DE VET, J. M. (1993), 'Globalisation and Local and Regional Competitiveness', *Science, Technology, Industry Review*, 13: 89–121, OECD.

DEAKIN, S. and WILKINSON, F. (1991*a*), 'Labour Law, Social Security and Economic Inequality', *Cambridge Journal of Economics*, 15.

—— —— (1991*b*), *The Economics of Employment Rights*, London: Institute of Employment Rights.

DEAN, A., DURAND, M., FALLON, J., and HOELLER, P. (1989), 'Savings Trends and Behaviour in OECD Countries', OECD Department of Economics Working Paper, no. 67.

Deregulierungskommission (1991), 'Marktöffnung und Wettbewerb', *Zweiter Bericht der Unabhängigen Expertenkommission zum Abbau marktwidriger Regulierungen*, Bonn, Mar.

DERTOUZANI, M. L., LESTER, R. K., and SOLOW, R. M. (1990), *Made in America*, Cambridge, Mass.: MIT Press.

DIAMOND, D. (1984), 'Financial Intermediation and Delegated Monitoring', *Review of Economic Studies*, 1984, 393–414.

DIAZ-ALEJANDRO, C. (1985), 'Good-Bye Financial Repression, Hello Financial Crash', *Journal of Development Economics*, 19/1–2.

DICKEN, P. (1992*a*), 'International Production in a Volatile Regulatory Environment: the Influence of National Regulatory Policies on the Spatial Strategies of Transnational Corporations', *Geoforum*, 23: 303–16.

—— (1992*b*), *Global Shift: The Internationalization of Economic Activity*, 2nd edn., New York: Guilford Publications.

DICKEN, P. (1994), 'Global-Local Tensions: Firms and States in the Global Space-Economy', *Economic Geography*, 70.

DONE, K. (1994), 'Tomorrow the World', *Financial Times*, 22 April.

DOWRICK, S. and GEMMELL, N. (1991), 'Industrialisation, Catching Up and Economic Growth: A Comparative Study across the World's Capitalist Economies', *The Economic Journal*, 101: 263–75.

—— and NGUYEN, D.-T. (1989), 'OECD Comparative Economic Growth 1950–85: Catch Up and Convergence', *American Economic Review*, 79: 1010–30.

DREZE, J. H. and MALINVAUD, E. (1993), 'Growth and Employment. The Scope of a European Initiative', Louvain-la-Neuve and Paris: mimeo, July.

DUNNING, J. (1983a), 'Changes in the Level and Structure of International Production: The Last One Hundred Years', in Casson, M. (ed.), *The Growth of International Business*, London: Allen and Unwin.

—— (ed.) (1993b), 'The Theory of Transnational Corporations', *The United Nations Library on Transnational Corporations*, i, London: Routledge.

—— (1994), 'Globalisation, Economic Restructuring and Development', Raul Prebisch lecture, UNCTAD, Geneva.

DWYER jun., G. P. and HAFER, R. W. (1988), 'Are National Stock Markets Linked?', *Federal Reserve Bank of St Louis*, Nov./Dec., 3–14.

EATWELL, J. (1994), 'The Coordination of Macroeconomic Policy in the European Community', Ch. 13 of Michie, J. and Grieve Smith, J. (eds.), *Unemployment in Europe*, London: Academic Press.

ECKES, A. (1975), 'A Search for Solvency—Bretton Woods and the International Monetary System, 1941–1971', Austin, Texas: University of Texas Press.

EDWARDS, R. W. (1985), *International Monetary Collaboration*, Dobbs Ferry, New York: Transnational Publishers.

EICHENGREEN, B. (1991), 'The Interwar Economy in a European Mirror', Centre for Economic Performance, Discussion Paper 589, Oct.

—— (1992), *Golden Fetters; The Gold Standard and the Great Depression, 1919–1939*, Oxford: Oxford University Press.

—— (1994a), 'History of the International Monetary System: Implications for Research in International Macroeconomics and Finance', in Van Der Ploeg, F. (ed.), *The Handbook of International Macroeconomics*, Oxford, Blackwell.

—— (1994b), 'Deja Vu All Over Again: Lessons from the Gold Standard for European Monetary Unification', Working Paper No. C94–032, Department of Economics, University of California at Berkeley.

—— IRWIN, D. A. (1993), 'Trade Blocs, Currency Blocs and the Disintegration of World Trade in the 1930s', mimeo.

—— and Wyplosz, C. (1993), 'The Unstable EMS', *Brookings Papers in Economic Activity*, i: 51–143.

FAZZARI, S., HUBBARD, R. G., and PETERSEN, B. (1988), 'Finance Constraints and Corporate Investment', *Brookings Papers on Economic Activity*, 141–95.

FEINSTEIN, C. H. (1972), *Statistical Tables of National Income and Expenditure and Output of the UK, 1855–1965*, Department of Applied Economics, Cambridge and Royal Economic Society.

FELDSTEIN, M. (1983), 'Domestic Saving and International Capital Movements in the Long Run and the Short Run', *European Economic Review*, 21: 129–51.

—— and BACCHETTA, P. (1991), 'National Saving and International Investment', in D. Bernheim and J. Shoven (eds.), *National Saving and Economic Performance*, Chicago: University of Chicago Press.

—— and HORIOKA, C. (1980), 'Domestic Savings and International Capital Flows', *Economic Journal*, 90/2.

FELIX, D. (1993), 'Suggestions for International Collaboration to Reduce Destabilizing Effects of International Capital Mobility on the Developing Countries', in *International Monetary and Financial Issues for the 1990s. Research Papers for the Group of Twenty-Four, Vol. III*, New York: United Nations.

FERENCZI, I. (1929), *International Migration*, New York: National Bureau of Economic Research.

FFORDE, J. S. (1983), 'Setting Monetary Objectives', *Bank of England Quarterly Bulletin*, 23: 200–8.

FIELDS, G. S. (1990), 'Labour Standards, Economic Development and International Trade', in Herzenberg, S. and Perez-Lopez, J. F. (eds.), *Labour Standards and Development in the Global Economy*, Washington: Department of Labour.

FINCH, C. D. (1993), 'IMF Surveillance and the G24', *International Monetary and Financial Issues for the 1990s*, II, UNCTAD.

FISHLOW, A. (1992a), 'Some Reflections on Comparative Latin American Economic Performance and Policy', in Banuri, T. (ed.), *Economic Liberalisation: No Panacea*, Oxford: Oxford University Press.

—— (1992b), 'Comment', on Kuczynski, M. 'International Capital Flows to Latin America: What is the Promise?', *Proceedings of the World Bank Annual Conference on Development Economics*, Washington D.C.: World Bank.

FLOOD, R. P. and ROSE, A. K. (1994), 'Fixing Exchange Rates: A Volatile Quest for Fundamentals', London School of Economics Financial Markets Group Discussion Paper no. 163.

FORSTNER, H. and BALLANCE, R. (1990), *Competing in a Global Economy*, London: Unwin.

FOX, A. (1974), *Beyond Contract: Work, Power and Trust Relations*, London: Faber and Faber.

FRANKEL, J. A. (1988), 'Obstacles to International Policy Coordination', *Princeton Studies in International Finance*, no. 64, Dec.

FREEMAN, R. (1993), 'Is Globalisation Impoverishing Low Skill American Workers', mimeo, Harvard University.

FRIEDEN, J. A. (1994), 'Exchange Rate Politics: Contemporary Lessons from American History', *Review of International Political Economy*, 1/1, Spring, 81–103.

FRÖBEL, F., HEINRICHS, J., KREYE, O. (1977), *Die neue internationale Arbeitsteilung*, Rowohlt: Reinbek bei Hamburg.

—— et al. (1980), *The New International Division of Labour*, Cambridge: Cambridge University Press.

FUNABASHI, Y. (1989), *Managing the Dollar: From the Plaza to the Louvre*, Washington DC: Institute for International Economics.

GALBRAITH, J. K. (1992), *The Culture of Contentment*, Boston: Houghton Mifflin.

GARDNER, R. N. (1980), *Sterling–Dollar Diplomacy in Current Perspective: The Origins and Prospects of Our International Economic Order*, New York: Columbia University Press.

GHILARDUCCI, T. (1992), *Labour's Capital*, Cambridge, Mass.: MIT, Press.

GHOSHAL, S. (1987), 'Global Strategy: An Organising Framework', *Strategic Management Journal*, 8: 425–40.

GIAVAZZI, F. and SPAVENTA, L. (1990), 'The "new" EMS', in de Grauwe, P. and Papademos, L. (eds.), *The European Monetary System in the 1990s*, Harlow: Longman.

GILBERT, C. (1990), 'Primary Commodity Prices and Inflation', *Oxford Review of Economic Policy*, 6/4, Winter, 77–99.

GLYN, A., HUGHES, A., LIPIETZ, A., and SINGH, A. (1990), 'The Rise and Fall of the Golden Age', in: Marglin, S. and Schor, J. (eds.), *The Golden Age of Capitalism: Reinterpreting the Postwar Experience*, Oxford: Clarendon Press, 39–125.

—— and MILIBAND, D. (eds.) (1994), *Paying for Inequality: The Economic Cost of Social Injustice*, London: Rivers Oram Press/Institute for Public Policy Research.

—— and Rowthorn, R. (1994), 'European Employment Policies'. Ch. 12 of Michie, J. and Grieve Smith, J. (eds.), *Unemployment in Europe*, London: Academic Press.

—— and SUTCLIFFE, R. (1992), 'The New World Order: Global but Leaderless', in *Socialist Register, 1992*.

GOMES, L. (1993), *The International Adjustment Mechanism—From the Gold Standard to the EMS*, London: Macmillan.

GOODMAN, R. (1979), *The Last Entrepreneurs: America's Regional Wars for Jobs and Dollars*, Boston: South End Press.

GRAHL, J. and TEAGUE, P. (1989), 'The Cost of Neo-Liberal Europe', *New Left Review*, 174, 33–50.

GREISING, D. and MORSE, L. (1991), *Brokers, Bagmen and Moles. Fraud and Corruption in the Chicago Futures Markets*, New York: John Wiley and Sons.

GRIEVE SMITH, J. (1994*a*), 'Policies to Reduce European Unemployment', in Michie, J. and Grieve Smith, J. (eds.), *Unemployment in Europe*, London: Academic Press.

—— (1994*b*), 'Economic Policy and Constitutional Change after Maastricht', in *Proceedings of Seventh Lothian Foundation Conference*, London: Lothian Foundation Press.

GROSSMAN, G. M. and HELPMAN, E. (1992), *Innovation and Growth in the Global Economy*, Cambridge, Mass.: MIT Press.

GRUNWALD, J. and FLAMM, K. (1985), *The Global Factory: Foreign Assembly in International Trade*, Washington, D.C.: Brookings Institute.

GUGLER, P. and DUNNING, J. (1993), 'Technology-Based Cross-Border Alliances', in Culpan, R. (ed.), *Multinational Strategic Alliances*, New York: International Business Press.

HABERMAN, G. (1987), 'Capital Requirements of Commercial and Investment Banks: Contrasts in Regulation', *Federal Reserve Bank of New York Quarterly Review*, Autumn.

HALL, M. (1992), 'Legislating for Employee Participation: A Case Study of the European Works Councils Directive', Warwick Papers in Industrial Relations, 39, Mar.

HARASZTI, S. (1981), *The Worker in the Workers' State*, London: Penguin.

HARCOURT, G. C. (1994), 'A "Modest Proposal" for Taming Speculators and Putting the World on Course to Prosperity', mimeo, University of Cambridge.

HARRIS, L. (1994), 'Financial Integration and Economic Policy in Europe', in Brouwer, F., Lintner, V. and Newman, M. (eds.), *Economic Policy Making and the European Union*, London: Federal Trust.

HARRISON, B. and BLUESTONE, B. (1988), *The Great U-Turn: Corporate Restructuring and the Polarisation of America*, New York: Basic Books.

HAYES, R. H. and ABERNATHY, W. J. (1985), 'Managing our Way to Industrial Decline', *Harvard Business Review*, July–Aug.

HENDERSON, H. D. (1955), *The Interwar Years and Other Papers*, Oxford: Clarendon Press.

HENDERSON, J. (1992), 'International Economic Integration: Progress, Prospects and Implications', *International Affairs*, 68: 633–53.

HIRST, P. and THOMPSON, G. (1992), 'The Problem of Globalization: International Economic Relations, National Economic Management and the Formation of Trading Blocs', *Economy and Society*, 21, Nov., 357–96.

HOLTHAM, G. (1989), 'Foreign Exchange Markets and Target Zones', *Oxford Review of Economic Policy*, 5/3, Autumn.

—— (1990), 'World Current Account Balances', *Oxford Review of Economic Policy*, 6/3, Autumn.

HORRELL, S., RUBERY, J. and BURCHELL, B. (1989), 'Unequal Jobs or Unequal Pay?' ,*Industrial Relations Journal*, 20/3: 176–91.

HOWELLS, J. (1990), 'The Internationalization of R&D and the Development of Global Research Networks', *Regional Studies*, 18: 495–512.

HU, Y-S. (1992), 'Global Firms are National Firms with International Operations', *California Management Review*, 34: 107–26.

HUFFMAN, W. E. and LOTHIAN, J. R. (1984), 'The Gold Standard and the Transmission of Business Cycles 1833–1932', in Bordo, M. D. and Schwartz, A. J., *A Retrospective on the Classical Gold Standard 1821–1931*, NBER Conference Volume, Chicago: University of Chicago Press, 455–507.

HUGHES, A. and SINGH, A. (1992), 'The World Economic Slowdown and Asian and Latin American Economies', in Banuri, T. (ed.), *The Limits of Economic Liberalization*, Oxford: Clarendon.

HUGHES HALLET, A., HOLTHAM, G. and HUTSON, G. (1989), 'Exchange-Rate Targeting As Surrogate International Co-operation', in Miller, M., Eichengreen, B. and Portes, R. (eds.), *Blueprints for Exchange Rate Management*, London: CEPR/Academic Press.

HYMER, S. (1976), *The International Operations of National Firms: A study of Direct Foreign Investment*, Cambridge, Mass.: MIT Press.

—— and ROWTHORN, R. E. (1970), 'Multinational Corporations and International Oligopoly: The Non-American Challenge', in Kindelberger, C., *The International Corporation*, Cambridge: MIT Press.

International Labour Office (1981), *Employment Effects of Multinational Enterprises in Industrialised Countries*, Geneva: ILO.

International Labour Organisation (ILO) (1976), *Employment Growth and Basic Needs: A One World Problem*, Geneva.

—— (1994), *Defending Values, Promoting Change, Report of the Director General*, International Labour Conference, 81st Session, Geneva.

320 BIBLIOGRAPHY

International Monetary Fund (IMF) (1993*a*), *World Economic Outlook*, Washington DC, Oct.
—— (1993*b*), *International Capital Markets, Part 1. Exchange Rate Management and International Capital Flows*, Washington, D.C.
—— (1994), *World Economic Outlook*, Washington DC, Mar.
International Confederation of Free Trade Unions (1994), *Annual Survey of Violations of Trade Union Rights 1994*, Brussels: ICFTU.
ITOH, M. (1994), 'Is the Japanese Economy in Crisis?', *Review of International Political Economy*, 1/1, Spring, 29–51.
JACQUEMIN, A. (1991), 'Strategic Competition in a Global Environment', in *Trade, Investment and Technology in the 1990s*, OECD, Paris.
JOHNSTON, W. B. (1991), 'Global Work Force 2000: The New World Labor Market', *Harvard Business Review*, Mar.–Apr., 115–27.
JURGENSON, P. (1983), *Report of the Working Group on Exchange Market Interventions*, Washington: U.S. Treasury Department, Mar.
KALDOR, N. (1972), 'The Irrelevance of Equilibrium Economics', *Economic Journal*, Dec.
—— (1978), *Further Essays on Applied Economics*, London: Duckworth.
—— (1985), *Economics Without Equilibrium*, Cardiff: University College Cardiff Press.
KALECKI, M. (1932), 'Is a Capitalist Overcoming of the Crisis Possible', and 'On the Papen Plan', in Osiatynski, J. (ed.), *Collected Works of Michal Kalecki*, Oxford: Oxford University Press, 1990.
—— (1943), 'Political Aspects of Full Employment', in *Selected Essays on the Dynamics of the Capitalist Economy*, Cambridge: Cambridge University Press, 1971.
KAMINSKY, G. L. and LEWIS, K. K. (1993), 'Does Foreign Exchange Intervention Signal Future Monetary Policy?', NBER Working Paper no. 4298, Mar.
KASMAN, B. and PIGOTT, C. (1988), 'Interest rate Divergence among the Major Industrial Nations', *Federal Reserve Bank of New York Quarterly Bulletin*, Autumn.
KAZIS, R. and GROSSMAN, L. G. (1982), *Fear at Work: Job Blackmail, Labour and the Environment*, New York: Pilgrim Press.
KELLY, R. (1994), 'A Framework for European Exchange Rates in the 1990s', Ch. 14 of Michie, J. and Grieve Smith, J. (eds.), *Unemployment in Europe*, London: Academic Press.
KENEN, P. B. (1988), *Managing Exchange Rates*, London: Chatham House Papers.
—— (1989), *Exchange Rates and Policy Coordination*, Manchester: Manchester University Press.
—— (1992), 'Bretton Woods System', in Newman, P., Milgate, M., and Eatwell, J. (eds.), *The New Palgrave Dictionary of Money and Finance*, i, London and Basingstoke: Macmillan.
KENNEDY, P. (1989), *The Rise and Fall of the Great Powers*, Glasgow: Fontana Press.
KENWOOD, A. G. and LOUGHEED, A. L. (1983), *The Growth of the International Economy 1820–1980*, London: Allen and Unwin.
KEYNES, J. M. (1926), 'The End of *Laissez Faire*', in *The Collected Writings of John

Maynard Keynes, Vol. IX, Essays in Persuasion, Cambridge: Macmillan and Cambridge University Press for the Royal Economic Society, 1984, 272–94.

—— (1930), *A Treatise on Money*, II, London: Macmillan, 1971.

—— (1936), *The General Theory of Employment, Interest and Money*, London: Macmillan.

—— (1943a), Speech before the House of Lords, 18 May 1943, in Moggridge, D. (ed.), *The Collected Writings of John Maynard Keynes*, XXV, Ch. 1, London: Macmillan, 1980.

—— (1943b), *Proposals for an International Clearing Union*, Cmnd 6437.

—— (1971), *The Economic Consequences of the Peace*, London: Macmillan.

—— (1980), *The Collected Writings of John Maynard Keynes*, xxv, Macmillan.

KHAN, M. S. and KNIGHT, M. D. (1988), 'Import Compression and Export Performance in Developing Countries', *Review of Economics and Statistics*, May.

KINDLEBERGER, C. (1973), *The World in Depression, 1929–39*, London: Allen Lane.

—— (1986), 'International Public Goods Without International Government', *American Economic Review*, Mar., 1–14.

—— (1988), 'The New Multinationalization of Business', *Asean Economic Bulletin*, 5: 113–24.

—— (1992), 'Why did the Golden Age Last so Long?', in Cairncross, A. and Cairncross, F., *The Legacy of the Golden Age: The 1960s and their Economic Consequences*, London: Routledge.

KING, M. A. and WHADWHANI, S. (1990), 'Transmission of Volatility Between Stock Markets', *Review of Financial Studies*, 3/1: 5–33.

KITSON, M. (1992), 'The Move to Autarchy: The Political Economy of Nazi Trade Policy', Department of Applied Economics, Cambridge, Working Paper 9201.

—— and MICHIE, J. (1994), 'Depression and Recovery: Lessons from the Interwar Period', Ch. 5 of Michie, J. and Grieve Smith, J. (eds.), *Unemployment in Europe*, London: Academic Press.

—— and SOLOMOU, S. (1990), *Protectionism and Economic Revival: The British Interwar Economy*, Cambridge: Cambridge University Press.

—— —— (1991), 'Bilateralism in the Interwar World Economy', DAE Working Paper, No. 9101, Department of Applied Economics, University of Cambridge.

KLINE, J. (1993), 'International Regulation of Transnational Business: Providing the Missing Leg of Global Investment Standards', *Transnational Corporation*, 2, February: 153–64.

KREGEL, J. (1994), 'Capital Flows, Globalisation of Production and Financing Development', *UNCTAD Review*, no. 5.

KRUGMAN, P. (1979), 'A Model of Balance of Payments Crises', *Journal of Money Credit and Banking*, 11/3.

—— (1989a), 'The Case for Stabilizing Exchange Rates', *Oxford Review of Economic Policy*, 5/3, Autumn.

—— (1989b), *Exchange Instability*, Cambridge, Mass., MIT Press.

—— (1991), 'Target Zones and Exchange Rate Dynamics', *Quarterly Journal of Economics*, 669–81.

—— (1993), 'Integration, Specialization and Adjustment', CEPR Discussion Paper no. 886, London.

KRUGMAN, P. (1994), 'Competitiveness: A Dangerous Obsession', *Foreign Affairs*, no. 2: 28–44.

—— and Lawrence, R. (1993), 'Trade, Jobs, and Wages', NBER Working Paper no. 4478.

KUH, E. and MEYER, J. (1963), 'Investment, Liquidity and Monetary Policy', in Commission on Money and Credit, *Impacts of Monetary Policy*, Englewood Cliffs NJ: Prentice Hall.

KUZNETS, S. (1966), *Modern Economic Growth: Rate, Structure and Spread*, New Haven: Yale University Press.

LALL, S. (1993), 'Transnational Corporations and Economic Development', *The United Nations Library on Transnational Corporations*, ii, London: Routledge.

LAMFALUSSY, A. (1985), 'The Changing Environment of Central Bank Policy', *American Economic Review Papers and Proceedings*, 75/2, (May).

LANDESMANN, M. (1986), 'UK Policy and the International Economy: An Internationalist Perspective', in Nolan, P. and Paine, S. (eds.), *Rethinking Socialist Economics*, Cambridge: Polity.

LANG, T. and HINES, C. (1993), *The New Protectionism: Protecting the Future Against Free Trade*, London: Earthscan Publications.

LAWRENCE, R. (1992), 'Japan's Low Levels of Inward Investment: The Role of Inhibitions on Acquisitions', *Transnational Corporations*, 3: 47–75.

—— and SLAUGHTER, M. (1993), 'Trade and US Wages: Giant Sucking Sound or Small Hiccup?', *Brooking Papers on Economic Activity: Microeconomics*, NBER.

League of Nations (1939), *World Economic Survey 1938/9*, Geneva: League of Nations.

—— (1942), *The Network of World Trade*, Geneva: League of Nations.

—— (1944), *International Currency Experience*, Geneva: League of Nations.

LEVITAN, S. and SHAPIRO, I. (1987), *Working But Poor: America's Contradiction*. Baltimore: The John Hopkins University Press.

LEVY, D. (1993), 'International Production and Sourcing: Trends and Issues', *Science, Technology, Industry Review*, 13: 13–59.

LEWIS, A. (1978), *Growth and Fluctuations, 1870–1913*, London: George Allen and Unwin.

—— (1981), 'The Rates of Growth of World Trade, 1830–1973', in Grassman, S. and Lundberg, E. (eds.), *The World Economic Order: Past and Prospects*, London and Basingstoke: Macmillan.

LIM, L. Y. C. (1990), 'Singapore', in: Herzenberg, S. and Perez-Lopez, J. F. (eds.), *Labour Standards and Development in the Global Economy*, Washington, DC: US Department of Labour.

LIM, T. B. and TSUI, K. Y. (1991), *Industrial Restructuring: The Case of Hong Kong's Manufacturing Sector*, Asian HRD Networking Paper, ILO, ARTEP, New Delhi.

LLOYD, P. J. (1992), 'Regionalisation and World Trade', *OECD Economic Studies*, 18, Spring, 7–44.

LUKE, R. (1985), 'The Schacht and the Keynes Plans', *Banca Nazionale del Lavoro Quarterly Review*, Mar.

McCAULEY, R. N. and ZIMMER, S. A. (1989), 'Explaining International Differences in the Cost of Capital', *Federal Reserve Bank of New York Quarterly Bulletin*, Summer.

McCLOSKEY, D. M. and ZECHER, J. R. (1984), 'The Success of Purchasing-Power Parity: Historical Evidence and its Implications for Macroeconomics', in Bordo, M. D. and Schwartz, A. J., *A Retrospective on the Classical Gold Standard, 1821–1931*, NBER Conference Volume, Chicago: University of Chicago Press, 121–62.

McKINNON, R. (1993), 'International Money in Historical Perspective', *Journal of Economic Literature*, XXXI, Mar., 1–44.

MACHLUP, F. (1977), *A History of Thought on Economic Integration*, London: Macmillan.

MADDISON, A. (1962), 'Growth and Fluctuations in the World Economy, 1870–1960', *Banca Nazionale del Lavoro Quarterly Review*, 15/61, June, 127–95.

—— (1982), *Phases of Capitalist Development*, Oxford: Oxford University Press.

—— (1984), 'Origins and Impact of the Welfare State, 1883–1983', *Banca Nazionale del Lavoro Quarterly Review*, Mar., 55–87.

—— (1989), *The World Economy in the 20th Century*, Paris: OECD Development Centre.

—— (1991), *Dynamic Forces in Capitalist Development*, Oxford: Oxford University Press.

MAGAZINER, I. C. and REICH, R. B. (1983), *Minding America's Business: The Decline and Rise of the American Economy*, New York: Vintage.

MAIZELS, A. (1963), *Growth and Trade*, Cambridge: Cambridge University Press.

—— (1994), 'The Functioning of International Markets for Commodities: Key Policy Issues for Developing Countries', Queen Elizabeth House, Oxford, mimeo.

MANN, F. A. (1982), *The Legal Aspect of Money*, Oxford: Clarendon Press.

MARGINSON, P. (1992), 'European Integration and Transnational Management–Union Relations in the Enterprise', *British Journal of Industrial Relations*, 30: 529–46.

MARRIS, S. (1985), 'Deficits and the Dollar: the World Economy at Risk', *Policy Analyses in International Economics*, 14, Washington DC: Institute for International Economics.

—— (1991), 'Why No Hard Landing?', in Bergsten (ed.), *International Adjusting and Financing*.

MARSHALL, A. (1982), *Principles of Economics*, Philadelphia: Porcupine Press.

MARSHALL, R. (1988a), *How to Expand World Trade and Protect Workers' Rights*, Geneva: International Metalworkers' Federation.

—— (1988b), 'Linking Workers' Rights and Trade', Paper presented to the International Metalworkers' Federation Central Committee Meeting, Madrid, June.

MARX, K. and ENGELS F. (1848), *The Communist Manifesto*.

MASON, E. S. and ASHER, R. E. (1973), *The World Bank since Bretton Woods*, Washington, DC: The Brookings Institution.

MATHEWSON, S. (1931), *Restriction of Output Amongst Unorganised Workers*, New York: Viking Press.

MATTHEWS, R. C. O. and BOWEN, A. (1987), 'Keynesian and Other Explanations of Post-War Macro-Economic Trends', Paper prepared for Keynes General Theory After Fifty Years Conference held at the National Economic Development Office, London, Sept.

MAYER, C. (1987), 'The Assessment: Financial Systems and Corporate Investment', *Oxford Review of Economic Policy*, 3/4.

—— (1988), 'New Issues in Corporate Finance', *European Economic Review*, 32/5: 1167–89.

MEEKS, G. (1981), 'Cash Flow and Investment', in Martin, W. E. (ed.), *The Economics of the Profits Crisis*, London: HMSO.

MEHAUT, F. (1988), 'New Firms' Training Policies and Changes in the Wage-Earning Relationship', *Labour and Society*, 4.

MICHALET, C.-A. (1989), 'Global Competition and its Implications for Firms', *Technology and Productivity: The Challenge for Economic Policy*, Paris: OECD.

MICHIE, J. (ed.) (1992), *The Economic Legacy: 1979–1992*, London: Academic Press.

—— (1994), 'Global Shocks and Social Corporatism', in Delorme, R. and Dopfer, K. (eds.), *The Political Economy of Complexity: Evolutionary Approaches to Economic Order and Disorder*, Aldershot: Edward Elgar.

—— and GRIEVE SMITH, J. (eds.) (1994), *Unemployment in Europe*, London: Academic Press.

MICKESELL, R. F. (1994), 'The Bretton Woods Debates: A Memoir', *Princeton Essays in International Finance*, Princeton: Princeton University Press.

MILLS, R. W. (1976*a*), 'An Evaluation of Measures to Influence Volatile Capital Flows', ch. 6 of Swoboda, A. K. (ed.), *Capital Movements and their Control*, Leiden: A. W. Sijthoff.

—— (1976*b*), 'The Regulation of Short-Term Capital Movements in Major Industrial Countries', ch. 9 of Swoboda (ed.), *Capital Movements and their Control*.

MILNER, C. and GREENAWAY, D. (1979), *An Introduction to International Economics*, London: Longman.

MILWARD, A. S. (1987*a*), *The Reconstruction of Western Europe 1945–51*, London: Methuen.

—— (1987*b*), *War, Economy and Society 1939–1945*, Harmondsworth, Middlesex: Penguin Books.

MOGGRIDGE, D. E. (1972), *British Monetary Policy 1924–1931*; *The Norman Conquest of $4.86*, Cambridge: Cambridge University Press.

—— (1986), 'Keynes and the International Monetary System 1909–1946', in Cohen, J. S. and Harcourt, G. C. (eds.), *International Monetary Problems and Supply-Side Economics—Essays in Honour of Lorie Tarshis*, London: Macmillan.

—— (1992), *Maynard Keynes: An Economist's Biography*, London: Routledge.

MONTGOMERY, D. (1979). *Workers' Control in America*, New York: Cambridge University Press.

MORGAN, G. (1989), *World Financial Markets*, no. 5, Nov.

MORGENSTERN, O. (1959), *International Financial Transactions and Business Cycles*, Princeton: Princeton University Press.

MORRIS, D. and HEIGERT, M. (1987), 'Trends in collaborative agreements', *Columbia Journal of World Business*, xxii: 15–21.

MUSSA, M. (1981), 'The Role of Official Intervention', *Group of Thirty Occasional Papers*, no. 6, Group of Thirty, New York.

MYRDAL, G. (1957), *Economic Theory and Underdeveloped Regions*, London: Duckworth.

NURKSE, R. (1944), *International Currency Experience*, Princeton: League of Nations.

O'BRIEN, R. (1992), *Global Financial Integration: The End of Geography*, New York: Council on Foreign Relations Press.

OBSTFELD, M. (1983), 'Exchange Rates, Inflation and the Sterilisation Problem', *European Economic Review*, 21: 161–89.

Office of Technology Assessment (OTA) (1993), *Multinationals and the National Interest*, Washington DC: United States Congress.

OHMAE, K. (1990), *The Borderless World: Power and Strategy in the Interlinked Economy*, London: Collins.

OMAN, C. (1994), *Globalisation and Regionalisation*, Paris: OECD Development Centre.

Organisation for Economic Co-operation and Development (OECD) (1964), *Statistics of Balance of Payments*, Paris: OECD.

—— (1979), *The Impact of Newly Industrialising Countries on Production and Trade of Manufactures*, Paris: OECD.

—— (1985), *Costs and Benefits of Protection*, Paris: OECD.

—— (1991), *Employment Outlook*, July, Paris: OECD.

—— (1992), *Historical Statistics*, Paris: OECD.

—— (1993), *Economic Outlook*, 53, June, Paris: OECD.

OSTRY, S. (1990), *Governments and Corporations in a Shrinking World*, New York: Council on Foreign Relations.

—— (1992), 'The Domestic Domain: The New International Policy Arena', *Transnational Corporations*, 1, 7–26.

OSHY, S. and GERMIN, M. (1994), 'Foreign Direct Investment, Technology Transfer and the Innovation Network Model', *Transnational Corporations*, forthcoming.

OUDIZ, G. and SACHS, J. (1984), 'Macroeconomic Policy Co-ordination Among the Industrial Economies', *Brookings Papers on Economic Activity*, 1: 1–64.

Overseas Development Council (1989), *Pulling Together: The IMF in a Multipolar World*, Washington DC.

OZAWA, T. (1992), 'Foreign Direct Investment and Economic Development', *Transnational Corporations*, 1, Feb., 27–54.

PANIĆ, M. (1988), *The National Management of the International Economy*, London: Macmillan.

—— (1991a), 'Managing Reforms in the East European Countries: Lessons from the Postwar Experience of Western Europe', *UN Discussion Paper*, no. 3, New York: United Nations.

—— (1991b), 'The Impact of Multinationals on National Economic Policies', in Burgenmeier, B. and Mucchielli, J. L. (eds.), *Multinationals and Europe 1992*, London: Routledge.

PANIĆ, M. (1992), *European Monetary Union: Lessons from the Classical Gold Standard*, London: Macmillan.

—— (1993), 'The State as an Agent of Change', paper presented at WIDER conference on the State and Economic Development, University of Cambridge.

—— (forthcoming), 'International Economic Integration and the Changing Role of National Governments', in Chang, H. J. and Rowthorn, B. (eds.), *The Role of the State in Economic Change*.

PARISOTTO, A. (1993), 'Direct Employment in Multinational Enterprises in Industrialised and Developing Countries in the 1980s: Main Characteristics and Trends', in Bailey, P. *et al.* (eds.), *Multinationals and Employment—The Global Economy of the 1990s*, Geneva: ILO.

PATEL, S. J. (1992), 'In Tribute to the Golden Age of the South's Development', *World Development*, 20/5: 767–77.

PEKKARINEN, J., POHJOLA, M. and ROWTHORN, R. (1992), *Social Corporatism: A Superior Economic System?*, Oxford: Oxford University Press.

PETRELLA, R. (1991). 'Mondialisation de l'Economie et Contrat Social—Une même Logique Inégalitaire sur Toute la Planète', in *Le Monde Diplomatique*, Jan.

PETRI, P. (1994), 'The Regional Clustering of Foreign Direct Investment and Trade', *Transnational Corporations*, forthcoming.

PFEFFER, R. M. (1979), *Working For Capitalism*, New York: Columbia University Press.

PIGOTT, C. (1993), 'International Interest Rate Convergence: A Survey of the Issues and Evidence', *Federal Reserve Bank of New York Quarterly Bulletin*, Winter.

PILBEAM, K. (1992), *International Finance*, London: Macmillan.

PIORE, M. and SABEL, C. (1984), *The Second Industrial Divide: Possibilities for Prosperity*, New York: Basic Books.

PIVETTI, M. (1993), 'Bretton Woods, Through the Lens of State-of-the-Art Macrotheory and the European Monetary System', *Contributions to Political Economy*, 12: 99–110.

POHL, R. (1993), 'Money Supply, Interest Rate and Exchange Rate Targets: Conflicting Issues in an Open Economy', in Frowen, S. F. (ed.), *Monetary Theory and Monetary Policy*, Basingstoke: Macmillan.

POLAK, J. J. (1984), 'Comment on Andrew Crockett, The Role of International Institutions in Surveillance and Policy Coordination', in Bryant, *Macro-Economic Policies in an Interdependent World*.

POLANYI, K. (1957), *The Great Transformation*, Boston: Beacon Press.

POLLARD, S. (1981), *Peaceful Conquest: The Industrialisation of Europe, 1760–1790*, Cambridge: Cambridge University Press.

POMFRET, R. (1988), *Unequal Trade: The Economics of Discretionary International Trade Policies*, Oxford: Basil Blackwell.

PONTUSSON, J. (1993), *The Limits of Social Democracy*, Cornell: Cornell University Press.

PORTER, M. E. (1990), *The Competitive Advantage of Nations*, London: Macmillan.

POTERBA, J. M. and SUMMERS, L. H. (1988), 'Mean Reversion in Stock Prices: Evidence and Implications', *Journal of Financial Economics*, 22: 27–59.

—— (1991), 'Comparing the Cost of Capital in the United States and Japan: A

Survey of Methods', *Federal Reserve Bank of New York Quarterly Review*, Winter.

Presidential Task Force on Market Mechanisms, (1988), *Report*, Washington DC: US Government Printers Office, January.

QIAN, Y. and XU, C. (1992), 'Innovation and Financial Constraints in Centralized and Decentralized Economies', *Discussion Paper 109*, Centre for Economic Performance, Dec.

REICH, R. (1992), *The Work of Nations: Preparing Ourselves for 21st Century Capitalism*, New York: Vintage Books.

REICH, S. (1989), 'Roads to Follow: Regulating Direct Foreign Investment', *International Organization*, 43: 543–84.

REMOLONA, E. M. (1991), 'Do International Reactions of Stock and Bond Markets reflect Macroeconomic Fundamentals?', *Federal Reserve Bank of New York Quarterly Review*, Autumn, 1–13.

REYNOLDS, L. G. (1983), 'The Spread of Economic Growth to the Third World: 1850–1980', *Journal of Economic Literature*, Sept.

RICHARDSON, H. W. (1967), *Economic Recovery in Britain, 1932–9*, London: Weidenfeld and Nicholson.

ROBBINS, L. (1940), 'The Economic Aspects of Federalism', in Channing Pearce, M. (ed.), *Federal Union*, London: Lothian Foundation Press.

ROBBINS, S. M. and STOBAUGH, P. B. (1974), *Money and the Multinational Enterprise—A Study of Financial Policy*, New York: Basic Books.

ROBSON, P. (1984), *The Economics of International Integration*, London: George Allen & Unwin.

—— (1993), 'Transnational Corporations and Regional Economic Integration', *United Nations Library on Transnational Corporations*, xiii, London: Routledge.

RODRICK, D. (1986), 'Macroeconomic Policy and Debt in Turkey During the 1970s: A Tale of Two Policy Phases', *Discussion Paper*, Harvard University John Fitzgerald School of Government, Nov.

ROLL, R. (1989), 'Price Volatility, International Market Links and their Implications for Regulatory Policies', *Journal of Financial Services Research*, 3: 211–46.

ROSE, A. K. and SVENSSON, L. (1994), 'European Exchange Rate Credibility before the Fall', *European Economic Review*.

ROSS, S. A. (1989), 'Commentary: Using Tax Policy to Curb Speculative Short-Term Trading', *Journal of Financial Services Research*, 3.

ROWTHORN, R. E. (1971), 'Imperialism in the 1970s—Unity or Rivalry?', *New Left Review*, 69: 31–51.

—— (1992), 'Centralisation, Employment and Wage Dispersion', *Economic Journal*, May.

—— and GLYN, A. (1988), *The Diversity of Unemployment Experience Since 1973*, Helsinki: WIDER.

—— and WELLS, J. R. (1987), *De-Industrialization and Foreign Trade*, Cambridge: Cambridge University Press.

RUBERY, J. (1992), *The Economics of Equal Value*, Manchester: Equal Opportunities Commission.

SACHS, J. (1985), 'External Debt and Macroeconomic Performance in Latin America and East Asia', *Brookings Papers on Economic Activity*, no. 2.

SAINT-PAUL, G. (1992), 'Technological Choice, Financial Markets, and Economic Development', *European Economic Review*, 36: 763–81.

SALTER, W. E. G. (1966), *Productivity and Technical Change*, Cambridge: Cambridge University Press.

SAWYER, M. (1994), 'Obstacles to the Achievement of Full Employment in Capitalist Economies', in Arestis, P. and Marshall, M. (eds.), *The Political Economy of Full Employment*, Aldershot: Edward Elgar.

SAYERS, R. S. (1965), *The Vicissitudes of an Export Economy: Britain since 1880.* Sydney: University of Sydney Press.

SCAMMELL, W. M. (1987), *The Stability of the International Monetary System*, London: Macmillan.

SCARAMOZZINO, P. (1994), 'Investment Irreversibility and Finance Constraints', mimeo.

SCHADLER, S., CARKOVIC, M., BENNETT, A. and KAHN, R. (1993), 'Recent Experiences with Surges in Capital Inflows', *IMF Occasional Paper 108*, Washington, DC: IMF.

SCHOR, J. (1992), 'Introduction', in Banuri, T. and Schor, J., *Financial Openness and National Autonomy: Opportunities and Constraints*, Oxford: Clarendon Press.

SCHWARTZ, A. J. (1986), 'Alternative Monetary Regimes: The Gold Standard', in Campbell, C. D. and Dougan, W. R. (eds.), *Alternative Monetary Regimes*, Baltimore: John Hopkins University Press.

SCOTT, Bruce (1992), 'Economic Strategy and Economic Performance', mimeo, Harvard Business School.

SCOTT, M. (1989), *A New View of Economic Growth*, Oxford: Oxford University Press.

SCRANTAN, P. (1991), 'Diversity in Diversity: Flexible Production and American Industrialisation, 1880–1930', *Business History Review*, 65, Spring.

SENGENBERGER, W. (1990), *On the Role of Labour Standards in Industrial Restructuring of: Participation, Protection and Promotion*, Geneva: International Institute for Labour Research.

—— (1994), 'Participation, Protection, Promotion: The systemic nature and effects of labour standards', in Sengenberger, W. and Campbell, D., *Providing Economic Opportunities—The Role of Labour Standards in Industrial Restructuring*, Institute for Labour Studies, Geneva.

SERVAIS, J. M. (1989), 'The Social Clause in Trade Agreements: Wishful Thinking or an Instrument of Social Progress?', in: *International Labour Review*, 128/4.

SHILLER, R. (1989), 'Comment' on von Furstenberg, G. M. and Jeon, B. N., 'International Stock Price Movements: Links and Messages', *Brookings Papers on Economic Activity,* 1: 1989.

SHIRREFF, D. (1993), 'Can Anyone Tame the Currency Market', *Euromoney*, Sept.

SHONFIELD, A. (1965), *Modern Capitalism*, Oxford: Oxford University Press.

SHOSTAK, A. B. (1980), *Blue-Collar Stress*, Reading, M.A.: Addison-Wesley.

SILLITOE, A. (1959), *Saturday Night and Sunday Morning*, New York: Knopk.

SINGH, A. (1977), 'UK Industry and the World Economy: A Case of Deindustrialization?', *Cambridge Journal of Economics*, June.

—— (1979), 'The "Basic Needs" Approach to Development vs the New International Economic Order: The Significance of Third World Industrialisation', *World Development*, 7: 585–606.

—— (1984), 'The Interrupted Industrial Revolution of the Third World: Prospects and Policies for Resumption', *Industry and Development*, no. 12.

—— (1986), 'The World Economic Crisis, Stabilisation and Structural Adjustment: An Overview', *Labour and Society*, Sept.

—— (1987), 'Manufacturing and De-Industrialization', in Eatwell, J., Milgate, M. and Newman, P. (eds.), *The New Palgrave*, London: Macmillan.

—— (1989), 'Third World Competition and De-Industrialization in Advanced Countries', *Cambridge Journal of Economics*.

—— (1990), 'Southern Competition, Labor Standards and Industrial Development in the North and South', in Hergenberg, S. and Perez-Lopez, J. F. (eds.), *Labour Standards, Development and the Global Economy*, Washington DC: US Department of Labour, 239–69.

—— (1992*a*), 'The Political Economy of Growth', in Michie, J. (ed.), *The Economic Legacy: 1979–1992*, London: Academic Press.

—— (1992*b*), 'The Actual Crisis of Economic Development in the 1980s: An Alternative Policy Perspective for the Future', in Dutt, A. K. and Jameson, K. P. (eds.), *New Directions in Development Economics*, Edward Elgar, Aldershot, 81–116.

—— (1993), 'Asian Economic Success and Latin American Failure in the 1980s: New Analyses and Future Policy Implications', *International Review of Applied Economics*, Sept.

—— (1994). 'Global Economic Changes, Skills and International Competitiveness', *International Labour Review*, 133/2.

SINGH, R. D. (1988), 'The Multinationals' Economic Penetration, Growth, Industrial Output and Domestic Savings in Developing Countries: Another Look', *Journal of Development Studies*, 25 Oct., 55–82.

SMITH, A. (1986), *An Inquiry into the Nature and Causes of the Wealth of Nations*, London: Penguin.

SOLOMON, R. (1982), *The International Monetary System, 1945–81*, 2nd ed., New York: Harper and Row.

SOLOMOU, S. (1988), *Phases of Economic Growth, 1850–1973: Kondratieff Waves and Kuznets Swings*, Cambridge: Cambridge University Press.

SPENCE, M. (1973), 'Job Market Signalling', *Quarterly Journal of Economics*, Aug., 355–74.

SPERO, J. E. (1981), *The Politics of International Economic Relations*, 2nd edn., London: Allen and Unwin.

STANNERS, W. (1993), 'Is Low Inflation an Important Condition for High Growth?', *Cambridge Journal of Economics*, 17/1, Mar.

STERNE, G. and BAYOUMI, T. (1993), 'Regional Trading Blocs, Mobile Capital and Exchange Rate Coordination', *Working Paper 12*, Bank of England, Apr.

STEWART, F. (1994), 'Biasses in Global Markets: Can the Forces of Inequity and Marginalisation be Modified?', Queen Elizabeth House, Oxford, Mimeo.

STIGLITZ, J. (1985), 'Credit Markets and the Control of Capital', *Journal of Money, Credit and Banking*, 17/2: 133–52.

STIGLITZ, J. (1989), 'Using Tax Policy to Curb Speculative Short-Term Trading', *Journal of Financial Services Research*, no. 3.

STOPFORD, J. M. and STRANGE, S. (1991), *Rival States, Rival Firms: Competition for World Market Shares*, Cambridge: Cambridge University Press.

STORPER, M. and WALKER, R. (1989), *The Capitalist Imperative: Territory, Technology and Industrial Growth*, Oxford: Blackwell.

STEETEN, P. (1992), 'Interdependence and Integration of the World Economy: The Role of States and Firms', *International Corporations*, 3, 125–36.

SUMMERS, L. (1991), 'Regionalism and the World Trading System', Federal Reserve Bank of Kansas.

SUMMERS, L. H. and SUMMERS, V. P. (1989), 'When Financial Markets Work Too Well: A Cautious Case For A Securities Transactions Tax', *Journal of Financial Services Research*, no. 3.

SVEDBERG, P. (1978), 'The Portfolio-Direct Composition of Private Foreign Investment in 1914, Revisited', *The Economic Journal*, Dec. 763–77.

SVENSSON, R. (1993), *Production in Foreign Affiliates: Effects on Home Country Exports and Modes of Entry*, Stockholm: IUI.

SWARY, I. and TOPF, B. (1992), *Global Financial Deregulation. Commercial Banking at the Crossroads*, Cambridge, Mass.: Blackwell.

TAYLOR, M. P. and ARTIS, M. J. (1988), 'What has the European Monetary System Achieved?', in Bank of England Discussion Papers, no. 31, Mar.

TEECE, D. (1993), 'Review of Alfred Chandler's Economies of Scale and Scope', *Journal of Economic Literature*, 31, Mar., 199–225.

TEMIN, P. (1989), *Lessons from the Great Depression*, Cambridge, Mass.: MIT Press.

TESAR, L. L. (1991), 'Savings, Investment and International Capital Flows', *Journal of International Economics*, 31, 55–78.

TEW, B. (1988), *The Evolution of the International Monetary System*, London: Hutchinson.

TEWELES, R. J., HARLOW, C. V. and STONE, H. L. (1974), *The Commodity Futures Game. Who Wins? Who Loses? Why?*, New York: McGraw-Hill Book Company.

THIRLWALL, A. P. (1979), 'The Balance of Payments Constraint as an Explanation of International Growth Rate Differences', *Banca Nazionale del Lavoro Quarterly Review*, Mar.

THUROW, L. (1994), *Head to Head*, London: Nicholas Brealey Publishing.

TOBIN, J. (1978), 'A Proposal for International Monetary Reform', *The Eastern Economic Journal*, July–Oct., 155–9; reprinted in Tobin, J., *Essays in Economics: Theory and Policy*, Cambridge, Mass.: The MIT Press, 1982.

—— (1984), 'On the Efficiency of the Financial System', *Lloyds Bank Review*, no. 153, July, 14–15.

TRIFFIN, R. (1960), *Gold and the Dollar Crisis*, New Haven: Yale University Press.

United Nations (UN) (1981), *Transnational Banks—Operations, Strategies and their Effects in Developing Countries*, New York.

—— (1993), *World Social Report*, Geneva.

—— (1993/4), *The United Nations Library on Transnational Corporations*, 21 vols., London: Routledge.

UN-TCMD (1992), *World Investment Report 1992, Transnational Corporations as Engines of Growth*, New York: United Nations.

—— (1993), *Transnational Corporations from Developing Countries: Impact on Their Home Countries*, New York: United Nations.

UNCTAD (1981), *Trade and Development Report*, Geneva: United Nations.

—— (1985), *Trade and Development Report*, Geneva: United Nations.

—— (1987), *International Monetary and Financial Issues for the Developing Countries*, New York: United Nations.

—— (1988), *Trade and Development Report*, Geneva: United Nations.

—— (1989), *Trade and Development Report*, Geneva: United Nations.

—— (1991), *Trade and Development Report*, Geneva: United Nations.

—— (1993*a*), *Trade and Development Report*, Geneva: United Nations.

—— (1993*b*), *World Investment Report 1993: Transnational Corporations and Integrated International Production*, New York, United Nations Conference on Trade and Development, United Nations Publications.

UNCTAD, DTCI (1994*a*), *Transnational Corporations and the Transfer of New Management Practices to Developing Countries*, Geneva: United Nations.

—— (1994*b*), *The Transnationalisation of Economic Activity*, Geneva: United Nations.

UNCTC (1988), *Transnational Corporations in World Development: Trends and Prospects*, New York: United Nations.

—— (1991), *World Investment Report 1991, The Triad in Foreign Direct Investment*, New York: United Nations.

US Department of State (1948*a*), *Proceedings and Documents of United Nations Monetary and Financial Conference—Bretton Woods, New Hampshire July 1–22, 1944, vol. I*, Washington, DC: United States Government Printing Office.

—— (1948*b*), *Proceedings and Documents of United Nations Monetary and Financial Conference—Bretton Woods, New Hampshire July 1–22, 1944, vol. II*, Washington, DC: United States Government Printing Office.

VAN DORMAEL, A. (1978), *Bretton Woods—Birth of a Monetary System*, London: Macmillan.

VAN LIEMT, G. (1989), 'Minimum Labour Standards and International Trade: Would a Social Clause Work?', in *International Labour Review*, 128/4.

—— (1992), 'Economic Globalization: Labour Options and Business Strategies in High Labour Cost Countries', *International Labour Review*, 131/4–5: 453–70.

VASAN, P. S. (1986), *Credit Rationing and Corporate Investment*, unpublished Ph.D., Harvard University.

VAUBEL, R. (1980), 'International Shifts in the Demand for Money, their Effects on Exchange Rates and Price Levels and their Implications for the Pre-Announcement of Monetary Expansion', *Weltwirtschaftliches Archiv*, 1–44.

VILLEVAL, M. C. (1988), 'Destructuring of an Industry and Local Changes in the Wage-Earning Relationship', *Labour and Society*, 13/4.

VOLCKER, P. and GYOHTEN, T. (1992), *Changing Fortunes: The World's Money and the Threat to American Leadership*, New York: Times Books.

VON FURSTENBERG, G. M. and JEON, B. N. (1989), 'International Stock Price Movements: Links and Messages', *Brookings Papers on Economic Activity*, 1: 125–79.

WALMSLEY, J. (1992), *The Foreign Exchange and Money Markets Guide*, New York: John Wiley and Sons.

WALTER, A. (1993), *World Power and World Money*, Hemel Hempstead: Harvester Wheatsheaf.

WATSON, A. and ALTRINGHAM, R. (1986), *Treasury Management: International Banking Operations*, London: The Chartered Institute of Bankers.

WELLS, J. (1993), 'Factors Making for Increasing International Economic Integration', unpublished manuscript, University of Cambridge.

WHADWHANI, S. and SHAH, M. (1994), 'Emerging Giants, Globalisation and Equity', Goldman Sachs International Ltd., London.

WHEELER, D. and MODY, A. (1992), 'International Investment Location Decision: The Case of US Firms', *Journal of International Economics*, 33: 57–76.

WHITLEY, R. (1992a), *Business Systems in East Asia: Firms, Markets and Societies*, London: Sage Publications.

—— (ed.) (1992b), *European Business Systems: Firms and Markets in their National Contexts*, London: Sage Publications.

WILKINS, M. (1988), 'European and North American Multinationals, 1870–1914: Comparisons and Contrasts', *Business History*, 30: 8–45.

WILKINSON, F. (1988), 'Real Wages, Effective Demand and Economic Development', *Cambridge Journal of Economics*, 12.

—— (1991a), 'The Structuring of Economic and Social Deprivation and the Working of the Labour Market in Industrial Countries', *Labour and Society*, 16/2.

—— (1991b), 'Industrial Organisation, Collective Bargaining and Industrial Efficiency', *International Contributions to Labour Studies*.

—— (1992), *Why Britain Needs a Minimum Wage*, London: Institute for Public Policy Research.

—— and YOU, J. (1992), *Competition and Cooperation: Towards Understanding Industrial Districts*, Small Business Research Centre, Working paper No. 18, Cambridge, Department of Applied Economics.

WILLIAMSON, J. (1983), *The Exchange Rate System*, Washington: Institute for International Economics, Rev. edn., June 1985.

—— (1985a), *The Exchange Rate System*, Washington DC: Institute for International Economics.

—— (1985b), 'On the Systems in Bretton Woods', *American Economic Review* (Papers and Proceedings), 75/2: 74–9.

—— (1991), 'FEERs and the ERM', *National Institute Economic Review*, no. 137, Aug.

—— (1993), 'Exchange Rate Management', *Economic Journal*, 103: 188–97.

—— and Miller, M. H. (1987), *Targets & Indicators: A Blueprint for the Coordination of Economic Policy*, Institute for International Economics, Washington DC: Policy Analyses in International Economics no. 22, Sept.

WOOD, A. (1994), *North–South Trade, Employment and Inequality: Changing Fortunes in a Skill-Driven World*, Oxford: Oxford University Press.

WOOLCOCK, S. (1991), *Market Access Issues in EC–US Relations: Trading Partners or Trading Blocs?*, London: Royal Institute of International Affairs.

World Bank (1987), *World Development Report*, Washington, DC.

—— (1988), *World Development Report 1988*, Oxford: Oxford University Press.

—— (1991), *The World Development Report 1991*, New York: Oxford University Press.

—— (1993), *The East Asian Miracle: Economic Growth and Public Policy*, New York: Oxford University Press.

WORSWICK, G. D. N. (1984), 'The Recovery in Britain in the 1930s', in Bank of England Panel of Academic Consultants, *The UK Economic Recovery in the 1930s*, Panel Paper no. 23: 5–28.

YOFFIE, D. B. (ed.) (1993), *Beyond Free Trade: Firms, Governments and Global Competition*, Boston: Harvard Business School Press.

YOU, J. (1990), 'South Korea', in Herzenberg, S. and Perez-Lopez, J. F. (eds.), *Labour Standards and Development in the Global Economy*, Washington, DC: US Department of Labour.

YOUNG, Allyn (1928), 'Increasing Returns and Economic Progress', *Economic Journal*. 38: 527–40.

ZEVIN, R. (1988), 'Are Financial Markets More Open? If So Why and With What Effects?', paper presented at WIDER conference on Financial Openness, Helsinki, July.

ZIMMER, S. A. and McCAULEY, R. N. (1991), 'Bank Cost of Capital and International Competitiveness', *Federal Reserve Bank of New York Quarterly Bulletin*, Winter.

INDEX